Born in 1955, **Purushottam Agrawal** served as member, Union Public Service Commission of India from 2007 to 2013. Before this, he was Chairperson, Centre of Indian Languages, Jawaharlal Nehru University, New Delhi. He has also been Visiting Professor at the Faculty of Oriental Studies, Cambridge University (UK) and at El Colegio de Mexico. His book *Akath Kahani Prem Ki: Kabir Ki Kavita Aur Unka Samay* (2009) has been widely acclaimed as a path-breaking study of Kabir and his work. His other books include *Hindi Serai: Astrakhan via Yerevan* (2013), a travelogue which traces the history of Indian traders who settled in the Russian city of Astrakhan between the sixteenth and eighteenth centuries; and *Padmavat: An Epic Love Story* (2018), an English translation of and commentary on Malik Muhammad Jayasi's epic poem. In 2016 he published his first novel, *NACOHUS,* which constructs a Kafkaesque fantasy around the politics of hurt sentiments. Its English and Marathi translations will be published in late 2019.

A well-known panelist on TV debates, Agrawal hosted a unique show on books called 'Kitab' on Rajya Sabha TV. He has also delivered several talks across the country. One of the most celebrated of these, also published as a monograph, was his Gandhi Peace Foundation lecture 'Majbooti ka naam Mahatma Gandhi' (2005), which throws new light on the issues of violence and power.

‘WHO IS BHARAT MATA?’

On History, Culture and the Idea of India

Writings by and on

JAWAHARLAL NEHRU

Edited and with an Introduction by

Purushottam Agrawal

SPEAKING TIGER

SPEAKING TIGER BOOKS LLP
125 A, Ground Floor, Shahpur Jat, Near Asiad Village
New Delhi 110049

First published in India by Speaking Tiger in paperback 2019
Copyright for excerpts from *An Autobiography*, *Glimpses of World History* and *The Discovery of India* vests in Sonia Gandhi
Copyright for all essays from *Jawaharlal Nehru: Centenary Volume* vests in Nehru Portal, Nehru Memorial Museum and Library
Copyright for all other pieces vests in the individual authors.
Introduction copyright © Purushottam Agrawal

ISBN: 978-93-86702-84-5
eISBN: 978-93-86702-85-2

10 9 8 7 6 5 4 3 2 1

Typeset in Arno Pro by Jojy Philip, New Delhi
Printed at Sanat Printers, Kundli, Haryana

All rights reserved.

No part of this publication may be reproduced, transmitted, or stored in a retrieval system, in any form or by any means, electronic, mechanical, photocopying, recording or otherwise, without the prior permission of the publisher.

This book is sold subject to the condition that it shall not, by way of trade or otherwise, be lent, resold, hired out, or otherwise circulated, without the publisher's prior consent, in any form of binding or cover other than that in which it is published.

Contents

BOOK II
ON NEHRU

Introduction

Discarding Extremes in Favour of the Enlightened Middle Way

1

I write this introduction in May 2019, just days after the Narendra Modi-led Bharatiya Janata Party (BJP) was voted back to power with an impressive majority. Jawaharlal Nehru, the country's first prime minister, passed away exactly fifty-five years ago. But if you were a dispassionate observer from another world covering the recently concluded elections, you would likely have come to the conclusion that Nehru was leading the opposition. He continues to be so *alive* to his detractors that he—his persona, his legacy, his worldview—was attacked day in and day out during the political campaign, and even more assiduously in 'apolitical' propaganda spread by every means of communication. Now that the most tireless and vocal of these detractors have emerged victorious in the national elections, you would expect the propaganda, abuse and hatred to recede. But it will not. Indeed, it cannot, for as long as any trace of Nehru's legacy remains, the victors will continue to feel defeated.

The renewed mandate for Narendra Modi, with an increased vote share despite indifferent performance, cannot be made light of by saying that 'he has not won the battle of ideas'. That would be ignorance at best, delusion at worst—either way, it would be missing the thick woods for the trees. Narendra Modi, ubiquitous and larger-than-life today, is only a part of a far larger machine. The fact is, many commentators had failed to comprehend the real significance of the 2014 election result. It was not a mere regime change, it was—as PM Modi himself put it back then—the culmination of 'five generations of sustained work' by the Rashtriya Swaymasevak Sangh (RSS). Since then, all government institutions and a pliant media have been enlisted to carry on the 'sustained work'—through institutional subversion, silencing or shouting down of dissent and an ideological blitzkrieg through electronic and social media, of which the demonization of Nehru is a crucial component. The 2014 election verdict, which gave the BJP a full majority on its own, was an important stage in the journey towards 'the Hinduization of all politics', to quote the 'father of Hindutva', Vinayak Damodar Savarkar. For Savarkar, 'Hindutva is *not* identical' with 'that vague, more limited, sectarian term Hinduism'. What Savarkar desired and what the RSS and the entire Sangh-parivar has been attempting for 'five generations' is not to make people more religious or more nationalistic, but to make them *Hindu nationalists*. Their true cause has been neither Hinduism nor nationalism, but Hindutva—and their aim is to use the state apparatus to consolidate the Hindutva idea of India, which is necessarily opposed to a democratic Indian nationalism. This is where Nehru becomes a problem: his idea of 'Bharat Mata' is a powerful challenge to the idea of 'Bharat Mata' that the Sangh-parivar has used to try and claim India for itself, and itself alone.

Our freedom movement was unique in the sense that it harnessed patriotic feelings and anti-colonial sentiment to build a democratic, inclusive nationalism. It was described by the remarkable freedom fighter and social reformer Dada Dharmadhikari as '*Maanavnishtha Bhartiyata*', or humane Indian nationalism. Reactionary, communal forces of all hues have always been opposed to this version of nationalism, and that is why Nehru and other leaders of our independence movement counterposed their nationalism to communalism—Hindu, Muslim or any other. Instead of shying away from nationalism, they tried to bring people on board to the idea of *Maanavnishtha Bhartiyata* as a shared vision, and they were successful. Nehru is vilified by the Hindu right because after Independence, he had the historic opportunity and responsibility to lead the process of channelling the innate patriotism of his fellow citizens into a modern version of *Maanavnishtha Bhartiyata*—an Indian nationalism which was forward-looking yet rooted in our tradition and heritage; which was inclusive and assertive of national interest and pride. And in this he succeeded spectacularly, defying the doom-and-gloom predictions of many political pundits within and outside India.

In the Hindutva view, Nehru's 'main crime' was and is unwavering commitment to and a pragmatic vision of such an enlightened nationalism. The Hindutva generals realize fully well that without distorting Nehru's memory and tarnishing his image, without belittling his towering personality—in fact, without erasing his impressions on the Indian mind—the Hindutva project cannot have lasting success.

And let us also be absolutely clear that to the trolls and their political gurus it is not merely Nehru the person who has to be 'finished'; the very idea of India associated with this person has to be destroyed. The question that all democratic-minded citizens have to ask themselves is this: Is the inclusive, enlightened and genuinely modern idea of India—which has come to be known as the 'Nehruvian' idea of India—worth defending and preserving or not?

This book is an attempt to help us answer that question.

2

One of the most poignant memories from my childhood belongs to the hot and dusty afternoon of 27 May, 1964. We children, having been fed, were forcibly put to bed, to save us from heatstroke and to give Jiji (as we addressed our mother) a few moments of much-needed rest after tiring household chores. I was just on the threshold of sleep when I felt a warm drop on my cheek, and heard the trembling, broken voice of Jiji: '*Utth, Nehru nahi rahe* (Wake up, Nehru is no more).'

After a while, Babuji was also back, having closed his shop. Looking dejected, trying hard to hold back his tears, he handed over the shop-keys to Jiji and lay down quietly on the charpai. No food was cooked that evening, though us children were given something to eat.

My parents, far from being admirers, were usually quite critical of Nehru. They were particularly harsh on him in the wake of the humiliating India-China war of 1962. But today, they were behaving as if they had lost a near and dear one, a member of the family.

Our mohalla in Gwalior was known to be a stronghold of the Hindu Mahasabha. There were some people who were jubilant at the death of 'that shatru'—arch enemy—of the 'Hindu rashtra', and they were asking people to light lamps of celebration ('*Jalao diye ghee ke*...'). But even these voices were soon muted; they were embarrassed at themselves given the grief and sadness all around. Those were not the days of 24x7 TV and social media, but for many days a great sense of loss was palpable all over the city, across communities and classes.

Even in the Vaishnava matth, to which my family professed spiritual allegiance, something quite unexpected happened. This is the famous matth whose Mahant, Gangadas ji, had performed the last rites of Lakshmibai, the famed Rani of Jhansi, in 1858. Jagannathdas ji, the mahant in 1964, apparently hated Nehru—for a number of reasons, but primarily because the matth had lost large patches of *maafidari* (rent-free) land due to 'that man's wretched policies'. But that afternoon, far from being jubilant, far even from being his usual overbearing and almost fearsome self, mahant ji was a study in grief and sadness. No food was cooked in the matth kitchen either that evening. And three days' *sootak*—ritual mourning—was duly observed.

Decades later, on 15 August 2014, I was on a TV panel discussion on the live telecast of the Prime Minister's customary address to the nation from the ramparts of the Red Fort. As soon as the new PM, Narendra Modi, finished, the young anchor, who could not contain her bubbling self, gushed to the camera: 'I'm sure no PM in the history of India has enjoyed this kind of *connect* with the people... what do you say, Professor Agrawal?'

I wished for a moment that I had the terrible temper of Mahant Jagannathdas ji, and also the licence he enjoyed, so that I could deliver the tongue-lashing such a question deserved. But I controlled myself.

'Well,' I replied, 'who can deny the popularity of the honourable PM. But *no* other PM? You may well ignore Nehru and Indira Gandhi, but only very recently there was a gentleman known as Atal Bihari Vajpayee for whose speech people of my age in our youth, before the TV-yuga of journalism, waited patiently all night.'

The anchor was obviously not very happy with this, and after a short exchange I was sort of forced to tell her, 'The problem, actually, is that for people like you, the history of India starts in May 2014....Fortunately, that is not the case. India has a long history and a long memory.'

The aggressive adulation coming from an uncritical, almost servile mindset and the genuine 'connect' of those who love and respect a leader (despite criticizing certain acts and policies) are two very different things. Sadly, like that gushing anchor, many people are incapable of recognizing this difference and understanding the far-reaching implications of what can only be described as a willing and complete surrender of their rights as citizens. Mindless, militant adulation cannot exist without distortion of history and erasure of memory. Erasing the kind of memories that millions of Indians like me have of that May afternoon of 1964 is a precondition for the success of the 'hate Nehru project', which in turn is one of the preconditions for converting India from a democracy into an authoritarian, majoritarian state.

Coming back to my childhood, the paradox of Mahant ji, who was almost always very critical of Nehru, being so grief-stricken at the same man's demise as to order a *sootak*, continued to flummox me for days. A couple of weeks later, I put my confusion to him: 'Baba, you were so critical of him, then why were you so sad that day?' Baba was used to my un-childlike questions, and also quite encouraging. He kept quiet for a while, and then slowly explained,

'Yes, some things he did were not at all good. For example, taking away lands even from *maafidars* like us, and the Hindu Code Bill ... But you know, such people are not ordinary human beings. Some of what they do we'll denounce and oppose—but let me tell you, he was a great yogi in his previous birth who could not complete his sadhana, so he had to choose rebirth. We will criticize many of his actions, but how can I forget his sufferings for the nation? How can I ignore the difference he made to people's lives? ... He should have lived longer, but for this wretched, perfidious China.'

And then Baba exploded in pained anger, '*Aur Jawaharlal ko khujli kya uthi Yamaraj ko chunauti dene ki?* (What was the itch that made Jawaharlal challenge the god of death?) Why did he have to declare "My life isn't coming to an end so soon"! Yama does not spare anyone, not even avatars, what to talk of yogis.... Nehru should not have said that.'

The 'Yogi in a previous birth' legend has been part of the popular lore about Nehru. Shashi Tharoor mentions it at the very beginning of *Nehru: The Invention of India,* and so does M.J. Akbar in his biography. According to this legend, during a trip to the Himalayas, Motilal Nehru, Madan Mohan Malviya and Pandit Deen Dayal Shastri ran into a yogi and asked him to bless Motilal with a son. The yogi told them bluntly, 'Motilal is not destined to have a son.' Malviya and Shastri urged the yogi to do something about it. Unable to decline the request, the yogi blessed Motilal against destiny, left for his heavenly abode, and exactly ten months later Jawaharlal was born. Needless to add, Nehru himself dismissed the story as 'apocryphal'. The point, however, is that to numerous people like Mahant Jagannathdas ji this legend provided a way to comprehend their affection for Nehru in spite of irritation with, even anger at, his policies.

Mahant ji's explanation also gives us a clue to the fascinating paradox of the 'irreligious' Nehru having such a deep emotional 'connect' not only with ordinary devout Hindus like my parents but also members of orthodox religious establishments like Mahant ji. To them, in certain matters he was certainly 'adharmik'; but then, they conceded, he had to be if he was to shape the destiny of his people and bequeath them a modern nation. He was a yogi, after all, and yogis had the privilege to act differently from ordinary mortals.

In this, even a traditionalist like Mahant ji was in fact endorsing Nehru himself. Reflecting on the 'arrested growth of India and urgent necessity for change', Nehru had written in *The Discovery of India*, 'It is probable that in this process many vital changes may be introduced in the old outlook, but they will not be superimposed from outside and will seem rather to grow naturally from the cultural background of the people.'

~

I was nine the year Nehru passed away and, for a child I was unusually interested in un-childlike activities like reading obsessively and indiscriminately, which made me somewhat antisocial. In any case, there was hardly any avenue for social and cultural activity and bonding, except the ubiquitous Rashtriya Swaymasevak Sangh—the RSS.

The local *shakhachalak*, the man in charge of the RSS shakha, or branch, tried to convince Jiji and Babuji to send me to the shakha every morning. 'He will get an opportunity to learn our religion, our culture and tradition ...' My parents finally agreed, although they were neither too busy nor too ignorant—even if not highly 'educated'—to give their children an adequate sense of religion, culture and tradition on their own. Their logic in sending me to the shakha was entirely different—they probably said to themselves, 'This lonely introverted boy will learn some social skills and engage in some sports.'

I attended the shakha for a couple of years, quite regularly and enthusiastically in the beginning but reluctantly as the months passed. Nehru was a constant topic of the daily *bauddhikas*, the 'intellectual' sermons delivered at the end of the morning drill and sports. The attempt was to cleanse the young minds of any good impressions of the man who was indisputably—and depressingly for extremists of all persuasions—the most popular and respected leader of the time, with a genuine pan-Indian appeal. Apart from 'criticism'—if at all this can be a suitable word for what was done—of Nehru's politics, we were given strange information regarding his *aacharan* and *charitra*, his conduct and character. For the more inquisitive ones like me, there was some suggested reading as well, the most important being a hyper-critical 'study' of Nehru penned by a certain Gurudutt—not to be confused with the legendary film-maker and actor, or with Gurudutt M.Sc., a great Arya Samaj activist. This particular Gurudutt was a full-time Ayurvedic physician and part-time novelist and essayist (or may be the other way around), and what a writing machine he was, churning out a thick novel almost every month, each bereft of any literary merit but carrying industrial doses of political Hindutva. Within six months of Nehru's demise, Gurudutt published *Jawaharlal Nehru: Ek Vivechnatmak Vritt*, i.e., 'an analytical appraisal'. It had lengthy quotations, printed in English and followed by Hindi translation. This was the author's way of giving his work a touch of authenticity. But Gurudutt's book failed to satisfy my basic queries and answer simple questions like 'Was it really wrong of Nehru to admire English authors because India was under British rule?'

And then came *Simhavlokan*—'In Retrospect'—the memoirs of Yashpal, a leading Hindi novelist and a comrade of Bhagat Singh. We were encouraged in the shakha to celebrate Bhagat Singh and other 'manly' revolutionaries and condemn the 'effeminate' ways of Gandhi and his followers, chiefly Nehru. We were also told that Bhagat Singh et al. were very critical of, in fact full of contempt for, 'characters like that Nehru'. But this book written by a close comrade of Bhagat Singh had an entirely different story to tell. Bhagat Singh criticized Gandhi and Nehru all right, but not from the standpoint of Hindutva at all. According to our shakha elders, Nehru was not sufficiently Indian, he was an effete compromiser; while Patel and Lajpat Rai were authentically Indian and Bose was a true, unbending revolutionary. But according to Yashpal, Bhagat Singh seemed to prefer Nehru over everyone else (See p. 322).

This was perplexing, to say the least. And there was more. We were told to treat the communists as '*kaumnasht*'—'destroyers of the nation', or 'anti-nationals', to borrow from the lexicon of twenty-first-century Hindutva (do note the irony of the 'impure', 'foreign' word *kaum* sitting pretty with the 'pure' and 'Bharatiya' *nasht*). But here was our manly hero Bhagat Singh talking like the communists! What was more, even when he criticized Gandhi and Nehru, he did so with the kind of touching reverence one would have for a father or an elder brother.

I could not contain myself and took my confusion to our *shakhachalak* repeatedly, till he gave up and decided to present me to a senior local functionary of the Sangh. The gentleman already had a sense of my 'deviation' and in just a while was utterly exasperated and snapped, 'Anyway, whatever be his views, Bhagat Singh after all was a Hindu.'

I should have pointed out to the RSS worthy that Bhagat Singh was Sikh by birth and irreligious by choice. Instead, I retorted, 'But then, so was Nehru.'

'*No*, he was *not*,' the worthy shot back. 'He hated Hindus! In fact, he described himself as "Hindu merely by accident".'

'But wasn't he right? Aren't we all Hindu, Muslim, Christian, whatever merely by accident of birth?'

'We must be proud of our culture, our ancestors.'

'Nehru seems to be quite proud of that, he wrote such moving words about the Ganga in his will—'

'All that is nonsense. He and Gandhi were anti-Hindu…you must realize this, you talk too much. Have you not attended any *bauddhikas*? Have you not read the book by Gurudutt ji?'

'Yes, I have, but…'

'Well, then? It is not good to ask too many questions. Learn to respect your elders and love your culture. Stay away from *kaumnashts* like Yashpal and their poisonous books. Listen to your gurus. Know this once and for all—Nehru was the greatest enemy of the Hindu nation.'

'But Bhagat Singh himself talked like the communists—'

'Enough of this nonsense. Go and play. I'm told you are quite good at kho-kho. Now run along…'

That was my last day at the shakha.

3

The *bauddhikas* given at the RSS shakhas of my childhood have metamorphosed into sermons on WhatsApp, Twitter, Facebook and Youtube in this post-truth era. Today, it would be hard to find a bigger victim of trolling than Nehru. He was, of course, trolled even before this term got currency. There was venom spewed against him in his lifetime, and he was not spared even in death. But it wasn't done with such insistence, as publicly and with as much nasty pride as in the age of social media that has been upon us for about a decade now. No amount of calumny is too much, and no low is low enough. From Nehru's family life to his eating habits to his personal tragedies—everything is fair game.

The psychopathic condition behind such 'sermons' issued from the WhatsApp university is a matter to be investigated by psychologists, but their political aim is clear: to demolish Nehru's image. The nine years he spent in jail as part of the freedom struggle are sought to be dismissed as 'propaganda'; his death is attributed to sexually transmitted diseases. No disinformation is ridiculous or disgusting enough to be avoided. Consider just two examples: In a speech delivered by Rajiv Dixit, a champion of 'Bharatiya sanskriti' and a late close associate of a TV yoga instructor turned Fast Moving Consumer Goods manufacturer, it was claimed that Nehru was a classmate of Muhammad Ali Jinnah's and Edwina Mountbatten's at Harris college, London. The speech is available on Youtube[1] and as of late April 2019, it had had almost 57 lakh views. Dixit's sermon is about the dismemberment of India—the creation of Pakistan. The person responsible for it, he tells his audience, was the wily Englishwoman Edwina, who found in Jinnah and Nehru, both senseless with desire for her, willing soldiers to fulfil her mission. Here are the exact words Dixit uses, some four minutes into the video:

> ...yeh jo Pakistan bana, usmein Muhammad Ali Jinnah ki bhoomika itni badi nahin thi—uss-se jaada badi bhoomika

---

[1] https://www.youtube.com/watch?time_continue=33&v=5XtcFiZwENY

Lady Mountbatten ki thi. Edwina Mountbatten ka naam aap jaante hain, nahin jaante hain toh jaan lijiye, woh Bharat ka antim Angrez adhikari jiska naam tha Louis Mountbatten, uski patni thi… Pakistan ban-ne ka sabse bada kaaran woh Edwina thi. Aap jaante hain kya khel khela usne? Edwina Mountbatten London ke Harris College mein padhti thi jismein yeh Jinnah padha karta tha. Aur usi college mein Bharat ke pehle pradhan mantri Pandit Jawaharlal Nehru bhi padhte the. Harris College mein teen log padhte the saath mein, ek hi class mein—ek hi class mein, dhyan dena—Jinnah Muhammad Ali, Pandit Jawaharlal Nehru aur Edwina… uss samey woh Mountbatten nahin thi, shaadi uski baad mein hui. … Toh Edwina, Jinnah aur Nehru ek hi class mein padhte the, aur record aur dastaawej bataate hain ki Edwina se donon lage hue the. Yeh documents batate hain. Aur Edwina itni chaalaak mahila thi ki donon ko handle karti thi woh. Itni chaalaak thi. Ek ko sabere morning mein, doosre ko sham ko. Aur Jinnah aur Nehru ka sabse bada jo jhagda hota tha woh Edwina ko lekar. Yeh jhagda wahan se shuru hua, Harris College se…

(… the role that Jinnah played in the creation of Pakistan wasn't as big as that played by Edwina Mountbatten. You would have heard of Edwina Mountbatten, if you haven't, you must—she was the wife of the last English administrator of India, Louis Mountbatten. … This Edwina was the biggest reason for the creation of Pakistan. Can you guess what game she played? Edwina Mountbatten was studying in London's Harris College, where this Jinnah was a student, too. As was India's first prime minister, Pandit Jawaharlal Nehru. Three people studying together in Harris College, in the same class—please note, in the same class—Jinnah Muhammad Ali, Pandit Jawaharlal Nehru and Edwina—at that time she wasn't Mountbatten, she married him later. … So, Edwina, Jinnah and Nehru were together in the same class, and records and documents tell us that they were both 'doing' Edwina. This is what documents tell us. Edwina was such a crafty woman, she handled them both—one man in the morning, the other at night. And the biggest quarrel Jinnah and Nehru ever had was to do with Edwina. The quarrels began there, in Harris College…)

Dixit's sermon goes on to talk about Motilal Nehru setting up a political party with the sole purpose of striking a deal with the British that when they finally left India, they would make his son, Jawaharlal, the prime minister; and about the British secret service, years later, getting Louis Mountbatten married to the seductress Edwina—'*Nehru aur Jinnah ki weakness*' ('Nehru's and Jinnah's weakness')—before they sent him to preside over India's Independence and the creation of Pakistan. There is a lot else, about alcohol, bedrooms, blackmail and the villainous 'Nehru ji' contracting a mysterious AIDS-like sexually transmitted disease that caused his body to rot long before he died.

Let us not concern ourselves with the juvenile prurience and misogyny of the sermon—these have long been part of a certain kind of right-wing discourse and now infect the language of people elected to our highest offices. Let us only consider the facts—actually, just three: there is no Harris college in London; Jinnah, thirteen years older than Nehru, had returned from England almost a decade before Nehru reached its shores; and poor Edwina never had any education beyond high school. But why have any qualms about uttering plain lies in the service of a 'cause', especially when the cause is as tough as making Indians, particularly Hindus, hate Nehru!

And the second example: In late 2017, the head of the BJP's IT cell, Amit Malviya, tweeted a collage of pictures of Jawaharlal Nehru with different women in order to portray him as a philanderer.[2] In three of the nine pictures, Nehru is hugging his sister Vijayalakshmi Pandit and being kissed on the cheek by his niece Nayantara. In a fourth, he's congratulating a family friend, Mrinalini Sarabhai, after her classical dance performance. In the rest, he is receiving or seeing off public figures and official guests like Jackie Kennedy and the Mountbattens' young daughter Pamela.

---

[2] https://www.altnews.in/bjp-cell-head-amit-malviya-shares-affectionate-pictures-nehru-sister-niece-claims-hardik-patels-dna/

The RSS, BJP and their ideological associates have, of late, realized that they cannot publicly denounce and denigrate Gandhi, Patel, Bose and Ambedkar, so they have tried to appropriate these icons. But Nehru remains anathema to the Hindu right. Even after half a century of his death, he continues to give them nightmares. Why? It is because he was a rationalist and a modernizer but also deeply rooted in his tradition, and hence very effective with the people. Despite his 'atheism' and 'western ways'—two attributes overemphasized by friends and foes alike—Nehru could connect with the Indian people magnificently: he could describe dams and industries as the 'temples of modern India' without leading to any hurt sentiments. He could speak openly about the dangers of both Hindu and Islamic fundamentalism and remain popular across communities. He was stridently opposed to the mystification of the political process and to the politics of religious identity. He earned his connect with his people the hard way. This connect reached magical proportions during the national movement and later became the greatest hurdle in the path of those who wanted to impose upon India the politics of religion, including political Hindutva.

The Nehru-haters also find it irritating that he continues to command world-wide respect as a tall leader who dared to articulate in world affairs the core of the Indian wisdom of discarding extremes in favour of an enlightened middle. In this, the economic right has as much of a problem with Nehru as the cultural right.

Despite his supposed indifference to religion and his insistence that 'the country must conduct itself through political principles, not through religious sentiments', Nehru won the faith and respect of his deeply religious compatriots and even today continues to be a figure of reverence and fond remembrance. But it is also true that as India's population gets younger and first-hand knowledge of the freedom struggle and the early years of Independence fades, the hate campaign has succeeded to the extent that misconceptions like Nehru's 'ignorance' of Indian culture and 'contempt' for Hinduism, and his 'rejection' of religion in general, have become widespread among lay people.

And even among academics: way back in 2004, I was attending a conference of scholars of Indian religions and cultures at Esalen Institute, California and was amazed to hear from a very respected scholar of philosophy and history that 'the rise of Hindutva politics in India is due to the fact that Nehru suppressed religion, particularly its public display'.

Any Indian born and brought up in 'Nehru's India' would find this statement bizarre. Nehru and his colleagues were farsighted, and in continuation of Gandhi's idea that 'every religion has some element of Truth', tried to evolve a state which sought to neither privilege nor suppress any religion and its public display, and provided space to atheists as well. This was in continuity with the Indian way of looking at these things. Even after Nehru's demise, when the word 'secular' was explicitly inserted into the preamble of the Indian Constitution through the 42nd amendment, care was taken to translate it in Hindi not as '*Dharma-nirpeksha*' but '*Panth-nirpeksha*'; because in Indian linguistic usage the term 'dharma' stands not for a religious doctrine, dogma or faith system, but for the 'inherent nature' of things, or for law.

I cannot claim to have read everything written or spoken by Nehru, but I have read a lot by and about him, and I haven't come across a single word that can be construed as contemptuous of the Hindu—or for that matter any cultural or religious—tradition. As for the peculiar self-definition that has been attributed to him—'English by education, Muslim by culture and Hindu by accident'—it is not to be found anywhere in Nehru's writings or records of his speeches and conversations. This 'quote' was imposed on him in the 1950s by the Hindu Mahasabha leader N. B. Khare, a fact duly noted by the well-known journalist and author, and now a member of the BJP, M.J. Akbar, among others.[3] Recently, the web portal Alt News has delved deep into the history of this quote and traced it to N.B. Khare beyond any doubt.[4]

---

[3] M.J. Akbar, *Nehru: The Making of India* (New Delhi: Roli Books, 2002), 27.

[4] https://www.altnews.in/did-jawaharlal-nehru-ever-say-i-am-english-by-education-muslim-by-culture-and-hindu-by-accident/

The rumour-mongering only underlines the rumour-mongers' fear of Nehru. This fear is rooted in hatred for an inclusive idea of India that was a natural evolution of the varied and rich cultural experience of the Indian people and was articulated politically during the freedom movement. The challenge that the leaders of our freedom movement faced was to evolve a modern national consciousness out of the traditionally given solidarities of religious and caste identities. The leaders of the Indian national movement knew well that only an inclusive and enlightened nationalism could sustain the struggle for Independence and give us a viable and stable free nation. They were certainly not fully and always successful, but while noting their failures, one must never forget that the task was not easy. And it is important to remember that this was not merely a vague cultural idea or only a political stance. Nehru espoused this idea of India vigorously, and came to symbolize it as a leader of the Independence movement and later as prime minister.

4

In *The Discovery of India* (1945), Nehru elaborates upon his understanding of religion which he had put forward in *An Autobiography* (1936) in the context of Gandhi's fast against untouchability. He writes of his aversion to the 'superstitious practices and dogmatic beliefs' and 'uncritical credulousness' that often go with religion. At the same time, he also notes that 'religion had supplied some deeply felt inner need of human nature, and the vast majority of people all over the world could not do without some form of religious belief. It had produced many fine types of men and women, as well as bigoted, narrow-minded, cruel tyrants. It had given a set of values to human life, and though some of these values had no application today, or were even harmful, others were still the foundation of morality and ethics.'[5]

[5] Jawaharlal Nehru, *The Discovery of India* (New Delhi: Penguin, 2010), 13.

This nuanced understanding is rooted in the insight that 'Life does not consist entirely of what we see and hear and feel, the visible world which is undergoing change in time and space; it is continually touching an invisible world of other and possibly more stable or equally changeable elements, and no thinking person can ignore this invisible world.'[6] Along with this insight, Nehru also felt a 'sense of the mysterious, of unknown depths', and confessed, '[b]ut the way to that understanding seems to me essentially the way of science.'[7]

The 'sense of the mysterious, of [the] unknown depths' of existence is part of human consciousness and so is the need to relate with it. This comes out beautifully in hymns like the Nasadiya Sukta from the *Rigveda* (quoted in *The Discovery of India* in full) and in ancient Tao teachings from China. This sense was described as the sense of 'cosmic wonder' by Einstein. It is precisely this need of the human spirit that humankind has so far tried to satisfy through various religions. At the same time, creative expressions of the human spirit like in the arts, music and literature have also played a major role in the process. After Independence, Nehru was as insistent on having autonomous institutions to promote literature, fine arts, music, drama and film—the national academies of letters, fine arts, music and drama, the National School of Drama and the Film Institute—as he was eager to have institutes of technology and nuclear reactors. These initiatives were not only about promoting superior culture; in Nehru's vision, their more important function was to address the 'spiritual emptiness facing our technological civilization'.

Elaborating on his 'philosophy of life', Nehru underlines his 'feeling at home' in a 'pantheistic atmosphere' and his attraction to 'the *advaita* philosophy of Vedanta' and the 'appeal of the ethical approach to life':

> What is the mysterious? I do not know. I do not call it God because God has come to mean much that I do not believe in. I

---

[6] Ibid., pp. 13–14.

[7] Ibid., pp. 15–16.

> find myself incapable of thinking of a deity or of any unknown supreme power in anthropomorphic terms, and the fact that many people think so is continually a source of surprise to me. Any idea of a personal God seems very odd to me. Intellectually, I can appreciate to some extent the conception of monism, and I have been attracted towards the *advaita* (non-dualist) philosophy of the Vedanta ... I realize that merely an intellectual appreciation of such matters does not carry one far. ... The diversity and fullness of nature stir me and produce a harmony of the spirit, and I can imagine myself feeling at home in the old Indian or Greek pagan and pantheistic atmosphere, but minus the conception of God or gods that was attached to it.
>
> Some kind of ethical approach to life has a strong appeal for me, though it would be difficult for me to justify it logically. I have been attracted by Gandhiji's stress on right means and I think one of his greatest contributions to our public life has been this emphasis.'[8]

Not only my parents and Mahant Jagannathdas ji, but anyone nurtured within the Indian religious sensibility would immediately relate to what Nehru is saying here. Indic religious traditions celebrate multitudes of gods and goddesses and other divinities. The Hindu tradition has been quite happy with its 'pantheistic atmosphere', and has left the question of choosing or not choosing anthropomorphic personal gods or God to each individual. Even the theoretically monotheistic faiths—Islam and Christianity—in practice have a number of divinities providing spiritual solace and pragmatic solutions to the faithful. Celebration of diversity, tolerance of difference and respect for others' faiths are not politically motivated slogans. These have been facts of India's social life, the gist of its cultural and spiritual *sadhana*, i.e., purposeful practice.

And this *sadhana*, with all its brooding reflection, is no synonym for sadness. Nehru quotes Arrian, the Greek historian of Alexander's campaign to north India: 'No nation is fonder

---

[8] Ibid., p. 16.

of singing and dancing than the Indian.'[9] He calls himself a 'pagan' yet again, contrasting his nature to the pessimist's: 'I was somewhere at the back of my mind, a pagan, with a pagan's liking for the exuberance of life and nature, and not very much averse to the conflicts life provides.'[10]

Ordinary, practising Hindus, as also scholarly ones, many even belonging to orthodox institutions, hardly found anything alien in Nehru's approach. In fact, some of the leading sadhus and acharyas of Nehru's time, and even later, were quite vocal in their admiration of him. You will read an excerpt from the autobiography of Bhagwadacharya—a prominent figure of the Ramanandi sampraday—who in spite of some peoples' opposition, insisted on beginning his religious discourse by paying tributes to 'Mahatma ji and Pandit ji' (See p. 391).

It is only the votaries of political Hindutva and the followers of the peculiar 'Amrikapanthi' branch of Hinduism—both of which suffer from a deep inferiority complex—who are violently troubled by Nehru's enlightened approach. In the 'pantheistic atmosphere' of Indian tradition, one is judged not for which God, or gods and goddesses, one believes in, but for one's *aacharan* and *charitra,* conduct and character. It is not at all surprising that the self-appointed guardians of Hinduism attack their targets precisely on these counts. But due to their own Victorian and Protestant puritanism, these poor souls are forced to reduce the idea of character merely to matters of sex, to what one eats and drinks and what one wears. Unfortunately for them, Indian tradition has been remarkably mature on this count. Indians do not reject their leaders—social, political, cultural and intellectual—merely on the basis of slander campaigns.

Nehru had a far truer and more mature understanding of Indian culture and tradition than the Hindutva lot. What he could not really tolerate was the political use of religious identity. He continued to fight against the use of religion for political power—

---

[9] Ibid., p. 119.

[10] Ibid., p. 133.

'communalism', as it is known in the politics of modern India. It is singularly important to remember that Nehru sought to counter communalism—Hindu, Muslim, Sikh, Christian or any other—not merely with 'secularism' but with 'Indian nationalism', which for him was based on diversity and was much more than mere emotionalism. Being a keen observer of the world, and with his robust ethical sense, Nehru, more than many of his contemporaries, could see through the emotional manipulation underlying the 'nationalism' of Hitler and Mussolini, and also understood that 'communalism' (of whatever variety) in Indian politics was the Indian version of that same politics. Six years before World War II erupted, Nehru was telling his daughter Indira about the 'strange Nazi philosophy' which propagated by all means fair or foul not only German superiority but also the 'culling' of the inferior races, and held that 'the age of pure reason and unprejudiced science is over'.[11]

Interestingly, around this time, Subhash Chandra Bose was imagining a party called Samyavadi Sangha, based on a synthesis of Marxism and Fascism, and was also taking Nazi philosophy at face value. He 'seemed to believe that Nazis were only interested in the elimination of Jewish influence', and was 'astounded when Jawaharlal presented a resolution to the Congress Working Committee proposing that the Congress offer employment to Jewish refugees who were experts and specialists'.[12]

Nehru noted repeatedly that not only Hindu but also Muslim communalism was full of admiration for Hitler. Both shared (as they continue to share) antipathy towards democratic nationalism, but with a difference (which is as crucial to understand today as it was then), clearly articulated by Nehru: 'That the Muslim organizations have shown themselves to be quite extraordinarily communal has been [apparent] to everybody. *The*

---

[11] Letter dated July 31, 1933, "The Nazi Triumph in Germany," *Glimpses of World History* (New Delhi: Penguin, 2004), 1065.

[12] Rudrangshu Mukherjee, *Nehru and Bose: Parallel Lives* (New Delhi: Penguin-Viking, 2014), 128.

[Hindu] Mahasabha's communalism has not been so obvious, as it masquerades under a nationalist cloak.'[13]

5

Historian Ramchandra Guha, in the prologue to his thought-provoking study *India after Gandhi*, states 'two fundamental ambitions' of his work: 'to pay proper respect to the social and political diversity of India, and to unravel the puzzle that has for so long confronted the scholar and citizen, foreigner as well as native—namely, why there is an India at all?'[14]

It was a version of this query—'why there is an India at all?'—which in various shades was motivating most of India's freedom fighters and intellectuals through the first half of the twentieth century. India is not merely a geographical spread, nor just a political unit. Its vibrant diversity and its resilience despite many axes of conflict make it a major 'outlier' to standard academic definitions—rooted in western historical experience—of 'nation'. And yet, India exists as a nation, and continues to be a civilizational entity. The idea of India is the product of the belief, born during the freedom movement, of being destined to offer something significant to the whole world. This idea implies an experiment of a very different kind of nation-building, from which the whole world can learn a lot—as Dr Zakir Hussain once put it. This was the idea that guided Nehru—and gave him confidence—in the gigantic task of transforming an ancient and continuing civilization into a modern nation-state defined by diversity, accommodation and the best, most humane and enlightened elements of tradition and modernity.

This confidence is entirely different from the deep sense of inferiority masquerading as pride that is behind the claims to the status of '*vishvaguru*', or 'world guru', that some people have been

---

[13] Jawaharlal Nehru, *An Autobiography* (New Delhi: Penguin, 2004), 484; emphasis added.

[14] Ramchandra Guha, *India after Gandhi: The History of the World's Largest Democracy* (New Delhi: Picador, 2008), xxvi.

making for India these days. The claim of being a receptacle for the 'great ocean of humanity'—Tagore's famous metaphor for India—and being instinctively inclusive was rooted in historic experience and resulted in the self-confident project of building a modern and genuinely multi-cultural democratic nation-state that still holds many lessons for the world. The Hindutva claims of vishvagurudom, on the other hand, emanate from a diffident mindset which fantasizes the ancient Indian origin of every western discovery and invention, from aircraft and space shuttles to television and the Internet. They imagine a golden age—of which no trace remains and after which, if the Hindutva historians stop to think about what their claims imply, the story of Indian civilization has been one of only decline; a self-engineered decline for at least a few thousand years, for Hindutva history believes our forefathers were 'pure' and masters of their own destiny until the twelfth century.

Nehru suffered from no sense of inferiority as an Indian. To him, the story of our great civilization was not one of unending loss. His favourite metaphor for India is that of a palimpsest, a page from a manuscript reused or altered but still bearing visible traces of its earlier form. Reflecting on its 'depth of soul', he writes about India:

> It was not her wide spaces that eluded me, or even her diversity, but some depth of soul which I could not fathom, though I had occasional and tantalizing glimpses of it. She was like some ancient palimpsest on which layer upon layer of thought and reverie had been inscribed, and yet no succeeding layer had completely hidden or erased what had been written previously. All of these existed in our conscious or subconscious selves, though we may not have been aware of them, and they had gone to build up the complex and mysterious personality of India.[15]

This indeed is an apt description of a society where you can still find not only the bullock cart, but also more subtle

---

[15] Jawaharlal Nehru, *The Discovery of India*, 51.

traces of the Indus Valley civilization along with impressions of later developments, and where you find traces of almost every human race.

The political and intellectual leadership of the Indian freedom movement were very conscious of, were in fact emphatic about, this 'depth of soul' and a clear sense of India's destiny. They articulated it in many ways, in words and in a variety of symbols and metaphors. Bharat Mata—Mother India—was a central metaphor. The slogan '*Bharat Mata ki Jai*' (victory to mother India) was a way to constantly renew the emotional bond with the idea of India. It signified the anti-imperialistic unity of all Indians coming from diverse cultural traditions.

Nehru reflected a lot on this slogan. He writes in his autobiography, 'India becomes *Bharat Mata,* Mother India, a beautiful lady, very old but ever youthful in appearance, sad-eyed and forlorn, cruelly treated by aliens and foreigners ... And yet, India is in the peasant and the worker, not beautiful to look at, for poverty is not beautiful.' Continuing with his reflection, Nehru boldly raises the question of the nature of the 'love' for Mother India: 'Does the beautiful lady of our imaginations represent the bare-bodied and bent workers in the fields and factories? Or the small group of those who have from ages past crushed the masses and exploited them, imposed cruel customs on them and made many of them even untouchable?'[16] This was in 1936; nine years later Nehru recalls how he engaged his audiences on the question 'who is this Bharat Mata, whose victory you wish in this slogan?' and also notes the idea he sought to convey to them: 'The mountains and the rivers of India, and the forests and the broad fields, which gave us food, water, were all dear to us, but what counted ultimately were the people of India ... who were spread out all over this vast land. Bharat Mata, Mother India, was essentially these millions of people, and victory to her meant victory to these people.'[17] (*The Discovery of India*, p. 53)

[16] Jawaharlal Nehru, *An Autobiography*, 448.

[17] *The Discovery of India*, 53.

Mother India was essentially these millions of people, and victory to her meant victory to these people—that is how not only Nehru but all progressive and liberal leaders of the national movement saw India.

This book carries the title that it does in order to remind us that India exists for a purpose; the Indian 'nation' consists of the Indian people—irrespective of creed, caste and gender, or any cultural or ethnic marker and social status. In the vision of the Independent Indian nation that Gandhi, Sarojini Naidu, Subhash Bose, Patel, Maulana Azad, Bhagat Singh and Ambedkar, among many others, had, and which was the vision Nehru championed and, indeed, lived. The slogan 'Bharat Mata ki Jai' could never be used as a violent challenge to the integrity of any religious group of the nation, or anyone who has some other metaphor to express her or his love of the country. The victory cry for Mother India cannot consist of the tortured laments of some of her daughters and sons.

6

The avoidance of extremes is the crux of the rich and varied cultural experience of the Indian people over millennia. The Nasadiya Sukta of the *Rig Veda* forecloses any possibility of conceited claims of finality on the part of any knowledge system. It goes to the extent of boldly declaring that all mysteries are not revealed even to the One who presides over all existence. The Upanishads make the same point even more forcefully. The intent of the *Mahabharata* is to exhort people to follow dharma—the right path—by underlining the devastating consequences of the extremes of personal passions: Vedavyasa, the poet, is heard lamenting at the end of the gigantic text—'I have been telling them to follow dharma, everything else will follow it; but who listens to me?'

Buddha strongly advocated the *Madhyama Pratipada*—'golden middle path'—which is the avoidance of extremes in action and ideas. Mahavira, through his '*Anekantatvada*', made people realize the potential multiplicity of Truth-realization and hence the need for openness and dialogue. Abhinavagupta—the great Shaiva scholar of Tantra and aesthetics from Kashmir—put the gist of this entire tradition most succinctly: नहि एकया दृष्ट्या सम्यंगं निर्वर्णनं निर्वहति ('No single view can claim to describe it all adequately.'). He was making this observation in the context of poetics (in his commentary on Anandwardhana's *Dhwanyaloka),* but its resonances are of much wider significance in the context of the evolution of Indian genius. Later on, this traditional genius impacted even the Semitic, monotheistic theologies and world-views of Christianity and Islam through mutually enriching interactions. The continuing genius of negotiating through give and take manifests itself in the vernacular Bhakti and Sufi poetry on the one hand and in the statecraft of rulers like Ashoka and Akbar, on the other.

Nehru represents this essence of 'Indianness' which is anathema to those who claim to know the whole truth, which, naturally, is nothing but *their* truth. His policies of non-alignment and mixed economy and the nation-building project undertaken by him and his colleagues have been under attack from sections of the Right *and* the Left.

The unending project of belittling the leaders of India's freedom movement, spreading hatred against Nehru and pitying Gandhi for the 'dreadful mistake' of choosing him as his political heir has, of course, been crucial for the economic and politico-cultural right wing in India. But some liberals share this hatred, too. There is a trend in western academia which denies the devastating effects of colonization, and locates the causes of all the problems facing India in its own tradition and culture. Terrible, man-made famines during the colonial period are normalized as a natural calamity recurrent in Indian history; deliberate de-industrialization and de-urbanization is projected as an eternal characteristic of the Indian landscape; and ruthless economic exploitation is shown as a 'service charge' for the West's civilizing mission.

Gandhi has grown too big to be easily maligned, at least in India, so he has to be projected as a politically harmless if eccentric saint;

but, his 'protége' Nehru has to be projected as a power-hungry hypocrite. Some love to contrast the 'compromising' Nehru with the 'revolutionary' Subhash Bose; some the 'anglophile' Nehru with the 'authentically Indian' Sardar Patel; and some others the Brahmin Nehru with the Dalit Ambedkar. This Nehru-hating convergence of colonization deniers and Hindutva votaries on the one hand and ultra-left and ultra-right analysts on the other is quite revealing of the challenge Nehru and his legacy pose to extremists and arm-chair rebels of all hues.

Writing for the *New York Times* (11 August, 2017), author and columnist Pankaj Mishra recalls African-American writer W.E.B. Du Bois describing August 15, 1947 'as the greatest historical date' of modern history. Mishra informs us, 'Du Bois believed the event was of "greater significance" than even the establishment of democracy in Britain, the emancipation of slaves in the United States or the Russian Revolution. The time "when the white man, by reason of the colour of his skin, can lord it over coloured people" was finally drawing to a close.' But something went terribly wrong, according to Mishra: 'Gandhi was determined not to let postcolonial India replicate the injustices built into modern civilization or, as he put it, "English rule without the Englishman." From that perspective, Gandhi may seem to have chosen his protégé unwisely: Nehru was the scion of a family of rich Brahmin Anglophiles.'

Interestingly, this is exactly the charge made by the RSS (minus the 'Brahmin' bit). RSS professes great respect for Gandhi, and so does Mishra. Neither can come to terms with the fact that as late as January 1942, Gandhi was telling the All India Congress Committee (AICC) in his speech at Wardha, 'Not Rajaji, not Sardar, but Jawahar will be my successor' (See p. 318).

Mishra then tells us, 'Nehru never let go of the British-created colonial state and its well-oiled machinery of repression. The brute power of the Indian police and army was used in 1948 to corral the princely state of Hyderabad into the Indian Union. Up to 40,000 Muslims were killed, and the episode remains the single-largest massacre in the history of independent India.' This pontification against the 'brute power' of the Indian state takes no note of the Nizam's and Jinnah's intrigues and the terror of the Razakars in the 'princely state of Hyderabad' (See Nehru's letter to V.K. Krishna Menon, p. 91). Also, Mishra completely ignores the Nehru-Liaquat pact (1950) through which Nehru committed the governments of India and Pakistan to guaranteeing the security of minorities in their jurisdictions. For this, he had to adopt the policy of 'persuasion' coupled with the warning of using force. Not only at this particular juncture, but in general, Nehru knew that 'power should never be divorced from legitimacy', as Shrinath Raghavan puts it in his study, and rightly advises, 'As India prepares to join the club of great powers, it is essential that its policy-makers and citizens re-acquaint themselves with Nehru's subtle understanding of power.'[18]

'Scholars' pretending sympathy with Muslims after seven decades of Partition from their safe heavens in the West appear to have no idea at all how tough the Nehru government was with Hindu trouble-makers in West Bengal (of course, using the 'brute power' of the state) who wanted to 'retaliate' against the attacks on Hindus in the then East Pakistan. They cannot even imagine the pressure Nehru had to withstand within his party and government at this point. There was a clamour for 'transfer of population'—something that not only Savarkar but even Ambedkar had proposed as 'the only lasting remedy for communal peace'. The argument was clear enough: 'There is no reason why the Hindus and the Muslims should keep on trading in safeguards which have proved so unsafe.'[19] Temperatures were so high that not only the 'hardliner' Patel, but also the 'pacifist' Acharya Kripalani advocated a 'tit-for-tat' policy. Protesting against the Nehru-Liaquat pact, the Hindutva icon S.P. Mukherjee resigned from Nehru's cabinet.

---

[18] Shrinath Raghavan, *War and Peace in Modern India: A Strategic History of the Nehru Years* (Ranikhet: Permanent Black, 2017), 320.

[19] B.R. Ambedkar, "Pakistan or the Partition of India," in *Writings and Speeches Vol. 8* (Bombay: Education Department, Government of Maharashtra, 1990), 116.

Nehru was so distraught at the environment within his cabinet and the Congress party that he even thought of relinquishing office and travelling to East Pakistan as a private citizen to convey the message of humanity, just as the Mahatma (who was rather wise and prescient in choosing his 'protégé') had done a couple of years earlier. Nehru wrote to Patel on 21 February, 1950 that such an action would 'strike the imagination of people both in West and East Bengal and make them pause and think'. [20]

We must understand clearly that in a multi-religious country like India, no ruler not confident of the faith and support of the majority community can ensure the democratic rights for the minorities. The basic reason for the Hindutva hatred of Nehru lies precisely here—this 'irreligious' 'Anglophile' had the trust of his compatriots, and he earned this faith the hard way, refusing to cater to baser instincts and phony sentiments.

No one is beyond valid criticism. (Nehru himself, writing under the pen-name 'Chanakya' in the 1930s, cautioned against 'hero-worship of Jawaharlal', telling fellow Indians bluntly, 'We want no Caesars' (See p. 312). It cannot be denied that some of Nehru's policies have been damaging. Yet, on the whole, in any serious assessment sensitive to historical context, Nehru ranks very high on the ethical scale of a statesman, which is different from individual ethics. As the leader of a country, one has to do things which as a private citizen one would not like to do. This is as true of an Akbar as of a Frederick (of 'honesty is the best policy' fame), and of course of a Nehru. To help Pankaj Mishra understand this fact, one would recommend an elementary course in political theory, beginning with the great Indian text *Arthashastra*, or the more accessible *Shukranitisara*—a work on which the 'Anglophile' Nehru dwells in detail in his writings.

Analysts and scholars like Mishra who refuse to see the discontinuity between Hindu religious traditions and Hindutva have contributed to the success of Hindutva in no small measure. In his *New York Times* piece, for instance, Mishra brackets Nehru

---

[20] Srinath Raghavan, *War and Peace in Modern India,* 160.

with Hindu 'nationalists' because of the sin of having faith in 'the essential continuity of India from ancient civilization to modern nation'. Nehru indeed had faith in that continuity, but unlike Hindu 'nationalists', his was not a faith born of ignorant fantasies of the past and distorted imaginations of the future. As already noted, his favourite metaphor for India was that of a palimpsest, carrying traces of multiple cultural memories, signifying continuity with change. He says unequivocally, 'A blind reverence for the past is bad and so also is a contempt for it, for no future can be founded on either of these.'[21] Further, 'Indian history is a striking record of... continuous adaptation of old ideas to a changing environment, of old patterns to new. Because of this, there is no cultural break in it and there is that continuity, in spite of repeated change, from the far distinct days of Mohenjo Daro to our own age. There was a reverence for the past and for traditional forms, but there was also a freedom and flexibility of the mind and tolerance of the spirit. So, while forms often remained, the inner content continued to change.'[22]

~

The 'golden middle path' was Nehru's golden rule. And in his world view, this was not a kind of 'fence-sitting' or a path-of-least-resistance compromise for all seasons. That would be dishonesty or pure cynicism, and even Nehru's critics have been hard-pressed for the slightest evidence of this in his private or public life. To Nehru, especially as prime minister, the middle path was about balance, accommodation and tempering revolutionary zeal with necessary checks and balances; it was an essential condition for democracy and for development.

Let us look only at his economic policy to understand this approach. Writing *The Discovery of India* just a couple of years before Independence, Nehru was clear that 'India, constituted as she is, cannot play a secondary part in the world. She will either

---

[21] *The Discovery of India*, 573.

[22] Ibid., 576.

count for a great deal or not count at all.'[23] In pursuance of 'India's destiny', he sought to foil neo-imperialist designs by creating a force of non-aligned nations challenging the convenient binary of the post-World-War II world. At the same time, domestically he created a strong public sector within the framework of the mixed economy and had a futuristic vision of scientific research and cultural development. His policies are paying off today, and only a very ungrateful bunch can ignore this.

A detailed discussion of the so-called 'mixed economy' is outside the purview of this introduction. Still, the fact remains that it was the wisest option in the given circumstances. A newly independent country, economically devastated by colonial loot and desirous of not aligning with either of the Cold-war era blocks, had to create a solid industrial base for political and economic independence. It had to use the resources of both the private and the public sector, had to seek foreign aid and still adopt protectionist policies to help domestic capital. And, at the same time, it could not have given short shrift to the issue of 'just redistribution of national resources'. To go in for a totally unregulated market economy would have been a betrayal of the ideals of the national movement and the principles of equality; and to go in for absolute state control would have made the creation of wealth impossible and, of course, would have compromised the ideal of democratic freedom.

'Nehrunomics', or the mixed economy, was ridiculed by puritan votaries of both the left and the right. As it happens, history has vindicated the basic idea and approach underlying Nehrunomics. Without going into much detail, one just needs to recall the demise of the Soviet Union and the transformation of the 'People's Republic of China' on the one hand, and the consequences in much of the West of total dependence on the free market, on the other. The worth of Nehrunomics—which sought redistributive justice, a democratic polity, individual freedom and national independence all at the same time—can

[23] Ibid., 48.

be better appreciated in the light of a recent statement by Francis Fukuyama. In an interview to the *New Statesman* (17 October, 2018) Fukuyama, who some years ago saw western capitalism as the 'end of history', says, 'If you mean redistributive programmes that try to redress this big imbalance in both incomes and wealth that has emerged, then, yes, I think not only can it [socialism] come back, it ought to come back. This extended period, which started with Reagan and Thatcher, in which a certain set of ideas about the benefits of unregulated markets took hold, in many ways it's had a disastrous effect.'

Of course, the Nehruvian mixed economy can be critiqued from the point of view of priorities and implementation, may be on many other counts too. But a genuine critique will be sensitive to its context, appreciative of its intent and orientation, and certainly mindful of the benefits of hindsight which were not available to Nehru and his colleagues.

7

Some people argue that Nehru's birth into relative wealth and privilege meant that he could never be truly representative of India, or be fully accepted by the Indian people, especially given the Hindus' reverence for ascetics and renunciants. Nehru did indeed come from a 'rich' family, but Hindus who love their Mahatmas do not hate successful householders, in fact, they look up to them. Contrary to modern mythology, Hindu tradition has *never* been 'other-worldly'. On p. 233 in this volume Nehru points out that other-worldliness was valorized by medieval European Christianity, not by Hindu tradition. Indian people don't dismiss someone merely because of her or his birth in a privileged environment. They of course admire those who deliberately renounce their privileges in search of Truth and the greater good.

After the Lahore Congress session of 1930 Jawaharlal had fully come out of Motilal Nehru's shadow and was tremendously popular in his own right. In *An Autobiography* he reflects seriously and yet with some enjoyment on this 'unusual degree of popularity with the masses'. Here, he records the legends which continued at least till my childhood, that is, up to the sixties of the last century—one of the most interesting being that the Nehru family sent its 'linen weekly from India to a Paris laundry'. Nehru's remark is quite characteristic of him: 'Anything more fantastic and absurd is difficult for me to imagine...'

'Fantastic' it is, but certainly not 'absurd'. Legends convey not the 'hard facts', but the popular and poetic reconstructions. The point of the legend is not the Paris laundry, but Nehru's willing renunciation of entitlement and comforts—his *tyaag*. It is partly irritating, partly amusing to see some people reducing everyone else to primordial identities of race, ethnicity, caste, religion or gender, keeping the privilege of individual agency only for themselves. Nehru, the 'scion of a family of rich brahmin Anglophiles' chose to discard the privileges of his caste and class status and lead the freedom movement. He chose to spend a decade of his life in British prisons in India, unlike some commentators who settle their own brahmin, Anglophile selves in the snug and safe confines of the capital city of the erstwhile Raj, untouched by the Indian heat and dust or the din of desperate struggle against the right-wing onslaught on democratic ideals and values.

~

There is also an argument that Nehru was too 'modern' and this prevented him from really understanding his country and its people. Not only Nehru-hating trolls and the often blinkered and sometimes disingenuous liberals, but also some serious scholars and well-meaning people assume a gulf between the 'traditionalist' Gandhi and the 'modernist' Nehru. At least scholars should know better.

What kind of 'traditional' practices were available to Gandhi and how did he relate with them? Having returned from South Africa, he established his first ashram on the bank of the Sabarmati river at Kocharab, Ahmedabad. Amongst the inmates of the ashram, there was an 'untouchable' couple—Dadubhai and his wife—belonging to the 'dhed' caste of hide-workers.

Even Kasturba was upset, and Gandhi's supporters warned of withholding contributions to his project. The 'traditionalist' Gandhi politely asked his supporters to keep their contributions, as there was no question of the 'untouchables' leaving the ashram.[24] Let us also not forget that the first attempt on Gandhi's life was made in Pune on June 25th, 1934 for the 'offence' of campaigning against the 'traditional' practice of untouchability.

Tradition also considered the home to be the proper place for a woman. Gandhi, starting from his first ashram and his first satyagraha in Champaran, made the participation of women not just a primary condition of any social and political activity, but the touchstone to judge its worth.

Gandhi knew that tradition is a living flow, not something frozen in time. Ancient texts and rituals are important, but they become 'tradition' precisely because of historical evolution reflected in everyday practices. In this process, they are transformed, sometimes beyond recognition. Gandhi related less with the dominant expressions of tradition and more with its dissenting, liberal voices. To him, blind submission at the cost of his own moral judgement was unacceptable. He looked at tradition through the prism of vernacular bhakti sensibility, in which lie the seeds of India's own early modernity. He discovered the Gujarati bhakta poet Narsi Mehta—whose song 'Vaishnav Jan to tene kahiye' became his signature tune—before the Bhagwad Gita (which, incidentally, he read first in English translation).

The assumption behind the binary of 'traditional' and 'modern' between Gandhi and Nehru is that while Gandhi took his tradition seriously, Nehru couldn't care less, and was even contemptuous of it. Nothing could be further from the truth, as the pieces in this volume will demonstrate. Nehru's family environment did not exclude intimate introduction to Hindu tradition and culture. Early exposure to theosophy apart from

---

[24] Rajmohan Gandhi, *Mohandas: A True Story of a Man, His People and an Empire* (New Delhi: Penguin, 2006), 195.

Christian and Islamic lore and practices only served as a very useful addition to his upbringing.

On the other hand, Gandhi never hid his gratitude to 'non-Indians' like Tolstoy, Ruskin and of course Jesus; and when pestered about the 'non-Indian' roots of his Ahimsa principle, he said bluntly: 'I have nothing to be ashamed of if my views on Ahimsa are the result of my western education. I have never tabooed all western ideas, nor am I prepared to anathematize everything that comes from the West as inherently evil.'[25]

Nehru knew India and its culture far better than many self-proclaimed lovers of the 'holy' Indian or Hindu tradition. In a conversation with R.K. Karanjia in 1960, when questioned about the need to make the Congress a cadre-based party, Nehru spontaneously recalled Kabir and the Panth established in his name, to underline the dangers of a 'movement' becoming a 'cadre-based' system: 'You know, first comes Kabir the reformer, and after Kabir comes Kabir Panth. I mean, the whole thing becomes a matter of conflicts and counter-conflicts and serves only to dissipate the nation's vitality.'[26]

Nehru tried to figure out the meaning of 'being Indian' both through participation in the freedom struggle and through deep study and reflection over decades. His doubts, questions and reflections can be seen permeating his articles, letters, *An Autobiography* and *Glimpses of World History* (fascinating letter-tutorials in history to his adolescent daughter Indira Priyadarshini). By the time he was writing *The Discovery of India* in Ahmednagar fort prison camp 'during the five months, April to September 1945', he had well-defined views on the queries, questions and discoveries that define Indian cultural experience. Having arrived at his idea of India after such serious and strenuous efforts, he didn't need to wear his Indianness

---

[25] *Young India*, October 11, 1928; quoted by Rajmohan Gandhi, *Mohandas*, 318.

[26] R.K. Karanjia, *The Mind of Mr. Nehru*, (London: George Allen and Unwin, 1960), 58.

on his sleeve. It came out spontaneously in the man's words and actions. Once, when Nehru was in Bihar, there was great pandemonium in a public meeting organized for him. Babu Jagjivan Ram in his welcome speech welcomed 'Pandit ji to the Bihar of Buddha and Ashoka'. Nehru, irritated with the enthusiastic, but undisciplined crowd started his address with these words: 'Babuji has welcomed me to the Bihar of Buddha and Ashoka, but your behaviour makes me feel that I have come to the Magadha of Jarasandha.'

One has to know the story of Jarasandha to appreciate the sobering wit here, and to imagine the impact it might have had on the crowd. According to the senior academic who related this incident to me, 'there was almost pin-drop silence in no time'. (Recall, in contrast, the famous speech in an election year by a leading Hindutva icon, who took Alexander to Pataliputra so that the fabled Greek conqueror could be pushed back by the great people of Bihar!)

A very graceful and confident cultural self speaks in Nehru's writings and conversations. In a letter written on January 20, 1931 to Indira, he gives a translation of a verse from the *Bhagavata* alluding to the 'desire' of king Rantidev who wanted nothing for himself, but only the end to the woes of all creatures—कामये दु;खतप्तानाम् प्राणिनामार्तिनाशनम्. Such indirect allusions and direct references to the Upanishads, *Bhagavata, Mahabharata, Ramayana, Panchatantra, Arthashastra, Shukranitisara, Rajatarangini* and other texts abound in Nehru's writing and conversations. In his autobiography, talking of the modern concept of 'law and order', Nehru recalls the 'thousand year old Kashmiri historic epic' *Rajatarangini* and its author Kalhana: 'I find in the *Rajatarangini*...that the phrase which is repeatedly used in the sense of law and order, something that it was the duty of ruler and the state to preserve, is *dharma* and *abhaya*—righteousness and absence of fear. Law was something more than mere law, and order was fearlessness of the people. How much more desirable is this idea of inculcating fearlessness than of enforcing "order" on a frightened populace.'

Dharma for Kalhana and others in Indic traditions was and is *not* defined by monopolistic claims on every aspect of human life. In Europe, after defeating paganism (with which Nehru felt an affinity), the Church insisted on and violently imposed its monopoly on the moral and emotional life of the individual as well as the political life of the community. It arrogated to itself the power to impose moral unanimity and provide spiritual guidance. In India, fortunately, such a thing could never happen. This good fortune of India and Hinduism is the greatest misfortune of political Hindutva, which fantasizes for itself a medieval Church-like monopoly over the moral and emotional life of every individual, along with an authoritarian political system.

In *Glimpses,* Nehru is actually trying to inculcate a sense of 'culture and civilization' in his adolescent daughter; as he makes clear quite early on. He ends his letter of 18 January 1931, with these words: 'Culture and civilization are difficult to define, and I shall not try to define them. But among the many things that culture includes are certainly restraint over oneself and consideration for others. If a person has not got this self-restraint and no consideration for others, one can certainly say that he is uncultured.' [27]

Culture includes many things, and which ones are emphasized depends on the person concerned. The above statement indicates Nehru's own idea of culture more than a 'standard' definition. It brings to mind the way Gandhi elaborated on his idea of Ahimsa: '*Ahimsa* is a comprehensive principle. We are helpless mortals caught in the configuration of *himsa.* The saying that life lives on life has a meaning to it. Man cannot for a moment live without consciously or unconsciously committing outward *himsa.* The very fact of his living—eating, drinking and moving about—necessarily involves some *himsa,* destruction of life, be it ever so minute. A votary of *Ahimsa* therefore remains true to his faith if the spring of all his actions is compassion ... He will be

[27] Jawaharlal Nehru, *Glimpses of World History* (New Delhi: Penguin, 2004), 40.

constantly growing in self-restraint and compassion, but he can never become entirely free from outward *himsa*.'[28]

What defines culture to Nehru, defines Ahimsa to Gandhi—self-restraint and compassion, i.e., consideration for others.

I have mentioned earlier Gandhi's speech at the Wardha session of the AICC in January 1942. It was held to discuss and ratify the resolution of the Congress Working Committee adopted in its meeting at Bardoli in December 1941. As you will see in the note preceding the extract from that speech later in this volume (p. 307), the context of the speech makes Gandhi's unequivocal declaration of Nehru as his successor most poignantly significant.

The Gandhi-Nehru relationship represents not a gulf, but a bridge connecting two ways to modernize tradition and transform an ancient civilization into a modern nation-state.

8

Nehru was a rationalist, and yet he kept a portion of the ashes of his late wife with him till the last, to be immersed along with his own. He composed a superbly moving, poetic paean to the Ganga—'the river of India'— in his final will and testament. Being a rationalist does not mean being a robot. As a matter of fact, Nehru's rationalism did not quite rule out the spiritual quest of human beings, as we have already seen. Similarly, being modern does not mean being unconcerned with or contemptuous of one's own or any tradition and culture. Quite the contrary, it means identifying and relating with, and accelerating the dynamism and modernizing tendencies in, tradition.

Gandhi and Nehru both tried to do the same in their own ways. They differed not in being 'traditionalist' and 'modernist' but in their attitude to industrialization and urbanization. Nehru never hid his preference for technology and industry, and his impatience with the 'glorification of village-life and poverty'. He

---

[28] M.K. Gandhi, *An Autobiography or The Story of my Experiments with Truth*, (Ahmedabad: Navjeevan, 2005), 321.

has documented with transparency his moments of confusion and frustration with Gandhi. In the wake of the sudden withdrawal of the Civil Disobedience Movement after the Gandhi-Irwin pact, Nehru had taken recourse to T.S. Eliot: 'This is the way the world ends/ Not with a bang, but with a whimper.' Throughout his autobiography Nehru is trying to come to terms with 'Gandhi ji's enigmatic and elusive personality'. On the one hand, he cannot hide his annoyance, even anger, when Gandhi withdraws the Non-Cooperation Movement or attributes the horrible Bihar earthquake of 1934 to the 'sin of untouchability'. On the other hand, he comes down heavily on those 'parlour socialists' who dismissed Gandhi as a 'reactionary'.

It is now clear that Gandhi's 'strange' views on industrial civilization provide some valid departures for its serious critique. There is no need to agree with the prognosis of *Hind-Swaraj*, but the spirit of that text is undoubtedly prophetic. It could have been moderated with Nehru's faith in technology and vice versa; Nehru seemingly tried to do precisely that but could not succeed. We must learn from his failures but that can be done only if we recognize his achievements as well as the gigantic problems that a nascent democracy was faced with. Would we have been able to pursue an independent policy without a strong industrial base? Could we have constructed that base without involving the private sector? Could we have maintained a welfare state if the private sector was given a free-for-all guarantee? It is very easy to be wise after the event and pass judgments with the benefit of hindsight, and it is futile as well. The correct thing is to understand the need for the Nehruvian path and then take corrective measures in the light of experiences.

Similarly, many of Gandhi's ideas regarding social organization and political systems remain deeply problematic, while some are quite thought-provoking, even if seemingly strange. This is not the place to discuss the issues involved, but it is clear that differences between 'Bapu' and 'Jawahar' must be seen as part of an animated dialogue between comrades, not as disputes between adversaries. In their correspondence, both leaders put forward their positions quite frankly, even sharply, not with any intent of scoring brownie points but in order to have a shared clarity of perspective. The 'real question', according to Nehru (as Gandhi put it, recalling their discussions) was 'how to bring about man's highest intellectual, economic, political and moral development', and how to ensure 'equal right and opportunity for all'. How could anybody with a moral sense, least of all Gandhi ji, disagree with this? Bapu wrote on 13 November 1945, from Pune, '[T]he impression that I have gathered from our yesterday's talk is that there is not much difference in our outlook.'[29]

Reading these letters, we can very well draw our own conclusions about the Gandhi-Nehru debate, the disagreements and agreements on the future vision of India and the world community, but obviously Gandhi had good reason to say with confidence, '[W]hen I am gone, Jawahar will speak my language.'

In chapter 47 of his autobiography, significantly titled 'What is religion?', Nehru reflects on the intuitive and 'irrational' aspects of a religious approach to life in the context of Bapu's 'mysterious' ways. Gandhi undertook a fast to create a moral pressure against untouchability in May 1933—the third in a series of fasts relating to the same question in less than a year. A few days before beginning his fast, Gandhi wrote a moving letter to Jawahar and asked for a reply. Nehru wrote back equally movingly: 'What can I say about matters I do not understand? I feel lost in a strange country, where you are the only familiar landmark and I try to grope my way in the dark but I stumble.'[30] Nehru was desperate emotionally and intellectually: 'Again I watched the emotional upheaval of the country during the fast, and I wondered more and more if this was the right method in politics. It seemed sheer revivalism, and clear thinking had not a ghost of a chance against it ... Gandhi ji did not encourage others to think; his insistence was only on purity and sacrifice. I felt

---

[29] Jawaharlal Nehru, *A Bunch of Old Letters* (Bombay: Asia Publishing House, 1960), 507.

[30] *An Autobiography*, 389.

that I was drifting away from him mentally, despite my strong emotional attachment to him.'[31]

In spite of Gandhi ji quite often providing occasions for such intellectual desperation—his reaction to the earthquake in Bihar for example—Nehru knew very well that Bapu did not 'strategically use' (as some commentators believe) the *dharmik* idiom, but actually looked at the world in a *dharmik* (not 'religious' but *ethical*) way, and this was the key to the mass appeal enjoyed by 'Bapu—the magician'. Gandhi's *tapasya* comes to Nehru's mind while writing about the Upanishads: 'This idea of some kind of penance, *tapasya*, is inherent in Indian thought, both among the thinkers at the top and the unread masses below. It is present today as it was present some thousands of years ago, and it is necessary to appreciate it in order to understand the mass movements which have convulsed India under Gandhiji's leadership.'[32]

On his own part, Nehru had realized the value of the 'ethical way' even before he grew close to Gandhi. Writing about the farmers' agitation in Awadh on 22 January 1921, he remarked, 'It is not the masses but we, nurtured in an atmosphere of the west, who talk glibly of the inefficiency of peaceful methods. The masses know the power of Ahimsa.'[33] Jawahar indeed was speaking the language of Bapu when, talking with R.K. Karanjia in 1960, he underlined 'the need to find some answer to the spiritual emptiness facing our technological civilization'.[34]

In his foreword to the eminent Hindi poet Ramdhari Singh Dinkar's *Sanskriti ke char Adhyay* (Four Chapters from Culture, 1955), Nehru reflected on Indian society's 'crisis of the spirit': 'We developed at one and the same time the broadest tolerance and catholicity of thought and opinion as well as the narrowest social forms of behaviour. This split personality has pursued us and we struggle against it even today. We overlook and excuse our

---

[31] Ibid., 390.

[32] *The Discovery of India*, 91.

[33] Jawaharlal Nehru, *Selected Works Vol.1*, ed. S. Gopal (New Delhi: Orient Longman, 1972), 211.

[34] *The Mind of Mr. Nehru*, 25.

own failings and narrowness of custom and habit by references to the great thoughts we have inherited from our ancestors. But there is an essential conflict between the two and so long as we do not resolve it, we will continue to have this split personality.

'In a more or less static period these opposed elements did not come into conflict with each other much. But, as the tempo of political and economic change has grown faster, these conflicts have come to be more in evidence.'[35]

No serious student of Indian history can fault this diagnosis. If anything, it requires even more urgent attention now, as the 'tempo of change' has only been accelerated; and at the same time, 'excuses' for 'moral failings and narrowness of custom' have increased manifold.

Nehru realized well the fundamental dilemma faced by a nascent nation-state in our modern, technological civilization. A country of the size and self-respect of India just could not move under the US or USSR umbrella. It had to have its own highest technology, including nuclear technology, and Nehru was clear on that even during the days of the interim government. India is a member of the nuclear club today, in important measure, due to Nehru's vision.

But, 'technological society', inevitable as it is, also breeds 'spiritual emptiness'. How to handle that? Nehru looked towards the arts and literature for making it possible for citizens to achieve the 'quality and character of a fully integrated person', as he put it to Karanjia. His approach to life was not merely 'scientific', it had a strong component of the poetic as well. He realized quite clearly the deep interconnection between the poetic and the spiritual. In 1922, lodged in Agra district jail, he read a lot of 'religious' works with the sensitivity of a poet. He read during this period the *Ramcharitmanas* with the renowned literary figure Ramnaresh Tripathi, a fact which Tripathi ji later related to Dinkar with pride. Nehru himself, in a letter to Gandhi giving a kind of progress

[35] Jawaharlal Nehru, *Jawaharlal Nehru's Speeches 1953–57* (New Delhi: Publications Division, 1958), 416.

report of his studies, made a remarkable observation about the 'Ramayana' of Tulsidas: '[It] is more a spiritual autobiography than a poetic history of Rama.'[36]

Given all this, it is not surprising at all that after Independence, the institutions to promote literature and arts were established with the same alacrity as was shown in establishing the IITs and IIMs; and their autonomy was ensured. Nehru himself was elected the first president of the national academy of letters—the Sahitya Akademi. Expressing his 'pride' at this honour, he emphasized, 'I would not like the Prime Minister to interfere with my work.' As we have noted before, separate academies for fine arts and music and drama were also established, as were the National School of Drama (NSD) and the Film Institute. Besides being the president of Sahitya Akademi, Nehru took active interest in the work of other academies as well. He occasionally came to watch NSD plays, and the old-timers recall that never was a show delayed for the arrival of the PM.

A letter written by Nehru, in his capacity as the president of the Sahitya Akademi, to the Akademi's secretary Krishna Kripalani on 13 March 1954, reflects his concern for the well-being of poets and writers, which went beyond formal rules and procedures. In the letter, he suggests a monthly support of Rs 100/- to the eminent Hindi poet Suryakant Tripathi 'Nirala', who had come upon difficult times (See p. 298). But he directs that the stipend should be made available through Mahadevi Verma (another eminent poet) as Nirala was famously careless of his possessions. (Rs. 100/- was an impressive sum those days, when the prestigious Akademi award carried a cash prize of Rs 5000/-, which was considered huge!)

Following the lead of the centre, the states also established their own similar institutions. To Nehru, the institutionalization of state support to culture with a commitment to autonomy was

---

[36] Cited from a letter preserved in the Gandhi papers in Ahmedabad, by Ramchandra Guha in 'Nehru The Spiritualist?', *The Telegraph*, 15 November 2014.

not a 'wasteful luxury' but one of the primary duties of a state. Andre Malraux, the Indophile French author, diplomat and traveller had good reason to describe Nehru as 'the nation's guru, as Gandhi had been'.[37]

9

Nehru performed the task of the 'nation's guru' by reiterating the traditional Indian respect for creative expression and scholarly vocation and by trying to instil democratic values amongst the people. This becomes particularly poignant these days, when the word 'intellectual' has been turned into a term of abuse, and democracy into a regressive soap-opera. Nehru, instead of asking for 'nationalist' credentials or personal loyalty from intellectuals, respected their autonomy and right to dissent. He respected intellectual and scholarly vocation, not with 'immediate utility' in mind but for its cultural significance. On 1 August 1956, releasing the volumes of *Shanti-Parva* of the critical edition of the *Mahabharata,* edited by V.S. Sukthankar and published by the Bhandarkar Institute of Pune, Nehru felt that 'this work may have a greater significance in the scheme of things than much of that we passing politicians of the day do'.[38]

Democracy is not merely a game of numbers. It is about norms, institutions and practices; rights and duties. Nehru conveyed this message to a variety of audiences in various ways. I can never forget the bit of 'Indian News Reel' (which I saw on TV sometime in the mid-1990s) showing Nehru, during an election speech, explaining to his audience '*Jamhooriyat ke Maani*', i.e., 'the meaning of democracy'.

> **'I am your prime minister,' says Nehru in this clip, 'but by no means your raja, not even your ruler. I am in fact**

[37] Andre Malraux, *Anti-Memoirs,* trans. T. Kilmartin (London: Penguin, 1968), 164.

[38] Jawaharlal Nehru, *Selected Speeches Vol. 3* (New Delhi: Publications Division, 1958), 419.

your servant, and when you see me fail in my duty, it will be your *duty* to pick me by my ear and remove me.' ('Kaan pakdein aur kursi se utaar dein.')

Before being a 'guru', one has to be a *sadhaka*, i.e., learner, which implies recognizing one's limitations. Nehru was aware of the distance between the masses and 'glib talkers nurtured in the atmosphere of the West'. He launched his own adventurous journey to discover India—internally as well externally. He noted with pride, in the context of an election-campaign in the mid-1930s, that 'every mode of transport' was used by him to reach out to the people. Internally also, he traversed the history of the whole world to 'discover' the meaning of India's past and its future destiny.

Ignoring all this, Hindutva politics accuses Nehru of being 'anti-Hindu and insufficiently Indian' because of its own condition of being ill at ease with the tradition it claims to stand for. The better known and amusing consequences of this condition are claims about space shuttles in the vedic era and Internet in the time of the *Mahabharata*; the less immediately apparent consequences are far more serious—a permanent sate of insecurity and a badly masked sense of inferiority, an internalization of hypocritical Victorian morality, a dangerous valorization of vacuous 'manliness', a contempt for civility and compassion, and so on.

This condition, like any condition of being in a state of 'dis-ease' in mind or body, must be properly diagnosed before recommending a cure.

This 'dis-ease' has a historical context—colonial rule and its system of knowledge, which led to a feeling among the ruled of being constantly under attack. What the historian Nicholas Dirks calls 'cultural technologies of rule' worked in many ways. One of them was to 'impose' the observations made in one part of the subcontinent as a 'general rule' across the entire land. This was the beginning of Indians, Hindus in particular, being pushed into a siege mentality, and a state of confusion and embarrassment about their cultural practices, lifestyles, mythology and faith structure.

Take for example the 'Hindu' taboo on crossing the sea. Yes, this was a taboo amongst the brahmins of Bengal and Bihar, but certainly not amongst the trading castes of West and South India. Hindu traders from the South traded in entire South East Asia; Hindu kings established their empires there. Traders from Rajasthan and Gujarat also regularly crossed the sea, and had contacts and settlements in places like Cairo and Astrakhan (Russia). I have visited Astrakhan myself, and consulted the city archives, which preserve the records of the census of the Hindu traders and document their activities, including their regular visits back home.[39] This trade was deliberately destroyed by the British Raj. Meanwhile, for well over a century, all Hindus were painted as insular, ignorant and blinded by superstition; completely lacking in enterprise and the spirit of adventure and inquiry. Inevitably, most Indians began to believe this about themselves, or were permanently on the defensive.

The leaders of our freedom movement, who also steered the nation immediately after Independence, never suffered from any complex about their land and their society; they were confident and proud of but never deluded about India. Nehru was among the tallest of these leaders, immensely proud of his Indianness and hugely knowledgeable. And yet, the irony is that a lot of the colonial constructs about Indian history, which Nehru criticized bitterly, continued to inform school text books under his prime ministership. This was indeed a failure; as was the fact that primary education in general suffered neglect due to the Nehru administration's focus on building institutes of higher learning. This failure to correct the imbalances and biases that had resulted from British colonial rule also affected the character and orientation of Independent India's civil services.

Any holistic critical appraisal of Nehru will have to consider such issues without succumbing to the temptation either of devoted rationalization or simplistic condemnation. Here is a

[39] I've written in detail about this in my travelogue *Hindi Serai: Astrakhan via Yerevan* (New Delhi: Rajkamal Prakashan, 2013).

clear hiatus between Nehru the rebel in the pre-Independence era and Nehru the ruler after Independence. This hiatus needs to be explored and critiqued of course, but for the purpose of making the ideas of the architects of our freedom and our Constitution more inclusive and sensitive, and not for the purpose of replacing them with a right or left variety of totalitarianism.

In the 'common sense' created by colonial knowledge systems, India immediately before the spread of British Raj in the eighteenth century was projected as not only politically unstable (which it was), but also culturally stagnant and intellectually moribund (which it was not). Vernacular wisdom was projected as merely good or bad translation of classical Sanskrit or Persian scholarship. Much of the Indian intelligentsia during and immediately after colonial rule internalized this understanding of their own history and culture, and a cultural and intellectual 'dissociation of sensibility' set in. The whole thing led both among Hindus and Muslims to a feeling of embarrassment about their present and immediate past. They looked for some release from this cultural siege in the remote, supposedly 'pure' Hindu or Muslim past.

This is the background to the kind of revivalism that has been upon us for some time and is at its worst now. This is also the background to the rejection of India's composite culture and shared heritage. This heritage wasn't, of course, always without strife and conflict, but it was dynamic, adaptive and allowed for diversity—for accommodation and co-existence—in a confident, even if not always enlightened and ideal, manner. This common heritage was not detached from the hoary past and classical legacy, but it was conscious of its autonomy, and simply accepted innovations for what they were—innovations. No Hindu poet or true scholar in early modern India, for instance, tried to prove that the sweet dish halwa or the word 'baba' or the architectural marvel that is the Taj Mahal existed in pre-Turk India.

The extremists of the right understand, or even acknowledge, none of this; nor do the extremists of the left. The 'radicals' of the left through their flat, simplistic condemnation of practically everything Hindu have only contributed to aggravating the 'disease' with being Indian that afflicts many Indians, and have thus immensely helped the radicals of the right in their regressive project. The contempt for anything Hindu (including, sometimes, even Gandhi)—so typical of many leftists, liberals and radicals—points not only to a purely instrumentalist understanding of history, but also to an abysmal poverty of imagination. Like their right-wing counterparts, they also look at tradition only through ancient texts, ignoring its complexity and constant evolution in everyday practices. That is why, while participating in the present-day political discourse on 'cow-protection', many left and liberal intellectuals put in considerable academic effort to 'prove' the consumption of beef amongst ancient Indians. They insist on ancient texts just as the right wing does, of course with different aims. The right wing assumes that after the 'golden' ancient (read 'pure' and Hindu) period, India saw nothing but decline; and the left wing 'beef in vedic India' enthusiasts assume that the Hindus after the ancient period somehow forfeited the right to develop new dietary preferences and taboos, and to go beyond the beliefs and practices of their ancestors.

Memory defines individual and collective identity. It implies a serious moral responsibility of choosing what to remember and what to forget. This choice obviously depends on the imagination of a future. If nurtured merely emotionally, without any rational negotiation of the past and an ethical imagination of the future, memory leads to disastrous delusions. The cultural memory of India cannot be narrow and exclusionist, because such a memory would only be violating the very object of memory—the real historical experience of the Indian people and their diverse traditions. Nehru understood this. His *Discovery of India* is indeed an expression of 'the nationalist imagination' as Sunil Khilnani puts it, 'but a highly unusual one, capacious, accepting and with no trace of a desire for purification and hardening of boundaries.'[40]

---

[40] Sunil Khilnani, *The Idea of India* (London: Hamish Hamilton, 1997), 168.

Indians need to gratefully celebrate the political and intellectual leadership of the national movement, even if with some reservations. The Indian freedom, or national, movement had an ethical side to it which made it self-confident enough to 'criticize' its society and try to purify it of evils like untouchability, misogyny and bigotry. The freedom fighters and 'founding parents' of the Republic of India respected the real nature of cultural memory and resisted the attempts to turn it into an instrument of regressive politics. Those liberals and radicals who bracket Nehru with the Hindutva lot for having a sense of the cultural continuity of India are not likely to realize this, but all sensible citizens must know that no political community can live with cultural amnesia. And no progressive and egalitarian nation can be built without a confident, rational and enlightened engagement with culture. This was what Nehru attempted.

10

Nehru might have been a yogi in his previous birth, but in this birth, he was a political person. It bears repeating here that Nehru ranks very high on the ethical scale of a leader, which is different from individual ethics. Still, the fact remains that he and his comrades were after all human. They had ambitions, strengths of mind and also weaknesses; moments of mutual distrust and mis-understanding, too. Nehru and Maulana Azad had very cordial relations, but in 1946, on the question of alliance with the Unionist Party in Punjab, they differed. Some people actively worked to spoil relations between Nehru and Maulana, and Maulana went to the extent of describing Nehru as someone who 'is very vain and cannot stand that anybody else should receive greater support and admiration than he.'[41]

While it is important to recall such disagreement, it is also important to know that this unpleasant interlude came to an end

---

[41] Abul Kalam Azad, *India Wins Freedom: The Complete Version* (Hyderabad: Orient Longman, 1988) 137–38.

very soon. Maulana enjoyed a very respected position in Nehru's government after Independence, and the book carrying the highly critical remark quoted above is yet dedicated to 'Jawaharlal Nehru—Friend and Comrade'.

Yes, there were genuine differences of opinion, sometimes very sharply expressed in private and in public, leading even to parting of ways. But some people have been trying to present a very distorted version of such political tensions with obvious intentions, and naturally Nehru has been the worst victim of such distortion and disinformation. In January, 2016, a leading national TV channel, citing official sources, aired a programme 'exposing' a 'letter written by Nehru', that allegedly compromised Subhash Chandra Bose's life, as Nehru had referred to Bose as a 'war criminal'. The letter, ridiculously enough, was addressed to the 'PM of England Clement Attle' of 'Down Street', and the anchor speaking immaculate English had found nothing amiss here, nor had his partners in fakery—Clement Attlee (not 'Attle') was prime minister of Britain (not 'England') and like his predecessors and successors, had his office on Downing (not 'Down') Street. Even if people were expected to ignore that Nehru, with his impeccable English and general knowledge could not have written such rubbish, were they really expected to take an unsigned letter seriously?

And just a couple of days before this, on Netaji jayanti, January 23, the spectacular event of declassifying the 'Netaji Files' had been organized by the BJP government, obviously with the hope of putting Nehru on the mat. But, quite contrary to such expectations, the files revealed a 'Tale of Nehru's Warmth – Not Sinister Conspiracy', as Anirban Mitra's story in the Wire was titled.[42] Anirban reconstructed the 'Tale' from the declassified documents of how Nehru moved, initially, the government for interim help and then the Congress party for a lasting mechanism

[42] Anirban Mitra, "The Netaji Files Reveal a Tale of Nehru's Warmth – Not Sinister Conspiracy," The Wire, May 27, 2017, https://thewire.in/137206/netaji-files-family-nehru/.

to financially help Netaji's wife and daughter, without making an 'event' of it.

I do not recall an Indian polity as divided as it is today, or an 'educated' public as misinformed and vulnerable as we have now. So it will be surprising for many today to learn that despite having broken up with Gandhi, Nehru and the Congress in general on the question of aligning with Hitler, Subhash Chandra Bose became the first person to refer to Gandhi as the 'father of our nation', in his broadcast from Rangoon (now Yangon) on 4 July, 1944.[43] He also named brigades in his Indian National Army after Gandhi, Nehru and Azad. After all, in spite of all their differences, they admired, in fact, loved each other. Their differences were as genuine as were their attempts to come to the broadest possible consensus. The Karachi Congress (1931) resolution on Fundamental Rights and Economic Programme is an illuminating metaphor of such attempts. This resolution embodies the spirit of the freedom movement and is actually a precursor to the Indian constitution's concern with justice and equality. It was drafted by Nehru and Bose, and moved by Gandhiji in a session presided over by Sardar Patel!

Patel has been projected by some people as an 'authentically Indian' contract and antidote to the 'Anglophile' Nehru. This happened in Patel's lifetime, too, and he characteristically saw through the game. He wrote: 'Contrary to impressions created by some interested persons and eagerly accepted in credulous circles, we have worked as life-long friends and colleagues, adjusting ourselves to each other's point of view…'[44]

'Adjusting to each other's point of view' is the key not only to governing a complex country like India, it is also the quintessence of democracy. Such adjustment must not be confused with compromise on fundamentals. One needs great 'navigation' talent to see socially progressive legislation through in the face of stiff conservative opposition. Nehru's 'navigation' talent came

---

[43] http://www.gandhi-manibhavan.org/main/q1.htm.

[44] From the *Nehru Abhinandan Granth: A Birthday Book*, 1949, xxix.

out brilliantly in the political and legislative process leading to the passage of laws relating to the matter of Hindu marriage and succession. These laws were passed gradually, not in one go, as Ambedkar desired. The details of this entire episode fall outside the scope of this volume; suffice here to note the way Nehru, speaking in the Lok Sabha on December 6, 1956 (the day Ambedkar passed away), remembered Ambedkar's contribution in this regard. Ambedkar will be remembered, said Nehru, '... for the great interest he took and the trouble he took over the question of Hindu law reform. I am happy that he saw that reform in a very large measure carried out, perhaps not in the form of that monumental tome that he had himself drafted, but in separate bits.'[45]

Ambedkar had resigned from Nehru's cabinet on this question, accusing him of not being sufficiently steadfast and consistent on the issue. On his part, Nehru had been aware that, 'Hindu law was largely custom' and customs are 'forced to adapt themselves to some extent to a changing environment'. He knew the dynamics of the 'natural alliance of the British power with the reactionaries' which had resulted in the perpetuation of outdated practices and 'law[s] unmodified by subsequent custom'. Contrary to believers of the 'progressive' protestations of the British Raj, Nehru was aware that 'change could only come by positive legislation, but the British government which was the legislative authority, had no wish to antagonize the conservative elements on whose support it counted.'[46]

The Nehru government did not count on the support of conservative elements of society, but it could not wish away their existence. On the Hindu Code Bill, he had to deal with conservative resistance in his government, party and society at large, including resistance from the President of the republic himself. It was prudent and far-sighted to first prove the popular support he and his government enjoyed through impressive victory in the general elections (of 1952) and then go ahead with

[45] Quoted by Guha, *India after Gandhi*, 240.

[46] *The Discovery of India*, 360–61.

the necessary reform. As on many other things, here also Nehru had to 'adjust without surrendering [the] basic position'. He had to navigate without rocking the boat, and hence was destined, just like his 'Bapu' to seem 'unfair' to many, including those for whom he was doing his best.

In domestic as well as in foreign affairs, in social and economic as well as in cultural matters, Nehru stuck to the core of Indian wisdom—doing the ethically right thing, but accommodating as many truth-perceptions as possible. Be it the question of the Hindu Code Bill or that of dealing with communalism, be it the matter of non-alignment or of a mixed economy, he dared go beyond the lure of extremes, tried to find the '*madhayma pratipada*'—enlightened middle—without compromising on fundamentally humanistic ethics.

Nehru was aware of the 'reverence, admiration and affection of all classes' for him, as he noted in his will, written on 21 June, 1954. This will is also a poetic paean to the Ganga—'a symbol and a memory of the past of India, running into the present, and flowing on to the great ocean of the future'.

For Jawaharlal, Ganga was the river not only of collective cultural memories, but also of personal memories connecting him to 'that unbroken chain that goes back to the dawn of history in the immemorial past of India'.

Along with fond memories, Nehru also reiterates in this will his desire that India 'rid herself of all shackles that divide her people and suppress vast numbers of them ...'

To rid oneself of the shackles that divide and suppress vast numbers of people is the right way to 'connect' with one's tradition and culture. This is also the right way to move on into the future.

This is the gist of Nehru's political and intellectual journey, and it is a pre-condition for India's survival as a democratic polity and as a humane, compassionate society.

Purushottam Agrawal
27 May, 2019
New Delhi

BOOK I

NEHRU ON INDIA AND THE WORLD

The Idea and the Making of India

UNDERSTANDING INDIA

The Search for India

(From The Discovery of India*)*

It was absurd, of course, to think of India or any country as a kind of anthropomorphic entity. I did not do so. I was also fully aware of the diversities and divisions of Indian life, of classes, castes, religions, races, different degrees of cultural development. Yet I think that a country with a long cultural background and a common outlook on life develops a spirit that is peculiar to it and that is impressed on all its children, however much they may differ among themselves. Can anyone fail to see this in China, whether he meets an old-fashioned mandarin or a Communist who has apparently broken with the past? It was this spirit of India that I was after, not through idle curiosity, though I was curious enough, but because I felt that it might give me some key to the understanding of my country and people, some guidance to thought and action. Politics and elections were day-to-day affairs when we grew excited over trumpery matters. But if we were going to build the house of India's future, strong and secure and beautiful, we would have to dig deep for the foundations.

'Bharat Mata'

Often, as I wandered from meeting to meeting, I spoke to my audience of this India of ours, of Hindustan and of Bharata, the old Sanskrit name derived from the mythical founder of the race. I seldom did so in the cities, for there the audiences were more sophisticated and wanted stronger fare. But to the peasant, with his limited outlook, I spoke of this great country for whose freedom we were struggling, of how each part differed from the other and yet was India, of common problems of the peasants from north to south and east to west, of the Swaraj that could only be for all and every part and not for some. I told them of my journeying from the Khyber Pass in the far north-west to Kanya Kumari or Cape Comorin in the distant south, and how everywhere the peasants put me identical questions, for their troubles were the same—poverty, debt, vested interests, landlords, moneylenders, heavy rents and taxes, police harassment, and all these wrapped up in the structure that the foreign government had imposed upon us—and relief must also come for all. I tried to make them think of India as a whole, and even to some little extent of this wide world of which we were a part. I brought in the struggle in China, in Spain, in Abyssinia, in Central Europe, in Egypt and the countries of Western Asia. I told them of the wonderful changes in the Soviet Union and of the great progress made in America. The task was not easy; yet it was not so difficult as I had imagined, for our ancient epics and myths and legends, which they knew so well, had made them familiar with the conception of their country, and some there were always who had travelled far and wide to the great places of pilgrimage situated at the four corners of India. Or there were old soldiers who had served in foreign parts in World War I or other expeditions. Even my references to foreign countries were brought home to them by the consequences of the great depression of the Thirties.

Sometimes as I reached a gathering, a great roar of welcome would greet me: Bharat Mata ki Jai—'Victory to Mother India.' I would ask them unexpectedly what they meant by that cry, who was this Bharat Mata, Mother India, whose victory they wanted? My question would amuse them and surprise them, and then, not knowing exactly what to answer, they would look at each other and at me. I persisted in my questioning. At last a vigorous Jat, wedded to the soil from immemorial generations, would say that it was the dharti, the good earth of India, that they meant. What earth? Their particular village patch, or all the patches in the district or province, or in the whole of India? And so question and answer went on, till they would ask me impatiently to tell them all about it. I would endeavour to do so and explain that India was all this that they had thought, but it was much more. The mountains and the rivers of India, and the forests and the broad fields, which gave us food, were all dear to us, but what counted ultimately were the people of India, people like them and me, who were spread out all over this vast land. Bharat Mata, Mother India, was essentially these millions of people, and victory to her meant victory to these people. You are parts of this Bharat Mata, I told them, you are in a manner yourselves Bharat Mata, and as this idea slowly soaked into their brains, their eyes would light up as if they had made a great discovery.

~

The Indian Philosophical Approach

(From The Discovery of India*)*

Though one thought leads to another, each usually related to life's changing texture, and a logical movement of the human mind is sometimes discernible, yet thoughts overlap and the new and the old run side by side, irreconcilable and often contradicting each other. Even an individual's mind is a bundle of contradictions and it is difficult to reconcile his action one with another. A people, comprising all stages of cultural development, represent in themselves and in their thoughts, beliefs, and activities, different ages of the past leading up to the present. Probably their activities may conform more to the social and cultural pattern of the present day, or else they would be stranded and isolated from life's moving stream, but behind these activities lie primitive beliefs and unreasoned convictions. It is astonishing to find in countries industrially advanced, where every person automatically uses or takes advantage of the latest modern discovery or device, beliefs and set ideas which reason denies and intelligence cannot accept. A politician may of course succeed in his business without being a shining example of reason or intelligence. A lawyer may be a brilliant advocate and jurist and yet be singularly ignorant of other matters. Even a scientist, that typical representative of the modern age, often forgets the method and outlook of science when he goes out of his study or laboratory.

This is so even in regard to the problems that affect our daily lives in their material aspects. In philosophy and metaphysics the problems are more remote, less transient and less connected with our day's routine. For most of us they are entirely beyond our grasp unless we undergo a rigid discipline and training of the mind. And yet all of us have some kind of philosophy of life, conscious or unconscious, if not thought out then inherited or accepted from others and considered as self-evident. Or we may seek refuge from the perils of thought in faith in some religious creed or dogma, or in national destiny, or in a vague and comforting humanitarianism. Often all these and others are present together, though with little to connect them, and we develop split personalities, each functioning in its separate compartment.

Probably there was more unity and harmony in the human personality in the old days, though this was at a lower level than today except for certain individuals who were obviously of a very high type. During this long age of transition through which humanity has been passing, we have managed to break up that unity, but have not so far succeeded in finding another. We cling still to the ways of dogmatic religion, adhere to outworn practices and beliefs, and yet talk and presume to live in terms of the scientific method. Perhaps science has been too narrow in its approach to life and has ignored many vital aspects of it, and hence it could not provide a suitable basis for a new unity and harmony. Perhaps it is gradually broadening this basis now, and we shall achieve a new harmony for the human personality on a much higher level than the previous one. But the problem is a more difficult and complex one now, for it has grown beyond the limits of the human personality. It was perhaps easier to develop some kind of a harmonious personality in the restricted spheres of ancient and medieval times. In that little world of town and village, with fixed concepts of social organization and behaviour, the individual and the group lived their self-contained lives, protected, as a rule, from outer storms. Today the sphere of even the individual has grown worldwide, and different concepts of social organization conflict with each other and behind them are different philosophies of life. A strong wind arising somewhere creates a cyclone in one place and an anti-cyclone in another. So if harmony is to be achieved by the individual, it has to be supported by some kind of social harmony throughout the world.

In India, far more so than elsewhere, the old concept of social organization and the philosophy of life underlying it have persisted, to some extent, to the present day. They could not have done so unless they had some virtue which stabilized society and made it conform to life's conditions. And they would not have failed ultimately and become a drag and a hindrance, divorced from life, if the evil in them had not overcome that virtue. But, in any event, they cannot be considered today as isolated phenomena; they must be viewed in that world context and made to harmonize with it.

'In India,' says Havell, 'religion is hardly a dogma, but a working hypothesis of human conduct, adapted to different stages of spiritual development and different conditions of life. A dogma might continue to be believed in, isolated from life, but a working hypothesis of human conduct must work and conform to life, or it obstructs life. The very raison d'etre of such a hypothesis is its workableness, its conformity to life, and its capacity to adapt itself to changing conditions. So long as it can do so it serves its purpose and performs its allotted function. When it goes off at a tangent from the curve of life, loses contact with social needs, and the distance between it and life grows, it loses all its vitality and significance.

Metaphysical theories and speculations deal not with the ever-changing stuff of life but with the permanent reality behind it, if such exists. Hence they have a certain permanence which is not affected by external changes. But, inevitably, they are the products of the environment in which they grow and of the state of development of the human minds that conceived them. If their influence spreads they affect the general philosophy of life of a people. In India, philosophy, though in its higher reaches confined to the elect, has been more pervasive than elsewhere and has had a strong influence in moulding the national outlook and in developing a certain distinctive attitude of mind.

Buddhist philosophy played an important part in this process and, during the medieval period, Islam left its impress upon the national outlook, directly as well as indirectly, through the evolution of new sects which sought to bridge the gap between Hinduism and the Islamic social and religious structure. But, in the main, the dominating influence has been that of the six systems of Indian philosophy, or darshanas, as they are called. Some of these systems were themselves greatly affected by Buddhist thought. All of them are considered orthodox and yet they vary in their approach and their conclusions, though they have many common ideas. There is polytheism, and theism with a personal God, and pure monism, and a system which ignores God altogether and bases itself on a theory of evolution. There is both idealism and realism. The various facets of the complex and inclusive Indian mind are shown in their unity and diversity. Max Müller drew attention to both these factors: '... the more have I become impressed with the truth ... that there is behind the variety of the six systems a common fund of what may be called national and popular philosophy... from which each thinker was allowed to draw for his own purposes.'

There is a common presumption in all of them: that the universe is orderly and functions according to law, that there is a mighty rhythm about it. Some such presumption becomes necessary, for otherwise there could hardly be any system to explain it. Though the law of causality, of cause and effect, functions, yet there is a measure of freedom to the individual to shape his own destiny. There is belief in rebirth and an emphasis on unselfish love and disinterested activity. Logic and reason are relied upon and used effectively for argument, but it is recognised that often intuition is greater than either. The general argument proceeds on a rational basis, in so far as reason can be applied to matters often outside its scope. Professor Keith has pointed out that 'The systems are indeed orthodox and admit the authority of the sacred scriptures, but they attack the problems of existence with human means, and scripture serves for all practical purposes but to lend sanctity to results which are achieved not only without its aid, but often in very dubious harmony with its tenets.'

~

India Old and New

(From An Autobiography*)*

It was natural and inevitable that Indian nationalism should resent alien rule. And yet it was curious how large numbers of our intelligentsia, to the end of the nineteenth century, accepted, consciously or unconsciously, the British ideology of empire. They built their own arguments on this, and only ventured to criticise some of its outward manifestations. The history and economics and other subjects that were taught in the school and colleges were written entirely from the British imperial veiwpoint, and laid stress on our numerous failings in the past and present and the virtues and high destiny of the British. We accepted to some extent this distorted version, and even when we resisted it instinctively we were influenced by it. At first there was no intellectual escape from it for we knew no other facts or arguments, and so we sought relief in religious nationalism, in the thought that at least in the sphere of religion and philosophy we were second to no other people. We comforted ourselves in our misfortune and degradation with the notion that though we did not possess the outward show and glitter of the West we had the real inner article, which was far more valuable and worth having. Vivekananda and others, as well as the interest of Western scholars in our old philosophies, gave us a measure of self-respect again and roused up our dormant pride in our past.

Gradually we began to suspect and examine critically British statements about our past and present conditions, but still we thought and worked within the framework of British ideology. If a thing was bad, it would be called 'un-British'; if a Britisher in India misbehaved, the fault was his, not that of the system. But the collection of this critical material of British rule in India, in spite of the moderate outlook of the authors, served a revolutionary purpose and gave a political and economic foundation to our nationalism. Dadabhai Naoroji's *Poverty and Un-British Rule in India*, and books by Romesh Dutt and William Digby and others thus played a revolutionary role in the development of our nationalist thought. Further researches in ancient Indian history revealed brilliant and highly civilised periods in the remote past, and we read of these with great satisfaction. We also discovered that the British record in India was very different from what we had been led to believe from their history books.

Our challenge to the British version of history, economics, and administration in India grew, and yet we continued to function within the orbit of their ideology. That was the position of Indian nationalism as a whole at the turn of the century. That is still the position of the Liberal group and other small groups as well as a number of moderate Congressmen, who go forward emotionally from time to time, but intellectually still live in the nineteenth century. Because of that the Liberal is unable to grasp the idea of Indian freedom, for the two are fundamentally irreconcilable. He imagines that step by step he will go up to higher offices and will deal with fatter and more important files. The machinery of government will go on smoothly as before, only he will be at the hub, and somewhere in the background, without intruding themselves too much, will be the British Army to give him protection in case of need. That is his idea of Dominion Status within the Empire. It is a naive notion impossible of achievement, for the price of British protection is Indian subjection. We cannot have it both ways, even if that was not degrading to the self-respect of a great country. Sir Frederick Whyte (no partisan of Indian nationalism) says in a recent book:[1] "He (the Indian) still believes that England will stand between him and disaster, and as long as he cherishes this delusion he cannot even lay the foundation of his own ideal of self-government." Evidently he refers to the Liberal or the reactionary and communal types of Indians, largely with whom he must have come into contact when he was President of the Indian Legislative Assembly. This is not the Congress belief, much less is it that of other advanced groups. They agree with Sir Frederick, however, that there can be no freedom till this delusion goes and India is left to face disaster, if that is her fate, by herself. The complete withdrawal of British military control of India will be the beginning of Indian freedom.

It is not surprising that the Indian intelligentsia in the nineteenth century should have succumbed to British ideology; what is surprising is that some people should continue to suffer that delusion even after the stirring events and changes of the twentieth century. In the nineteenth century the British ruling classes were the aristocrats of the world, with a long record of wealth and success and power behind them. This long record and training gave them some of the virtues as well as failings of aristocracy. We in India can comfort ourselves with the thought that we helped substantially during the last century and three-quarters in providing the wherewithal and the training for this superior state. They began to think themselves, as so many races and nations have done, the chosen of God and their Empire as an earthly Kingdom of Heaven. If their special position was acknowledged and their superiority not challenged, they were gracious and obliging, provided that this did them no harm. But opposition to them became opposition to the divine order, and as such was a deadly sin which must be suppressed...

If this was the general British attitude to the rest of the world, it was most conspicuous in India. There was something fascinating about the British approach to the Indian problem,

[1] Sir Frederick Whyte, *The Future of East and West,* Sidgwick and Jackson Limited (1932).

even though it was singularly irritating. The calm assurance of always being in the right and of having borne a great burden worthily, faith in their racial destiny and their own brand of imperialism, contempt and anger at the unbelievers and sinners who challenged the foundations of the true faith—there was something of the religious temper about this attitude. Like the Inquisitors of old, they were bent on saving us regardless of our desires in the matter. Incidentally they profited by this traffic in virtue, thus demonstrating the truth of the old proverb: "Honesty is the best policy". The progress of India became synonymous with the adaptation of the country to the imperial scheme and the fashioning of chosen Indians after the British mould. The more we accepted British ideals and objectives the fitter we were for 'self-government'. Freedom would be ours as soon as we demonstrated and guaranteed that we would use it only in accordance with British wishes.

Indians and Englishmen are, I am afraid, likely to disagree about the record of British rule in India. That is perhaps natural, but it does come as a shock when high British officials, including Secretaries of State for India, draw fanciful pictures of India's past and present and make statements which have no basis in fact. It is quite extraordinary how ignorant English people, apart from some experts and others, are about India. If facts elude them, how much more is the spirit of India beyond their reach? They seized her body and possessed her, but it was the possession of violence. They did not know her or try to know her. They never looked into her eyes, for theirs were averted and hers downcast through shame and humiliation. After centuries of contact they face each other, strangers still, full of dislike for each other.

And yet India with all her poverty and degradation had enough of nobility and greatness about her, and though she was overburdened with ancient tradition and present misery, and her eyelids were a little weary, she had "a beauty wrought out from within upon the flesh, the deposit little cell by cell, of strange thoughts and fantastic reveries and exquisite passions". Behind and within her battered body one could still glimpse a majesty of soul. Through long ages she had travelled and gathered much wisdom on the way, and trafficked with strangers and added them to her own big family, and witnessed days of glory and of decay, and suffered humiliation and terrible sorrow, and seen many a strange sight; but throughout her long journey she had clung to her immemorial culture, drawn strength and vitality from it, and shared it with other lands. Like a pendulum she had swung up and down; she had ventured with the daring of her thought to reach up to the heavens and unravel their mystery, and she had also had bitter experience of the pit of hell. Despite the woeful accumulations of superstition and degrading custom that had clung to her and borne her down, she had never wholly forgotten the inspiration that some of the wisest of her children, at the dawn of history, had given her in the Upanishads. Their keen minds, ever restless and ever striving and exploring, had not sought refuge in blind dogma or grown complacent in the routine observance of dead forms or ritual and creed. They had demanded not a personal relief from suffering in the present or a place in a paradise to come, but light and understanding: "Lead me from the unreal to the real, lead me from darkness to light, lead me from death to immortality."[2] In the most famous of the prayers recited daily even to-day by millions, the gayatri mantra, the call is for knowledge, for enlightenment.

Though often broken up politically her spirit always guarded a common heritage, and in her diversity there was ever an amazing unity.[3] Like all ancient lands she was a curious mixture of the good and bad, but the good was hidden and had to be sought after, while the odour of decay was evident and her hot, pitiless sun gave full publicity to the bad.

---

[2] *Brihadaranyak Upanishad*, i. 3, 27.

[3] "The greatest of all the contradictions in India is that over this diversity is spread a greater unity, which is not immediately evident because it failed historically to find expression in any political cohesion to make the country one, but which is so great a reality, and so powerful, that even the Musulman world of India has to confess that it has been deeply affected by coming within its influence."—From Sir Frederick Whyte's *The Future of East and West*.

There is some similarity between Italy and India. Both are ancient countries with long traditions of culture behind them, though Italy is a newcomer compared to India, and India is a much vaster country. Both are split up politically, and yet the conception of Italia, like that of India, never died, and in all their diversity the unity was predominant. In Italy the unity was largely a Roman unity, for that great city had dominated the country and been the fount and symbol of unity. In India there was no such single centre or dominant city, although Benares might well be called the Eternal City of the East, not only for India but also for Eastern Asia. But, unlike Rome, Benares never dabbled in empire or thought of temporal power. Indian culture was so widespread all over India that no part of the country could be called the heart of that culture. From Cape Comorin to Amarnath and Badrinath in the Himalayas, from Dwarka to Puri, the same ideas coursed, and if there was a clash of ideas in one place, the noise of it soon reached distant parts of the country.

Just as Italy gave the gift of culture and religion to Western Europe, India did so to Eastern Asia, though China was as old and venerable as India. And even when Italy was lying prostrate politically, her life coursed through the veins of Europe. It was Metternich who called Italy a "geographical expression", and many a would-be Metternich has used that phrase for India, and, strangely enough, there is a similarity even in their geographical positions in the two continents. More interesting is the comparison of England with Austria, for has not England of the twentieth century been compared to Austria of the nineteenth, proud and haughty and imposing still, but with the roots that gave strength shrivelling up and decay eating its way into the mighty fabric.

It is curious how one cannot resist the tendency to give an anthropomorphic form to a country. Such is the force of habit and early associations. India becomes Bharat Mata, Mother India, a beautiful lady, very old but ever youthful in appearance, sad-eyed and forlorn, cruelly treated by aliens and outsiders, and calling upon her children to protect her. Some such picture rouses the emotions of hundreds of thousands and drives them to action and sacrifice. And yet India is in the main the peasant and the worker, not beautiful to look at, for poverty is not beautiful. Does the beautiful lady of our imaginations represent the bare-bodied and bent workers in the fields and factories? Or the small group of those who have from ages past crushed the masses and exploited them, imposed cruel customs on them and made many of them even untouchable? We seek to cover truth by the creatures of our imaginations and endeavour to escape from reality to a world of dreams.

~

The Culture of the Masses

(From The Discovery of India*)*

...Thus I saw the moving drama of the Indian people in the present, and could often trace the threads which bound their lives to the past, even while their eyes were turned towards the future. Everywhere I found a cultural background which had exerted a powerful influence on their lives. This background was a mixture of popular philosophy, tradition, history, myth, and legend, and it was not possible to draw a line between any of these. Even the entirely uneducated and illiterate shared this background. The old epics of India, the Ramayana and the Mahabharata and other books, in popular translations and paraphrases, were widely known among the masses, and every incident and story and moral in them was engraved on the popular mind and gave a richness and content to it. Illiterate villagers would know hundreds of verses by heart and their conversation would be full of references to them or to some story with a moral, enshrined in some old classic. Often I was surprised by some such literary turn given by a group of villagers to a simple talk about present-day affairs. If my mind was full of pictures from recorded history and more-or-less ascertained fact, I realised that even the illiterate peasant had a picture gallery in his mind, though this was largely drawn from myth and tradition and epic heroes and heroines, and only very little from history. Nevertheless, it was vivid enough. I looked at their faces and their figures and watched their movements. There was many a sensitive face and many a sturdy body, straight and clean-limbed; and among the women there was grace and suppleness and dignity and poise and, very often, a look that was full of melancholy. Usually the finer physical types were among the upper castes, who were just a little better off in the economic sense. Sometimes, as I was passing along a country road, or through a village, I would start with surprise on seeing a fine type of man, or a beautiful woman, who reminded me of some fresco of ancient times. And I wondered how the type endured and continued through ages, in spite of all the horror and misery that India had gone through. What could we not do with these people under better conditions and with greater opportunities opening out to them?

There was poverty and the innumerable progeny of poverty everywhere, and the mark of this beast was on every forehead. Life had been crushed and distorted and made into a thing of evil, and many vices had flowed from this distortion and continuous lack and ever-present insecurity. All this was not pleasant to see; yet that was the basic reality in India. There was far too much of the spirit of resignation and acceptance of things as they were. But there was also a mellowness and a gentleness, the cultural heritage of thousands of years, which no amount of misfortune had been able to rub off.

~

Ends and Means

Address on the occasion of the conferment of the degree of Doctor of Law at Columbia University, New York, 17 October, 1949.[4]

I have come to you not so much in my capacity as Prime Minister of a great country or a politician but rather as a humble seeker

[4] Jawaharlal Nehru, *Jawaharlal Nehru's Speeches 1949–1953* Volume Two (New Delhi: Publication Division, 1954), 391–398.

after truth and as one who has continuously struggled to find the way, not always with success, to fit action to the objectives and ideals that he has held. The process is always difficult but it becomes increasingly so in this world of conflict and passion. Politicians have to deal with day-to-day problems and they seek immediate remedies. Philosophers think of ultimate objectives and are apt to lose touch with the day-to-day world and its problems. Neither approach appears to be adequate by itself. Is it possible to combine those two approaches and function after the manner of Plato's philosopher kings? You, Sir, who have had the experience of the role of a great man of action and also that of a philosopher as head of this university, should be able to help us to answer this question.

In this world of incessant and feverish activity, men have little time to think, much less to consider ideals and objectives. Yet how are we to act, even in the present, unless we know which way we are going and what our objectives are? It is only in the peaceful atmosphere of a university that these basic problems can be adequately considered. It is only when the young men and women, who are in the university today and on whom the burden of life's problems will fall tomorrow, learn to have clear objectives and standards of values that there is hope for the next generation. The past generation produced some great men but as a generation it led the world repeatedly to disaster. Two world wars are the price that has been paid for the lack of wisdom on man's part in this generation. It is a terrible price and the tragedy of it is that, even after that price has been paid, we have not purchased real peace or a cessation of conflict and an even deeper tragedy is that mankind does not profit by its experience and continues to go the same way that led previously to disaster.

We have had wars and we have had victory and we have celebrated that victory; yet, what is victory and how do we measure it? A war is fought presumably to gain certain objectives. The defeat of the enemy is not by itself an objective but rather the removal of an obstruction towards the attainment of the objective. If that objective is not attained, then that victory over the enemy brings only negative relief and indeed is not a real victory. We have seen, however, that the aim in wars is almost entirely to defeat the enemy and the other and real objective is often forgotten. The result has been that the victory attained by defeating the enemy has only been a very partial one and has not solved the real problem; if it has solved the immediate problem, it has, at the same time, given rise to many other and sometimes worse problems. Therefore, it becomes necessary to have the real objective clear in our minds at all times whether in war or in peace and always to aim at achieving the objective.

I think also that there is always a close and intimate relationship between the end we aim at and the means adopted to attain it. Even if the end is right but the means are wrong, it will vitiate the end or divert us in a wrong direction. Means and ends are thus intimately and inextricably connected and cannot be separated. That, indeed, has been the lesson of old taught us by many great men in the past but unfortunately it is seldom remembered.

I am venturing to place some of these ideas before you, not because they are novel but because they have impressed themselves upon me in the course of my life which has been spent in alternating periods of incessant activity and conflict and enforced leisure.

The great leader of my country, Mahatma Gandhi, under whose inspiration and sheltering care I grew up, always laid stress on moral values and warned us never to subordinate means to ends.

We were not worthy of him and yet, to the best of our ability, we tried to follow his teaching. Even the limited extent to which we could follow his teaching yielded rich results. After a generation of intense struggle with a great and powerful nation, we achieved success and, perhaps, the most significant part of it for which credit is due to both parties, was the manner of its achievement. History hardly affords a parallel to the solution of such a conflict in a peaceful way, followed by friendly and co-operative relations. It is astonishing how rapidly bitterness and ill-will between the two nations have faded away, giving place to cooperation. And we in India have decided of our own free will to continue this cooperation as an independent nation.

I would not presume to offer advice to other and more experienced nations in any way. But may I suggest for your consideration that there is some lesson in India's peaceful involution which might be applied to the larger problems before the world today? That revolution demonstrated to us that physical force need not necessarily be the arbiter of man's destiny and that the method of waging a struggle and the way of its termination are of paramount importance. Past history shows as the important part that physical force has played. But it also shows us that no such force can ultimately ignore the moral forces of the world; and if it attempts to do so, it does so at its peril. Today, this problem faces us in all its intensity, because the weapons that physical force has at its disposal are terrible to contemplate. Must the twentieth century differ from primitive barbarism only in the destructive efficacy of the weapons that man's ingenuity has invented for man's destruction? I do believe, in accordance with my master's teaching, that there is another way to meet this situation and solve the problem that faces us.

I realize that a statesman or a man who has to deal with public affairs cannot ignore realities and cannot act in terms of abstract truth. His activity is always limited by the degree of receptivity of the truth by his fellow men. Nevertheless, the basic truth remains truth and is always to be kept in view and, as far as possible, it should guide our actions. Otherwise we get caught up in a vicious circle of evil where one evil action leads to another.

India is a very old country with a great past. But she is a new country also, with new urges and desires. Since August 1947, she has been in a position to pursue a foreign policy of her own. She was limited by the realities of the situation which we could not ignore or overcome. But even so, she could not forget the lesson of her great leader. She has tried to adapt, however imperfectly, theory to reality in so far as she could. In the family of nations she was a newcomer and could not influence them greatly to begin with. But she had a certain advantage. She had great potential resources that could, no doubt, increase her power and influence. A greater advantage lay in the fact that she was not fettered by the past, by old enmities or old ties, by historic claims or traditional rivalries. Even against her former rulers there was no bitterness left. Thus, India came into the family of nations with no prejudices or enmities, ready to welcome and be welcomed. Inevitably, she had to consider her foreign policy in terms of enlightened self-interest but at the same time she brought to it a touch of her idealism. Thus, she has tried to combine idealism with national interest. The main objectives of that policy are: the pursuit of peace, not through alignment with any power or group of powers but through an independent approach to each controversial or disputed issue, the liberation of subject peoples, the maintenance of freedom, both national and individual, the elimination of racial discrimination and the elimination of want, disease and ignorance, which afflict the greater part of the world's population. I am asked frequently why India does not align herself with a particular nation or a group of nations and told that because we have refrained from doing so we sitting on the fence. The question and the comment are easily understood, because in times of crisis it is not unnatural for those who are involved in it deeply to regard calm objectivity in others as irrational, short-sighted, negative, unreal or even unmanly. But I should like to make it clear that the policy India has sought to pursue is not a negative and neutral policy. It is a positive and a vital policy that flows from our struggle for freedom and from the teaching of Mahatma Gandhi. Peace is not only an absolute necessity for us in India in order to progress and develop but is also of paramount importance to the world. How can that peace be preserved? Not by surrendering to aggression, not by compromising with evil or injustice but also not by talking and preparing for war! Aggression has to be met, for it endangers peace. At the same time, the lesson of the last two wars has to be remembered and it seems to me astonishing that in spite of that lesson, we go the same way. The very process of marshalling the world into two hostile camps precipitates the conflict which it has sought to avoid. It produces a sense of terrible fear and that fear darkens men's minds and leads them into wrong courses. There is perhaps nothing so bad and so dangerous in life as fear. As a great President of the United States said, there is nothing really to fear except fear itself.

Our problem, therefore, becomes one of lessening and ultimately putting an end to this fear. That will not happen if all the world takes sides and talks of war. War becomes almost certain then.

We are a member of the family of nations and we have no wish to shirk any of the obligations and burdens of that membership. We have accepted fully the obligations of membership in the United Nations and intend to abide by them. We wish to make our full contribution to the common store and to render our full measure of service. But that can only be done effectively in our own way and of our own choice. We believe passionately in the democratic method and we seek to enlarge the bounds of democracy both on the political and the economic plane, for no democracy can exist for long in the midst of want and poverty and inequality. Our immediate needs are economic betterment and raising the standards of our people. The more we succeed in this, the more we can serve the cause of peace in the world. We are fully aware of our weaknesses and failings and claim no superior virtue; but we do not wish to forfeit the advantage that our present detachment gives us. We believe that the maintenance of that detachment is not only in our interest but also in the interest of world peace and freedom. That detachment is neither isolationism nor indifference nor neutrality when peace or freedom is threatened. When man's liberty or peace is in danger we cannot and shall not be neutral; neutrality then would be a betrayal of what we have fought for and stand for.

If we seek to ensure peace we must attack the root causes of war and not merely the symptoms. What are the underlying causes of war in the modern world?

One of the basic causes is the domination of one country by another or an attempt to dominate. Large parts of Asia were ruled till recently by foreign and chiefly European Powers. We ourselves were part of the British Empire, as were also Pakistan, Ceylon and Burma. France, Holland and Portugal still have territories over which they rule. But the rising tide of nationalism and the love of independence have submerged most of the Western Empires in Asia. In Indonesia, I hope that there will soon be an independent Sovereign State. We hope also that French Indo-China will achieve freedom and peace before long under a government of its own choice. Much of Africa, however, is subject to foreign Powers, some of whom still attempt to enlarge their dominions. It is clear that all remaining vestiges of imperialism and colonialism will have to disappear.

Secondly, there is the problem of racial relations. The progress of some races in knowledge or in invention, their success in war and conquest, has tempted them to believe that they are racially superior and has led them to treat other nations with contempt. A recent example of this was the horrible attempt, so largely successful, to exterminate the Jews. In Asia and Africa, racial superiority has been most widely and most insolently exhibited. It is forgotten that nearly all the great religions of mankind arose in the East and that wonderful civilizations grew up there when Europe and America were still unknown to history. The West has too often despised the Asian and the African and still, in many places, denies them not only equality of rights but even common humanity and kindliness. This is one of the great danger points of our modern world; and now that Asia and Africa are shaking off their torpor and arousing themselves, out of this evil may come a conflagration of which no man can see the range of consequences. One of your greatest men said that this country cannot exist half slave and half free. The world cannot long maintain peace if half of it is enslaved and despised. The problem is not always simple nor can it be solved by a resolution or a decree. Unless there is a firm and sincere determination to solve it, there will be no peace.

The third reason for war and revolution is the misery and want of millions of people in many countries and, in particular, in Asia and Africa. In the West, though the war has brought much misery and many difficulties, the common man generally lives in some measure of comfort—he has food, clothing and shelter to some extent. The basic problem of the East, therefore, is to obtain these necessaries of life. If they are lacking, then there is the apathy of despair or the destructive rage of the revolutionary. Political subjection, racial inequality, economic inequality and misery—these are the evils that we have to remove if we would ensure peace. If we can offer no remedy, then other cries and slogans will make an appeal to the minds of the people.

Many of the countries of Asia have entered the family of nations; others, we hope, will soon find a place in this circle. We have the same hopes for the countries of Africa. This process should proceed rapidly and America and Europe should use their great influence and power to facilitate it. We see before us vast changes taking place, not only in the political and economic spheres but even more so in the minds of men. Asia is becoming dynamic again and is passionately eager to progress and raise the economic standards of her vast masses. This awakening of a giant continent is of the greatest importance to the future of mankind and requires imaginative statesmanship of a high order. The problems of this awakening will not be solved by looking at it with fear or in a spirit of isolationism by any of us. It requires a friendly and understanding approach, clear objectives and a common effort to realize them.

The colossal expenditure of energy and resources on armaments is an outstanding feature of many national budgets today but that does not solve the problem of world peace. Perhaps, even a fraction of that outlay, utilized in other ways and for other purposes, will provide a more enduring basis for peace and happiness.

That is India's view, offered in all friendliness to all thinking men and women, to all persons of goodwill in the name of our common humanity. That view is not based on wishful thinking but on a deep consideration of the problems that afflict us all and on its merits I venture to place it before you.

I should like to add a few words, Sir. I have been deeply moved by what you have said, by what was said about me in the previous citation and I have felt very humble as I listened to these remarks.

The scene that I see here under your distinguished presidentship will long remain in my mind. Indeed, I do not think that I shall ever forget it. I shall remember the scene and above all I shall remember the great courtesy, kindliness and generosity with which you have received me here and made me one of yourselves.

I shall prize the honour of being a fellow member with you of this great university, above the other honours that have come my way. I shall prize it, not only in my individual capacity as I believe that this honour was, perhaps, meant for more than an individual and that, for the moment, you have treated me not as an individual but also as a symbol and representative of India. And here, Sir, forgetting myself for a moment, I thank you on behalf of my country and my people.

~

INDIAN HISTORY AND ICONS

Ashoka, the Beloved of the Gods

(From Glimpses of World History*)*

I am afraid I am a little too fond of running down kings and princes. I see little in their kind to admire or do reverence to. But we are now coming to a man who, in spite of being a king and emperor, was great and worthy of admiration. He was Ashoka, the grandson of Chandragupta Maurya. Speaking of him in his *Outline of History,* H.G. Wells (some of whose romances you must have read) says:

> Amidst the tens of thousands of names of monarchs that crowd the columns of history, their majesties and graciousnesses and serenities and royal highnesses and the like, the name of Ashoka shines, and shines almost alone, a star. From the Volga to Japan his name is still honoured. China, Tibet, and even India, though

> it has left his doctrine, preserve the tradition of his greatness. More living men cherish his memory today than have ever heard the names of Constantine or Charlemagne.

This is high praise indeed. But it is deserved, and for an Indian it is an especial pleasure to think of this period of India's history.

Chandragupta died nearly 300 years before the Christian era began. He was succeeded by his son Bindusara, who seems to have had a quiet reign of twenty-five years. He kept up contacts with the Greek world, and ambassadors came to his Court from Ptolemy of Egypt, and Antiochus, who was the son of Seleucus of western Asia. There was trade with the outside world and, it is said, the Egyptians used to dye their cloth with indigo from India. It is also stated that they wrapped their mummies in Indian muslins. Some old remains have been discovered in Bihar which seem to show that some kind of glass was made there even before the Mauryan period.

It will interest you to know that Megasthenes, the Greek ambassador who came to the Court of Chandragupta, writes about the Indian love of finery and beauty, and specially notes the use of the shoe to add to one's height. So high heels are not entirely a modern invention.

Ashoka succeeded Bindusara in 268 BC to a great empire, which included the whole of north and central India and extended right up to Central Asia. With the desire, perhaps, of bringing into his empire the remaining parts in the south-east and south, he started the conquest of Kalinga in the ninth year of his reign. Kalinga lay on the east coast of India, between the Mahanadi, Godavari and Kistna rivers. The people of Kalinga fought bravely, but they were ultimately subdued after terrible slaughter. This war and slaughter affected Ashoka so deeply that he was disgusted with war and all its works. Henceforth there was to be no war for him. Nearly the whole of India, except a tiny tip in the south, was under him; and it was easy enough for him to complete the conquest of this little tip. But he refrained. According to H.G. Wells, he is the only military monarch on record who abandoned warfare after victory.

Fortunately for us, we have Ashoka's own words, telling us of what he thought and what he did. In numerous edicts which were carved out in the rock or on metal, we still have his messages to his people and to posterity. You know that there is such an Ashoka Pillar in the fort at Allahabad. There are many others in our province.

In these edicts Ashoka tells us of his horror and remorse at the slaughter which war and conquest involve. The only true conquest, he says, is the conquest of self and the conquest of men's hearts by the Dharma. But I shall quote for you some of these edicts. They make fascinating reading and they will bring Ashoka nearer to you.

> "Kalinga was conquered by His Sacred and Gracious Majesty", so runs an edict, "when he had been consecrated eight years." One hundred and fifty thousand persons were thence carried away captive, one hundred thousand were there slain, and many times that number died.
>
> Directly after the annexation of the Kalingas began His Sacred Majesty's zealous protection of the Law of Piety, his love of that Law, and his inculcation of that Law *(Dharma)*. *Thus* arose his sacred Majesty's remorse for having conquered the Kalingas, because the conquest of a country previously unconquered involves the slaughter, death and carrying away captive of the people. That is a matter of profound sorrow and regret to His Sacred Majesty.

The edict goes on to say that Ashoka would not tolerate any longer the slaughter or captivity of even a hundredth or thousandth part of the number killed and made captive in Kalinga.

> Moreover, should any one do him wrong, that too must be borne with by His Sacred Majesty', so far as it can possibly be borne with. Even upon the forest folk in his dominions His Sacred Majesty looks kindly and he seeks to make them think aright, for, if he did not, repentance would come upon His Sacred Majesty. For His Sacred Majesty desires that all animate beings should have security, self-control, peace of mind, and joyousness.

Ashoka further explains that true conquest consists of the conquest of men's hearts by the Law of Duty or Piety, and to relate that he had already won such real victories, not only in his own dominions, but in distant kingdoms.

The Law to which reference is made repeatedly in these edicts was the Law of the Buddha. Ashoka became an ardent Buddhist and tried his utmost to spread the Dharma. But there was no force or compulsion. It was only by winning men's hearts that he sought to make converts.

> **Men of religion have seldom, very seldom, been as tolerant as Ashoka. In order to convert people to their own faith they have seldom scrupled to use force and terrorism and fraud. The whole of history is full of religious persecution and religious wars, and in the name of religion and of God perhaps more blood has been shed than in any other name. It is good therefore to remember how a great son of India, intensely religious, and the head of a powerful empire, behaved in order to convert people to his ways of thought. It is strange that anyone should be so foolish as to think that religion and faith can be thrust down a person's throat at the point of the sword or a bayonet.**

So Ashoka, the beloved of the gods—devanampriya, as he is called in the edicts—sent his messengers and ambassadors to the kingdoms of the West in Asia, Europe and Africa. To Ceylon, you will remember, he sent his own brother Mahendra and sister Sanghamitra, and they are said to have carried a branch of the sacred peepal tree from Gaya. Do you remember the peepal tree we saw in the temple at Anuradhapura? We are told that this was the very tree which grew out of that ancient branch.

In India Buddhism spread rapidly. And as the Dharma was for Ashoka not just the repetition of empty prayers and the performance of pujas and ceremonies, but the performance of good deeds and social uplift, all over the country public gardens and hospitals and wells and roads grew up. Special provision was made for the education of women. Four great university towns—Takshashila or Taxila in the far north, near Peshawar; Mathura, vulgarly spelt Muttra now by the English; Ujjain in Central India; and Nalanda near Patna in Bihar—attracted students not only from India, but from distant countries—from China to western Asia—and these students carried back home with them the message of Buddha's teaching. Great monasteries grew up all over the country—Vihara they were called. There were apparently so many round about Pataliputra or Patna that the whole province came to be known as Vihara, or, as it is called now, Bihar. But, as often happens, these monasteries soon lost the inspiration of teaching and of thought, and became just places where people followed a certain routine and worship.

Ashoka's passion for protecting life extended to animals also. Hospitals especially meant for them were erected, and animal-sacrifice was forbidden. In both these matters he was somewhat in advance of our own time. Unhappily, animal-sacrifice still prevails to some extent, and is supposed to be an essential part of religion; and there is little provision for the treatment of animals.

Ashoka's example and the spread of Buddhism resulted in vegetarianism becoming popular. Till then Kshattriyas and Brahmans in India generally ate meat and used to take wines and alcoholic drinks. Both meat-eating and wine-drinking grew much less.

So ruled Ashoka for thirty-eight years, trying his utmost to promote peacefully the public good. He was always ready for public business "at all times and at all places, whether I am dining or in the ladies' apartments, in my bedroom or in my closet, in my carriage or in my palace gardens, the official reporters should keep me constantly informed of the people's business". If any difficulty arose, a report was to be made to him immediately "at any hour and at any place", for, as he says, "work I must for the commonwealth".

Ashoka died in 226 BC. Some time before his death he became a Buddhist monk.

We have few remains of Mauryan times. But what we have are practically the earliest so far discovered of Aryan civilization in India—for the moment we are not considering the ruins of Mohenjodaro. In Sarnath, near Benares, you can see the beautiful Ashoka pillar with the lions on the top.

Of the great city of Pataliputra, which was Ashoka's capital, nothing is left. Indeed over 1500 years ago, 600 years after Ashoka, a Chinese traveller, Fa-Hien, visited the place. The city flourished then and was rich and prosperous, but even then Ashoka's palace of stone was in ruins. Even these ruins impressed Fa-Hien, who says in his travel record that they did not appear to be human work. The palace of massive stone is gone, leaving no trace behind, but the memory of Ashoka lives over the whole continent of Asia, and his edicts still speak to us in a language we can understand and appreciate. And we can still learn much from them. This letter has grown long and may weary you. I shall finish it with a small quotation from one of Ashoka's edicts: "All sects deserve reverence for one reason or another. By thus acting a man exalts his own sect and at the same time does service to the sects of other people."

~

The Influence of Indian Art Abroad

(From The Discovery of India*)*

These records of ancient empires and dynasties have an interest for the antiquarian, but they have a large interest in the history of civilization and art. From the point of view of India they are particularly important, for it was India that functioned there and exhibited her vitality and genius in a variety of ways. We see her bubbling over with energy and spreading out far and wide, carrying not only her thought but her other ideals, her art, her trade, her language and literature, and her methods of government. She was not stagnant, or standing aloof, or isolated and cut off by mountain and sea. Her people crossed those high mountain barriers and perilous seas and built up, as M. Grousset says, 'a Greater India politically as little organized as Greater Greece, but morally equally harmonious.' As a matter of fact even the political organization of these Malayasian states was of a high order, though it was not part of the Indian political structure. But M. Grousset refers to the wider areas where Indian culture spread: 'In the high plateau of eastern Iran, in the oases of Serindia, in the arid wastes of Tibet, Mongolia, and Manchuria, in the ancient civilized lands of China and Japan, in the lands of the primitive Mons and Khmers and other tribes in Indo-China, in the countries of the Malayo-Polynesians, in Indonesia and Malay, India left the indelible impress of her high culture, not only upon religion, but also upon art and literature, in a word, all the higher things of spirit.'[5]

Indian civilization took root especially in the countries of south-east Asia and the evidence for this can be found all over the place today. There were great centres of Sanskrit learning in Champa, Angkor, Srivijaya, Majapahit, and other places. The names of the rulers of the various states and empires that arose are purely Indian and Sanskrit. This does not mean that they were pure Indian, but it does mean that they were Indianized. State ceremonies were Indian and conducted in Sanskrit. All the officers of the state bear old Sanskrit titles and some of these titles and designations have been continued up till now, not only in Thailand but in the Moslem states of Malaya. The old literatures of these places in Indonesia are full of Indian myth and legend. The famous dances of Java and Bali derive from India. The little island of Bali has indeed largely maintained its old Indian culture down to modern times and even Hinduism has persisted there. The art of writing went to the Philippines from India.

In Cambodia the alphabet is derived from South India and numerous Sanskrit words have been taken over with minor variations. The civil and criminal law is based on the Laws

---

[5] Rene Grousset *Civilizations of the East* Volume II (UK: Lightning Source, 2002), 276.

of Manu, the ancient law-giver of India, and this has been codified, with variations due to Buddhist influence, in modern Cambodian legislation.[6]

But above all else it is in the magnificent art and architecture of these old Indian colonies that the Indian influence is most marked. The original impulse was modified, adapted, and fused with the genius of the place and out of this fusion arose the monuments and wonderful temples of Angkor and Borobudur. At Borobudur in Java, the whole life story of Buddha is carved in stone. At other places bas-reliefs reproduce the legends of Vishnu and Rama and Krishna. Of Angkor, Mr Osbert Sitwell has written: 'Let it be said immediately that Angkor, as it stands, ranks as chief wonder of the world today, one of the summits to which human genius has aspired in stone, infinitely more impressive, lovely and, as well, romantic, than anything that can be seen in China .... The material remains of a civilization that flashed its wings, of the utmost brilliance, for six centuries, and then perished so utterly that even his name has died from the lips of man.'

Round the great temple of Angkor Vat is a vast area of mighty ruins with artificial lakes and pools, and canals and bridges over them, and a great gate dominated by 'a vast sculptured head, a lovely, smiling but enigmatic Cambodian face, though one raised to the power and beauty of a god.' The face with its strangely fascinating and disturbing smile—the 'Angkor smile'—is repeated again and again. This gate leads to the temple: 'the neighbouring Bayon can be said to be the most imaginative and singular in the world, more lovely than Angkor Vat, because more unearthly in its conception, a temple from a city in some other distant planet,,, imbued with the same elusive beauty that often lives between the lines of a great poem.'[7]

The inspiration for Angkor came from India but it was the

---

[6] A. Leclire, 'Recherches sur les origines brahmaniques des lois Cambodgiennes' as quoted in B.R. Chatterji's *Indian Cultural Influence in Cambodia* (Calcutta: University of Calcutta, 1928).

[7] These extracts have been taken from Osbert Sitwell's *'Escape with Me—An Oriental Sketch Book*, Literary Licensing LLC (1941).

Khmer genius that developed it, or the two fused together and produced this wonder. The Cambodian king who is said to have built this great temple is named Jayavarman VII, a typical Indian name.

Dr. Quaritch Wales says that, 'when the guiding hand of India was removed, her inspiration was not forgotten, but the Khmer genius was released to mould from it vast new conceptions of amazing vitality different from, and hence not properly to be compared with anything matured in a purely Indian environment... It is true that Khmer culture is essentially based on the inspiration of India, without which the Khmers at best might have produced nothing greater than the barbaric splendour of the Central American Mayas; but it must be admitted that here, more than anywhere else in Greater India, this inspiration fell on fertile soil'.[8]

This leads one to think that in India itself that original inspiration gradually faded because the mind and the soil became over-worked and undernourished for lack of fresh currents and ideas. So long as India kept her mind open and gave of her riches to others, and received from them what she lacked, she remained fresh and strong and vital. But the more she withdrew into her shell, intent on preserving herself, uncontaminated by external influences, the more she lost that inspiration and her life became increasingly a dull round of meaningless activities all centred in the dead past. Losing the art of creating beauty, her children lost even the capacity to recognize it.

It is to European scholars and archaeologists that the excavations and discoveries in Java, Angkor and elsewhere in Greater India are due, more especially to French and Dutch scholars. Great cities and monuments probably still lie buried there awaiting discovery. Meanwhile it is said that important sites in Malaya containing ancient ruins have been destroyed by mining operations or for obtaining material for building roads. The war will no doubt add to this destruction.

---

[8] From Dr. H.G. Quartich Wales' *Towards Angkor,* Harrap (1933).

Some years ago I had a letter from a Thai (Siamese) student who had come to Tagore's Santiniketan and was returning to Thailand. He wrote: 'I always consider myself exceptionally fortunate in being able to come to this great and ancient land of Aryavarta and to pay my humble homage at the feet of grandmother India in whose affectionate arms my mother country was so lovingly brought up and taught to appreciate and love what was sublime and beautiful in culture and religion.' This may not be typical, but it does convey some idea of the general feeling towards India which, though vague and overladen with much else, still continues in many of the countries of South-East Asia. Everywhere an intense and narrow nationalism has grown, looking to itself and distrustful of others; there is fear and hatred of European domination and yet a desire to emulate Europe and America; there is often some contempt for India because of her dependent condition; and yet behind all this there is a feeling of respect and friendship for India, for old memories endure and people have not forgotten that there was a time when India was a mother country to these and nourished them with rich fare from her own treasure house. Just as Hellenism spread from Greece to the countries of the Mediterranean and in Western Asia, India's cultural influence spread to many countries and left its powerful impress upon them.

~

Mathematics in Ancient India

(From The Discovery of India*)*

Highly intellectual and given to abstract thinking as they were, one would expect the ancient Indians to excel in mathematics. Europe got its early arithmetic and algebra from the Arabs—hence the 'Arabic numerals'—but the Arabs themselves had previously taken them from India. The astonishing progress that the Indians had made in mathematics is now well known and it is recognized that the foundations of modern arithmetic and algebra were laid long ago in India. The clumsy method of using a counting frame and the use of Roman and such like numerals had long retarded progress when the ten Indian numerals, including the zero sign, liberated the human mind from these restrictions and threw a flood of light on the behaviour of numbers. These number symbols were unique and entirely different from all other symbols that had been in use in other countries. They are common enough today and we take them for granted, yet they contained the germs of revolutionary progress in them. It took many centuries for them to travel from India, via Baghdad, to the western world.

A hundred and fifty years ago, during Napoleon's time, La Place wrote: 'It is India that gave us the ingenious method of expressing all numbers by means of ten symbols, each symbol receiving a value of position, as well as an absolute value; a profound and important idea which appears so simple to us now that we ignore its true merit, but its very simplicity, the great ease which it has lent to all computations, puts our arithmetic in the first rank of useful inventions; and we shall appreciate the grandeur of this achievement when we remember that it escaped the genius of Archimedes and Apollonius, two of the greatest men produced by antiquity.'[9]

The origins of geometry, arithmetic, and algebra in India go back to remote periods. Probably to begin with there was some kind of geometrical algebra used for making figures for Vedic altars. Mention is made in the most ancient books of the geometrical method for the transformation of a square into a rectangle having a given side: $ax = c$. Geometrical figures are even now commonly used in Hindu ceremonies. Geometry made progress in India but in this respect Greece and Alexandria went ahead. It was in arithmetic and algebra that India kept the lead. The inventor or inventors of the decimal place-value system and the zero mark are not known. The earliest use of the zero symbol,

---

[9] As quoted in Lancelot Hogben's *Mathematics for the Million*, (London: 1942).

so far discovered, is in one of the scriptural books dated about 200 B.C. It is considered probable that the place-value system was invented about the beginning of the Christian era. The zero, called shunya or nothing, was originally a dot and later it became a small circle. It was considered a number like any other. Professor Halsted thus emphasizes the vital significance of this invention: 'The importance of the creation of the zero mark can never be exaggerated. This giving to airy nothing, not merely a local habitation and a name, a picture, a symbol but helpful power, is the characteristic of the Hindu race from whence it sprang. It is like coining the Nirvana into dynamos. No single mathematical creation has been more potent for the general on-go of intelligence and power.'[10]

Yet another modern mathematician has grown eloquent over this historic event. Dantzig in his 'Number' writes: 'This long period of nearly five thousand years saw the rise and fall of many a civilization, each leaving behind it a heritage of literature, art, philosophy, and religion. But what was the net achievement in the field of reckoning, the earliest art practised by man? An inflexible numeration so crude as to make progress well-nigh impossible, and a calculating device so limited in scope that even elementary calculations called for the services of an expert... Man used these devices for thousands of years without making a single worthwhile improvement in the instrument, without contributing a single important idea to the system.... Even when compared with the slow growth of ideas during the dark ages, the history of reckoning presents a peculiar picture of desolate stagnation. When viewed in this light the achievements of the unknown Hindu, who sometime in the first centuries of our era discovered the principle of position, assumes the importance of a world event.'[11]

---

[10] B. Halsted: *On the Foundation and Technique of Arithmetic*, p. 20 (Chicago: 1912), as quoted in B. Datta and A.N. Singh's *History of Hindu Mathematics* (1935).

[11] Quoted in L. Hogben's *Mathematics for the Million* (London, 1942).

Dantzig is puzzled at the fact that the great mathematicians of Greece did not stumble on this discovery. 'Is it that the Greeks had such a marked contempt for applied science, leaving even the instruction of their children to slaves? But if so, how is it that the nation that gave us geometry and carried this science so far did not create even a rudimentary algebra? Is it not equally strange that algebra,that corner-stone of modern mathematics, also originated in India, and at about the same time that positional numeration did?'

The answer to this question is suggested by Professor Hogben: 'The difficulty of understanding why it should have been the Hindus who took this step, why it was not taken by the mathematicians of antiquity, why it should first have been taken by practical man, is only insuperable if we seek for the explanation of intellectual progress in the genius of a few gifted individuals, instead of in the whole social framework of custom thought which circumscribes the greatest individual genius. What happened in India about A.D. 100 had happened before. Maybe it is happening now in Soviet Russia.... .To accept it (this truth) is to recognise that every culture contains within itself its own doom, unless it pays as much attention to the education of the mass of mankind as to the education of the exceptionally gifted people.'[12]

We must assume then that these momentous inventions were not just due to the momentary illumination of an erratic genius, much in advance of his time, but that they were essentially the product of the social milieu and that they answered some insistent demand of the times. Genius of a high order was certainly necessary to find this out and fulfil the demand, but if the demand had not been there the urge to find some way out would have been absent, and even if the invention had been made it would have been forgotten or put aside till circumstances more propitious for its use arose. It seems clear from the early Sanskrit works on mathematics that the demand was there, for these books are full of problems of trade and social relationship

[12] Ibid.

involving complicated calculations. There are problems dealing with taxation, debt, and interest; problems of partnership, barter and exchange, and the calculation of the fineness of gold. Society had grown complex and large numbers of people were engaged in governmental operations and in an extensive trade. It was impossible to carry on without simple methods of calculation.

The adoption of zero and the decimal place-value system in India unbarred the gates of the mind to rapid progress in arithmetic and algebra. Fractions come in, and the multiplication and division of fractions; the rule of three is discovered and perfected; squares and square-roots (together with the sign of the square-root, V) J cubes and cube-roots; the minus sign; tables of sines; π is evaluated as 3.1416; letters of the alphabet are used in algebra to denote unknowns; simple and quadratic equations are considered; the mathematics of zero are investigated. Zero is defined as - a = 0; a + 0 = a; a - 0 = a; a x 0=0; a 0 becomes infinity. The conception of negative quantities also comes in, thus: 4 = ± 2.

These and other advances in mathematics are contained in books written by a succession of eminent mathematicians from the fifth to the twelfth century B.C. There are earlier books also (Baudhayana, eighth century B.C.; Apastamba and Katyayana, both fifth century B.C.) which deal with geometrical problems, especially with triangles, rectangles, and squares. But the earliest extant book on algebra is by the famous astronomer, Aryabhata, who was born in B.C. 476. He wrote this book on astronomy and mathematics when he was only twenty-three years old. Aryabhata, who is sometimes called the inventor of algebra, must have relied, partly at least, on the work of his predecessors. The next great name in Indian mathematics is that of Bhaskara I (B.C. 522), and he was followed by Brahmagupta (B.C. 628), who was also a famous astronomer, and who stated the laws applying to shunya or zero and made other notable advances. There follow a succession of mathematicians who have written on arithmetic or algebra. The last great name is that of Bhaskara II, who was born in B.C. 1114. He wrote three books, on astronomy, algebra, and arithmetic. His book on arithmetic is known as *Lilavati*, which is an odd name for a treatise on mathematics, as it is the name of a woman. There are frequent references in the book to a young girl who is addressed as 'O Lilavati' and is then instructed on the problems stated. It is believed, without any definite proof, that Lilavati was Bhaskara's daughter. The style of the book is clear and simple and suitable for young persons to understand. The book is still used, partly for its style, in Sanskrit schools.

Books on mathematics continued to appear (Narayana 1150, Ganesha 1545), but these are mere repetitions of what had been done. Very little original work on mathematics was done in India after the twelfth century till we reach the modern age. In the eighth century, during the reign of the Khalif Al-Mansur (753–774), a number of Indian scholars went to Baghdad, and among the books they took with them were works on mathematics and astronomy. Probably even earlier than this, Indian numerals had reached Baghdad, but this was the first systematic approach, and Aryabhata's and other books were translated into Arabic. They influenced the development of mathematics and astronomy in the Arab world, and Indian numerals were introduced. Baghdad was then a great centre of learning and Greek and Jewish scholars had gathered there bringing with them Greek philosophy, geometry, and science. The cultural influence of Baghdad was felt throughout the Moslem world from central Asia to Spain, and a knowledge of Indian mathematics in their Arabic translations spread all over this vast area. The numerals were called by the Arabs 'figures of Hind' (or India), and the Arabic word for a number is 'Hindsah', meaning 'from Hind'.

From this Arab world the new mathematics travelled to European countries, probably through the Moorish universities of Spain, and became the foundation for European mathematics. There was opposition in Europe to the use of the new numbers, as they were considered infidel symbols, and it took several hundred years before they were in common use. The earliest known use is in a Sicilian coin of 1134; in Britain the first use is in 1490.

It seems clear that some knowledge of Indian mathematics, and especially of the place-value system of numbers, had penetrated into western Asia even before the formal embassy carried books to Baghdad. There is an interesting passage in a complaint made by a Syrian scholar-monk who was hurt at the arrogance of some Greek scholars who looked down on Syrians. Severus Sebokht was his name, and he lived in a convent situated on the Euphrates. He writes in A.D. 662 and tries to show that the Syrians were in no way inferior to the Greeks. By way of illustration he refers to the Indians: 'I will omit all discussion of the science of the Hindus, a people not the same as the Syrians; their subtle discoveries in the science of astronomy, discoveries that are more ingenious than those of the Greeks and the Babylonians; their computing that surpasses description. I wish only to say that this computation is done by means of nine signs. If those who believe, because they speak Greek, that they have reached the limits of science, should know of these things, they would be convinced that there are also others who know something.'[13]

Mathematics in India inevitably makes one think of one extraordinary figure of recent times. This was Srinivasa Ramanujam. Born in a poor brahmin family in south India, having no opportunities for a proper education, he became a clerk in the Madras Port Trust. But he was bubbling over with some irrepressible quality of instinctive genius and played about with numbers and equations in his spare time. By a lucky chance he attracted the attention of a mathematician who sent some of his amateur work to Cambridge in England. People there were impressed and a scholarship was arranged for him. So he left his clerk's job and went to Cambridge and during a very brief period there did work of profound value and amazing originality. The Royal Society of England went rather out of their way and made him a Fellow, but he died two years later, probably of tuberculosis, at the age of thirty-three. Professor Julian Huxley has, I believe, referred to him somewhere as the greatest mathematician of the century.

---

[13] As quoted in *History of Hindu Mathematics*. I am indebted to this book for much information on this subject.

Ramanujam's brief life and death are symbolic of conditions in India. Of our millions how few get any education at all, how many live on the verge of starvation; of even those who get some education how many have nothing to look forward to but a clerkship in some office on a pay that is usually far less than the unemployment dole in England? If life opened its gates to them and offered them food and healthy conditions of living and education and opportunities of growth, how many among these millions would be eminent scientists, educationists, technicians, industrialists, writers and artists, helping to build a new India and a new world?

~

South India Colonizes

(From Glimpses of World History*)*

...You will remember the borderland empire of the Kushans—the great Buddhist State comprising the whole of northern India and a good bit of Central Asia—with its capital at Purushapura or Peshawar. You will also perhaps remember that about this period in the south of India there was a great state stretching from sea to sea—the Andhra State. For about 300 years the Kushans and the Andhras flourished. About the middle of the third century after Christ these two empires ceased to be, and for a period India had a number of small states. Within 100 years, however, another Chandragupta arose in Pataliputra and started a period of aggressive Hindu imperialism. But before we go on to the Guptas, as they are called, we might have a look at the beginnings of great enterprises in the south, which were to carry Indian art and culture to distant islands of the East.

You know well the shape of India, as she lies between the Himalayas and the two seas. The north is far removed from the sea. Its main preoccupation in the past has been the land frontier, over which enemies and invaders used to come. But in the east and west and south we have a tremendous sea-coast, and India narrows down till the east meets the west at

Kanyakumari or Cape Comorin. All these people living near the sea were naturally interested in it, and one would expect many of them to be seafaring folk. I have told you already of the great trade which South India had from the remotest times with the West. It is not surprising therefore to find that from early times shipbuilding existed in India and people crossed the seas in search of trade, or maybe adventure. Vijaya is supposed to have gone from India and conquered Ceylon about the time Gautama the Buddha lived here. In the Ajanta caves, I think there is a representation of Vijaya crossing to Ceylon, with horses and elephants being carried across in ships. Vijaya gave the name Sinhala to the Island—"Sinhala Dweep". Sinhala is derived from Sinha, a lion, and there is an old story about a lion, current in Ceylon, which I have forgotten. I suppose the word Ceylon is derived from Sinhala.

The little crossing from South India to Ceylon was, of course, no great feat. But we have plenty of evidence of shipbuilding and people going across the seas from the many Indian ports which dotted the coastline from Bengal to Gujrat. Chanakya, the great Minister of Chandragupta Maurya, tells us something about the navy in his *Arthashastra,* about which I wrote to you from Naini. Megasthenes, the Greek ambassador at Chandragupta's Court, also mentions it. Thus it appears that even at the beginning of the Mauryan period shipbuilding was a flourishing industry in India. And ships are obviously meant to be used. So quite a considerable number of people must have crossed the seas in them. It is strange and interesting to think of this, and then to think of some of our people even today who are afraid of crossing the seas and think it against their religion to do so. We cannot call these people relics of the past, for, as you see, the past was much more sensible. Fortunately, such extraordinary notions have largely disappeared now, and there are few people who are influenced by them.

The south naturally looked more to the sea than the north. Most of the foreign trade was with the south, and Tamil poems are full of references to "yavana" wines and vases and lamps. "Yavana" was chiefly used for Greeks, but perhaps vaguely for all foreigners. The Andhra coins of the second and third centuries bear the device of a large two-masted ship, which shows how very much interested the old Andhras must have been in shipbuilding and sea-trade.

It was the south, therefore, which took the lead in a great enterprise which resulted in establishing Indian colonies all over the islands in the East. These colonizing excursions started in the first century after Christ and they continued for hundreds of years. All over Malay and Java and Sumatra and Cambodia and Borneo they went, and established themselves and took Indian culture and Indian art with them. In Burma and Siam and Indo-China there were large Indian colonies. Many even of the names they gave to their new towns and settlements were borrowed from India—Ayodhya, Hastinapur, Taxila, Gandhara. Strange how history repeats itself! The Anglo-Saxon colonists who went to America did likewise, and in the United States today the names of old English cities are repeated.

No doubt these Indian colonists misbehaved wherever they went, as all such colonists do. They must have exploited the people of the islands and lorded it over them. But after a while the colonists and the old inhabitants must have intermixed, for it was difficult to keep up regular contacts with India. Hindu States and empires were established in these eastern islands, and then Buddhist rulers came, and between the Hindu and the Buddhist there was a tussle for mastery. It is a long and fascinating story—the history of Further or Greater India, as it is called. Mighty ruins still tell us of the great buildings and temples that adorned these Indian settlements. There were great cities, built by Indian builders and craftsmen—Kamboja, Sri Vijaya, Angkor the Magnificent, Madjapahit.

For nearly 1400 years these Hindu and Buddhist States lasted in these islands, contending against each other for mastery, changing hands, and occasionally destroying each other. In the fifteenth century the Muslims finally obtained control, and soon after came the Portuguese and the Spaniards, the Dutch and the English, and last of all the Americans. The Chinese, of course, had always been close neighbours, sometimes interfering and conquering; oftener living as friends and exchanging gifts; and all the time influencing them with their great culture and civilization.

These Hindu colonies of the East have many things to interest us. The most striking feature is that the colonization was evidently organized by one of the principal governments of the day in southern India. At first many individual explorers must have gone; then later as trade developed, families and groups of people must have gone on their own account. It is said that the early settlers were from Kalinga (Orissa) and the eastern coast. Perhaps some people went from Bengal also. There is also a tradition that some people from Gujrat, pushed out from their own homelands, went to these islands. But these are conjectures. The principal stream of colonists went from the Pallava country—the southern portion of the Tamil land, where a great Pallava dynasty was ruling. And it was this Pallava government that seems to have organized this colonization of Malaysia. Perhaps there was pressure of population owing to people pushing down from northern India. Whatever the reason may have been, settlements in widely scattered places, far from India, were deliberately planned and colonies were started in these places almost simultaneously. These settlements were in Indo-China, Malay Peninsula, Borneo, Sumatra, Java and in other places. All these were Pallava colonies bearing Indian names. In Indo-China the settlement was called Kamboja (the present Kambodia), a name which came all the way from a Kamboja in the Kabul Valley in Gandhara.

For 400 or 600 years these settlements remained Hindu in religion; then gradually Buddhism spread all over. Much later came Islam and spread in part of Malaysia, part remaining Buddhist.

Empires and kingdoms came and went in Malaysia. But the real result of these colonizing enterprises of southern India was to introduce Indo-Aryan civilization in this part of the world, and to a certain extent the people of Malaysia today are the children of the same civilization as we are. They have had other influences also, notably the Chinese, and it is interesting to observe the mixture of these two powerful influences—the Indian and the

Chinese—on the different countries of Malaysia. Some have been more Indianized; in others the Chinese element is more in evidence. On the mainland, in Burma, Siam and Indo-China, the Chinese influence is predominant—but not in Malay. In the islands, Java, Sumatra and others, Indian influence is more obvious, with a recent covering of Islam.

But there was no conflict between the Indian and the Chinese influences. They were very dissimilar, and yet they could work on parallel lines without difficulty. In religion, of course, India was the fountainhead, whether it was Hinduism or Buddhism. Even China owed her religion to India. In art also Indian influence was supreme in Malaysia. Even in Indo-China, where Chinese influence was great, the architecture was wholly Indian. China influenced these continental countries more in regard to their methods of government and their general philosophy of life. So that today the people of Indo-China and Burma and Siam seem to be nearer akin to the Chinese than to the Indian. Of course, racially they have more of Mongolian blood in them, and this makes them resemble, to some extent, the Chinese.

In Borobodur in Java are to be seen now the remains of great Buddhist temples built by Indian artisans. The whole story of the Buddha's life is carved on the walls of these buildings, and they are a unique monument not only to the Buddha, but to the Indian art of that day.

Indian influence went farther still. It reached the Philippines and even Formosa, which were both part, for a time, of the Hindu Sri Vijaya kingdom of Sumatra.

~

Akbar

(From Glimpses of World History*)*

Babar had conquered a great part of northern India by his generalship and military efficiency. He had defeated the Afghan Sultan of Delhi, and later, and this was the more difficult task, the Rajput clans under the leadership of the gallant Rana Sanga of Chittor, a famous hero in Rajput history. But he left a difficult task for his son Humayun. Humayun was a cultured and learned person, but no soldier like his father. He had trouble all over his new empire, and ultimately in 1540, ten years after Babar's death, an Afghan chief in Bihar, named Sher Khan, defeated and drove him out of India. So the second of the Great Moghals became a wanderer, hiding himself and suffering all manner of privations. It was during these wanderings in the Rajputana desert that his wife gave birth to a son in November 1542. This son, born in the desert, was to become Akbar.

Humayun escaped to Persia, and Shah Tamasp, the ruler of the place, gave him shelter. Meanwhile Sher Khan was supreme in northern India, and for five years he ruled as Sher Shah. Even during this brief period he showed that he was a very capable person. He was a brilliant organizer, and his government was active and efficient. In the midst of his wars he found time to start a new and a better land-revenue system for assessing taxes on the cultivators. He was a stern and hard man, but of all the Afghan rulers of India, and of many others also, he was certainly the ablest and best. But, as often happens with efficient autocrats, he was all in all in his government, and with his death the whole structure went to pieces.

Humayun took advantage of this disorganization and returned from Persia in 1556 with an army. He won, and after an interval of sixteen years he was again on the throne of Delhi. But not for long. Six months later he fell down a staircase and died.

It is interesting to contrast the tombs or mausoleums of Sher Shah and Humayun. The Afghan's tomb is at Sahasram in Bihar, a stern, strong, imperious-looking building, like the man. Humayun's tomb is at Delhi. It is a polished and elegant building. And from these structures of stone one can form a good idea of these two rivals for empire in the sixteenth century.

Akbar was only thirteen years old then. Like his grandfather, he came to the throne early. He had a guardian and protector, Bairam Khan—the Khan Baba, he was called. But within four years Akbar wearied of guardianship and other people's direction and took the government into his own hands.

For nearly fifty years Akbar ruled India, from early in 1556 to the end of 1605. This was the period of the revolt of the Netherlands in Europe, and of Shakespeare in England. Akbar's name stands put in Indian history, and sometimes, and in some ways, he reminds one of Ashoka. It is a strange thing that a Buddhist Emperor of India of the third century before Christ, and a Muslim Emperor of India of the sixteenth century after Christ, should speak in the same manner and almost in the same voice. One wonders if this is not perhaps the voice of India herself speaking through two of her great sons. Of Ashoka we know little enough, except what he has himself left carved in stone. Of Akbar we know a great deal. Two contemporary historians of his Court have left long accounts, and the foreigners who visited him, and especially the Jesuits who tried hard to convert him to Christianity, have written at length.

He was the third in the line from Babar. But the Moghals were still new to the country. They were regarded as foreigners and their hold was military. It was Akbar's reign that established the Moghal dynasty and made it of the soil and wholly Indian in outlook. It was in his reign that the title of Great Moghal came to be used in Europe. He was very autocratic and had uncontrolled power. There seems to have been no whisper in India then of checking a ruler's powers. As it happened,

> **Akbar was a wise despot, and he worked hard for the welfare of the Indian people. In a sense he might be considered to be the father of Indian nationalism. At a time when there was little of nationality in the country and religion was a dividing factor, Akbar deliberately placed the ideal of a common Indian nationhood above the claims of separatist religion.**

He did not wholly succeed in his attempt. But it is amazing how far he did go and what great success attended his efforts.

And yet Akbar's success, such as it was, was not due entirely to his unaided self. No man can succeed in great tasks unless the time is ripe and the atmosphere is favourable. A great man often forces the pace and creates his own atmosphere. But the great man himself is a product of the times and of the prevailing atmosphere. So Akbar also was the product of the times in India.

In a previous letter I told you how silent forces in India worked for the synthesis of the two cultures and religions that had been thrown together in this country. I told you of new styles of architecture and of the growth of the Indian languages, and especially of Urdu or Hindustani. And I also told you of reformers and religious leaders, like Ramananda and Kabir and Guru Nanak, who sought to bring Islam and Hinduism nearer to each other by laying stress on the common features and attacking their rites and ceremonials. This spirit of synthesis was abroad, and Akbar, with his finely sensitive and receptive mind, must have absorbed it and reacted to it greatly. Indeed, he became its chief exponent.

Even as a statesman he must have come to the conclusion that his strength, and the nation's strength, would he in this synthesis. He was a brave enough fighter and an able general. He was, unlike Ashoka, never averse to fighting. But he preferred the gains of affection to the gains of the sword, and he knew that they would be more enduring. So he set himself out deliberately to win the goodwill of the Hindu nobles and the Hindu masses. He abolished the jizya poll tax on non-Muslims and the tax on Hindu pilgrims. He married himself a girl of a noble Rajput family; later he married his son to a Rajput girl also; and he encouraged such mixed marriages. He appointed Rajput nobles to the highest posts in his Empire. Several of his bravest generals and most capable ministers and governors were Hindus. Raja Man Singh was even sent for a while as governor to Kabul. Indeed, in his attempts to conciliate the Rajputs and the Hindu masses, he went to such lengths that he was occasionally unjust to his Muslim subjects. He succeeded, however, in winning the goodwill of the Hindus, and the Rajputs flocked to serve him and do him honour—nearly all, except one unbending figure, Rana Pratap Singh of Mewar.

Rana Pratap refused to acknowledge Akbar's suzerainty, even nominally. Beaten in battle, he preferred to live a hunted life in the jungle to pampered ease as Akbar's vassal. All his life this proud Rajput fought the great Emperor of Delhi and refused to bow down to him. Towards the end of his days he even met with some success. The memory of this gallant Rajput is treasured in Rajputana, and many a legend has grown round his name.

So Akbar won over the Rajputs, and became very popular with the masses. He was indulgent to the Parsees and even to the Jesuit missionaries who came to his Court. But this indulgence and a certain disregard of Muslim observances made him unpopular with the Muslim nobles, and there were several revolts against him.

I have compared him to Ashoka, but do not be misled by this comparison. In many ways he was unlike him. He was very ambitious, and to the end of his days he was a conqueror, intent on extending his empire. The Jesuits tell us that he,

> 'possessed an alert and discerning mind; he was a man of sound judgment, prudent in affairs, and above all, kind, affable, and generous. With these qualities he combined the courage of those who undertake and carry out great enterprises... He was interested in, and curious to learn about many things, and possessed an intimate knowledge not only of military and political matters, but of many of the mechanical arts...the light of clemency and mildness shone forth from this prince, even upon those who offended against his own person. He seldom lost his temper. If he did so, he fell into a violent passion; but his wrath was never of long duration.'

Remember that this description is not by a courtier, but by a stranger from another land who had plenty of opportunities to observe Akbar.

Physically, Akbar was extraordinarily strong and active, and he loved nothing better than hunting wild and dangerous animals. As a soldier he was brave to the point of recklessness. His amazing energy can be judged from a famous march of his from Agra to

Ahmedabad in nine days. A revolt had broken out in Gujrat, and Akbar rushed with a little army across the desert of Rajputana, a distance of 450 miles. It was an extraordinary feat. There were no railways or motor cars then, I need hardly remind you.

But great men have something besides all these qualities: they have, it is said, a magnetism which draws people to them. Akbar had this personal magnetism and charm in abundant measure; his compelling eyes were, in the wonderful description of the Jesuits, "vibrant like the sea in sunshine". Is it any wonder that this man should fascinate us still, and that his most royal and manly figure should tower high above the crowds of men who have been but kings?

As a conqueror, Akbar triumphed all over North India and even the South. He added Gujrat, Bengal, Orissa, Kashmir and Sindh to his Empire. He was victorious in Central India and South India also and took tribute. His defeat of Rani Durgavati, a ruler in the Central Province, does him little credit. The Rani was a brave and good ruler and she did him no harm. But ambition and the desire for empire care little for such obstacles. In South India his armies fought another woman ruler, the famous Chand Bibi, regent of Ahmednagar. This lady had courage and ability, and the fight she put up impressed the Moghal army so much that they granted her a favourable peace. Unfortunately she was killed later by some discontented soldiers of her own.

Akbar's armies also laid siege to Chittor—this was before Rana Pratap's time. Chittor was defended very gallantly by Jaimal. On his death there was the terrible jauhar ceremony again, and Chittor fell.

Akbar managed to gather round himself many efficient lieutenants who were devoted to him. Chief among these were the two brothers, Faizi and Abul Fazl, and Birbal, about whom innumerable stories are still told. Todar Mai was his finance minister. It was he who revised the whole revenue system. In those days, you may be interested to know, there was no zamindari system and no zamindars or taluqdars. The State settled with the individual cultivators or ryots. It is what is called now the ryotwari system. Present-day zamindars are the creation of the British.

Raja Man Singh of Jaipur was one of Akbar's best generals. Another famous person in Akbar's Court was Tansen, the great singer, who has become the patron saint of all singers in India.

Akbar's capital was at Agra to begin with and he built the fort there. Then he built a new city at Fatehpur-Sikri, which is about fifteen miles from Agra. He chose this site as a saintly person, Shaikh Salim Chishti, lived there. Here he built a splendid city, "much greater than London", according to an English traveller of the day, and for over fifteen years this was the capital of his Empire. Later he made Lahore his capital. "His Majesty", says Abul-Fazl, the friend and minister of Akbar, "plans splendid edifices, and dresses the work of his mind and heart in the garment of stone and clay" Fatehpur-Sikri still stands with its beautiful mosque and great *Bulatid Darwaza* and many other fine buildings. It is a deserted city and there is no life in it; but through its streets and across its wide courts the ghosts of a dead empire still seem to pass.

Our present city of Allahabad was also founded by Akbar, but of course the site is a most ancient one and Prayaga has flourished there since the days of the *Ramayana*. The fort at Allahabad was built by Akbar.

It must have been a busy life of conquest and consolidation of a vast empire. But right through it one can see another of Akbar's remarkable traits. This was his boundless curiosity and his search for truth. Whoever could throw light on any subject was sent for and questioned. The men of different religions gathered round him in the *Ibadat Khana,* each hoping to convert this mighty monarch. They often quarrelled with each other, and Akbar sat by, listening to their arguments and putting many questions to them. He seems to have been convinced that truth was no monopoly of any religion or sect, and he proclaimed that his avowed principle was one of universal toleration in religion.

A historian of his reign, Badauni, who must have participated in many of these gatherings himself, gives an interesting account of Akbar, which I shall quote. Badauni himself was an orthodox

Muslim, and he thoroughly disapproved of these activities of Akbar.

> His Majesty [he says] collected the opinions of everyone, especially of such as were not Muslims, retaining whatever he approved of, and rejecting everything which was against his disposition and ran counter to his wishes. From his earliest childhood to his manhood, and from his manhood to old age, his Majesty has passed through the most various phases, and through all sorts of religious practices and sectarian beliefs, and has collected everything which people can find in books, with a talent of selection peculiar to him, and a spirit of enquiry opposed to every (Islamic) principle. Thus a faith based on some elementary principles traced Itself on the mirror of his heart, and as a result of all the influences brought to bear on his Majesty, there grew, gradually as the outline on a stone, the conviction in his heart that there were sensible men in all religions, and abstemious thinkers, and men endowed with miraculous powers, among all nations. If some true knowledge was thus everywhere to be found, why should truth be confined to one religion?

At this time, you will remember, there was the most extraordinary intolerance in Europe in matters of religion. The Inquisition flourished in Spain and the Netherlands and elsewhere, and both Catholic and Calvinist thought tolerance of the other a deadly sin.

Year after year Akbar continued his religious talks and arguments with the professors of all faiths, till these professors got rather tired of it and gave up hope of converting him to their particular faith. When each faith had something of the truth, how could he fix upon one? "For the Gentiles", he is reported by the Jesuits to have remarked, "regard their law as good; and so likewise do the Saracens and the Christians. To which, then, shall we give our adherence?" (By the Gentiles, the Jesuits meant the Hindus, and the Saracens referred, of course, to the Muslims. The Jesuit fathers, being Portuguese, knew the Saracens of Spain, and called the Indian Muslims by the same name.) Akbar's question was a very pertinent one, but it annoyed the Jesuits, who say, in their book, that

> thus we see in this Prince the common fault of the atheist, who refuses to make reason subservient to faith, and, accepting nothing as true which his feeble mind is unable to fathom, is content to submit to his own imperfect judgment matters transcending the highest limits of human understanding.

If this is the definition of an atheist, the more we have of them the better.

What Akbar was aiming at is not clear. Did he look upon the question purely as a political one? In his desire to evolve a common nationality did he want to force the different religions into one channel? Or was he religious in his motives and his quest? I do not know. But I am inclined to think that he was more of a statesman than a religious reformer. Whatever his object may have been, he actually proclaimed a new religion—the *Din Ilahi*—of which he himself was the head. In religion, as in other matters, his autocracy was to be unchallenged, and there was a lot of disgusting prostration and kissing the feet and the like. The new religion did not catch. All it did was to irritate the Muslims.

Akbar was the very essence of authoritarianism. And yet it is interesting to speculate what his reaction to politically liberal ideas might have been. If there was to be liberty of conscience, why not greater political freedom for the people? To science he would certainly have been greatly attracted. Unhappily, these ideas, which were beginning to trouble some people in Europe then, were not current in India at the time. Nor does there seem to have been any use of the printing press, and education was thus very limited. Indeed, you will be amazed to learn that Akbar was illiterate—that is, he could not read or write! But none the less he was highly educated and was very fond of having books read to him. Under his orders many Sanskrit books were translated into Persian.

It is interesting to note that he issued orders forbidding the practice of sati by Hindu widows, and also the practice of making prisoners of war slaves.

Akbar died in October 1605 in his sixty-fourth year, after a reign of nearly fifty years. He lies buried in a beautiful mausoleum at Sikandra, near Agra.

In Akbar's reign there flourished in northern India—mostly in Benares—a man whose name is known to every villager in the United Provinces. He is far better known there, and is more popular, than Akbar or any king can be. I refer to Tulsi Das, who wrote the *Ramacharitmanas* or the *Ramayana* in Hindi.

~

Ranjit Singh and Jai Singh

(From The Discovery of India*)*

It seems clear that India became a prey to foreign conquest because of the inadequacy of her own people and because the British represented a higher and advancing social order. The contrast between the leaders on both sides is marked; the Indians, for all their ability, functioned in a narrow, limited sphere of thought and action, unaware of what was happening elsewhere and therefore unable to adapt themselves to changing conditions. Even if the curiosity of individuals was roused they could not break the shell which held them and their people prisoners. The Englishmen, on the other hand, were much more worldly wise, shaken up and forced to think by events in their own country and in France and America. Two great revolutions had taken place. The campaigns of the French revolutionary armies and of Napoleon had changed the whole science of war. Even the most ignorant Englishman who came to India saw different parts of the world in the course of his journey. In England itself great discoveries were being made, heralding the industrial revolution, though perhaps few realised their far-reaching significance at the time. But the leaven of change was working powerfully and influencing the people. Behind it all was the expansive energy which sent the British to distant lands.

Those who had recorded the history of India are so full of wars and tumults and the political and military leaders of the day, that they tell us very little of what was happening in the mind of India and how social and economic processes were at work. Only occasional and accidental glimpses emerge from this sordid record. It appears that during this period of terror the people generally were crushed and exhausted, passively submitting to the decrees of a malevolent fate, dazed and devoid of curiosity. There must have been many individuals, however, who were curious and who tried to understand the new forces at play, but they were overwhelmed by the tide of events and could not influence them.

One of the individuals who was full of curiosity was Maharaja Ranjit Singh, a Jat Sikh, who had built up a kingdom in the Punjab, which subsequently spread to Kashmir and the Frontier Province. He had failings and vices; nevertheless he was a remarkable man. The Frenchman, Jacquemont, calls him 'extremely brave' and 'almost the first inquisitive Indian I have seen, but his curiosity makes up for the apathy of the whole nation.' 'His conversation is like a nightmare.'[14] It must be remembered that Indians as a rule, are a reserved people, and more so the intellectuals amongst them. Very few of these would have cared to associate then with the foreign military leaders and adventurers in India, many of whose actions filled them with horror. So these intellectuals tried to preserve their dignity by keeping as far as possible from the foreign elements and met them only on formal occasions when circumstances compelled them to do so. The Indians whom Englishmen and other foreigners usually met were of the opportunist and servile class that surrounded them or the ministers, frequently corrupt and intriguing, of the Indian courts.

Ranjit Singh was not only intellectually curious and inquisitive, he was remarkably humane at a time when India and the world seethed with callousness and inhumanity. He built up a kingdom and a powerful army and yet he disliked bloodshed. 'Never was so large an empire founded by one man with so little criminality,' says Prinsep. He abolished the death sentence for every crime, however heinous it might be, when in England even petty pilferers

---

14 As quoted by Edward Thompson in *The Making of Indian Princes* (1943), 158.

had to face death. 'Except in actual warfare,' writes Osborne, who visited him, 'he has never been known to take life, though his own has been attempted more than once, and his reign will be found freer from any striking acts of cruelty and oppression than those of many more civilized monarches.'[15]

Another but a different type of Indian statesman was Sawai Jai Singh, of Jaipur in Rajputana. He belongs to a somewhat earlier period and he died in 1743. He lived during the period of disruption following Aurungzeb's death. He was clever and opportunist enough to survive the many shocks and changes that followed each other in quick succession. He acknowledged the suzerainty of the Delhi Emperor. When he found that the advancing Marathas were too strong to be checked, he came to terms with them on behalf of the emperor. But it is not his political or military career that interests me. He was a brave warrior and an accomplished diplomat, but he was something much more than this. He was a mathematician and an astronomer, a scientist and a town-planner, and he was interested in the study of history.

Jai Singh built big observatories at Jaipur, Delhi, Ujjain, Benares, and Mathura. Learning through Portuguese missionaries of the progress of astronomy in Portugal, he sent his own men, with one of the missionaries, to the court of the Portuguese King Emmanuel. Emmanuel sent his envoy, Xavier de Silva, with De la Hire's tables to Jai Singh. On comparing these with his own tables, Jai Singh came to the conclusion that the Portuguese tables were less exact and had several errors. He attributed these to the 'inferior diameters' of the instruments used.

Jai Singh was of course fully acquainted with Indian mathematics; he had studied the old Greek treatises and also knew of recent European developments in mathematics. He had some of the Greek books (Euclid, etc.) as well as European works on plane and spherical trigonometry and the construction and use of logarithms translated into Sanskrit. He also had Arabic books on astronomy translated.

[15] Ibid., 157, 158.

He founded the city of Jaipur. Interested in town planning, he collected the plans of many European cities of the time and then drew up his own plan. Many of these plans of the old European cities of the time are preserved in the Jaipur museum. The city of Jaipur was so well and wisely planned that it is still considered a model of town-planning.

Jai Singh did all this and much more in the course of a comparatively brief life and in the midst of perpetual wars and court intrigues, in which he was himself often involved. Nadir Shah's invasion took place just four years before Jai Singh's death. Jai Singh would have been a remarkable man anywhere and at any time. The fact that he rose and functioned as a scientist in the typically feudal milieu of Rajputana and during one of the darkest periods of Indian history, when disruption and war and tumults filled the scene, is very significant. It shows that the spirit of scientific inquiry was not dead in India and that there was some ferment at work which might have yielded rich results if only an opportunity had been given to it to fructify. Jai Singh was no anachronism or solitary thinker in an unfriendly and uncomprehending environment. He was a product of his age and he collected a number of scientific workers to work with him. Out of these he sent some in the embassy to Portugal, and social custom or taboo did not deter him from doing so. It seems probable that there was plenty of good material for scientific work in the country, both theoretical and technical, if only it was given a chance to function. That opportunity did not come for a long time. Even when the troubles and disorders were over, there was no encouragement of scientific work by those in authority.

~

Vivekananda, Tagore and Gandhi

(*From* The Discovery of India)

Vivekananda, together with his brother disciples, founded the non-sectarian Ramakrishna Mission of service. Rooted in the past and full of pride in India's heritage, Vivekananda was yet modern in his approach to life's problems and was a kind of bridge between the past of India and her present. He was a powerful orator in Bengali and English and a graceful writer of Bengali prose and poetry. He was a fine figure of a man, imposing, full of poise and dignity, sure of himself and his mission, and at the same time full of a dynamic and fiery energy and a passion to push India forward. He came as a tonic to the depressed and demoralized Hindu mind and gave it self-reliance and some roots in the past. He attended the Parliament of Religions in Chicago in 1893, spent over a year in the U.S.A., travelled across Europe, going as far as Athens and Constantinople, and visited Egypt, China, and Japan. Wherever he went, he created a minor sensation not only by his presence but by what he said and how he said it. Having seen this Hindu Sanyasin once it was difficult to forget him or his message. In America he was called the 'cyclonic Hindu.' He was himself greatly influenced by his travels in western countries; he admired British perseverance and the vitality and spirit of equality of the American people. 'America is the best field in the world to carry on any idea,' he wrote to a friend in India. But he was not impressed by the manifestations of religion in the west and his faith in the Indian philosophical and spiritual background became firmer. India, in spite of her degradation, still represented to him the Light.

He preached the monism of the Advaita philosophy of the Vedanta and was convinced that only this could be the future religion of thinking humanity. For the Vedanta was not only spiritual but rational and in harmony with scientific investigations of external nature. 'This universe has not been created by any extra-cosmic God, nor is it the work of any outside genius. It is self-creating, self-dissolving, self-manifesting, One Infinite Existence, the Brahma.' The Vedanta ideal was of the solidarity of man and his inborn divine nature; to see God in man is the real God-vision; man is the greatest of all beings. But 'the abstract Vedanta must become living—poetic—in everyday life; out of hopelessly intricate mythology must come concrete moral forms;

and out of bewildering Yogi-ism must come the most scientific and practical psychology.' India had fallen because she had narrowed herself, gone into her shell and lost touch with other nations, and thus sunk into a state of 'mummified' and 'crystallized' civilization. Caste, which was necessary and desirable in its early forms, and meant to develop individuality and freedom, had become a monstrous degradation, the opposite of what it was meant to be, and had crushed the masses. Caste was a form of social organization which was and should be kept separate from religion. Social organizations should change with the changing times. Passionately, Vivekananda condemned the meaningless metaphysical discussions and arguments about ceremonials and especially the touch-me-notism of the upper caste. 'Our religion is in the kitchen. Our God is the cooking-pot, and our religion is: "don't touch me, I am holy."'

He kept away from politics and disapproved of the politicians of his day. But again and again he laid stress on the necessity for liberty and equality and the raising of the masses. 'Liberty of thought and action is the only condition of life, of growth and well-being. Where it does not exist, the man, the race, the nation must go.' 'The only hope of India is from the masses. The upper classes are physically and morally dead.' He wanted to combine western progress with India's spiritual background. 'Make a European society with India's religion.' 'Become an occidental of occidentals in your spirit of equality, freedom, work, and energy, and at the same time a Hindu to the very backbone in religious culture, and instincts.' Progressively, Vivekananda grew more international in outlook: 'Even in politics and sociology, problems that were only national twenty years ago can no longer be solved on national grounds only. They are assuming huge proportions, gigantic shapes. They can only be solved when looked at in the broader light of international grounds. International organizations, international combinations, international laws are the cry of the day. That shows solidarity. In science, every day they are coming to a similar broad view of matter.' And again: 'There cannot be any progress without the whole world following in the wake, and it is becoming every day clearer that the solution of any problem can never be attained on racial, or national, or narrow grounds. Every idea has to become broad till it covers the whole of this world, every aspiration must go on increasing till it has engulfed the whole of humanity, nay the whole of life, within its scope.' All this fitted in with Vivekananda's view of the Vedanta philosophy, and he preached this from end to end of India. 'I am thoroughly convinced that no individual or nation can live by holding itself apart from the community of others, and wherever such an attempt has been made under false ideas of greatness, policy or holiness—the result has always been disastrous to the secluding one.' 'The fact of our isolation from all the other nations of the world is the cause of our degeneration and its only remedy is getting back into the current of the rest of the world. Motion is the sign of life.'

He once wrote: 'I am a socialist not because I think it is a perfect system, but half a loaf is better than no bread. The other systems have been tried and found wanting. Let this one be tried—if for nothing else, for the novelty of the thing.'

Vivekananda spoke of many things but the one constant refrain of his speech and writing was abhay—be fearless, be strong. For him man was no miserable sinner but a part of divinity; why should he be afraid of anything? 'If there is a sin in the world it is weakness; avoid all weakness, weakness is sin, weakness is death.' That had been the great lesson of the Upanishads. Fear breeds evil and weeping and wailing. There had been enough of that, enough of softness. 'What our country now wants are muscles of iron and nerves of steel, gigantic wills which nothing can resist, which can penetrate into the mysteries and the secrets of the universe, and will accomplish their purpose in any fashion, even if it meant going down to the bottom of the ocean and meeting death face to face.' He condemned 'occultism and mysticism ... these creepy things; there may be great truths in them, but they have nearly destroyed us ... And here is the test of truth—anything that makes you weak physically, intellectually, and spiritually, reject as poison, there is no life in it, it cannot be true. Truth is strengthening. Truth is purity, truth is all-knowledge…These mysticisms, in spite of some grains of truth in them, are generally weakening…Go back to your Upanishads, the shining, the strengthening, the bright philosophy; and part from all these mysterious things, all these weakening things. Take up this philosophy; the greatest truths are the simplest things in the world, simple as your own existence.' And beware of superstition. 'I would rather see everyone of you rank atheists than superstitious fools, for the atheist is alive, and you can make something of him. But if superstition enters, the brain is gone, the brain is softening, degradation has seized upon the life…Mystery-mongering and superstition are always signs of weakness.'[16]

So Vivekananda thundered from Cape Comorin on the southern tip of India to the Himalayas, and he wore himself out in the process, dying in 1902 when he was thirty-nine years of age.

---

[16] Most of these extracts have been taken from 'Lectures from Colombo to Almora' by Swami Vivekananda (1933) and 'Letters of Swami Vivekananda' (1942) both published by the Advaita Ashrama, Mayavati, Almora, Himalayas. In the 'Letters' p. 390, there is a remarkable letter written by Vivekananda to a Moslem friend. In the course of this he writes: 'Whether we call it Vedantism or any ism, the truth is that Advaitism is the last word of religion and thought and the only position from which one can look upon all religions and sects with love. We believe it is the religion of the future enlightened humanity. The Hindus may get the credit of arriving at it earlier than other races, they being an older race than either the Hebrew or the Arab; yet practical Advaitism, which looks upon and behaves to all mankind as one's own soul, is yet to be developed among the Hindus universally.

'On the other hand our experience is that if ever the followers of any religion approach to this equality in an appreciable degree in the plane of practical work-a-day life—it may be quite unconscious generally of the deeper meaning and the underlying principle of such conduct, which the Hindus as a rule so clearly perceive—it is those of Islam and Islam alone….

'For our own motherland a junction of the two great systems, Hinduism and Islam—Vedanta brain and Islam body—is the only hope.

'I see in my mind's eye the future perfect India rising out of this chaos and strife, glorious and invincible, with Vedanta brain and Islam body.' This letter is dated Almora, June 10, 1898.

A contemporary of Vivekananda, and yet belonging much more to a later generation, was Rabindranath Tagore. The Tagore family had played a leading part in various reform movements in Bengal during the nineteenth century. There were men of spiritual stature in it and fine writers and artists, but Rabindranath towered above them all, and indeed all over India his position gradually became one of unchallenged supremacy. His long life of creative activity covered two entire generations and he seems almost of our present day. He was no politician, but he was too sensitive and devoted to the freedom of the Indian people to remain always in his ivory tower of poetry and song. Again and again he stepped out of it, when he could tolerate some development no longer, and in prophetic language warned the British Government or his own people. He played a prominent part in the Swadeshi movement that swept through Bengal in the first decade of the twentieth century, and again when he gave up his knighthood at the time of the Amritsar massacre. His constructive work in the field of education, quietly begun, has already made Santiniketan one of the focal points of Indian culture. His influence over the mind of India, and specially of successive rising generations, has been tremendous. Not Bengali only, the language in which he himself wrote, but all the modern languages of India have been moulded partly by his writings. More than any other Indian, he has helped to bring into harmony the ideals of the east and the west, and broadened the bases of Indian nationalism. He has been India's internationalist par excellence, believing and working for international cooperation, taking India's message to other countries and bringing their message to his own people. And yet with all his internationalism, his feet have always been planted firmly on India's soil and his mind has been saturated with the wisdom of the Upanishads. Contrary to the usual course of development, as he grew older he became more radical in his outlook and views. Strong individualist as he was, he became an admirer of the great achievements of the Russian Revolution, especially in the spread of education, culture, health, and the spirit of equality. Nationalism is a narrowing creed, and nationalism in conflict with a dominating imperialism produces all manner of frustrations and complexes. It was Tagore's immense service to India, as it has been Gandhi's in a different plane, that he forced the people in some measure out of their narrow grooves of thought and made them think of broader issues affecting humanity. Tagore was the great humanist of India.

Tagore and Gandhi have undoubtedly been the two outstanding and dominating figures of India in this first half of the twentieth century. It is instructive to compare and contrast them. No two persons could be so different from one another in their make up or temperaments. Tagore, the aristocractic artist turned democrat with proletarian sympathies, represented essentially the cultural tradition of India, the tradition of accepting life in the fullness thereof and going through it with song and dance. Gandhi, more a man of the people, almost the embodiment of the Indian peasant, represented the other ancient tradition of India, that of renunciation and asceticism. And yet Tagore was primarily the man of thought, Gandhi of concentrated and ceaseless activity. Both, in their different ways had a world outlook, and both were at the same time wholly Indian. They seemed to present different but harmonious aspects of India and to complement one another.

Tagore and Gandhi bring us to our present age. But we were considering an earlier period and the effect produced on the people, and especially the Hindus, by the stress laid by Vivekananda and others on the past greatness of India and their pride in it. Vivekananda himself was careful to warn his people not to dwell too much on the past, but to look to the future. 'When, O Lord,' he wrote, 'shall our land be free from this eternal dwelling upon the past?' But he himself and others had evoked that past, and there was a glamour in it, and no getting away from it.

MAKING A NEW INDIA

Address to the Prayag Mahila Vidyapitha[17]

(From Selected Works of Jawaharlal Nehru: Volume Six)

Many years ago—so much has happened during recent years that I have almost lost the exact count of time and even a few years seem long ago—I had the honour of laying the foundation stone of the hall of the Mahila Vidyapitha.[18] Since then I have been engrossed in the dust and tumble of politics and direct action, and the struggle for India's freedom has filled my mind. I have lost touch with the Mahila Vidyapitha. During the last four months that I have been in the wider world outside the prison walls many a call has come to me and I have been invited to participate in a variety of public activities. I have not listened to these calls and have kept away from these activities, for my ears were open to only one call and all my energy was directed to one end. That call was the call of India, our unhappy and long oppressed motherland, and especially of our suffering and exploited masses, and that end was the complete freedom of the Indian people.

I have refused therefore to be drawn away from the main issue to other and minor activities, important as some of these were in their own limited spheres. But when Shri Sangam Lal came to me and pressed me to address the convocation of the Mahila Vidyapitha, I found it difficult to resist his appeal. For behind that appeal I saw the girls and young women of India, on the threshold of life, trying to free themselves from an age-long bondage and peeping into the future with diffidence and yet, as youth will, with the eyes of hope.

I agreed, therefore, provisionally and diffidently for I was not sure if a more urgent call would not call me elsewhere. And now I find that urgent call has come from the sorely afflicted province

---

[17] 'The Leader', 24 January 1934. Reprinted in *Recent Essays and Writings,* (Allahabad: 1934), 148–153. As Jawaharlal could not be present, the address was read out on his behalf on 20 January 1934.

[18] See *Selected Works,* Vol. 3, p. 361.

of Bengal[19] and I must go there and I may not be back in time for the convocation of the Mahila Vidyapitha. I regret this and all I can do is to leave this message behind.

If our nation is to rise, how can it do so if half the nation, if our womankind, lag behind and remain ignorant and uneducated? How can our children grow up into self-reliant and efficient citizens of India if their mothers are not themselves self-reliant and efficient? Our history tells us of many wise women and many that were true and brave even unto death. We treasure their examples and are inspired by them, and yet we know that the lot of women in India and elsewhere has been an unhappy one. Our civilization, our customs, our laws, have all been made by man and he has taken good care to keep himself in a superior position and to treat woman as a chattel and a plaything to be exploited for his own advantage and amusement. Under this continuous pressure woman has been unable to grow and to develop her capacities to her fullest, and then man has blamed her for her backwardness.

Gradually, in some of the countries of the West, woman has succeeded in getting a measure of freedom, but in India we are still backward, although the urge to progress has come here too. We have to fight many social evils; we have to break many an inherited custom that enchains us and drags us down. Men and women, like plants and flowers, can only grow in the sunlight and fresh air of freedom; they wilt and stunt themselves in the dark shadow and suffocating atmosphere of alien domination.

For all of us, therefore, the first problem that presents itself is how to free India and remove the many burdens of the Indian masses. But the women of India have an additional task and that is to free themselves from the tyranny of man-made customs and laws. They will have to carry on this second struggle by themselves for man is not likely to help them.

Many of the girls and young women present at the convocation will have finished their courses, taken their degrees, and prepared

---

[19] Jawaharlal had been invited to address a public meeting at Calcutta to protest against the repression in Chittagong and Midnapur.

themselves for activities in a larger sphere. What ideals will they carry with them to this wider world, what inner urge will fashion them and govern their actions? Many of them, I am afraid, will relapse into the humdrum day-to-day activities of the household and seldom think of ideals or other obligations; many will think only of earning a livelihood. Both these are no doubt necessary, but if this is all that the Mahila Vidyapitha has taught its students, it has failed in its purpose. For a university that wishes to justify itself must train and send out into the world knight errants in the cause of truth and freedom and justice, who will battle fearlessly against oppression and evil. I hope there are some such amongst you, some who prefer to climb the mountains, facing risk and danger, to remaining in the misty and unhealthy valleys below.

But our universities do not encourage the climbing of mountains; they prefer the safety of the lowlands and valleys. They do not encourage initiative and freedom; like true children of our foreign rulers, they prefer the rule of authority and a discipline imposed from above. Is it any wonder that their products are disappointing and ineffective and stunted, and misfits in this changing world of ours?

There have been many critics of our universities and most of their criticisms are justified. Indeed hardly anyone has a good word for the Indian universities. But even the critics have looked upon the university as an upper class organ of education. It does not touch the masses. Education to be real and national must have roots in the soil and reach down to the masses. That is not possible today because of our alien government and our old-world social system. But some of you who go out of the Vidyapitha and help in the education of others must bear this in mind and work for a change.

It is sometimes said, and I believe the Vidyapitha itself lays stress on this, that woman's education should be something apart from that of man's. It should train her for household duties and for the widely practised profession of marriage. I am afraid I am unable to agree to this limited and one-sided view of women's education.

I am convinced that women should be given the best of

education in every department of human activity and be trained to play an effective part in all professions and spheres. In particular, the habit of looking upon marriage as a profession almost and as the sole economic refuge for woman will have to go before woman can have any freedom.

> **Freedom depends on economic conditions even more than political and if woman is not economically free and self-earning she will have to depend on her husband or someone else, and dependents are never free. The association of man and woman should be of perfect freedom and perfect comradeship with no dependence of one on the other.**

What will you do, graduates and others of the Vidyapitha, when you go out? Will you just drift and accept things as they are, however bad they may be? Will you be content with pious and ineffective expressions of sympathy for what is good and desirable and do nothing more? Or will you justify your education and prove your mettle by hurling defiance at the evils that encompass you? The purdah, that evil relic of a barbarous age, which imprisons the body and mind of so many of our sisters—will you not tear it to bits and burn the fragments? Untouchability and caste, which degrade humanity and help in the exploitation of one class by another—will you not fight them and end them and thus help in bringing a measure of equality in this country? Our marriage laws and many of our out-of-date customs which hold us back and especially crush our womenfolk—will you not combat them and bring them in line with modern conditions? Will you not also fight with energy and determination for the physical improvement of our women by games in the open air and athletics and sane living so that India may be full of strong and healthy and beautiful women and happy children? And, above all, will you not play a gallant part in the struggle for national and social freedom that is convulsing our country today?

I have put these many questions to you, but the answers to them have already come from thousands of brave girls and women who have played a leading part in our freedom struggle during the last four years. Who has not been thrilled at the sight of our sisters, unused as they were to public activity, leaving the shelter of their homes and standing shoulder to shoulder with their brothers in the fight for India's freedom? They shamed many a person who called himself a man, and they proclaimed to the world that the women of India have arisen from their long slumber and would not be denied their rights.

The women of India have answered, and so I greet you, girls and young women of the Mahila Vidyapitha, and I charge you to keep that torch of freedom burning brightly till it spreads its lustre all over this ancient and dearly loved land of ours.

~

Hindu and Muslim Communalism[20]

(From Selected Works of Jawaharlal Nehru: Volume Six*)*

...It must be remembered that the communalism of a majority community must of necessity bear a closer resemblance to nationalism than the communalism of a minority group. One of the best tests of its true nature is what relation it bears to the national struggle. If it is politically reactionary or lays stress on communal problems rather than national ones then it is obviously anti-national.

The Simon Commission,[21] as is well known, met with a widespread and almost unanimous boycott in India. Bhai Parmanandji,[22] in his recent presidential address at Ajmer,

---

[20] 27 November 1933. *The Tribune,* 30 November 1933. Reprinted in *Recent Essays and Writings,* (Allahabad, 1934), 47–61.

[21] The Simon Commission was a group of 7 British MPs sent to India in 1928 to study constitutional reforms and make recommendations to the government.

[22] Bhai Parmanand was an Indian nationalist and a prominent leader of the Hindu Mahasabha.

says that this boycott was unfortunate for the Hindus, and he approvingly mentions that the Punjab Hindus (probably under his guidance) cooperated with the Commission. Thus Bhaiji is of opinion that, whatever the national aspect of the question might have been, it was desirable for the Hindus to cooperate with the British Government in order to gain some communal advantages. This is obviously an anti-national attitude. Even from the narrow communal point of view it is difficult to see its wisdom, or communal advantages can only be given at the expense of another community, and when both seek the favours of the ruling power, there is little chance of obtaining even a superficial advantage.

Bhaiji's argument, repeatedly stated, is that the British Government is so strongly entrenched in India that it cannot be shaken by any popular movement and therefore it is folly to try to do so. The only alternative is to seek its favours. That is an argument which I can only characterise, with all respect to him, as wholly unworthy of any people however fallen they might be.

Bhaiji's view is that the cry of Hindu-Muslim unity is a false cry and a wrong ideal to aim at because the power of gift is in the hands of the government. Granting this power of gift, every cry other than one of seeking the government's favours is futile. And if the possibility of Hindu-Muslim cooperation and collaboration is ruled out,[23] nationalism is also ruled out in the country-wide sense of the word. The inevitable consequence, and Bhaiji accepts this, is what the calls "Hindu nationalism", which is but another name for Hindu communalism. What is the way to this? Cooperation with British imperialism. "I feel an impulse within me," says Bhaiji in his presidential address, "that the Hindus would willingly cooperate with Great Britain if their status and responsible position as the premier community in India is recognised in the political institutions of new India."

This attitude of trying to combine with the ruling power

---

[23] Bhai Parmanand stated that "we have reached a stage when the Congress with its theory of Swaraj through Hindu-Moslem unity and civil disobedience goes entirely out of the field."

against another community or group is the natural and only policy which communalism can adopt. It fits in of course entirely with the wishes of the ruling power which can then play off one group against another. It was the policy which was adopted by the Muslim communalists with some apparent temporary advantages to themselves. It is the policy which the Hindu Mahasabha partly favoured from its earliest days but could not adopt wholeheartedly because of the pressure of nationalist Hindus, and which its leaders now seem to have definitely adopted.

Dr Moonje,[24] presiding over the C.P. Hindu Conference on May 17, 1933 made it clear that "the Mahasabha never had any faith in the kind of noncooperation which Mahatma Gandhi has been preaching and practising. It believes in the eternal Sanatan Law of stimulus and response, namely, responsive cooperation. The Mahasabha holds that whatever may be the constitution of the legislatures, they should never be boycotted." Dr. Moonje is an authority on Sanatan Law, but I hope it does not lay down that the response to a kick should be grovelling at the feet of him who kicks. This speech was made when a widespread national struggle was going on and there was unprecedented repression under the ordinance regime. I shall not discuss here the wisdom of stating, long before the British-made constitution had taken shape, that whatever happens they would work it. Was this not an invitation to the government to ignore the Mahasabha for in any event it would accept the new dispensation?

Dr Moonje himself went to the Round Table Conference in 1930, at the height of the civil disobedience movement, though in justice to him it must be stated that he had declared that he went in his individual capacity. Subsequently of course the Mahasabha took full part in the London conferences and committees.

Of the part taken by the Mahasabha representatives in these deliberations, especially by those from the Punjab and Sind, I wish only to say that it was a most painful one. Politically it was most reactionary and efforts were made to increase the reserved powers

---

[24] Another Mahasabha leader

and safeguards of the British Government or the Governors in order to prevent the Muslim majorities in certain provinces from exercising effective power. The identical policy and argument of the Muslim communalists in regard to the whole of India were repeated by Hindu communalists in regard to certain provinces. But of course the special powers of Governors were not going to be confined to some provinces. They would inevitably apply to all the provinces. The reason for this reactionary attitude in both the cases was of course fear of the majority. Whatever the reason, this played entirely into the hands of the British Government.

The whole of the case of the Sind Hindu Sabha is a negation of the principle of democracy,[25] except in so far as joint electorates are demanded. It is an attempt to prevent the will of the majority from prevailing because the minority might suffer. The anti-social arguments of greater wealth and education of the minority are advanced, and financial reasons based entirely on the continuation of the top-heavy British system are made a prop. Wealth and economic control are not only sufficient protection under modern conditions, but have to be protected against. Almost every argument that has been advanced by the Sind Hindu communalists can be advanced by the Muslim minority in India as a whole with this difference that the Hindus are generally the richer and more educated community and have thus greater economic power.

In their attempts to show the backwardness of the Muslims in Sind, the Sind Hindu Sabha memorandum to the Joint Parliamentary Committee has made sweeping statements about Muslims which are astonishing and most painful to read.[26] They remind one of Katherine Mayo's methods of denunciation.

I do not know what the Punjab Hindu Sewak Sabha is. Probably it is not connected with the Hindu Sabha, and it may

---

[25] Its contention was that Sind, whose connection with Bombay had proved beneficial, was now being made over to a Council "dominated by a ... medieval oligarchy."

[26] The memorandum of 17 July 1933 stated that "the organized gang dacoities in the Sukkur district show that the Sind Muslims continue to be almost as intolerant as they were in the forties of the last century."

only be a mushroom growth fathered by our benign government. On the eve of Bhai Parmanand's departure for England last May, to give evidence before the Joint Committee, this Sabha sent him a message which laid stress on the retention of safeguards by Governors in order to protect the Hindus of the Punjab. "The only thing," it said, "that can protect the Punjab Hindus is the effective working of safeguards as provided in the constitution." "Let not any endeavours of the politicians lead to the abrogation of these safeguards....The judicious discharge of their special responsibility by our Governors has been greatly helpful."

Another organization, of which I know nothing, the Punjab Hindu Youth League of Lahore, stated as follows in a public statement dated 29 May, 1933: "We feel that the time has now come for unity not so much between Moslems and Hindus as between the British and Indians ... Hindu leaders ... should insist on having safeguards for the Hindu minority in the constitutions and cabinets."

I cannot hold the Mahasabha responsible for these statements but as a matter of fact they fit in with, and are only a slight elaboration of the Mahasabha attitude.

And they bear out that many Hindu communalists are definitely thinking on the lines of cooperation with British imperialism in the hope of getting favours. It requires little argument to show that this attitude is not only narrowly communal but also antinational and intensely reactionary.

If this is the attitude when the Hindu Mahasabha feels that it has lost all along the line, in so far as the Communal Award is concerned, one wonders what its attitude will be when a petty favour is shown to it by the government.

It is perfectly true that the Hindu Mahasabha has stood for joint electorates right through its career and this is obviously the only national solution of the problem. It is also true that the Communal Award is an utter negation of nationalism and is meant to separate India into communal compartments and give strength to disruptive tendencies and thus to strengthen the hold of British imperialism. But it must be borne in mind that nationalism cannot be accepted only when it profits the majority community. The test comes in the provinces where there is a Muslim majority and in that test the Hindu Mahasabha has failed.

Nor is it enough to blame Muslim communalists. It is easy enough to do so, for Indian Muslims as a whole are unhappily very backward and compare unfavourably with Muslims in all other countries. The point is that a special responsibility does attach to the Hindus in India both because they are the majority community and because economically and educationally they are more advanced. The Mahasabha, instead of discharging that responsibility has acted in a manner which has undoubtedly increased the communalism of the Muslims and made them distrust the Hindus all the more. The only way it has tried to meet their communalism is by its own variety of communalism.

One communalism does not end the other; each feeds on the other and both fatten.

The Mahasabha at Ajmer has passed a long resolution on the Communal Award pointing out its obvious faults and inconsistencies.[27] But it has not, so far as I am aware, said a word in criticism of the White Paper scheme. I am not personally interested in petty criticisms of that scheme because I think that it is wholly bad and is incapable of improvement. But from the Mahasabha's point of view to ignore it was to demonstrate that it cared little, if at all, about the political aspect of Indian freedom. It thought only in terms of what the Hindus got or did not get. It has been reported that a resolution on independence was brought forward but this was apparently suppressed. Not only that, no resolution on the political or economic objective was considered. If the Mahasabha claims to represent the Hindus of India, must it be said that the Hindus are not interested in the freedom of India?

Ordinarily this would be remarkable enough. But in present-day conditions and with the background of the past few years

[27] The resolution pointed out that even the Hindus of the minority provinces were opposed, in principle, to communal electorates.

of heroic struggle and sacrifice, such a lapse can have only one meaning—that the Mahasabha has ceased to think even in terms of nationalism and is engrossed in communal squabbles. Or it may be that the policy is a deliberate one so as to avoid irritating the government with which the Mahasabha wishes to cooperate.

This view is strengthened by the fact that no reference is made in the resolutions or in the presidential address to the ordinance rule and the extraordinary measures of repression which the government has indulged in and is still indulging in. The Mahasabha seems to live in a world of its own unconnected with the struggles and desires and sufferings of the Indian people.

Even more significant was the refusal (if newspaper reports are to be credited) to pass a resolution of condolence on the death, under tragic circumstances, of Syt. J.M. Sen Gupta.[28] This was a harmless resolution, a formal tribute to the memory of a great patriot and a Hindu, and yet the Mahasabha sensed danger in it.

Our friends, the moderates or liberals, though they may be lacking in action and though their methods and ideology may be utterly inadequate, still consider these questions and pass resolutions on them. Not so the Mahasabha which has moved away completely from the political and national plane and rests itself solely on the communal issue, thereby weakening even its communal position. I submit that this attitude is wholly reactionary and anti-national. I have some contacts with the outside world, through foreign newspapers and other means, and I should like to tell the Mahasabha leaders that, whatever their motives or methods may have been, they have succeeded in creating a considerable amount of prejudice abroad against the Mahasabha and the communally inclined Hindus.

I cannot say what following the Hindu or Muslim communal organizations have. It is possible that in a moment of communal excitement each side may command the allegiance of considerable numbers. But I do submit that on both sides

[28] The president disallowed it on the ground that it was not proposed in the subjects committee.

these organizations represent the rich upper class groups and the struggle for communal advantages is really an attempt of these groups to take as big a share of power and privilege for themselves as possible. At the most it means jobs for a few of our unemployed intellectuals. How do these communal demands meet the needs of the masses? What is the programme of the Hindu Mahasabha or the Muslim League for the workers, the peasants, and the lower middle classes, which form the great bulk of the nation? They have no programme except a negative one, as the Mahasabha hinted at Ajmer, of not disturbing the present social order. This in itself shows that the controlling forces of these communal organizations are the upper class, possessing social groups today. The Muslim communalists tell us a great deal about the democracy of Islam but are afraid of democracy in practice; the Hindu communalists talk of nationalism and think in terms of a 'Hindu nationalism'.

Personally I am convinced that nationalism can only come out of the ideological fusion of Hindu, Muslim, Sikh and other groups in India. That does not and need not mean the extinction of any real culture of any group, but it does mean a common national outlook, to which other matters are subordinated. I do not think that Hindu-Muslim or other unity will come merely by reciting it like a mantra. That it will come, I have no doubt, but it will come from below, not above, for many of those above are too much interested in English domination, and hope to preserve their special privileges through it. Social and economic forces will inevitably bring other problems to the front. They will create cleavages along different lines, but the communal cleavage will go.

I have been warned by friends, whose opinion I value, that my attitude towards communal organizations will result in antagonizing any people against me. That is indeed probable. I have no desire to antagonize any countryman of mine for we are in the midst of a mighty struggle against a powerful opponent. But that very struggle demands that we must check harmful tendencies and always keep the goal before us. I would be false to myself, to my friends and comrades, so many of whom have sacrificed their all at the altar of freedom, and even to those who disapprove of what I say, if I remained a silent witness to an attempt to weaken and check our great struggle for freedom. Those who, in my opinion, are helping in this attempt, may be perfectly honest in the beliefs they hold. I do not challenge their bona fides. But none the less the beliefs may be wrong, anti-national and reactionary.

~

Reality and Myth[29]

(*From* Selected Works of Jawaharlal Nehru: Volume Six)

The suggestion made by me that both political and communal problems in India should be solved by means of a constituent assembly has met with considerable favour. Gandhiji has commended it and so have many others. Others again have misunderstood it or not taken the trouble to understand it.

Politically and nationally, if it is granted, as it must be, that the people of India are to be the sole arbiters of India's fate and must therefore have full freedom to draw up their constitution, it follows that this can only be done by means of a constituent assembly elected on the widest franchise. Those who believe in independence have no other choice. Even those who talk vaguely in terms of a nebulous Dominion Status must agree that the decision has to be made by the Indian people. How then is this decision to be made? Not by a group of so-called leaders or individuals. Not by these self-constituted bodies called All Parties Conferences which represent, if anybody at all, small interested groups and leave out the vast majority of the population. Not even, let us admit, by the National Congress, powerful and largely representative as it is. It is of course open to the Congress to influence and largely control the constituent assembly if it can

---

[29] Statement to the press, Allahabad, 5 January 1934. *The Tribune,* 8 January 1934. Reprinted in *Recent Essays and Writings,* (Allahabad, 1934), 72-81.

carry the people with it. But the ultimate political decision must be with the people of India acting through a popularly elected constituent assembly.

This assembly of course can have nothing in common with the sham and lifeless councils and assemblies imposed on us by an alien authority. It must derive its sanction from the people themselves without any outside interference. I have suggested that it should be elected under adult or near-adult franchise. What the method of election should be can be considered and decided later. Personally I favour the introduction, as far as possible, of the functional system of election as this is far more representative of real interests. The geographical system often covers up and confuses these interests. But I am prepared to agree to either or to a combination of both. I see no difficulty, except one, and that is an important one, in the way of such a constituent assembly being elected and functioning. This functioning will be limited to drawing up of a constitution and then fresh elections will have to be held on the basis of the new constitution.

The one difficulty I referred to is the presence and dominance of an outside authority, that is the British Government. It is clear that so long as this dominance continues no real constituent assembly can meet or function. So thus an essential preliminary is the development of sufficient strength in the nation to be able to enforce the will of the Indian people. Two opposing wills cannot prevail at the same time; there must be conflict between them and a struggle for dominance, such as we see today in India. Essentially, this struggle is for the preservation of British vested interests in India and the White Paper effort is an attempt to perpetuate them. No constituent assembly can be bound down by these chains, and so long as the nation has not developed strength enough to break these chains, such an assembly cannot function.

This assembly would also deal with the communal problem, and I have suggested that, in order to remove all suspicion from the minds of a minority, it may even, if it so chooses, have its representatives elected by separate electorates. These separate electorates would only be for the constituent assembly. The future method of election, as well as all other matters connected with the constitution, would be settled by the assembly itself.

I have further added that if the Muslim elected representatives for this constituent assembly adhere to certain communal demands I shall press for their acceptance. Much as I dislike communalism I realise that it does not disappear by suppression but by a removal of the feeling of fear, or by a diversion of interest. We should therefore remove this fear complex and make the Muslim masses realise that they can have any protection that they really desire. I feel that this realisation will go a long way in toning down the feeling of communalism.

But I am convinced that the real remedy lies in a diversion of interest from the myths that have been fostered and have grown up round the communal question to the realities of today. The bulwark of communalism today is political reaction and so we find that communal leaders inevitably tend to become reactionaries in political and economic matters.

Groups of upper class people try to cover up their own class interests by making it appear that they stand for the communal demands of religious minorities or majorities.

A critical examination of the various communal demands put forward on behalf of Hindus, Muslims or others reveals that they have nothing to do with the masses. At the most they deal with some jobs for a few of the unemployed intellectuals but it is obvious that the problem even of the unemployed middle class intellectuals cannot be solved by a redistribution of state jobs. There are far too many unemployed persons of the middle class to be absorbed in state or other services and their number is growing at a rapid pace. So far as the masses are concerned there is absolutely no reference to them or to their wants in the numerous demands put forward by communal organizations. Apparently the communalists do not consider them as worthy of attention. What is there, in the various communal formulae, in regard to the distress of the agriculturists, their rent or revenue or the staggering burden of debt that crushes them? Or in regard to the factory or railway or other workers who have to face continuous cuts in wages and a vanishing standard of living? Or the lower middle classes who, for want of employment and work, are sinking in the slough of despair? Heated arguments take place about seats in councils and separate and joint electorates and the separation of provinces which can affect or interest only a few. Is the starving peasant likely to be interested in this when hunger gnaws his stomach? But our communal friends take good care to avoid these real issues, for a solution of them might affect their own interests, and they try to divert people's attention to entirely unreal and, from the mass point of view, trivial matters.

Communalism is essentially a hunt for favours from a third party—the ruling power. The communalist can only think in terms of a continuation of foreign domination and he tries to make the best of it for his own particular group. Delete the foreign power and the communal arguments and demands fall to the ground. Both the foreign power and the communalists, as representing some upper class groups, want no essential change of the political and economic structure; both are interested in the preservation and augmentation of their vested interests. Because of this, both cannot tackle the real economic problems which confront the country, for a solution of these would upset the present social structure and devest the vested interests. For both, this ostrich-like policy of ignoring real issues is bound to end in disaster. Facts and economic forces are more powerful than governments and empires and can only be ignored at peril.

Communalism thus becomes another name for political and social reaction and the British Government, being the citadel of this reaction in India, naturally throws its sheltering wings over a useful ally. Many a false trail is drawn to confuse the issue; we are told of Islamic culture and Hindu culture, of religion and old custom, of ancient glories and the like. But behind all this lies political and social reaction, and communalism must therefore be fought on all fronts and given no quarter. Because the inward nature of communalism has not been sufficiently realised, it has often sailed under false colours and taken in many an unwary person. It is an undoubted fact that many a Congressman has almost unconsciously partly succumbed to it and tried to reconcile his nationalism with this narrow and reactionary creed. A real appreciation of its true nature would demonstrate that there can be no common ground between the two. They belong to different species. It is time that Congressmen and others who have flirted with Hindu or Muslim or Sikh or any other communalism should understand this position and make their choice. No one can have it both ways, and the choice lies between political and social progress and stark reaction. An association with any form of communalism means the strengthening of the forces of reaction and of British imperialism in India; it means opposition to social and economic changes and a toleration of the present terrible distress of our people; it means a blind ignoring of world forces and events.

What are communal organizations? They are not religious although they confine themselves to religious groups and exploit the name of religion. They are not cultural and have done nothing for culture although they talk bravely of a past culture. They are not ethical or moral groups for their teachings are singularly devoid of all ethics and morality. They are certainly not economic groupings for there is no economic link binding their members and they have no shadow of an economic programme. Some of them claim not to be political even. What then are they?

As a matter of fact they function politically and their demands are political, but calling themselves non-political, they avoid the real issues and only succeed in obstructing the path of others. If they are political organizations then we are entitled to know exactly where they stand. Do they stand for the complete freedom of India or a partial freedom, if such a thing exists? Do they stand for independence or what is called Dominion Status? The best of words are apt to be misleading and many people still think that Dominion Status is something next door to independence. As a matter of fact they are two different types entirely, two roads going in opposite directions. It is not a question of fourteen annas and sixteen annas but of different species of coins which are not interchangeable.

Dominion Status means continuing the steel framework of British finance and vested interests; from this stranglehold there is no relief under Dominion Status. Independence means a possibility of relief from these burdens and the freedom to decide about our social structure. Therefore whatever measure of limited freedom we may get under Dominion Status it will always be subject to the paramount claims of the Bank of England and British capital, and it will also be subject to the continuation of our present economic structure. That means that we cannot solve our economic problems and relieve the masses of their crushing burdens; we can only sink deeper and deeper into the morass. What then do the communal organizations stand for: independence or Dominion Status?

We need not refer to that travesty of a constitution which the White Paper is supposed to embody. It is only an ungentle reminder to us that British capital and interests in India will be preserved at all costs, so long as the British Government has power to preserve them. Only those who are interested in the preservation of these British vested interests or those who are very simple and unsophisticated can go anywhere near the White Paper or its offshoots.

Even more important than the political objective is the economic objective. It is notorious that the era of politics has passed away and we live in an age when economics dominate national and international affairs. What have the communal organizations to say in regard to these economic matters? Or are they blissfully ignorant of the hunger and unemployment that darken the horizon of the masses as well as of the lower middle classes? If they claim to represent the masses they must know that the all-absorbing problem before these unfortunate and unhappy millions is the problem of hunger, and they should have some answer, some theoretical solution at least for this problem. What do they propose should be done in industry and in agriculture? How do they solve the distress of the worker and the peasant; what land laws do they suggest? What is to happen to the debt of the agricultural classes; is it to be liquidated or merely toned down, or is it to remain? What of unemployment? Do they believe in the present capitalist order of society or do they think in terms of a new order? These are a few odd questions that arise and an answer to them, as well as to other similar questions, will enlighten us as to the true inwardness of the claims and demands of the communalists. Even more so I think will the masses be enlightened if the answers manage to reach them. The Muslim masses are probably even poorer than the Hindu masses but the 'fourteen points' say nothing about these poverty-stricken Muslims. The Hindu communalists also lay all their stress on the preservation of their own vested interests and ignore their own masses.

I am afraid I am not likely to get clear, or perhaps any answers to my questions, partly because the questions are inconvenient, partly because communal leaders know little about economic facts and have never thought in terms of the masses. They are experts only in percentages and their battle ground is the conference room, not the field or factory or market place. But whether they like them or not the questions will force themselves to the front and those who cannot answer them effectively will find little place for themselves in public affairs. The answer of many of us can be given in one comprehensive word—socialism—and in the socialist structure of society.

But whether socialism or communism is the right answer or some other, one thing is certain—that the answer must be in terms of economics and not merely politics. For India and the world are oppressed by economic problems and there is no escaping them. So long as the fullest economic freedom does not come to us there can be no freedom whatever the political structure may be. Economic freedom must of course include political freedom. That is the reality today; all else is myth and delusion, and there is no greater myth than the communal myth.

To go back to the constituent assembly. If a really popular assembly met with freedom to face and decide the real issues, immediately these real economic problems would occupy attention. The so-called communal problem will fade into the background for the masses will be far more interested in filling their hungry stomachs than in questions of percentages. This assembly will release the vital forces in the country which are at present suppressed by our foreign rulers as well as by Indian vested interests. The lead will go to the masses and the masses, when free, though they may sometimes err, think in terms of reality and have no use for myths. The workers and the peasantry will dominate the situation, and their decisions, imperfect though they may be, will take us a long way to freedom. I cannot say what the constituent assembly will decide. But I have faith in the masses and am willing to abide by their decision. And I am sure that the communal problem will cease to exist when it is put to the hard test of real mass opinion. It has been a hothouse of growth nurtured in the heated atmosphere of conference rooms and so-called All Parties Conferences. It will not find a solution in that artificial environment, but it will wilt and die in the fresh air and the sunlight.

~

Paradoxes

(*From* An Autobiography)

...The industrial age has brought many evils that loom large before us; but we are apt to forget that, taking the world as a whole, and especially the parts that are most industrialised, it has laid down a basis of material well-being which makes cultural and spiritual progress far easier for large numbers. This is not all evident in India or other colonial countries as we have not profited by industrialism. We have only been exploited by it and in many respects made worse, even materially, and more so culturally and spiritually. The fault is not of industrialism but of foreign domination. The so-called Westernisation in India has actually, for the time being, strengthened feudalism, and instead of solving any of our problems has simply intensified them.

That has been our misfortune, and we must not allow it to colour our vision of the world today. For under present conditions the rich man is no longer a necessary or a desirable part of the productive system or of society as a whole. He is redundant and he is always coming in the way. And the old business of the priest to ask the rich to be charitable and the poor to be resigned, grateful for their lot, thrifty and well behaved, has lost its meaning. Human resources have grown tremendously and can face and solve the world's problems. Many of the rich have become definitely parasitical and the existence of a parasite class is not only a hindrance but an enormous waste of these resources. That class and the system that breeds them actually prevent work and production and encourage the workless at either end of the scale, both those who live on other people's labour and those who have no work to do and famish. Gandhiji himself wrote some time ago: "To a people famishing and idle, the only acceptable form in which God dare appear is work and promise of food as wages. God created man to work for his food, and said that those who ate without work were thieves."

To try to understand the complex problems of the modern world by an application of ancient methods and formulae when these problems did not exist, to use out-of-date phrases in regard to them, is to produce confusion and to invite failure. The very idea of private property, which seems to some people one of the fundamental notions of the world, has been an ever-changing one. Slaves were property at one time, and so were women and children, the seigneur's right to the bride's first night, roads, temples, ferries, bridges, public utilities, air and land. Animals are still property, though legislation has in many countries limited the rights of ownership. During war-time there is a continuous infringement of property rights. Property today is becoming more and more intangible, the possession of shares, a certain amount of credit, etc. As the conception of property changes, the State interferes more and more, public opinion demands, and the law enforces a limitation of the anarchic rights of property-owners. All manner of heavy taxes, which are in the nature of confiscation, swallow up individual property rights for the public good. The public good becomes the basis of public policy, and a man may not act contrary to the public good even to protect his property rights. After all, the vast majority of people had no property rights in the past, they were themselves property owned by others. Even today a very small number have such rights. We hear a great deal of vested interests. Today a new vested interest has come to be recognised, that of every man and woman to live and labour and enjoy the fruits of labour. Because of these changing conceptions property and capital do not vanish, they are diffused, and the power over others, which a concentration of them gave to a few, is taken back by society as a whole.

Gandhiji wants to improve the individual internally, morally and spiritually, and thereby to change the external environment. He wants people to give up bad habits and indulgences and to become pure. He lays stress on sexual abstinence, on the giving up of drink, smoking, etc. Opinions may differ about the relative wickedness of these indulgences, but can there be any doubt that even from the individual point of view, and much more so from the social, these personal failings are less harmful than covetousness, selfishness, acquisitiveness, the fierce conflicts of individuals for personal gain, the ruthless struggles of groups and classes, the inhuman suppression and exploitation of one group by another, the terrible wars between nations. Of course he detests all this violence and degrading conflict. But are they not inherent in the acquisitive society of today with its law that the strong must prey on the weak, and its motto, that, as of old, "they shall take who have the power and they shall keep who can "? The profit motive today inevitably leads to conflict. The whole system protects and gives every scope to man's predatory instincts; it encourages some finer instincts no doubt, but much more so the baser instincts of man. Success means the knocking down of others and mounting on their vanquished selves. If these motives and ambitions are encouraged by society and attract the best of our people, does Gandhiji think that he can achieve his ideal, the moral man, in this environment? He wants to develop the spirit of service; he will succeed in the case of some individuals, but so long as society puts forward as exemplars the victors of an acquisitive society and the chief urge as the personal profit motive, the vast majority will follow this course.

~

The Importance of the National Idea; Changes Necessary in India

(From The Discovery of India*)*

A blind reverence for the past is bad and so also is a contempt for it, for no future can be founded on either of these. The present and the future inevitably grow out of the past and bear its stamp, and to forget this is to build without foundations and to cut off the roots of national growth. It is to ignore one of the most powerful forces that influence people. Nationalism is essentially a group memory of past achievements, traditions, and experiences, and nationalism is stronger today than it has ever been. Many people thought that nationalism had had its day and must inevitably give place to the ever-growing international tendencies of the modern world. Socialism with its proletarian background derided national culture as something tied up with a decaying middle-class. Capitalism itself became progressively international with its cartels and combines and overflowed national boundaries. Trade and commerce, easy communications and rapid transport, the radio and cinema, all helped to create an international atmosphere and to produce the delusion that nationalism was doomed.

Yet whenever a crisis has arisen nationalism has emerged again and dominated the scene, and people have sought comfort and strength in their old traditions. One of the remarkable developments of the present age has been the rediscovery of the past and of the nation. This going back to national traditions has been most marked in the ranks of labour and the proletarian elements, who were supposed to be the foremost champions of international action. War or similar crisis dissolves their internationalism and they become subject to nationalist hates and fears even more than other groups. The most striking example of this is the recent development of the Soviet Union. Without giving up in any way its essential social and economic structure, it has become more nationalist-minded and the appeal of the fatherland is now much greater than the appeal of the international proletariat. Famous figures in national history have again been revived and have become heroes of the Soviet people. The inspiring record of the Soviet people in this war, the strength and unity they have shown, are no doubt due to a social and economic structure which has resulted in social advances on a wide front, on planned production and consumption, on the development of science and its functions, and on the release of a vast quantity of new talent and capacity for leadership, as also on brilliant leadership. But it may also be partly due to a revival of national memories and traditions and a new awareness of the past, of which the present was felt to be a continuation. It would be wrong to imagine that this nationalist outlook of Russia is just a reversion to old-style nationalism. It is certainly not that. The tremendous experiences of the revolution and all that followed it cannot be forgotten, and the changes that resulted from it in social structure and mental adjustment must remain. That social structure leads inevitably to a certain international outlook. Nevertheless nationalism has reappeared in such a way as to fit in with the new environment and add to the strength of the people.

It is instructive to compare the development of the Soviet state with the varying fortunes of the Communist Parties in other countries. There was the first flush of enthusiasm among many people in all countries, and especially in proletarian ranks, soon after the Soviet Revolution. Out of this grew communist groups and parties. Then conflicts arose between these groups and national labour parties. During the Soviet five-year plans there was another wave of interest and enthusiasm, and this probably affected middle-class intellectuals even more than Labour. Again there was a reaction at the time of the purges in the Soviet Union. In some countries Communist Parties were suppressed, in others they made progress. But almost everywhere they came into conflict with organized national Labour. Partly this was due to the conservatism of Labour, but more so to a feeling that the Communist Party represented a foreign group and that they took their policies from Russia. The inherent nationalism of Labour came in the way of its accepting the cooperation of the Communist Party even when many were favourably inclined towards communism.

The many changes in Soviet policy, which could be understood in relation to Russia, became totally incomprehensible as policies favoured by Communist Parties elsewhere. They could only be understood on the basis that what may be good for Russia must necessarily be good for the rest of the world. These Communist Parties, though they consisted of some able and very earnest men and women, lost contact with the nationalist sentiments of the people and weakened accordingly. While the Soviet Union was forging new links with national tradition, the Communist Parties of other countries were drifting further away from it.

I cannot speak with much knowledge of what happened elsewhere, but I know that in India the Communist Party is completely divorced from, and is ignorant of, the national traditions that fill the minds of the people. It believes that communism necessarily implies a contempt for the past. So far as it is concerned, the history of the world began in November, 1917, and everything that preceded this was preparatory and leading up to it. Normally speaking, in a country like India with large numbers of people on the verge of starvation and the economic structure cracking up, communism should have a wide appeal. In a sense there is that vague appeal, but the Communist Party cannot take advantage of it because it has cut itself off from the springs of national sentiment and speaks in a language which finds no echo in the hearts of the people. It remains an energetic, but small group, with no real roots.

It is not only the Communist Party in India that has failed in this respect. There are others who talk glibly of modernism and modern spirit and the essence of western culture, and are at the same time ignorant of their own culture. Unlike the communists, they have no ideal that moves them and no driving force that carries them forward. They take the external forms and outer trappings of the west (and often some of the less desirable features), and imagine that they are in the vanguard of an advancing civilization. Naive and shallow and yet full of their own conceits, they live, chiefly in a few large cities, an artificial life which has no living contacts with the culture of the east or of the west.

National progress can, therefore, neither lie in a repetition of the past nor in its denial. New patterns must inevitably be adopted but they must be integrated with the old. Sometimes the new, though very different, appears in terms of pre-existing patterns, and thus creates a feeling of a continuous development from the past, a link in the long chain of the history of the race. Indian history is a striking record of changes introduced in this way, a continuous adaptation of old ideas to a changing environment, of old patterns to new. Because of this there is no sense of cultural break in it and there is that continuity, in spite of repeated change, from the far distant days of Mohenjodaro to our own age. There was a reverence for the past and for traditional forms, but there was also a freedom and flexibility of the mind and a tolerance of the spirit. So while forms often remained, the inner content continued to change. In no other way could that society have survived for thousands of years. Only a living and growing mind could overcome the rigidity of traditional forms, only those forms could give it continuity and stability.

Yet this balance may become precarious and one aspect may overshadow, and to some extent, suppress this other. In India there was an extraordinary freedom of the mind allied to certain rigid social forms. These forms ultimately influenced the freedom of the mind and made it in practice, if not in theory, more rigid and limited. In western Europe there was no such freedom of the mind and there was also much less rigidity in social forms. Europe had a long struggle for the freedom of the mind and, as a consequence, social forms also changed.

In China the flexibility of the mind was even greater than in India and for all her love of, and attachment to, tradition, that mind never lost its flexibility and essential tolerance. Tradition sometimes delayed changes but that mind was not afraid of change, though it retained the old patterns. Even more than in India, Chinese society built up a balance and an equilibrium which survived through many changes for thousands of years. Perhaps one of the great advantages that China has had over other countries is her entire freedom from dogma, from the narrow and limited religious outlook, and her reliance on reason and common sense. No other country has based its culture less on religion and more on morality and ethics and a deep understanding of the variety of human life.

In India, because of the recognized freedom of the mind, howsoever limited in practice, new ideas are not shut out. They are considered and can be accepted far more than in countries which have a more rigid and dogmatic outlook on life. The essential ideals of Indian culture are broad-based and can be adapted to almost any environment. The bitter conflict between science and religion which shook up Europe in the nineteenth century would have no reality in India, nor would change based on the applications of science bring any conflict with those ideals. Undoubtedly such changes would stir up, as they are stirring up, the mind of India, but instead of combating them or rejecting them it would rationalize them from its own ideological point of view and fit them into its mental framework. It is probable that in this process many vital changes may be introduced in the old outlook, but they will not be super-imposed from outside and will seem rather to grow naturally from the cultural background of the people. This is more difficult today than it might have been, because of the long period of arrested growth and the urgent necessity for big and qualitative changes.

Conflict, however, there will be, with much of the superstructure that has grown up round those basic ideals and which exists and stifles us to-day. That superstructure will inevitably have to go, because much of it is bad in itself and is contrary to the spirit of the age. Those who seek to retain it do an ill service to the basic ideals of Indian culture, for they mix up the good and the bad and thus endanger the former. It is no easy matter to separate the two or draw a hard and fast line between them, and here opinions will differ widely. But it is not necessary to draw any such theoretical and logical line; the logic of changing life and the march of events will gradually draw that line for us. Every kind of development—technological or philosophical—necessitates contact with life itself, with social needs, with the living movements of the world. Lack of this contact leads to stagnation and loss of vitality and creativeness. But if we maintain these contacts and are receptive to them, we shall adapt ourselves to the curve of life without losing the essential characteristic which we have valued.

Our approach to knowledge in the past was a synthetic one, but limited to India. That limitation continued and the synthetic approach gave place gradually to a more analytical one. We have now to lay greater stress on the synthetic aspect and make the whole world our field of study. This emphasis on synthesis is indeed necessary for every nation and individual if they are to grow out of the narrow grooves of thought and action in which most people have lived for so long. The development of science and its applications have made this possible for us, and yet the very excess of new knowledge has added to its difficulty. Specialization has led to a narrowing of individual life in a particular groove, and man's labour in industry is often confined to some infinitesimal part of the whole product. Specialization in knowledge and work will have to continue, but it seems more essential than ever that a synthetic view of human life and man's adventure through the ages should be encouraged. This view will have to take into consideration the past and the present, and include in its scope all countries and peoples. In this way perhaps we might develop, in addition to our own national backgrounds and cultures, an appreciation of others and a capacity to understand and cooperate with the peoples of other countries. Thus also we might succeed to some extent in building up integrated personalities instead of the lopsided individuals of today. We might become, in Plato's words, 'spectators of all time and all being,' drawing sustenance from the rich treasures that humanity has accumulated, adding to them, and applying them in building for the future.

It is a curious and significant act that, in spite of all modern scientific progress and talk of internationalism, racialism and other separating factors are at least as much in evidence today, if not more so, than at any previous time in history. There is something lacking in all this progress, which can neither produce harmony between nations nor within the spirit of man. Perhaps more synthesis and a little humility towards the wisdom of the past, which, after all, is the accumulated experience of the human race, would help us to gain a new perspective and greater harmony. That is especially needed by those peoples who live a fevered life in the present only and have almost forgotten the past. But for countries like India a different emphasis is necessary, for we have too much of the past about us and have ignored the present. We have to get rid of that narrowing religious outlook, that obsession with the supernatural and metaphysical speculations, that loosening of the mind's discipline in religious ceremonial and mystical emotionalism, which come in the way of our understanding ourselves and the world. We have to come to grips with the present, this life, this world, this nature which surrounds us in its infinite variety.

Some Hindus talk of going back to the Vedas; some Moslems dream of an Islamic theocracy. Idle fancies, for there is no going back to the past; there is no turning back even if this was thought desirable. There is only one-way traffic in Time.

India must therefore lessen her religiosity and turn to science. She must get rid of the exclusiveness in thought and social habit which has become life a prison to her, stunting her spirit and preventing growth. The idea of ceremonial purity has erected barriers against social intercourse and narrowed the sphere of social action. The day-to-day religion of the orthodox Hindu is more concerned with what to eat and what not to eat, who to eat with and from whom to keep away, than with spiritual values. The rules and regulations of the kitchen dominate his social life. The Moslem is fortunately free from these inhibitions, but he has his own narrow codes and ceremonials, a routine which he rigorously follows, forgetting the lesson of brotherhood which his religion taught him. His view of life is, perhaps, even more limited and sterile than the Hindu view, though the average Hindu today is a poor representative of the latter view, for he has lost that traditional freedom of thought and the background that enriches life in many ways.

~

On Hyderabad and Kashmir: Forging a Nation

(From Selected Works of Jawaharlal Nehru Volume VI*)*

To
V.K. Krishna Menon[30]
New Delhi

26 June 1948

My dear Krishna,

This is the second letter I am dictating to you today.

You will be kept in touch with general developments in Kashmir and Hyderabad. There is one aspect of them which I should like again to bring to your notice because it is particularly affecting Indian opinion. This aspect is the help given by large numbers of Englishmen to every opponent of the Indian Union, whether it is Pakistan or Hyderabad or 'Azad Kashmir'. It is difficult to tie up this help with British governmental policy but the public, of course, cannot distinguish between the two and sometimes even we cannot distinguish.

British diplomatic and consular representatives in various parts of the world represent Pakistan interests. As such they do propaganda for Pakistan and they come in our way sometimes. Most of them are anti-Indian anyhow and whether they get

[30] V.K. Krishna Menon (1896–1974) was an Indian nationalist, diplomat, and politician. He led the Indian independence movement abroad, was the architect of India's foreign policy and a close ally of Nehru.

instructions from their Government or not they gladly act in an anti-Indian manner. Recently the Kashmir Story film was to be shown in Indonesia. The Dutch Government permitted this. At the last moment the British Consul there objected on behalf of Pakistan and the film was not shown. In Kashghar in Central Asia the British Consul again is coming in our way.

The Pakistan Army is full of British officers and cannot function without them. More and more Britishers are coming in. I have no doubt at all that many of these British officers are fully connected with Kashmir operations. It is quite impossible for the top ranking officers like Gracey, the Commander-in-Chief, to be unaware of what the Pakistan Army is doing in Kashmir. Bucher admitted this much. Till lately they denied any direct knowledge but now even that denial is not clearly forthcoming.

Apart from military officers, Pakistan is full of British civil officers and technicians. Some of these officers are of the worst type and are those who were kicked out from India. Mudie, of course, is a thoroughly bad person from every point of view.

In Hyderabad, the State Government has been receiving help from British sources for a long time past under various guises. We are informed by a responsible person that a number of high ranking Britishers are at present in Hyderabad incognito. At the end of last year a group of so-called British journalists visited Hyderabad. We are told that they were representatives of British armament makers and they advised Hyderabad about defence and attack, etc. In particular they told the Government there to keep squadrons of planes outside Indian territory so that they could be used when the time came against India. Many such planes have been purchased by Hyderabad during the last two years or so from British and American disposals in China, Burma and elsewhere. Hyderabad keeps these planes in Pakistan territory or even in the Middle East. Our information is that some bomber planes are kept in East Bengal, some in western Pakistan, a squadron in Basra and a squadron in Persia. The air crews are usually Poles or Czechs.

It is becoming notorious that there is constant gun-running between some place in the Middle East and Hyderabad via

Karachi. The aircraft used is a Halifax Bomber with a European crew, probably British. These air journeys serve two purposes—they take arms and bring back gold.

Of course, all this is done in complete cooperation with Pakistan. In fact it is a joint policy. There is some basis for saying that Hyderabad wants a war and might even instigate it.

Barton[31] went to Lisbon on behalf of Hyderabad chiefly in connection with Goa. Our report is that a secret treaty was signed authorising Hyderabad to use Goa as a port in case of need. For this purpose Hyderabad will spend a great deal of money in developing harbour and port facilities in Goa. The idea presumably is that Pakistan or Middle East troops could come via Goa to Hyderabad.

There is, of course, the active sympathy and help of the Conservative Party of Britain. I do not quite know what Monckton is doing now. He went away from here very angry with the Nizam and cursing him and his present government freely. Nevertheless, I do not feel at all happy about what he might do. There is talk of reference to U.N.O. and Monckton going to Lake Success to support them. I rather doubt if he will go, but very probably there will be a reference to U.N.O.

We are informed that British Secret Service men have been loaned to the Hyderabad Government. They are working in the London office of the Pakistan Embassy there. All this and more is creating a feeling of bitterness against the British Government and people and I want to apprise you of it. The British Government's attitude, as represented by Noel-Baker in the Security Council over the Kashmir issue, has, of course, done much to irritate Indian opinion against Britain and the British Government.

Yours,
Jawaharlal

~

---

[31] William Barton (1871–1956); entered I.C.S. 1893; served in N.W.F.P. in various capacities; Resident in Baroda, 1919, in Mysore, 1920–25, and in Hyderabad, 1925–30; came to India with Supply Mission, 1940–41; author of *The Princes of India* (1934), *India's North West Frontier* (1939) and *India's Fateful Hour* (1942).

To
Vallabhbhai Patel[32]

5 June 1948

My dear Vallabhbhai,

I have pressed Gopalaswami Ayyangar[33] to go to Jammu and Srinagar for two or three days and he has at last agreed to do so. He will go on the 8th, first to Jammu. While it is true that Sheikh Abdullah is not always tactful and sometimes says and does things which he should not, my last visit to Kashmir convinced me that he was trying hard to meet the Maharaja more than half way. He has to deal with a very difficult situation, the essence of which is to gain popular goodwill. Whatever happens, the ultimate decision in Kashmir will be greatly influenced by this popular feeling. If the present Kashmir Government cannot succeed in this then it fails utterly. The Maharaja is completely oblivious of this aspect or the international implications of the Kashmir issue. He behaves in a manner which is completely inexplicable to me and which irritates the people. There is at present a vitally urgent problem of arranging for the destitute refugees in Jammu—40,000 or more. Cholera has begun and typhoid is feared. Our Relief and Health Ministry people visited Jammu and came to the conclusion that the Maharaja's stud farm was ideally suited for a relief camp. The horses there could easily be put somewhere else or sent to Srinagar for a few months. The Maharaja refused to permit this even though Amrit Kaur and Lady Mountbatten begged him for it. Meanwhile, children are dying in Jammu streets. You can imagine the public reaction to this.

Again about certain barracks in Srinagar. They were empty and were urgently wanted for our troops. The Maharaja would not agree. He is unapproachable and cannot be reached even by

---

[32] *Sardar Patel's Correspondence 1945–50*, Vol. I (Ahmedabad: Navajivan Publishing House), 200-201.

[33] Rajya Sabha leader, a cabinet minister in the Government of India, who came to look after Kashmir Affairs.

telephone. Meanwhile, urgent situations develop which must be handled with rapidity. What is to be done then?[34]

Jammu has ceased to have any great importance from the military point of view. Srinagar is the nerve centre for all activities, civil or military. It is essential for the Maharaja to be there and to remain in constant touch with his Government. Otherwise work suffers and things are hung up, and inevitably he is ignored where urgency demands it. The effect on the public of his remaining away from Srinagar is also very bad.

About the army (State) I fear it can never improve if the Maharaja has anything to do with it. It is in a hopeless mess. I wrote to you about the disgraceful behaviour of the State troops in Ladakh etc.[35] There are Hindu Dogra troops. They, or their officers, have lost all morale and discipline and any further association with the Maharaja will worsen the position. If any effective State army is to be built up, as it must be, it must be by our officers and men. The matter is too serious for it to be left to the discretion of the Maharaja. We are playing for high stakes and we dare not take risks. This is the opinion of our army men also.

I cannot write more now as I have to go.

I hope you are progressing well.

V.P. Menon will accompany Gopalaswami to Jammu and Srinagar, unless the wretched Hyderabad affair comes in the way.

Yours affectionately.
Jawaharlal

~

[34] The Maharaja complained to Patel on 24 April 1948 that the building which housed his offices and the rest house at Rambagh had been vacated for military occupation by Sheikh Abdullah without consulting him.

[35] For example, Brigadier Fakir Singh, a senior officer of the Kashmir State Army, who was sent to Skardu, ran away leaving behind 65,000 rounds of ammunition and a large quantity of mortar, handgrenades and rifles.

Radio Address to the Nation Ahead of the 1951 General Election

(*From* Jawaharlal Nehru: Selected Speeches Volume Two 1949–1953)

I am going to speak to you tonight about the General Election. All of you know something about them and there is naturally a great deal of interest in the country on this subject. It is right that each one of you should take an interest in this democratic process which is taking place on a scale yet unknown to history. It is also important that you take interest as citizens of the Republic of India, the future of which will, no doubt, be affected by these elections. Democracy is based on the active and intelligent interest of the people in their national affairs and in the elections that result in the formation of governments.

Let us first have an idea of the extent to which the General Elections will affect the country. There are altogether 2,293 constituencies in India. These include constituencies for Parliament, that is, for the House of the People and the Council of States and for the Legislative Assemblies and Councils in the States. Altogether 4,412 representatives will be chosen for these various Legislatures.

The number of voters on our electoral rolls is about 176,600,000. The number of polling booths will approximately be 224,000.

Each polling booth will have to be manned by a Presiding Officer, five clerks and four policemen. As elections will not take place all over India simultaneously, part of the stall required will do duty in more than one place. A rough estimate of the specialized staff required is:

Presiding Officers	..	..	56,000
Clerks	..	..	280,000
Policemen	..	..	224,000

To these will be added vast numbers of Government servants and voluntary workers. Indeed, the whole machinery of the State will be especially geared for the elections. The estimated cost of the elections, both for the Central Government and State Governments, is approximately Rs 100,000,000.

I have referred only to the official staff; but in addition there will be an election agent for every candidate as well as other agents and assistants.

Thus, the number of people engaged in these elections, besides the voters, is very large. Indeed, the entire organization has been built on a colossal scale and is a test for all of us. The gigantic preparation for the actual business of polling has been preceded by a tremendous amount of human labour. To begin with, the electoral rolls had to be prepared. You can imagine what a great quantity of paper must have been required for these rolls and the vast amount of printing which had to be done.

Unfortunately, many of our voters are not literate and we have, therefore, to provide coloured boxes with emblems for different parties and candidates. This introduces a fresh burden- which the Governments at the Centre and in the States have to shoulder. For the purpose, they have had to build up a huge staff which functions under the Central Election Commission. But no amount of governmental organization can make these elections a success unless the people themselves cooperate. It is, therefore, of the utmost importance for our people that they understand all the processes which lead us to their vote and give us their intelligent cooperation.

Many organized parties are running candidates for these elections. It is also likely that there will be some independent candidates. Every party and every candidate must be given a fair and equal chance in these elections. The fact that one party happens to be in charge of government does not entitle it to any special privileges during the elections. Officers of the Government must function impartially. Strict instructions have been issued to all of them by the Central and the State Governments, that they should carry out their duties with the strictest neutrality. The law has laid down penalties for any improper conduct on the part of a public servant. The Election Commission has also issued similar warnings on several occasions and suitable action will certainly be taken in regard to improper or illegal conduct.

Candidates and their agents must remember their duties and obligations and make it a point to be well acquainted with the complicated law on the subject of elections. Any error or lapse may disqualify them.

The Ministers of the Government, many of whom will themselves be standing as candidates for election, have a difficult task before them. They must not utilize their official position to further their own election prospects in any way. They must try to separate, as far as possible, their official duties from their electoral or private work. Detailed instructions to this effect have been issued.

It should always be remembered that the National Flag must not be used or exploited for party purposes. Indeed, there are strict rules as to when the National Flag may be used officially. It must not be used for any election purpose.

The whole object of democratic elections is to ascertain the views of the electorate on major problems and to enable the electorate to select their representatives. Parties place their programmes before the public and carry on intensive propaganda to convince the electorate of the virtues of each individual programme as well as of the demerits of other programmes. These conflicting approaches are supposed to educate and enlighten the electorate and enable it to choose rightly.

For some reason, elections cause a great deal of excitement and sometimes even passion. Unfortunately, this excitement may also lead to improper behaviour and to a lowering of normal standards of democracy. We have to be on our guard against this. It is of the utmost importance that all of us, whatever the party to which we belong, should maintain a high level of propriety and decorous behaviour. Our propaganda by speech or in writing should not be personal but should deal with policies and programmes. It should on no account be allowed to degenerate into personal criticism and abuse. The standard we set up now will act as a precedent and govern future elections.

The elections have already begun and polling has taken place in some of the remote valleys of Himachal Pradesh. This had to be done now because in mid-winter the mountain passes are closed and travelling becomes very difficult. For the same reason, a few constituencies in the mountainous parts of Uttar Pradesh will poll next February. These are exceptional cases and polling will take place over the length and breadth of the country in January on the dates which have already been announced.

I have given you a simple and rather bald account of these elections. I should like you, however, to try and realize the deep significance of this great adventure of the Indian people. Hundreds of millions of people in India will determine the future of this country. They will put their voting papers in tens of thousands of ballot boxes indicating their choice and will or should do so peacefully. Out of these voting papers will emerge the Members of the Parliament of India and of the State Assemblies and we shall accept the result of this election without question.

> **That is the essence of democracy. All of us naturally want the cause we represent to triumph and we strive for that end. In a democracy, we have to know how to win and also how to lose with grace. Those who win should not allow this to go to their heads, those who lose should not feel dejected.**

The manner of winning or losing is even more important than the result. It is better to lose in the right way than to win in the wrong way. Indeed, if success comes through misconceived effort or wrong means, then the value of that success itself is lost.

There have been interminable arguments about ends and means in India. Do wrong means justify right ends? So far as we, in India, are concerned we decided long ago that no end, for which wrong means were employed, could be right. If we apply that principle to the elections, we must come to the conclusion that it is far better that the person with wrong ends in view be elected than that the persons whose aims are worthy should win through dubious methods. If dubious methods are employed, then the rightness of the aims becomes meaningless.

I lay stress upon this because it is important and because there is a tendency, during election time, to disregard all standards of behaviour. I earnestly hope that every candidate along with his supporters will remember that to some extent he has the honour of India in his keeping and conduct himself accordingly.

For the 4,412 seats to be filled, there are innumerable applicants. Out of these, a limited number will be chosen to contest the seats, so that there will be a large number of people who are not chosen as candidates or who, being chosen, do not succeed. I hope that those who fall out in the first or the second round will not take it too much to heart.

There is a mistaken impression that one can serve India only if one goes to the legislatures. No doubt people can serve India in the legislatures but perhaps they can do so much better outside. Elections will come again and there is no point in getting too excited about them. Let us face them calmly and take them in our stride.

I should like to add something I have often said before. We owe a special duty to our minority communities and to those who are backward economically or educationally and who form the largest part of the population of India. We are all clamouring for our rights and privileges. It is more important to remember our duties and responsibilities.

Let us then face this great adventure of our General Elections with good heart and spirit and try to avoid ill will even in regard to those who oppose us. Thus, we shall lay the firm foundations of the democratic structure of this great Republic.

~

The Tribal Folk

(Speech delivered at the opening session of the Scheduled Tribes and Schedule Areas Conference, New Delhi, June 7, 1952.)

Mr Chairman and Friends, this audience is more or less a select one since it consists largely of experts. I am not an expert and, I am afraid, I shall not be able to contribute much if we were to sit down and discuss your problems.

I suppose you have invited me here because I happen to occupy the office of Prime Minister but I think I have another and possibly greater, claim to participate in this Conference. The claim is that I have always—long before I became Prime Minister—felt very strongly attracted to the tribal people of this country. This feeling was not the curiosity an idle observer has for strange customs; nor was it the attraction of the charitably disposed who want to do good to other people. I was attracted to them simply because I felt happy and at home with them. I liked them without any desire to do them good or to have good done to me. To do good to others is, I think, a very laudable desire but it often leads to great excesses which do not result in good to either the doer or the recipient.

In the tribal people, I have found many qualities which I miss in the people of the plains, cities and other parts of India. It was these very qualities that attracted me.

The tribal people of India are a virile people who naturally went astray sometimes. They quarrelled and occasionally cut off one another's heads. These were deplorable occurrences and should have been checked. Even so, it struck me that some of their practices were perhaps less evil than those that prevail in our cities. It is often better to cut off a hand or a head than to crush and trample on a heart. Perhaps, I also felt happy with these simple folk, because the nomad in me found congenial soil in their company. I approached them in a spirit of comradeship and not like someone aloof who had come to look at them, examine them, weigh them, measure them and report about them or to try and make them conform to another way of life.

I am alarmed when I see—not only in this country but in other great countries, too—how anxious people are to shape others according to their own image or likeness and to impose on them their particular way of living. We are welcome to our way of living but why impose it on others? This applies equally to national and international fields. In fact, there would be more peace in the world, if people were to desist from imposing their way of living on other people and countries.

I am not at all sure which is the better way of living. In some respects I am quite certain theirs is better. Therefore, it is grossly presumptuous on our part to approach them with an air of superiority or to tell them what to do or not to do. There is no point in trying to make of them a second rate copy of ourselves.

Now, who are these tribal folk? A way of describing them is that they are the people of the frontiers or those who live away from the interior of this country. Just as the hills breed a somewhat different type of people from those who inhabit the plains, so also the frontier breeds a different type of people from those who live away from the frontier. My own predilection is for the mountains rather than for the plains, for the hill folk rather than the plains people. So also I prefer the frontier, not only in a physical sense but because the idea of living near a frontier appeals to me intellectually. I feel that it would prevent one from becoming complacent and complacency is a very grave danger, especially in a great country like India where the nearest frontier may be a thousand miles away.

We should have a receptive attitude to the tribal people. There is a great deal we can learn from them, particularly in the frontier areas; and having learnt, we must try to help and cooperate. They are an extremely disciplined people, often a great deal more democratic than most others in India.

Even though they have no constitution, they are able to function democratically and carry out the decisions made by their elders or representatives. Above all, they are a people who sing and dance and try to enjoy life; not people who sit in stock exchanges, shout at one another and think themselves civilized.

I would prefer being a nomad in the hills to being a member of stock exchanges, where one is made to sit and listen to noises that are ugly to a degree. Is that the civilization we want the tribal people to have? I hope not. I am quite sure that the tribal folk, with their civilization of song and dance, will last till long after stock exchanges have ceased to exist.

It is a very great pity that we in the cities have drifted so far away from the aesthetic side of life. We still have a good many folk songs and dances when we go to the villages, because modern civilization has more or less left them untouched. The progress of modern civilization in India involves both good things and bad. One of the things we have lost is the spirit of song and dance and the capacity for enjoyment and this is what the tribal people so abundantly have. We seem to pay too much attention to the cinema; it is undoubtedly an excellent medium for many good things but unfortunately it has not proved to be particularly inspiring. We must imbibe something of the spirit of the tribal folk instead of damping it with our long faces and black gowns.

For half a century or more, we have struggled for freedom and ultimately achieved it. That struggle, apart from anything else, was a great liberating force. It raised us above ourselves it improved us and hid for the moment some of our weaknesses. We must remember that this experience of hundreds of millions of Indian people was not shared by the tribal folk. Our struggle for freedom did influence the tribes in Central India to some extent but the frontier areas of Assam, for instance, remained almost unaffected by it. This was partly due to the inadequacy of the means of communication available to us in the old day. Of course, there were other reasons, too.

One of the reasons was that the city people were a little afraid to leave their familiar haunts and go into the mountains. The Christian missionaries went to various tribal areas and some of them spent practically all their lives there. I do not find many instances of people from the plains going to the tribal areas to settle down. Apart from our own lack of initiative, we were not allowed to go there by the British authorities then in power. That is why our freedom movement reached these people only in the shape of occasional rumours. Sometimes they reacted rightly and sometimes wrongly but that is beside the point. The essence of our struggle for freedom was the unleashing of a liberating force in India. This force did not even affect the frontier people in one of the most important tribal areas. The result is that while we have had several decades in which to prepare ourselves psychologically for basis changes, the tribal people have had no such opportunity. On the contrary, they were prepared the other way round through the efforts of the British officials and sometimes the missionaries. The missionaries did very good work there and I am all praise for them but, politically speaking, they did not particularly like the changes in India. In fact, just when a new political awareness dawned on India, there was a movement in north-eastern India to encourage the people of the north-east to form separate and independent States. Many foreigners in the area supported this movement. I do not understand how it could be considered practical or feasible from any point of view. My point is that the whole of the north-east frontier had been conditioned differently during the past generation and even in more recent years. The fault lay partly with us and partly with circumstances. These factors have an important bearing on any genuine understanding of the tribal folk. They are our own people and our work does not end with the opening of so many schools and so many dispensaries and hospitals. Of course, we want schools and hospitals and dispensaries and roads and all that but to stop there is rather a dead way of looking at things. What we ought to do is to develop a sense of oneness with these people, a sense of unity and understanding. That involves a psychological approach.

You may talk day after day about development programmes in regard to schools and other matters but you will fail completely if you do not touch the real core of the problem. The need today is to understand these people, make them understand us and thus create a bond of affection and understanding. After achievement of independence, the basic problem of India, taken as a whole, is one of integration and consolidation. Political integration is now complete but that is not enough. We must bring about changes much more basic and intimate than mere political integration. That will take time, because it is not merely a matter of law. All we can do is to nurture it and create conditions where it finds congenial soil. So, the greatest problem of India today is not so much political as psychological integration and consolidation. India must build up for herself a unity which will do away with provincialism, communalism and the various other 'isms' which disrupt and separate.

As I said, we must approach the tribal people with affection and friendliness and come to them as a liberating force. We must let them feel that we come to give and not to take something away from them. That is the kind of psychological integration India needs. If, on the other hand, they feel you have come to impose yourselves upon them or that we go to them in order to try and change their methods of living, to take away their land and to encourage our businessmen to exploit them, then the fault is ours for it only means that our approach to the tribal people is wholly wrong. The less we hear of this type of integration and consolidation of the tribal areas, the better it will be.

We ought to be careful about appointing officers anywhere but we must be doubly so when we appoint them in tribal areas. An officer in the tribal areas should not merely be a man who has passed an examination or gained some experience of routine work. He must be a man with enthusiasm, whose mind and even more so whose heart understands the problem it is his duty to deal with. He must not go there just to sit in an office for a few hours a day and for the rest curse his fate for being sent to an out of the way place. That type of man is completely useless. It is far better to send a totally uneducated man who has passed no examination, so long as he goes to these people with friendship and affection and lives as one of them. Such a man will produce better results than the brilliant intellectual who has no human understanding of the problem. The man who goes there as an officer must be prepared to share his life with the tribal folk. He must be prepared to enter their huts, talk to them, eat and smoke with them, live their lives and not consider himself superior or apart. Then only can he gain their confidence and respect and thus be in a position to advise them.

The language problem is almost always exceedingly important

from the psychological point of view. The best of solutions can come to nought if misunderstood or misinterpreted by the party concerned. It is absolutely clear to me that the Government must encourage the tribal languages. It is not enough simply to allow them to prevail. They must be given all possible support and the conditions in which they can flourish must be safeguarded. We must go out of our way to achieve this. In the Soviet Republic we have the example of a country that has adopted such a policy with success. Lenin and other leaders in his time were exceedingly wise in this respect. Regardless of their ultimate objective they wanted to win the goodwill of the people and they won it largely by their policy of encouraging their languages, by going out of their way to help hundreds of dialects, by preparing dictionaries and vocabularies and sometimes even by evolving new scripts where there were none. They wanted their people to feel that they were free to live their own lives and they succeeded in producing that impression. In the matter of languages there must be no compulsion whatever. I have no doubt at all that the West Bengal Government must have built special schools in places like Darjeeling and Kalimpong for the Tibetan-speaking people. If the tribal people have a script we must, of course, use it. But, normally, they do not have a script and the only script they have thus far learnt to some extent is the Roman script. It is a good script no doubt; and because many people have learnt it, I would not discourage it. But if we are to evolve script—here I do not speak with any assurance but am merely saying something that has occurred to me—it might be better, for the future, if we were to use the Devanagari script. It is a relatively easy script, apart from the fact that it can put the tribal folk more in touch with the rest of India than any other script. In areas where a majority of the people already know the Roman script, I would not suddenly force them to abandon it because I do not want them to feel compelled in any way.

I find that so far we have approached the tribal people in one of two ways. One might be called the anthropological approach in which we treat them as museum specimens to be observed and written about. To treat them as specimens for anthropological examination and analysis—except in the sense that everybody is more or less an anthropological specimen—is to insult them. We do not conceive of them as living human beings with whom it is possible to work and play. The other approach is one of ignoring the fact that they are something different requiring special treatment and of attempting forcibly to absorb them into the normal pattern of social life. The way of forcible assimilation or of assimilation through the operation of normal factors would be equally wrong. In fact, I have no doubt that, if normal factors were allowed to operate, unscrupulous people from outside would take possession of tribal lands. They would take possession of the forests and interfere with the life of the tribal people. We must give them a measure of protection in their areas so that no outsider can take possession of their lands or forests or interfere with them in any way except with their consent and goodwill. The first priority in tribal areas, as well as elsewhere in the country, must be given to roads and communications. Without that, nothing we may do will be effective. Obviously, there is need for schools, for health relief, for cottage industries and so on. One must always remember, however, that we do not mean to interfere with their way of life but want to help them live it.

~

The Dignity of Labour

(Translation of speech at the inauguration of the Harijan Convention, Wardha, November 1, 1952.)

I am glad to be present at this Sammelan. It will be out of place to talk of revolution here. It has become almost a habit with us to repeat old grievances and narrate old tales. I do not mean that we should not persist in righting wrongs, old though they be; but we must, at the same time, be alert and keep our heads on our shoulders. This country belongs to all of us. Before we attained independence our main object was to drive the foreigners out of this land. We talked of social and economic reforms then, too, but our struggle at that time was mainly political.

After the attainment of Swaraj, economic and social problems have begun to loom large before us. There may be differences of opinion about these problems but the question is how to solve them. We talk of Gandhivad and other vads or 'isms' but our chief defect is that we are more given to talking about things than to doing them. We seem to think that social and economic reforms can be achieved merely by resolutions or legislations.

You ought to give thought to your problems but I would ask you to broaden your vision and think of India, of Bharat Mata, as a whole. Who is Bharat Mata? It is you—the janata—and the question before us is how to raise the economic standard of the nation.

Giving government jobs to a few people will not solve the problem of the crores of Indians who are unemployed. It is not possible for the Government to find employment for everybody. If unqualified people are employed, the country will suffer. Let all those who are engaged in an occupation do their job well, for production is proportionate to the work done. The prosperity of a nation depends on its capacity for production and on a rational distribution of wealth. In order to ensure the latter, we must get rid of all the present bottle-necks.

A revolution cannot increase our wealth, which really calls for hard work. After the revolution of 1917, the Russians had to work tremendously hard before they could reach their present position. They had their Five Year Plans and laboured with diligence and patience for them. The people gladly endured hardship and suffering so that the foundation of their Republic may be true and strong. The Russian Revolution took place 35 years ago and it is only now that the people are beginning to gather the fruit of their labours. For the first decade, they had to work hard and suffer even more than they did under the old regime; but they had courage and confidence. Revolution can remove an old regime but it cannot make a nation wealthy overnight. To improve their lot, the Russians toiled and sweated and have now come into their own.

From Socialist Russia to Capitalist America is a far cry. It is true that America is two and a half times as big as India but the ratio of American production is far higher than ours. They have devised means of increasing their wealth. The average income of a working man is about a thousand rupees a month. The American people recognize the dignity of labour. Even the sons of the rich earn their living while they learn. They think it derogatory to live on the earnings of others.

We have got to change our mentality. At present we are apt to look down on manual labour and that tendency is responsible for our present plight. There are two kinds of unemployment in our country-there are people who do not find work and there are those who are not willing to work. During my recent tour of Assam I came across a young girl, who was carrying a load of firewood on her head. I stopped and spoke to her. I was surprised because she spoke perfect English. She had been educated in England. Her parents had lost their all in Pakistan and were reduced to penury. In spite of her background, she did not hesitate to do manual work. The most important thing is the will to work. The prosperity of a nation is judged by the number of people who are employed. Unemployment is the bane of a nation.

I shall now come to an important social problem. It cannot be gainsaid that the Harijans have been oppressed for ages. Certain cruel customs have sprung up and they cannot be eradicated merely by legislation. Even so, I am sure that the present world conditions are bound, sooner or later, to bring about a basic change in the situation. If we want to prosper as a nation, we must put a premium on efficiency and competence and, therefore, only those who are competent should be given employment in the Government. Nepotism, favouritism or reservation will lower the standard of government work. It worries me to find our standard of efficiency falling. It will be dangerous to allow this state of affairs to continue, because in the next four or five years new responsibilities will devolve on us.

It is wrong to think that government services are there to maintain the people. In advanced countries, it is no honour to be a government servant. It is only in backward countries, where there is a great deal of unemployment, that government services are given undue importance.

The test of competency is not merely a university degree. Our greatest responsibility today is to give every child—boy or girl—equal opportunity. My heart saddens when I see our young children going about half naked, half starved. It is our duty to supply them with proper nourishment and clothing. We have a glorious past and our history goes back thousands of years; but our civilization had its evils also, the caste system not the least of them. We must draw lessons from our past and rise to new heights.

~

The Middle Way

Address at the annual meeting of the Indian Chemical Manufacturers' Association, New Delhi, December 26, 1950.[36]

It has been a great pleasure to me to come here. I have done so chiefly because my old friend Dr Hamied37 invited me and also because I consider that the chemical industry is a very important one. I have also come on a mission of curiosity and intend to find out who the chemical manufacturers of this country are and what they are doing. I have learnt something from Dr Hamied's address, Of course, I do not mean to say that I was totally unaware of their activities. Dr Hamied's address added a great deal to my knowledge of what has been done or not done and also what the Government should and should not do. He has presumably asked me and others to appreciate and admire the work of both the chemical manufacturers and the other private interests engaged in industry in India.

---

[36] Jawaharlal Nehru, *Jawaharlal Nehru's Speeches 1949–1953* Volume Two (New Delhi: Publication Division, 1954), 44–49

[37] Scientist and founder of Cipla, he is also credited with conceptualizing the idea of the CSIR as an umbrella organization to run several labs in the country.

I have no doubt that much of their work is worthy of appreciation and occasionally some might even be worthy of admiration. Perhaps, it might be said that they have not yet attained the degree of perfection at which we aim and there might be some lapses on their part. We have, nevertheless, to look at this problem in relation to our country's economy and her needs. We have to keep before us the problem of how to build or develop our economy and, in a smaller sense, our chemical industry as well.

Looking at newspaper advertisements it seemed to me that one of the main industries in the country was the manufacture of some potent and powerful pills. Being unacquainted with the taste or effect of those pills and seeing the advertisements in the newspapers day after day, I began to dislike intensely the people who manufactured these things and advertised them so frequently. I may go a step further and say that I am a very bad product of the pharmaceutical age, because I have hardly ever taken any medicine, pills or drugs. However, I have no doubt that other people need these pills and I have no desire to deprive them.

Dr Hamied has referred to some large questions. He has laid down some excellent maxims and some extraordinary maxims.

He has stated as an obvious fact which admits of no dispute or argument that private enterprise and nationalization can be equated with democracy and that totalitarianism and nationalization are the same. It is for the first time that I have heard such a viewpoint. I am not going to enter into any controversy about this or about what he called the dual policy of the Government. Obviously, he wants us either to plump for absolute free enterprise or for hundred per cent nationalization.

I am afraid Dr Hamied is out of touch with what is happening in the world. There is no country in the world where the free enterprise of his dream exists. It does not exist even in the United States of America which is the high priest of free enterprise. On the contrary, it becomes less and less significant in spite of the country's policy and its aims. World conditions today create forces which compel a country to progress in a certain direction, whether it wants to or not.

There are countries like Soviet Russia and some others which have gone a long way in creating a State which is in complete control of industry. Everything else is also State-controlled. Dr Hamied wants us to choose between Soviet Russia and something which does not exist anywhere in the world. That is a very hard choice indeed and I do not see why I should be forced to make it. It is inevitable that those countries, which do not want either of the two extremes, must find a middle way. In that middle way, there is bound to be more emphasis on some factors than on others but obviously a middle way or a mixed economy, if you like to call it that, is inevitable. That is not a dogma or an axiom which can be applied to any country regardless of its conditions. It will have to be decided by each country individually with regard to its particular conditions. What may be suitable for India might not be suitable, let us say, for Burma or Afghanistan or a country in Europe. We have to base our actions on objective facts and our capacities. We cannot think of this country in terms of what is happening in the United States. We must take into consideration the facts that are peculiar to, and govern the situation.

The United States of America has had 150 years of consolidation and growth and its capacity for production today is colossal. All kinds of economic forces which have little relationship with the old idea of capitalism are active in that country. Of course, America is a capitalist country and she is proud of being one. But the fact is that modern capitalism in the United States of America is vastly different from what it was twenty or thirty or forty years ago. It has changed. Even economies can move in a particular direction with a momentum of their own. I was told the other day by someone who knows—I have no idea how far the figures are correct—that one person in every five in the United States of America is in some kind of State employment. That is a prodigious number and America, mind you, is a capitalist and not a socialist state. The fact that one person in five is in State employment in a capitalist country shows how the nature of the capitalist state is changing. This means that in a country where conditions are different and where the stresses of modern life are greater, the changes are also bound to be of a basic nature.

In England there has also been a considerable change. I should like to know what the response from Parliament or from the Government or from other people would be if Dr Hamied's axiom were to be stated in England. England is obviously pursuing a socialist policy and has been pursuing it with considerable courage during the last four or five years since the war ended.

So, the problem is not a simple one. There are in this world various policies, ideologies and theories. I suppose there is some truth in each of them. However, my personal feeling is that while it is very important to have a theory as the logical basis of our thought, it is not reasonable to apply it by force to all conditions. We can use a theory for the purpose of argument and for testing its validity. In practice, however, you have to take the facts of the situation and adapt either yourself or your theory accordingly. Most countries have to do it. If I may say so, even Soviet Russia which seeks to base herself on a very hard and rigid theory of Marxism, interprets Marxism in a manner that suits her. The result is that her brand of Marxism has little to do with Marx. I am quite certain that Marx would be astonished if he were to see the various interpretations of his theory. Whether you approve of this or not is immaterial. The important point is that Russians, in their own way, are hard realists and continue to adapt their policy to what they consider for the moment good for their country or their party.

Coming to India, we have to consider things as they are. We cannot lay down any slogan or watchword and try to force it through to its logical conclusion. Whether it is in India or anywhere else, only those policies can succeed which promise to deliver the goods. There are no other tests. Broadly speaking, the present conflict is between the various forces represented by communism on the one side and on the other by something to which I cannot quite give a name. I cannot call it capitalism because it has all kinds of variations. What is really developing in the world is some kind of democratic socialism. It is developing gradually and in varying degrees. Whatever the two conflicting forces may be, their real test is not going to be on the battlefield. They are ultimately going to be tested by the results achieved.

We should try to understand our problems in as realistic a manner as possible, avoiding for the moment words which have long histories behind them and which confuse the mind. When we throw these 'isms' about as arguments, we get lost. Passions are aroused and the hard facts are ignored. A person who calls himself a socialist naturally has a certain general outlook and a certain set of objectives. Another person may have quite a different point of view. If you put these two persons together, they hurl harsh words at each other and nothing results. If, on the other hand, they sat down together and said, 'Well, here is a job to be done,' something might result. Here in India, there is so much we want—food, clothing, housing, education, health—in fact, all the important things of life. How are we to get them? Surely, not by shouting slogans or passing resolutions about socialism or capitalism or any other 'ism'. We will have to produce the goods and distribute them properly. We must think how best to do it.

There is no doubt that American capitalism has an amazing capacity for production; in fact, it is colossal. This capacity of American capitalism was not always the same; it has changed and has been changing. Besides, the United States of America has had 150 years to achieve it in. It had a territory with huge economic resources. It had opportunity without the hampering background of conflict which other countries had to reckon with. It had neither a heavy population nor the relics of a feudal age. It was a new country with enormous space and it developed to its present level in 150 years. It is thus rather absurd to say, 'Do what has been done in America.' I would like to do it in my own way but how can I do it? I do not have the 150 years or even 100 years to settle down in and grow as America did. I have neither that enormous space nor that invaluable freedom from conflict and trouble. I have neither that much time nor the same opportunity. India is a big country with a background of all kinds of conflict. Many kinds of forces are at play. I have got to solve my problems in the immediate present or in the near future, not in the next hundred years. Private enterprise in America developed gradually till it built up for itself a very strong position with enormous resources. Has private enterprise in India got the capacity or the ability or the resources to do that? It has ability and it has resources but it just has not the strength or capacity to solve the situation by itself. It is a patent fact that you just cannot do it. Is our private enterprise going to take up our river valley schemes? It cannot, because they are too big for it. These schemes cannot pay dividends quickly. We have to wait for years and years. Therefore, the State inevitably has to take them up. In America the railways are owned by private companies. Here we own the railway. Are we not told, 'All this dislocates business. Let private enterprise have full play'? If private enterprise has full play, one of the first casualties in this country will be private enterprise itself. To be frank with you—I am talking in general terms—private enterprise in this country is not wise enough. It may be clever in making money but it just is not wise enough. It does not see what is happening all round. It does not see a changing world in turmoil but sees it in terms of an age that is dead and gone.

It so happens—and it amazes me—that here in India, in spite of enormous difficulties, we have conflicts and all kinds of unhelpful criticism and condemnation of the government. That very fact symbolizes a certain state of affairs in India and an attitude in the minds of her people which is far from critical. There is no doubt about it. When we talk of something critical like the food situation, for instance, we use strong language without showing any awareness of the crisis. We live our lives in the same old way and though large numbers of people suffer in the country for lack of food, lack of shelter or lack of other things, most of us, especially those of us who criticize, lead our lives unaffected in any way. Asia is on the verge of a crisis. In fact, the whole world is tense with a sense of urgency but we have no such sense yet! Unfortunately, this lightheartedness in understanding what is happening all round us is not good because then realization sometimes comes as a shock. We have to take the problems of India and look at them in the context of the world. Let us deal with them as realistically as possible, having certain aims and objectives, trying to go towards them, adopting our policies with a view to realizing those objectives, without arguing so much and without having recourse to slogans or terms.

The only objective that you can set before you in the modern world is a widespread raising of the people's standard of living. It is not the only objective but others are subject to it. No government can afford to ignore the urges of the common people. After all, democracy has its basis on those very urges and if any government flouts them, it is pushed aside and other governments take over. They may be better or worse. That is immaterial.

Dr Hamied, in his address, criticized heavy taxation on the one hand and on the other called upon the government to provide certain urgently needed things like a synthetic petrol plant which would cost thirty or forty crores. How can we reduce the revenue by lessening the taxes and still do everything that is necessary? I don't understand. Naturally, there is a limit to our capacity to do things and there is a limit to taxation. We cannot go beyond that without disturbing the whole structure of our economy. Important things have certainly to be done and if enough money is not forthcoming, those things are not done.

I should like you, gentlemen, to look at this picture and balance things. I want you to realize that in the modern age it is not possible to go back to the old days of a dead world. No country in the wide world can go back to those days. If you think in terms of going back then you are thinking in a vacuum and that is unreal thinking. How far the state can or should come in or how far there should be cooperation are matters for consideration but the real test is results which are not the accumulation of private fortunes but the advancement of the public generally.

~

Defining Foreign Policy

(Speech during the debate on the President's Address, Parliament, New Delhi, 17 February, 1953)

I must first of all apologize to this House for not being able to attend this debate in person. We, in the Government, have sometimes to attend to the business of two Houses and when something is before the two Houses simultaneously, it adds to the difficulty. I have tried, with the help of my colleague here, to keep in touch with the trend of the debate and have read reports of some of the speeches made here. Both here and in the other House, it is my business and duty to listen very carefully to the criticism that is made and to the suggestions that are offered. It is my desire to learn from them and to accept them where possible.

The public and sometimes the press have criticized the President's Address as a mere repetition of the policies of the Government. The President is not going to launch a new policy in the country and, therefore, his address is bound to be a repetition of our policy. It gives or purports to give a broad survey of foreign and domestic affairs and does so in language that becomes him as the head of the state.

Every government should have an integrated outlook consistent with its foreign and domestic policy. However, it is not particularly easy to have an integrated outlook because many unknown factors have to be dealt with. We are not in charge of the world and the other countries do not necessarily carry out our dictates or follow our wishes. We have to take things as they are and they are, I assure you, in a very difficult state. Vast changes are taking place; the whole world is in turmoil. Some countries are actually engaged in war; the rest live in constant fear of war and suffer the havoc fear brings with it. Enormous technological changes take place from day to day although they do not always come to our notice. The entire economic and social structure of the world is being changed by them. They change the structure of society and the thinking of man. Therefore, it may be that a policy which was good for us yesterday is not good today. A policy which was idealistic and advanced in the nineteenth century may be out of date today. All of us have been hurled suddenly into the middle of the twentieth century, irrespective of whether we wished it or not; but our minds lag behind in the remote past. Even economic and social problems are discussed in terms of the past, although the enormous changes that have taken place as a result of the last two great World Wars are obvious enough. At the end of the last war, we saw two mighty giants rise among the nations—the United States of America and the Soviet Union. Other countries are far behind them in terms of power and technological growth. This situation has upset all the old balances. Therefore, all theories and policies based on the old balances are of little use today. Yet, I find people still talking in old terms without realizing or appreciating that nothing in the world today can remain static.

The situation in the Far East is also completely different from what it was in the past. I merely mention this to point out to you that we must be alert about the changing conditions. It is true that we must have principles; we must have ideals and objectives. But that is not enough. The application, the implementation and the working of our principles and ideals depend, to a large extent, on external circumstances. Those circumstances are hardly ever wholly in our control. We have to accept things as they are.

I have no doubt that everyone here would like to build a new world according to his heart's desire. Similarly, we also aim to go in a particular direction but it is not always possible, because we cannot ignore certain factors, much less in a democratic society. Of course, rapid changes consistent with the aims of a government can be brought about in a country even though the wishes of considerable numbers of people have to be disregarded; but such a thing is conceivable only in a particular type of political and economic set-up where one group wields supreme power. We, for instance, cannot ignore large groups. Sometimes the majority has its way, as it should. When Hon'ble Members accuse us of complacency—even of smugness—I feel that they have little understanding of how my mind or that of my colleagues' functions. Even if we were so foolish as to be complacent, the circumstances we have to face every day make it impossible for those of us who are in responsible positions to be complacent.

I cannot speak for those who are responsible for the government of other countries but I can certainly speak for my colleagues and for myself. I want to tell you that we approach our problems in all humility of spirit and with feelings utterly devoid of complacency and smugness. We feel that, however small we might be as men, our problems, those of our country and those of the world, are big. We must approach them with all the wisdom we possess and with such experience as we have. Although we have to advance step by step, we must constantly be on the alert so that we can change our step wherever necessary. We must always take counsel with others and never forget to maintain our spirit of humility.

I am anxious to seek help and guidance in every important matter that comes up before this House. Apart from such knowledge as we may have of world history, most of us have been conditioned by India's national movement and have a common background of thought and a common approach to problems. Many of us, thus conditioned, subsequently took different paths and they were entitled to do this. It was not necessary that all of us should have thought alike. Our understanding of problems—ours as well as those of the world—necessarily influenced by our background which we have to adapt to new conditions as they develop. Having once been part of the nationalist movement, we cannot possibly think of functioning negatively. Of course, negation inevitably had its place during our fight for freedom but now that we are building India anew, it is imperative that we function positively.

Hon'ble Members of the Opposition will realize that positive functioning is more difficult because one wrong move can expose the country to danger. Independence has meant added responsibility. Besides our own, we have to try and help solve problems of the world. Not that we wanted to interfere with the affairs of other countries but in the present circumstances it cannot be avoided. A multitude of political, economic and social issues demand consideration in our own country. Large numbers of these problems had been overlooked for generations but when foreign rule was removed, new problems were added to the old ones and we are supposed to solve the whole lot of them at once. I want you to remember that it is not possible to consider our troubles in a vacuum; nor is it easy to decide what is right and what is wrong; even more difficult is the proper application of what one considers right in principle. In order to do that one must have full control over the situation in the country, if not, indeed, in the world.

Our foreign policy has been criticized from various points of view. The most common criticism is that it is not a policy at all because it is too vague. Some Hon'ble Members believe that we are tied up with the Anglo-American bloc because we expect help from it. Others talk frequently of building up a 'third force' or 'third bloc'. An Hon'ble Member wants us—he says so—to align ourselves with the rival bloc. It is not that he is against an alignment as such but he would rather that we had ties with the other bloc. According to the general consensus of opinion in this matter, we should follow a policy independent of this or that bloc. You may, of course, sympathize with one or the other; that is quite another thing. To become part of a power bloc means giving up the right to have a policy of our own and following that of somebody else. Surely, that is not the kind of future any self-respecting person would like to envisage for our great country. I am not saying that we should not cooperate with others or consult them but at the same time we must follow an independent policy. It is perfectly true that no country can function in a vacuum. To achieve anything, it has to take the rest of the world into account and then decide upon its course of action. Although our foreign policy is a continuation of the stand we took during our struggle for independence, we are, sometimes, unstrained to vary it according to circumstances.

A country's foreign policy is really a collection of different policies, though they have a common basic outlook. When we deal with America or England or Russia or Japan or China or Egypt or

Indonesia, we have to deal with the peculiar circumstances that obtain in the country concerned as well as with those in each of the rest. No single broad rule can apply in every case, because the nature of our relationship varies with each country. The only rule we can lay down is that we shall try to be friendly with all the countries.

Finally, a foreign policy is not just a declaration of fine principles; nor is it a directive to tell the world how to behave. It is conditioned and controlled by a country's own strength. If the policy does not take the capacity of the country into account, it cannot be followed up. If a country talks bigger than it is, it brings little credit to itself. It is easy for you or me to lay down beautiful maxims; but if that is done by a government or nations, it would probably come to nothing. In any case, what do we achieve except the satisfaction of having made fine speeches?

The strength which limits or, at any rate, conditions the foreign policy of a country may be military, financial or, if I may use the word, moral. It is obvious that India has neither military nor financial strength. Furthermore, we have no desire to—and we cannot impose our will on others. We are, however, anxious to prevent catastrophes and wars and, where possible, to help in the general progress of humanity. We do express our opinion and work for our goals with the limited strength that we have but if we adopt a policy which we are not in a position to implement, we would be discrediting ourselves in the eyes of other nations and be dubbed irresponsible. It is difficult for me to praise or even defend the foreign policy we are pursuing, for I have had a great deal to do with it. I hope I am not being vain when I say that our policy has, indeed, secured us the friendship of a large number of countries. I am confident that today there is no country which is actually hostile to us. Naturally, some countries are more friendly than others but those who are occasionally critical of us do not harbour any permanent resentment against us. We owe this to the policy we are pursuing and the manner in which we are pursuing it. We have tried not to join in the new diplomatic game of maligning, defaming and cursing other countries. That does not necessarily mean that we agree with what they say or do; we may not agree but merely shouting against them does not help, apart from the fact that it is indecorous, too. We have to deal not only with political and economic considerations but also with a large number of imponderables like fear for, for instance. It is alarming to see fear gripping some of the largest and most powerful countries in the world. It is heartening—and I think it is true—that although we cannot be compared with the great countries of the world in terms of power, yet, if I may say so, we as a people, are less influenced by the fear psychosis. Of course, some people may attribute this to our ignorance of the facts. Facts certainly have to be reckoned with; but imponderable things also come in the way of humanity and, if we are to deal with them effectively, the least we can do is to adopt a manner that would help rather than hinder. That is to say, we must refrain from merely running down other countries. We can certainly express our opinion when it is necessary; we can say that we do not agree with a country or that certain things are, in our opinion, wrong; but we must not go farther than that.

Mention has been made of a 'third force'. I have not been able to understand quite what it means. If by the term is meant a power bloc, military or other, I am afraid I do not consider it desirable, apart from the fact that it is not feasible either. The biggest countries today are small compared with the two giants. It would be absurd for a number of countries in Asia to come together and call themselves a third force or a third power in a military sense. It may, however, have a meaning in another sense. Instead of calling it a third force or a third bloc, it can be called a third area, an area which—let us put it negatively first—does not want war, works for peace in a positive way and believes in cooperation. I should like my country to work for that. Indeed, we have tried to do so but the idea of a third bloc or a third force inevitably hinders our work. It frightens people, especially those we wish to approach. Those countries, who do not want to align themselves with either of the two powerful blocs and who are willing to work for the cause of peace, should by all means come together; and we, on our part, should do all we can to make this possible. That is our general policy and I think we should follow it without too much of shouting. I am not afraid of shouting but we want to achieve certain things and shouting may embarrass the countries we have to approach.

The Far Eastern problem is on the agenda of UNO and is due for discussion at its next session. I cannot say now what our representatives may have to do then, because so much depends on the circumstances which may develop in the course of the next two weeks or so. All I can say is that they will broadly try to follow the policy we are pursuing. What I wanted was to refer briefly to the Korean Resolution which we sponsored at the United Nations. Ever since the Korean war started, we have been very much concerned with it, not because we wanted to interfere or bully others but because we were perhaps in a position to help more than any other country could. Our relations with the countries in conflict were cordial. This was not true of other countries and, therefore, it was difficult for them to do anything. We realized our peculiar responsibility to the poor people of Korea and strongly felt that the utter ruin and destruction in Korea should be stopped at any cost.

I do not want to go into past history; but several steps were taken by us which did not yield immediate results but which, it was subsequently realized, were the right steps. The very first thing that strikes us about the situation in the Far East and about which we are all agreed is that it is unreal and that unless we deal with that great country, China, we can do nothing effective. We, therefore, recognized the People's Republic of China right from the beginning and urged other countries in UNO and elsewhere to do the same regardless of whether or not they liked the policies of China. The fact of China is patent enough and not to recognize it was and is a fundamental breach—I do not know if 'breach' is the right word—and contrary to the very spirit and charter of the United Nations. Nobody can say that UNO was supposed only to represent countries subscribing to its policy. That, unfortunately, is the trend that has gradually come to exist at UNO. The result is that a country as tremendous as China has been treated as though it did not exist and a small island off the coast of China is accepted as representing China. That is very extraordinary. My contention is that this fact is the crux of the situation that has developed in the Far East. The non-recognition of realities naturally leads to artificial policies programmes and that is exactly what is happening.

We had been in continuous touch with the Government of China, the U.K. and the U.S.A. as well as those of other countries a few months before we sponsored the Korean Resolution at UNO. We were very anxious not to take any step which would embarrass us or some other party because that would only have made it more difficult for us to help. Occasionally we informed one party about the general outlook and point of view of another. We were in a position to do this because the heads of our missions abroad made it a point to keep in touch with the countries they were accredited to. That is why we were able to frame our resolution largely in accordance with the Chinese viewpoint as we thought it to be. I do not say it was a hundred per cent representative of the Chinese viewpoint but it was certainly an attempt to represent it. The burden of it was that in the matter of the exchange of prisoners, the Geneva Convention should be followed.

Let me not be understood to mean that we were committed to the statements made by our representatives to those of China. We only tried to find out how China would like things to be done. It is, of course, not possible for a party, however big, to have its own way in every respect and we did not overlook this aspect of the problem when we framed our resolution.

Now, another factor to be borne in mind is that this resolution dealt only with the problem of exchange of prisoners. Those who want to know why it did not deal with the question of a cease fire forget the facts of the case. All of us know that truce negotiations were being carried on at Panmunjon for a year and a half before this. After great difficulty an agreement was arrived at in every matter except that of the exchange of prisoners. Obviously, the primary aim of the truce negotiations was a cease fire and that was the first consequence of an agreement. Therefore, we took up only the still unsettled question of exchange of prisoners, subject to the settlement of which a cease fire had already been agreed upon. The principles which governed the resolution had been drawn up in great detail before it was actually framed. Those principles were communicated to the People's Government of China for their opinion early last November. A fortnight passed—I am speaking from memory about the period—and we were told that our communication was being carefully considered. I might say that on many occasions we had been encouraged by various governments, including the Chinese Government, to persevere in our endeavours for peace. It was not our desire to thrust ourselves where we were not wanted. It is true that the Chinese Government had not committed itself to cooperating with us but it had not refused to do so either and we felt that we might safely go ahead. It may have been a wrong decision but we made considerable progress and things were developing. There was no great difference between the principles we had drawn up and the final resolution. Anyhow, we sent the latter to the parties concerned and a few days elapsed—I forget how many—before we actually proposed the resolution. As the House will remember the first reaction to it was one of disapproval and an immediate rejection on the part of the United States Government. Till then we had no idea what the reaction of the Chinese and Soviet Governments would be. They, at length, informed us that they did not approve of it. Naturally, we were greatly disappointed. What were we to do then? Some people are of the opinion that we should have withdrawn the resolution at that stage. It is true that the mere passing of a resolution has little meaning when the aim is an agreed settlement. We realized that but, on the other hand, there were not many alternatives. Before we put our resolution to UNO there were a number of others, all of which were, if I may say so, aggressive and would certainly have made the situation much worse. We did not approve of them and would have voted against them had the occasion presented itself. A resolution proposed by the Soviet Union or by some other country of Eastern Europe laid stress on the importance of an immediate cease fire. We should have welcomed a cease fire but it was absolutely clear that the resolution would not be passed. Many countries felt that if the issue of prisoners could not be resolved after a whole year's argument, in spite of the pressure of a war, it would never be resolved even if a cease fire took place. Therefore, they preferred to continue negotiations till all the issues could be decided once and for all to the satisfaction of all parties concerned. This was the difficulty so far as our resolution was concerned. Furthermore, it had been very largely supported but some of the principal parties concerned unfortunately did not agree to it. As a matter of fact, the resolution was not ours but one that had been sponsored by the House. We had to adopt a realistic course but we did not know whether or not we should withdraw the resolution and let matters drift. The resolution, however, was not a mandate but in the nature of a proposal and we thought it might possibly help in the further consideration of the subject.

May I say one other thing in this connection? I understand that some Members have disapproved of our action in sending a medical unit to Korea. We sent this unit to Korea purely for medical relief work and, I must say, it has done remarkably well, gaining for itself, in addition, some very valuable experience. Of its kind, it is one of the best units in the world today. It did not take part in the fighting because, though we are prepared to give medical succour, we have nothing to do with the war as such.

I am afraid I have taken a long time over this matter and I should like to pass on to another subject. I am told that my friend, Acharya Narendra Dev, whose opinion I value very greatly, expressed himself in despondent tones about the economic situation in the country and said that the Five Year Plan is not likely to succeed.

It is not easy to take an overall view of the economic situation in the country and sum it up in a few sentences. None of us can take a complacent view of it but the point is how to overcome our difficulties in regard to food, land, industry and, ultimately, better production and better distribution. All this was considered at great length when the Five Year Plan was formulated.

The main virtue of the Five Year Plan is that we have come to grips with our problems for the first time. Theoretical approaches have their place and are, I suppose, essential but a theory must be tempered with reality. In this instance, we have to realize that we cannot go far beyond our resources. And I think that in the Five Year Plan we have come to realistic conclusions, not forgetting our objectives. I should like the pace at which we are making progress to increase and, indeed, I shall be very happy if Hon'ble Members would suggest practical measures to achieve this end.

I believe that the food situation has improved considerably and I am sure that, of the various factors responsible, government policy is certainly one. People refer to the famine or near-famine conditions that prevailed in Rayalaseema last year and do in parts of Karnataka and Bombay State this year. They are right. I would, however, like the House to remember that though we use the word 'famine' today—I do not like using the word—we do so in an entirely different sense than we did in the old days when the British were here. Then, a famine meant millions of people dying like flies. Whereas, if a person dies of hunger or from other causes today, there is an outcry of protest. There is, at the present moment, a new political consciousness and I am very glad about it. In the Bengal famine of 1942-43, 35 lakhs of people died. And I do suggest that the situation is vastly different now. I mention this because a foreign visitor went to the famine areas the other day. He said: 'You talk about famine in these areas! I do not find any people dead or dying. This is not a famine.' Doubtless, he had got his conception of famine from British days.

It is no small achievement that in spite of tremendous natural calamities, such as the failure of the rains and drought, which affected vast areas, the state governments, with the cooperation of the central government, have prevented the situation from deteriorating and have controlled it by giving work or doles. Unfortunately, they could not always prevent misery and hunger. The government of Bombay State, for instance, recognizes its responsibility of providing food in scarcity areas whether it is through work—which some Hon'ble Members must have seen in Rayalaseema and in the Karnataka areas—or other means. Two years ago, a huge administrative venture was undertaken with considerable success in Bihar. Unfortunately, we cannot deal satisfactorily with accidents, such as the failure of the monsoons. As I said, natural calamities have done considerable damage but we are building up our strength so as to be able to deal with the situation. It is difficult to cope with great disasters; but we should be able to overcome natural calamities in the course of the next two or three years. By then, I think, it should be possible—I dare not give any promise—to become more or less self-sufficient in food.

Some people say that we are always talking about agriculture to the neglect of industry. I attach the greatest importance to the development of industry but I doubt whether any real industrial development can take place in India till we have a firm basis for our agriculture. Of course, we must make progress on all fronts. The nation's economic growth is no simple matter. We have to plan the nation's savings and long term investments with great care. Saving for future generations means exerting some pressure on the present generation. It means, if I may say so, a certain austerity. It is all very well for an authoritarian government to dictate a policy it considers good for the country; but it is not so easy for a democratic country to do so. It is difficult to people who starve today to have jam tomorrow. Even great countries like the United Kingdom and the U.S.A. took 150 years to build themselves up. Those Hon'ble. Members who are acquainted with history know that this meant extreme suffering for their working classes. The proprietors themselves were not men who liked luxury; they were austere people who saved so that their industrial apparatus might grow and they did this at a terrible cost. It was not difficult to do this in England where Parliament at that time was controlled by a small group of propertied people. Conditions were different in America where there were vast areas. We are differently situated in many ways; for one thing, we have an enormous population which grows every year and which has to be maintained. Also, we have adult suffrage in a democratic set-up.

Some people suggest that we should have a capital levy in order to save for investment. Others want to improve the general standard of living which, apart from the psychological good it may do, will not gain much for us. What really counts is the increase in our rate of production. To build up an adequate apparatus for an increase in future production, you naturally have to save today. To do this and to solve our other problems, we must have definite industrial, financial and land policies. Therefore, we have inaugurated the Five Year Plan and the great point in its favour is that it has made people plan-conscious generally. It has also made us aware of the basic realities, such as the true nature of our position and resources. Of course, we can vary the Plan whenever we like, although it is dangerous to think of changing it constantly.

The House will remember that in the President's Address there is a reference to the welfare state. He has also said that the real test of progress lies in the growth of employment and in the ultimate ending of unemployment. Obviously, there can be no welfare state if there is unemployment. Anyhow, the unemployed themselves are not parties to the welfare state but just outside its pale. To realize the ideal of a welfare state requires hard work, tremendous effort and cooperation from us and I appeal to this House and to the country to give us that cooperation.

Finally, I should like to say a few words about the Praja Parishad agitation. My friend, the Hon'ble Acharya Narendra Dev, referred to it and said that in his opinion it was a wholly communal agitation initiated by those who had been supporters of the former Maharaja and the landed gentry. He also suggested that an investigation should be made to find out why this agitation, which was primarily a class agitation, should have affected other people. I agree that there should be an investigation but we must remember that some aspects of this question may not be as well known as others. To understand the significance of the agitation, we must distinguish its purely economic aspect from the other, which is political, constitutional and, perhaps, even international.

As the House knows, an official commission, with the Chief Justice of the State—a very responsible and able officer—as its president, has been appointed to deal with economic matters. Had the commission been non-official, it should immediately have been condemned as not being representative. I submit to the House that it was hardly possible for the Kashmir Government to appoint a commission constituted by the very people who were against the former. If it had appointed non-officials, other non-officials might have said: 'These are your party men'. I think the Kashmir Government very wisely appointed a purely official commission whose findings it can accept and give effect to.

Many things are said about other matters which are of a political nature. The Hon'ble Member who spoke before me said something about our National Flag. The Constituent Assembly of Kashmir has repeatedly said that the Union Flag is the supreme flag of Kashmir State as it is of the rest of India and it has, therefore, been displayed from time to time. It is interesting to note that many of those who talk about their respect for the National Flag have, in the past, openly declared their intention to replace it by their own party flag. Communal organizations, be they in Jammu or in Delhi, have seldom shown respect for our flag and now they exploit it in order to gain other people's goodwill for this agitation. My chief grievance and sorrow in this matter is that legitimate things have been exploited for unworthy objectives.

> **There is nobody here who does not want the state of Jammu and Kashmir to have the closest association with India. There is no difference of opinion on this objective but the way that has been pursued has made its realization very difficult. Our union with Jammu and Kashmir State can only be based on the wishes of the people of Jammu and Kashmir; we are not going to achieve a union at the point of the bayonet.**

Our policy, therefore, should be to try and win them over instead of frightening them. We must not disturb the status of Jammu and Kashmir State but let it remain a separate entity in the Union of India. The accession of Jammu and Kashmir State was identical with that of any other state in India, although it was thought at the time that there might be a variation in the degree to which states would be integrated with India in the future. We certainly did not think it possible that all the states could be integrated with India the same degree. I am talking of 1947 or perhaps early 1948. When Jammu and Kashmir State acceded, it did so as fully as any other state, so that the question of partial accession does not arise. I should especially like to point this out to people who talk about the reference to the United Nations on the possibility of plebiscite. This does not detract from Kashmir's accession to India in any way. The accession is complete. Accession must, however, be distinguished from integration. Jammu and Kashmir State acceded first and then integrated as the other States had done and in the same degree. However, the late Sardar Vallabhbhai Patel wisely followed a policy of fuller integration for the other States; but in the nature of things, we could not follow a similar policy in Kashmir where a war, which had almost become an international issue, was going on.

Last year, the question of further accession arose—not as such but in connection with certain other arrangements with Kashmir. The agreement between the Governments of India and Kashmir had to do with a number of things to which this House agreed and the implementation of which was tantamount to further degree of integration.

We are sometimes asked why that agreement has not been fully implemented yet. The question is apparently justified but the fact is that the Jammu and Kashmir Government is, even more than the others, an autonomous government. It is up to it to shoulder the responsibility for the situations it may have to face. If something happens in Bengal or Bombay or Madras, we can only give advice because they are autonomous states and must deal with the local situation themselves. The same is true of Kashmir also. We cannot order the Government of Kashmir about or foist a timetable on it. We leave it to it to judge its own affairs and take such action as it deems fit.

In view of the war and the other events which have given it an international significance, Kashmir had to be treated as a special case. The Jammu Praja Parishad agitation started the very day the agreement between the Governments of India and Kashmir was given effect to in part and when the new head of the state, the Sadar-e-Riyasat, elected by the Kashmir Assembly and approved by our President, arrived in Jammu. The Parishad workers tried to interfere with the welcome given to the Yuvaraj and tore the triumphal arch down. That was how it started but it has continued ever since. Had the Kashmir Government been anxious to implement the rest of the agreement, it could not have done so without dealing with the existing situation first. Its hands were thus tied to some extent because of the agitation. The history of Kashmir, going back a little over a hundred years, bears evidence that the state has had to experience repeated conquest, transfer, purchase and so on. The Jammu province of the state was most important from a political and other points of view just as Hyderabad was in the old days when the Muslim community dominated. Now, things are completely different.

Naturally, Hyderabad has changed. The feudal order that existed has gone, taking with it the big jagirs and inevitably causing considerable distress among those who depended on that feudal order as also among those who depended on the armed forces which were disbanded. I cannot compare the two; there are very great differences. But there are resemblances, too, because both Jammu and Hyderabad had dominant groups which resisted the political changes that were taking place and disapproved of the new land reform. Also, the background of the economic difficulties of both has some common features.

The agitation soon assumed a violent form. I have here with me particulars of over a hundred officers of the Jammu and Kashmir Government—Deputy Commissioners, Superintendents of Police, schoolmasters and constables—who have been injured. Numerous school buildings have been ransacked, furniture and other things destroyed and small Government offices and treasuries looted. This is a curious kind of 'peaceful' satyagraha.

However, the Kashmir Government has to deal with the situation but the agitation will, as the House must realize, have unfortunate repercussions. The demand of the Parishad is the complete integration of Jammu with India but if Jammu were to have its wishes carried out and Kashmir were left out of the picture it would obviously amount to the disruption of the state.

This is an extraordinary attitude to adopt and it can certainly aid and comfort the enemies of India. I am amazed when responsible people in India support an agitation which can only result in injury to India as a whole and the people of Jammu inevitably. If the agitation succeeds, it will be the people of Jammu who will suffer. I had occasion to read reports of some of the speeches made in the course of the agitation. Appeals were made to subvert the Government of India so that a different policy could be followed. Everybody has a right to ask for his own government but such demands on the part of the Jammu Parishad were merely an excuse for something bigger. Whether or not the demands are feasible is a matter which is being discussed at Geneva at the moment. Naturally, we are anxious that this conflict should end, normality should return and legitimate grievances be removed. I am certain that the Kashmir Government is as anxious as we are but how are we to decide complicated constitutional and international problems? It is difficult for us to discuss them with other people because we have to consult so many parties. We are supposed to discuss these problems in the market place with the Praja Parishad people! I just do not understand how this can be done.

Principal Devaprasad Ghosh suggested that the question of the aggressors and the plebiscite in Kashmir should be discussed at Geneva. I had discussions with the leaders of the Jan Sangh about how the aggressors can be got rid of. However, the question involves military matters, political matters, constitutional and national matters. Since Pakistan is the aggressor, the question involves the entire problem of war and peace between India and Pakistan. Let us realize the nature and depth of the problem and discuss it dispassionately. By connecting it with the Jammu Parishad agitation, we are giving it a communal outlook and that,

I think, is fatal for the whole country. It will disrupt the country and put an end to our freedom. And there is such a wide gap between the two approaches that one cannot be too optimistic at the possibility of an agreement.

My honourable friend Dr Kunzru[38] showed grave concern and expressed his disapproval of the fact that certain persons in the Punjab had been arrested and detained in the course of the past week or ten days. I believe about a dozen or so have been arrested. I do not know whether Dr Kunzru meant that under no circumstances should a person be so arrested and detained or whether he thought that in the peculiar circumstances now prevailing in the Punjab this should not have been done.

If he means the former, I would submit that it is difficult to agree with him and, indeed, I cannot do so; nor can any other country agree with him in a final sense. Of course, it is a thing which should not normally be done and I hope it is not normally done; but it is done under the stress of special circumstances. When the Punjab became a source of supply to the people of Jammu, the latter used all kinds of methods to excite the people there and to create trouble on communal lines. Their techniques are still being employed in Delhi and in some cities of western U.P. processions are being taken out with the shouting of explosive slogans. Surely, that can lead to a very grave situation. Some of the trouble occurred almost within a stone's throw of the cease fire line. Since the Pakistan forces were on the other side, we were anxious that our army should keep completely out of this. In fact, the disturbances were planned presumably to excite the army. I know that the Punjab Government was gravely concerned for weeks because the ultimate responsibility was theirs, whether they did anything or not.

I am sorry to have taken up so much of your time but the subjects before the House in connection with the President's Address cover not only India but the world and the responsibility

---

[38] Kashmiri freedom fighter who was also a member of the Constituent Assembly of India.

largely falls upon us, as a Parliament, to face our problems with dignity and restraint, always keeping our principles before us and always in a spirit of humility.

~

Freedom and Licence

(Speech at the All-India Newspaper Editors' Conference, New Delhi, 3 December, 1950.)

Mr President and friends, you have referred to me and addressed me as Prime Minister and, perhaps, you have also invited me in that capacity. Nevertheless, I would like to speak to you, not as Prime Minister, although I cannot be rid of that fact, but informally, as friends meeting together in earnest converse to consider difficult and baffling problems, for we do meet under the stress of heavy circumstances today.

Now, if this is so, it is easy enough for us or for anybody else to start criticizing people and condemning nations. But the whole point is: what are we driving at? If we have a clear objective before us, are we going towards it by what we say or do or are we moving away from it? That is the test. In normal times, it does not much matter—within limits, of course—what one says or does, because it cannot do very much harm; and even if it does harm, we can always pull ourselves together. But in times of crisis, in times of grave emergency, what is said or done does matter very much: a wrong word or a wrong action may have very far-reaching results.

The press, it is repeatedly said, performs a very essential function in our lives today, especially in the life of democratic countries. In other places, that function is performed under authoritarian direction, while in democratic countries it is supposed to say just what it likes within the limitations of the law which are—I must say—pretty wide. Now, this is a tremendous burden. The burden, of course, is inevitable when power or privilege comes to a group. We won our independence and we take pride in it. But, obviously, independence or freedom is not a one-sided affair; it carries enormous responsibilities, such as that of defending that independence when it is attacked—defending it, not only from external attack but, what is even more important, from an internal weakening.

After all, the thing that a nation must beware of—more than external danger—is internal rot. Freedom carries with it the obvious responsibility, which every one realizes, of defending it from external attack. But, ultimately, the other responsibility is more important and that is to maintain the inner strength, the morale, the self-confidence of a nation, which can be done only by following what I roughly call the right advice and, more especially, developing the habit of dispassionate thought and the calm consideration of problems. This becomes even more important in times of crisis, when people are apt to become excited and hysterical and are inclined to believe every vague rumour.

Newspapers are, of course, of all kinds and in India there are thousands of them. There are responsible newspapers; there are newspapers which are sometimes responsible, sometimes not; there are newspapers which are more irresponsible than responsible; and there are some sheets which seem to excel only in flights of imagination and other acts of irresponsibility. Fortunately, the latter are not important. In the old days, it was or at least was thought to be the function of the government to suppress the newspapers that had an evil tendency, in the opinion of the government. That, of course, is an utterly wrong approach, because you cannot cure the evil by trying to suppress it.

What, then, are we to do? For, sometimes, the evil may grow and become dangerous to public welfare. Obviously, the right way is for an organization like yours to interest itself in it directly, not, of course, in the sense of punishing people—there is no question of punishing—but of forming such a strong body of opinion among those who are responsible for the newspapers that any back-slider can be pulled up; or, at any rate, it can be made known to the public that the person concerned is a back-slider and is not acting rightly. I think that is very important, because while on the one hand the main organs of the Indian press have shown a fairly high standard of responsibility in dealing with news or situations generally, on the other there are some periodicals which amaze me by their utter irresponsibility. No doubt, people read them and, no doubt, they are affected by them. How we are going to deal with this matters. It concerns the wider question of privilege and power having to bear responsibility. Mr Stanley Baldwin, the Prime Minister of England, once became angry with the press in England and said that the press had the harlot's privilege and power without responsibility. That was an extreme way of putting the matter but the point is that when we have power or right, inevitably an obligation follows that right. You cannot separate the two.

We, who have been fighting for our rights and have finally achieved them, are apt to forget that a right by itself is incomplete and, in fact, cannot last long if the obligations which accompany that right are forgotten by the nation or by a greater part of it. Whether as individuals or citizens or groups, we still think too much in terms of rights and privileges and too little in terms of obligations. That weakens a nation and we become then merely critics and complain without anything constructive to contribute. That applies to the nation as a whole but much more so to the press. That is to say, the press fought for its own freedom from governmental interference in the old days and, gradually, step by step it has achieved wider freedom. I think I can say that whatever our other failings might be—by 'our' I mean the Government's—at the present moment the amount of freedom of expression that is allowed to or indulged in by the press can hardly be exceeded in any country in the world.

I shall be quite frank with you. Much that appears because of that freedom seems to me exceedingly dangerous. To my mind, the freedom of the press is not just a slogan from the larger point of view but it is an essential attribute of the democratic process. I have no doubt that even if the government dislikes the liberties taken by the press and considers them dangerous, it is

wrong to interfere with the freedom of the press. By imposing restrictions you do not change anything; you merely suppress the public manifestation of certain things, thereby causing the idea and thought underlying them to spread further. Therefore, I would rather have a completely free press with all the dangers involved in the wrong use of that freedom than a suppressed or regulated press.

Without responsibility, freedom gradually becomes something very near licence. Licence is a vague word and I do not like it; but it is being used in this connection and I can think of no better word at the moment. Licence ultimately means mental disintegration; and if there is mental disintegration in the body politic, obviously it affects every limb of it. That applies to the newspapers also. If, with the freedom they have, the element of licence and utter irresponsibility increases then not only will it endanger their freedom but injure their reputation. We should have freedom by all means but we should try to maintain a certain integrity of approach in public activities, including the press. Of course, we know that newspapermen and journalists of the past and in the present have laid down in high terms what the press should be and I have no doubt that responsible newspapermen, at any rate, are always trying to reach that standard. Anyhow, it seems to me that the only right approach to it is for newspapermen and their organization to tackle the problem and it is not within the competence of an external agency to do so, even though that agency is the government. They should raise their standards themselves, not by punishment—because they are not an executive branch of the government—but by making it clear to their erring brethren that what they do is bad. I have noticed that when certain periodicals behave in an irresponsible way, I seldom find any criticism of their conduct in the other periodicals. I know it is a bad thing for newspapers to call one another names; nor do I wish to encourage controversy between newspapermen. What I mean is that a responsible body has the right to pull up any member of that profession, if he is flagrantly wrong. Of course, every person has the right to express his views and I am not denying that; I am censuring only the utter irresponsibility and the vulgarity that newspapers of no great repute may descend to. I think such a body should firmly—politely if you like but firmly—make it clear that they do not approve of this kind of thing. Thus, they will be giving a lead to the public in this respect.

I mentioned vulgarity. It is an odd world we live in, a rapidly changing world. We all hope that, in spite of difficulties and disasters, something good will ultimately emerge; but the one very grave and disheartening feature of the present day is a rapid fall in mental and moral standards all over the world. We disintegrate; we gradually go to pieces. Ultimately, we become, because of the process of disintegration, somewhat neurotic and hysterical and quite unable to judge anything. After all, unless we have certain values in life, life becomes rather empty; unless we have certain values in our public and in our mental conduct, it becomes difficult to see whither we are going and what we are trying to do. Great countries cannot live from hand to mouth, so far as standards and basic objectives are concerned. Those of you who have had personal experience of the last thirty years or so of India's history will have noticed periods in this history in which, one might say, a high moral tone prevailed among the people. The people are still the same. They are not different. They have the same failings and the same virtues. It is not easy to change an entire nation suddenly. But you can make them think of their virtues and strength or of their weaknesses and railings. Well, during these past thirty years, we did, I think, in our public life attain, often enough, high standards—unusually high standards. That was due to a great man who led us and ho set those standards himself but the fact remains that we did attain them and because of that it is all the more noticeable and distressing to find such low standards at present. We have to fight against these. Vulgarity, however, is a world phenomenon and by no means peculiarly Indian. But, anyhow, we have to deal with it. Life, after all, may be considered from many points of view political, economic and other; these are very important but surely there is something beyond all this; otherwise, everything that you gain by political thought and economic welfare, would be without significance. It is most distressing to see the gradual passing of what was gracious in life and instead a gradual extension and increase of what is vulgar. An individual may be good or bad, vulgar or otherwise. But it is a dangerous thing for a country to go down the scale of values in this way. In this matter, the press can perform a most important function. It can render much help in combating vulgarity. The views of newspapers on political issues may not be accepted. I rather doubt myself if newspapers have any very great influence on political opinion. They give the news, of course; but I rather doubt if they have any great influence politically. You have seen in other countries—democratic countries—how a great number of newspapers have supported one party while another has won the elections. So, it appears that newspapers do not have the same effect on public opinion as people imagine they do. I am sure they wield tremendous power, not only through day-to-day news but through the colour they give it, through the restraint or looseness of expression, through vulgarity or its absence. The daily dose, regularly given, affects the reader's mind. If you tell him to do this or that, he may resist; but the slight daily dose, if it is right, improves his mind and, if it is wrong, corrupts it. There is a certain lack of social conscience in this country in spite of our high ideals. I react strongly against the idea of regimentation anywhere and much more so in a vast country like India, where there are so many different approaches, so many different aspects, to life. But I also stand against the loose and incorrect behaviour of the people their lack of discipline. This weakens us physically but, what worse, it weakens us psychologically, too. In this matter also, I think, the press can help tremendously, not only by building up a better and a higher social conscience but also a code of social behaviour in the little things of life. We tend to think that we need not worry about the little things of life because we are preoccupied with the big things of life. That is utterly and fundamentally wrong. If you are, let us say, wedded or attracted to the ideal of truth and beauty, you cannot follow that ideal if you deal with the ugly and untruthful in the small things of life. We take pride in saying that the civilization of the West is a material one and is opposed to ours which is spiritual. Having said so, we indulge in things which totally lack the normal social proprieties. We say we are above them but, as a matter of fact, it is not quite clear where the question of spirituality comes in. I do not believe that a person who ignores the small things of life, the small truths, the small decencies, the small pleasantnesses, the small graciousness, can undertake anything big in a big way.

It is not a question of show or, should I say, ostentation. Of course, ostentation itself is the height of vulgarity; but the deliberate rejection of all refinement can also be a deliberate and rather aggressive way of saying 'oh, we don't care for the fineries of life and, therefore, we go about, in unwashed condition and with our clothes and our appearance unkempt'.

I referred just now, in the few words I said in Hindi, to the news that was splashed in big headlines in the morning papers today. It was about the possibility of my going to Washington and said that I had been summoned there for discussions. Now, as far as I know, there is absolutely no foundation for all this. It is only excitement on the part of some people and a search for a way out or a remedy for the world's ills that leads them to these flights of imagination. This particular thing may not do much harm, although it does a little always. Even so, I beg of you, more especially in these days, to be careful. I will see that steps are taken about the development of a liaison machinery between the press and the Government, more especially the External Affairs Ministry of the Government. It is very desirable and, so far as we are concerned, we should like to help in every way. It is a difficult matter, of course, always to know where to draw the line in regard to matters which are considered secret and which, if they leak out, would embarrass us greatly in our relations with other countries. Now, it all depends ultimately, if I may say so quite frankly, on the measure of cooperation received from the press in keeping secrecy. You can, course, count on every cooperation from us.

We are meeting here today in the very extraordinary

circumstances of the world and there are very grave crises facing us. I confess that the only way I can see myself approaching these big questions is in a spirit of deep earnestness and a great deal of humility. There are big questions affecting the future of the world, affecting the future happiness or misery or destruction of millions of people and no man can consider them without deep misgivings about his own capacity to show the right path and I am quite frank with you about this matter. I rather doubt if any country, even the biggest of them all, can have an adequate sense of direction. The matter is too complicated, too big and all we can do is, first of all, to have an earnest desire for something. What is that something? We will surely find, in the immediate context of today, that that something is peace. There lie many other things besides. But today peace is most important. If that is so, then how are we to attain peace or, at any rate, help in realizing it and avoiding that terrible catastrophe—war? Surely, apart from any particular proposal that a country may put forward, a great deal depends on the basic approach. If you want peace among different countries, it is hardly a sensible or a logical thing to go about slanging one another, irritating one another, pointing out the faults and errors and sins of one another. Your argument may be perfectly valid and you may be justified in putting it forward. But my point is that the argument does not lead to the atmosphere of peace. It leads to the closing up of the people's minds and when minds are closed they become impervious to reason. Therefore, it seems to me, what is important today is that we should stop this business of running down one another and keep our feelings within ourselves and then try to find some way of stopping the rot.

The next step would be to consider these problems in this slightly new atmosphere and try to find a solution, even if it is a temporary one. The next step would, in that case, be towards a more durable solution. No country must endanger the world's peace merely on grounds of prestige or anger. That is all I can say. I feel and am quite sure that vast numbers of people, every country all over the world, desire peace. Personally, I prepared to go a step further and say that there is no government in the world which really desires war. There are, of course, governments which may be impelled by circumstances to believe that war is inevitable. That is a different thing and somehow we get entangled in a net and thus, without any desire, we are forced to go to war. Whether that is an example of determinism in human affairs, I do not know; but I do think that even individual in his individual capacity as also in larger groups, including nations, should fight against anything they consider evil and not submit to the fatal idea of determinism and thus allow themselves to be overwhelmed by disaster. So, I hope that the present-day India will throw all her weight in favour of a dispassionate consideration of the problems of peace.

We here and elsewhere are apt to say that this country is good or bad, as though countries were solid blocks which are good or bad. They consist of millions of human beings—very decent human beings, very peaceful human beings.

Governments may go wrong and more so politicians. But do not ever talk of countries and peoples as bad. It is misleading to talk like that.

There is a great deal of common humanity in all of us, in all the countries, although we may differ outwardly a great deal. Let us encourage that common humanity and that friendliness and let us not lose our heads, whatever happens.

~

Children of the World

(From The Unity of India*)*

What a troublesome person Shankar[39] is! Every few days I get a reminder from him that I must write something for the Children's Number or else he himself appears and looks at me with reproachful eyes. Here I am trying hard to get through a

---

[39] Kesava Shankar Pillai, considered the father of political cartooning in India. He also founded the Children's Book Trust.

great deal of work before I leave for England and on top of this I am expected to write articles! Shankar seems to forget that most of my writing has been done in the leisure of prison. Since I came out of that small prison and entered the larger prison of office, my freedom to read and write has been taken away from me. I cannot do many of the things that I would like to do and I have to do much that I intensely dislike.

I suppose Shankar knows all this but he has got an idea into his head that something from me must appear in the Children's Number. Well, I am bound to confess that I like the idea of a Children's Number very much and I should like to help it grow. I liked the last number and I am almost sure that the next number will be better. What pleases me most of all is the great interest that children in distant countries have taken in this venture. I was surprised and delighted to visit an exhibition where hundreds of pictures and cartoons sent for Shankar's Children's Number were exhibited.

As I looked at these pictures, I thought of the vast army of children all over the world, outwardly different in many ways, speaking different languages, wearing different kinds of clothes and yet so very like one another. If you bring them together, they play or quarrel. But even their quarrelling is some kind of play. They do not think of differences amongst themselves, differences of class or caste or colour or status. They are wiser than their fathers and mothers. As they grow up, unfortunately, their natural wisdom is often eclipsed by the teaching and behaviour of their elders. At school they learn many things which are no doubt useful but they gradually forget that the essential thing is to be human and kind and playful and to make life richer for ourselves and others. We live in a wonderful world that is full of beauty and charm and adventure. There is no end to the adventure that we can have if only we seek them with our eyes open. So many people seem to go about their life's business with their eyes shut. Indeed, they object to other people keeping their eyes open. Unable to play themselves, they dislike the play of others.

Our own country is a little world in itself with an infinite variety and places for us to discover. I have travelled a great deal in this country and I have grown in years. And yet I have not seen many parts of the country we love so much and seek to serve. I wish I had more time, so that I could visit the odd nooks and corners of India. I would like to go there in the company of bright young children whose minds are opening out with wonder and curiosity as they make new discoveries. I should like to go with them, not so much to the great cities of India as to the mountains and the forests and the great rivers and the old monuments, all of which tell us something of India's story. I would like them to discover for themselves that they can play about in the snow in some parts of India and also see other places where tropical forests flourish. Such a trip with children would be a voyage of discovery of the beautiful trees of our forests and hillsides and the flowers that grace the changing seasons and bring life and colour to us. We would watch the birds and try to recognize them and make friends with them. But the most exciting adventure would be to go to the forests and see the wild animals, both the little ones and the big. Foolish people go with a gun and kill them and thus put an end to something that was beautiful. It is far more interesting and amusing to wander about without a gun or any other weapon and to find that wild animals are not afraid and can be approached. Animals have keener instincts than man. If a man goes to them with murder in his heart, they are afraid of him and run away. But if he has any love for animals, they realize that he is a friend and do not mind him. If you are full of fear yourself, then the animal is afraid, too, and might attack you in self-defence. The fearless person is seldom, if ever, attacked.

Perhaps, that lesson might be applied to human beings also. If we meet other people in a friendly way, they also become friendly. But if we are afraid of them or if we show our dislike to them, then they behave in the same manner.

These are simple truths which the world has known for ages. But even so, the world forgets and the people of one country hate and fear the people of another country; and because they are afraid, they are sometimes foolish enough to fight each other.

Children should be wiser. At any rate, the children who read Shankar's Children's Number are expected to be more sensible.

~

Interview with the Prime Minister

(*From* The Mind of Mr Nehru: An Interview with R.K. Karanjia)

The Gandhian Heritage

Q. Mr Prime Minister, as I was waiting outside your office for this interview, I heard someone mention that next year happens to be your father Motilalji's centenary. I wonder if this is correct?

A. Quite so. He was born in 1861.

Q. I had no idea that a whole century had passed. What a fabulous period it has been!

A. Yes indeed—and do you know that father was born on the same day as Rabindranath Tagore?

Q. The same day, sir?

A. Yes, the same day, the same month, the same year—a remarkable coincidence!

Q. They must constitute two of the most vital influences with Gandhiji and, of course, yourself, on this Indian century. In fact, one thinks of Motilalji, yourself and Gandhiji in terms of the Father, Son and the Holy Mahatma in a sort of an Indian National Trinity.

A. I would not put it that way, but it is true that the three of us exercised considerable influence upon one another. And most of all, Gandhiji on both of us. He was a powerful and revolutionary personality and a very effective one too. So was father in his own way, very strong and stubborn, and, of course, of a very different mould, but Gandhiji persuaded him out of his ways and beliefs to join the freedom struggle. The way this change was brought about by persuasion, consent, and patient handling of human nature, without any coercion and at the same time, without any compromise on essentials, struck me as something very remarkable and also very effective. It was typical of Gandhiji's strategy of winning over opposition. It brought results, produced major changes, not only in relation to father but in relation to all people, the masses and, in fact, the whole country.

Q. And yourself most of all?

A. Yes, myself most of all. The transformation of father under Gandhiji's influence, as also the revolution he was producing in the minds and hearts of the people by truthful and honest means, non-violent means, peaceful and persuasive rather then coercive means, and yet effective means which brought about results, was something new and revolutionary. It gave me what I was searching for.

Q. A lever for your own solutions?

A. A lever certainly. My approach to problems was different, very different, from Gandhiji's at that time; but on the main issue of freedom and the strategy for the struggle we agreed completely, both in regard to the ends and the means. One doubted his way of going about the fight, but he bowled out all opposition by producing results, moving the masses in a big way and in the right direction, till we realized that he was a great revolutionary force in action.

Q. Would it be a correct analysis to say that this triangular relationship between Motilalji, Gandhiji and yourself produced the elements which have since fashioned what is known today as *the Indian approach* or *the Nehru line* in national and international affairs?

A. It is wrong to call it the Nehru line or anything of that sort. It was fundamentally *an Indian approach,* as you say, and Gandhiji, of course, represented it. That is why it was able to create such revolutionary changes.

Q. What I meant to suggest was that Motilalji was in some

ways the great Victorian representing the best traditions of European liberalism, while Gandhiji was the pure and simple nationalist with some kind of an atavistic approach. The link between these two vitally diverse personalities could perhaps have been Jawaharlal Nehru, come back to India deeply imbued with Marxist Socialism and conscious of social, scientific and historical forces. Perhaps, it could be said that the interaction of these three influences produced the Indian approach which we see functioning today in domestic as well as international affairs?

A. One cannot define personalities in such a sharp manner. Gandhiji, for example, was much more than the nationalist, pure and simple and atavistic, as you call him. He was a great man and a mighty leader. He had a deep social conscience, not in the socialist or class-struggle sense, but as reflected in the almost continuous struggle he waged against inequality for the underdog, the Harijans and the peasantry, for example. Take the caste system and consider how he used the lever of his challenge to untouchability to shake and overturn, as it were, the whole structure.

What I mean to say is that Gandhiji, too, had a social philosophy which emerged right from the beginning of his career in South Africa. This is one reason why our freedom struggle was never without its social content—in fact, the latter was its base and this is why the strategy produced such tremendous results. Gandhiji believed in the complete identification of the leadership with the masses, even if that meant falling behind somewhat and slowing down the pace of progress so as to carry the whole people forward with him.

Q. To carry the whole national mass continuum forward?

A. Yes that is, without dividing or splitting the movement and causing factional opposition by being unnecessarily aggressive or dogmatic. Gandhiji always sought to function within the social fabric in which the masses had been living for centuries and tried to bring about gradual but revolutionary changes, instead of destroying the fabric or uprooting the people from their soil. He insisted on continuity with the past and he accepted the existing social system as a base for his political and social strategy. Again, taking the caste system as an example, you can see how he functioned. He sought the weakest point in the armoury of the caste structure—that is, untouchability—and by undermining and dynamiting it, he shook the whole fabric without the people realizing the earthquake he had unleashed. In this way, Gandhiji introduced new and revolutionary processes in the mass mind and brought about mighty social changes.

Q. That may be so, sir. Nobody doubts Gandhiji's enormous influence on the Indian revolution, even though people of my way of thinking consider his philosophy to be somewhat confused and unscientific. However that may be, the Gandhian era ended with the assumption of political power by the Congress. The year 1947 ushered in what is universally hailed as the Nehru epoch in our country. Should I be right in the inference that from Freedom onwards, you used the Gandhian means to serve the Nehru ends—that is, socialism within the fabric of Parliamentary Democracy, first of all; secularism next; and, finally, and most importantly, your insistence on a foreign policy based on World Peace and Non-alignment?

A. You are wrong in using words like the Nehru epoch or the Nehru policy. I would call ours the authentic Gandhian era and the policies and philosophy which we seek to implement are the policies and philosophy taught to us by Gandhiji. There has been no break in the continuity of our thoughts before and after 1947, though, of course, new technological and scientific advances since have made us rethink in some ways and adapt our policies to the new times. But here also Gandhiji was in many ways prophetic. His thoughts and approaches and solutions helped us to cover the chasm between the Industrial Revolution and the Nuclear Era.

After all, the only possible answer to the Atom Bomb is nonviolence. Isn't it?

Q. If I may interrupt, sir, you have gone beyond nonviolence to the discovery of a more positive solution to this threat of the Atom Bomb in Panch Sheel or the Doctrine of Peaceful Coexistence.

A. All that was inherent in Gandhism. In fact, this approach of Panch Sheel, coexistence, peace, tolerance, the attitude of live and let live, has been fundamental to Indian thought throughout the ages and you find it in all religions. Great emperors like Ashoka practised it and Gandhiji organized it into a practical philosophy of action which we have inherited. There was no place for the 'cold war' in Ashoka's mind, and Gandhiji gave the world the most practical substitute for war and violence by bringing about a mighty revolution with the bloodless weapon of passive resistance. The most important thing about our foreign policy is that it is part of our great historical tradition. Do you know the story of Chanakya?

Q. I don't seem to remember it, sir.

A. It appears in a very interesting Sanskrit book translated by my brother-in-law, the late Mr Pandit, who was a Sanskrit scholar. You must get the English translation and read it if it is available. It tells a story of King Chandragupta and his Prime Minister Chanakya. Chanakya was typical of the Indian genius: peace-loving, shrewd, cunning, very scholarly, proud and selfless and reputed to be a very wise man. Now some kings and chieftains opposed Chandragupta and organized themselves into a confederation and declared war on the kingdom. Chandragupta called Chanakya to lead the defence, and this person, who appears to have been a great statesman and a superb diplomat, succeeded in confusing and defeating the enemy front without resorting to anything like a war or even a battle. Somehow the enemy was won over. Then came the test. Chandragupta asked Chanakya's advice as to what to do next. Chanakya replied that his job was done. He had dispersed the foe and won a victory for his king. All he desired now was to be relieved of his responsibility so that he may retire to the forest and attend to his reading and writing. The King was shocked. For who would substitute Chanakya as the Chief Minister? Chanakya's reply was classic and very symptomatic of Indian thought. He told the King to get the defeated leader of the enemy confederation to serve him as his Chief Executive. That was the only way to restore peace and goodwill to the Kingdom. Now that was coexistence some 2,000 years ago. Wasn't it?

Q. True enough, Mr Nehru. I stand corrected, but still the conviction remains amongst progressives that Gandhiji broke and emasculated your earlier faith in Scientific Socialism with his sentimental and spiritual solutions.

A. Some of Gandhiji's approaches were old-fashioned, and I disputed them, even combated them, as you know well enough. But on the whole it is wrong to say that he broke or emasculated me or anybody else. Any such thing would be against his way of doing things. The most important thing he insisted upon was the importance of means: ends were shaped by the means that led to them, and therefore the means had to be good, pure and truthful. That is what we learnt from him and it is well we did so.

On the other hand, what you say about sentimental and spiritual solutions may be true. I take it that by sentiment you mean humanity—that is, the deep human approach which has always been as much part of my thinking as it was of Gandhiji's. The spiritual approach, too, is necessary and good, and I have always shared it with Gandhiji, probably more so today when we see the need of finding some answer to the spiritual emptiness facing our technological civilization than I did yesterday. Scientific Socialism, as you call it—I take it your reference is to Marxist socialism—also has to be adapted to the new scientific era which has progressed beyond the Industrial Revolution which was responsible for Marxism. New changes pose new riddles which demand new answers.

Marxism in the Modern World

Q. Now here, I believe, we of India—I use the collective deliberately, since evidently mention of Jawaharlal Nehru embarrasses you!—have discovered the new answers, or, at least, some of them, to the new problems of the changing times. First and most important of them all, as I see it, is the adoption of the Marxist approach, which in our case has gone through the Gandhian influence, to the imperatives of the new scientific and technological era. In this context, India can boast of having evolved, first of all, *a new kind of socialism* and, secondly, *a new way to socialism,* both of which attempt to create a synthesis between Capitalist democracy, on the one hand, and Communist dictatorship, on the other.

Now, sir, without indulging in flattery, I would like to say that this constitutes a very remarkable experiment which affects one-seventh of humanity directly and the rest of the world indirectly, but very vitally. Besides, it provides some answers to the problems raised by the new epoch of nuclear discoveries and inter-planetary advances.

This is one side of the picture. On the other hand, your noble but somewhat abstract Manifestos on this New Socialism, or Socialist Humanism, have put your followers in an ideological dilemma. The reason is that you have not defined the goals and objectives of Indian Socialism, nor fashioned the means or instruments. Nevertheless, I believe you now have sufficient experience of both to give us something like a definition. Could you?

A. You are constantly referring to Indian Socialism and to manifestos on socialism by me. Well, the truth is that I do not think of the problem particularly in terms of *Indian* Socialism, nor have I issued any Manifestos....

Q. I am referring to your speeches, your writings, your hooks like *Whither India*. They have been our Manifestos....

A. Yes, I understand. But as I said, one cannot think of it particularly or specifically in terms of *Indian* Socialism, though I agree that each country has a particular genius, particular roots, and its social and economic structure is partly conditioned and moulded by these factors. To illustrate this, let us take the example of religion. Buddhism, for instance, spread to many countries from India putting on the garb as it were of each separate country. Chinese Buddhism, though derived from India, took on a Chinese orientation. So did the Burmese, the Japanese, etc. That means it was engrafted in to the roots of the national soul or whatever you like to call it. In that sense, national characteristics have to be borne in mind in any study of political philosophies as you have to take into account the climate and other physical features of each country. The study of a tropical region in the context of economic production may well be different from that of a non-tropical country.

Q. That is so. I would like you to submit the Marxist analysis to the Indian situation as also other objective conditions to which you have made references before.

A. I was coming to that. In considering what may be called the economic or social philosophy, one learns, of course, a great deal from past experience; and I have always considered the Marxist analysis of the past very scientific and very illuminating. I do not agree with everything Marx says, but broadly I have found it useful and rational. Nevertheless, the fact must be remembered that Marxism was the outcome of the beginnings of the Industrial Revolution in England, the early beginnings when conditions were rather peculiar and very special, conditions which have not been repeated elsewhere in the world and quite naturally so. Marx was influenced by the abnormal and, I should say, abominable conditions which prevailed in the first flush of industrialization when there was nothing like a democratic structure of the state and changes had to be made violently for the simple reason that they could not be made constitutionally or democratically. Hence his doctrine of revolutionary violence.

Now when we face the problem of production, change etc., dealt with by Marx, today, we have to think of them in the context of our own times, our own country and our peculiar circumstances and objective conditions. We cannot go back to conditions in early nineteenth century England in which Marx functioned. It is *our* conditions that prevail and fashion our thought. The Marxist solutions follow a brilliant line. They may have been right and proper for the times and the problems which brought them into being, but you cannot remove them from their historical context and apply them to a century where different conditions prevail. That is one argument against dogmatic insistence on the Marxist solutions.

Secondly, the Marxist analysis of many things, historical forces and the like, was *in vacuo* a correct analysis. Let me explain what I mean. If you do not think of other forces coming into the picture, the direction of Marxist economy, which says that given such and such conditions, this or that will happen, or should happen, is logically correct. But the trouble is that Marx does not take into account *other* forces that might come into play in the future. That, of course, was not the fault of Marx. He saw the conditions as they were during his period and used them as the premises for his conclusions. Then other forces came in. The most important of them was political democracy which made possible peaceful change. Remember that in Marx's lime there was no political democracy, even in the so-called democratic countries, where the land-owning class was in the government. Now the mere fact of the vote coming in, even though it does not solve all problems, does make and has made vital differences. When everybody has a vote it becomes a power exercising certain pulls, certain effective pressures, in the direction of social change to an extent that Marx could not have conceived simply because the picture was not before him.

Then other and further democratic factors came into the picture, like trade union organizations, workers' organizations, peasant organizations—all exercising powerful pressures upon the wealthy ruling classes in favour of what might be called the beginnings of economic democracy. The result was that the Marxist fear in the context of the Industrial Revolution that there would be greater and greater concentration of wealth and power in fewer and fewer hands, extending and widening poverty, did not really occur. These pressures—partly democratic, partly trade union and others that followed—had a powerful impact in limiting both. I do not dispute the fact that the economic tendency which Marx foresaw happened, but it was limited and inhibited all the time by these objective conditions.

There were new types of organizations growing in the political background which was changing, continuously and radically, on one side, accelerating the urge for social justice and the will to social change. On the other the world was being revolutionized by really big and tremendous technological developments, of which nobody in the nineteenth century, Marx or any other thinker, could have had any awareness.

These scientific and technological developments have in theory, you might say, solved the problems of wealth and production, bringing the goal of material prosperity within reach of all. That is, in theory at least, there is enough in the world to go round the entire human population, or enough can be produced in the world to satisfy every normal, primary want of humanity.

Marx was functioning at a time when the main economic question was one of the distribution of something that was not enough and this created all kinds of conflicts. The stronger and wealthier seized the most of what there was and the poor and the weak went to the wall....

[...]

Philosophy of Synthesis

Q. All that you have said about our heritage and development suggests an overall philosophy of *synthesis* as against the doctrine of *antithesis.* Am I correct, sir?

A. Yes, synthesis. Gandhiji always sought to build bridges and forge links between conflicting elements.

Q. Synthesis is all right as a practical philosophy, but it becomes somewhat odd in its application to fundamental contradictions of the class nature. For example, Gandhiji sought to bridge the class difference between the *Haves* and the *Have-nots* with the astounding theory of trusteeship and trust. Why, he almost handed over the trusting lamb to the trusteeship of the tiger! The question is: have you come around to accepting the Gandhian solution of *class synthesis* in preference to Marxist approach of *class struggle*?

A. Class struggle is there always. One cannot deny it or put it aside. But the solution need no longer be one of violence or struggle or hatred: and that's where Gandhiji's peaceful approach, friendly and constructive approach, comes in. As I have already explained to you, Marx was conditioned by his times where there was no democracy or franchise, no working-class movement and—well, simply no means of resolving inequalities and equalizing society other than struggle, don't you see? So while not denying or repudiating class contradictions, we want to deal with the problem in a peaceful and co-operative way by lessening rather than increasing these conflicts and trying to win over people instead of threatening to fight them or destroy them. Gandhiji perhaps wasn't conscious of this class I struggle aspect in the way you or I are. But his solutions are more applicable to our time and, particularly, our land. Our history and traditions show this way—that is, the advantage of the peaceful, friendly and co-operative solutions.

There is one more factor which comes into this picture of class struggles and wars and all that. It is the atom bomb and, of course, its positive aspect in nuclear energy. Now while nuclear energy holds out tremendous hopes for human advancement, the atom bomb threatens to blow up civilization with one or two or three bangs—thus this emergence of such a destructive weapon makes conflict or war, be it in the form of class struggle or capitalist-socialist conflict, simply so disastrous that it is impossible to think of solutions in terms of violence at all. Hence, from any point of view, the concept of class struggles or wars has been outdated as too dangerous at a time when not only nations but groups or even individuals can be put in possession of weapons of enormous destructive potentiality. So we have to appreciate and follow the Gandhian solution of synthesis, co-operation, co-existence and progressive equalization.

Q. I believe, Mr Nehru, there you have stated the genesis of the doctrine of Panch Sheel, or the Five Foundations of Peaceful Coexistence, whereby you have sought to resolve international conflicts and reorganize world relations in the spirit of Gandhism. Now what I would like to know from you is, *how you came to be such a faithful convert to the Gandhian outlook?* There appears to have been some change in your attitude from one of a critical follower to that of a passionate convert in the Forties. Since you have mentioned the atom bomb, is it possible that the emergence of this appalling weapon of destruction brought about a radical change in your pre-1940 thinking? Or was it perhaps the crucifixion of Gandhiji that transformed you into his most loyal disciple?

A. I don't know. It is difficult to analyse oneself. The atom bomb of course, affected my mental outlook a great deal but not in the particular aspect you mentioned. The transformation has been a gradual one. This atom bomb necessarily represents a very powerful influence not only in its painful consequences but by way of the advent of a new power, enormous energy which could be used or misused, and which does affect one's thinking and outlook. It changes anyone's thinking about the future and what can happen in the future.

Take this issue of class struggle we were discussing. Now there are classes, and obviously those classes are in conflict. Their interests are in conflict. Therefore, a struggle comes about. That cannot be denied. The point is whether in order to put an end to class struggle, you should intensify it and resolve it, or liquidate it, through conflict and violence. Well, that comes in the way, first of all of my basic approach that as far as possible conflict should be resolved and violence avoided. This is not a *denial* of class struggle, but the *removal* of class struggle through *other* means than conflict and violence. And that has always been part of our approach—not due to the atom bomb or Gandhiji's murder, but something basic and fundamental.

I think that to some extent we have succeeded in using this solution effectively, whether it be in the cases of princes or landlords. I don't imagine we have converted all the princes, but they are bound down to certain conditions and pressures which are rising all the time, pressures from the people, pressures from the Government, so that it becomes relatively easy to come to terms with them. In that sense, we have abolished Zamindari, the big landlord system. We gave them compensation, but that was no compensation for the standards they had been used to. They did not like it and there was conflict, but it was resolved without anything like a big struggle.

Now there is conflict between the Private Sector and the growing Public Sector, but I'm sure that too will be resolved peacefully and cooperatively.

So it can all be done in the Gandhian way. Sometimes conflict may come. That is a different matter. But that is not a big-scale conflict, but rather a local conflict. So while recognizing the fact that there is a class, a privileged class, a class dominating other classes, like the working people and the peasantry and the middle-classes, and having a genuine desire to put an end to all such inequalities and disparities, I do not think the right way to do it is by accentuating the differences and solving them by struggle. Even if apparently we succeed in doing so, you leave a bad train behind. It really comes back to the *means* and *ends* business.

Q. So this conversion of yours to the Gandhian solution was there before the atom bomb destroyed Hiroshima and Nagasaki and changed the course of History?

A. My outlook has always been against conflict, particularly conflict with violence. But I do think of the atom bomb—or rather atomic energy, which represents such vast power coming to the world, has changed the whole context of life—the prospect of future life and so all our theories of the past, whether economic or any other, have to be reviewed in this new context. First of all, of course, one has to think in the context of the possibility of war which can now put an end to almost everything.

Q. Hence comes your insistence on Coexistence?

A. Well, Coexistence was there all the time?

Q. Even before the Forties.

A. Naturally, it was there all the time and, in fact, it dates back to the days of Ashoka and Buddha. Gandhiji made it a part of the ends and means business. *It is a pan, if I may say so, of the basic process of Indian thought the basis of which is to live and let live.* I don't say Indians are angels, but anyhow Indian thought is good. So this philosophy of Coexistence flows from our history, though it receives powerful support from present day developments when war might mean the total destruction of humankind.

The National Movement

Inquilab Zindabad

(*From* Glimpses of World History)

Priyadarshini[1]—dear to the sight, but dearer still when sight is denied! As I sat here today to write to you, faint cries, like distant thunder, reached me. I could not make out at first what they were, but they had a familiar ring and they seemed to find an answering echo in my heart. Gradually they seemed to approach and grow in volume, and soon there was no doubt as to what they were. *"Inqilab zindabad!" "Inqilab zindabad!"* the prison resounded with the spirited challenge, and our hearts were glad to hear it. I do not know who they were who shouted our war cry so near us outside the gaol—whether they were men and women from the city or peasants from the villages. Nor do I know the occasion for it today. But whoever they were, they cheered us up, and we sent a silent answer to their greeting and all our good wishes went with it.

Why should we shout *"Inqilab zindabad"*? Why should we want revolution and change? India of course wants a big change today. But even after the big change that we all want has come and India is independent, we cannot rest quiescent. Nothing in the world that is alive remains unchanging. All Nature changes from day to day and minute to minute, only the dead stop growing and are quiescent. Fresh water runs on, and if you stop it, it becomes stagnant. So also is it with the life of man and the life of a nation. Whether we want to or not, we grow old. Babies

[1] Priyadarshini is Indira's second name and means 'dear to the sight'.

become little girls, and little girls big girls and grown-up women and old women. We have to put up with these changes. But there are many who refuse to admit that the world changes. They keep their minds closed and locked up and will not permit any new ideas to come into them. Nothing frightens them so much as the idea of thinking. What is the result? The world moves on in spite of them, and because they and people like them do not adapt themselves to the changing conditions, there are big burst-ups from time to time. Big revolutions take place, like the great French Revolution of a hundred and forty years ago, or the Russian Revolution thirteen years ago. Even so in our own country, we are today in the middle of a revolution. We want independence, of course. But we want something more. We want to clear out all the stagnant pools and let in clean fresh water everywhere. We must sweep away the dirt and the poverty and misery from our country. We must also clean up, as far as we can, the cobwebs from the minds of so many people which prevent them from thinking and cooperating in the great work before us. It is a great work, and it may be that it will require time. Let us, at least, give it a good push on—*Inqilab zindabad!*

We are on the threshold of our Revolution. What the future will bring we cannot say. But even the present has brought us rich returns for our labours. See the women of India, how proudly they march ahead of all in the struggle! Gentle and yet brave and indomitable, see how they set the pace for others. And the purdah, which hid our brave and beautiful women, and was a curse to them and to their country, where is it now? Is it not rapidly slinking away to take its rightful place in the shelves of museums, where we keep the relics of a bygone age?

See also the children—the boys and girls—the Vanar Senas and the Bal and Balika Sabhas. The parents of many of these children may have behaved as cowards or slaves in the past. But who dare doubt that the children of our generation will tolerate no slavery or cowardice?

And so the wheel of change moves on, and those who were down go up and those who were up go down. It was time it moved in our country. But we have given it such a push this time that no one can stop it.

Inqilab zindabad!

January 7, 1931

~

How Britain Ruled India

(*From* Glimpses of World History)

The tyranny of the British, we say. Whose tyranny is it, after all? Who profits by it? Not the whole British race, for millions of them are themselves unhappy and oppressed. And undoubtedly there are small groups and classes of Indians who have profited a little by the British exploitation of India. Where are we to draw the line, then? It is not a question of individuals, but that of a system. We have been living under a huge machine that has exploited and crushed India's millions. This machine is the machine of the new imperialism, the outcome of industrial capitalism. The profits of this exploitation go largely to England, but in England they go almost entirely to certain classes. Some part of the profits of exploitation remain in India also, and certain classes benefit by them. It is therefore foolish for us to get angry with individuals, or even with the British as a whole. If a system is wrong and injures us, it has to be changed. It makes little difference who runs it, and even good people are helpless in a bad system. With the best will in the world, you cannot convert stones and earth into good food, however much you may cook them. So it is, I think, with imperialism and capitalism. They cannot be improved; the only real improvement is to do away with them altogether. But that is my opinion. Some people differ from this. You need not take anything for granted, and, when the time comes, you can draw your conclusions. But about one thing most people do agree: that what is wrong is the system, and it is useless getting annoyed with individuals. If we want a change, let us attack and change the system. We have seen some of the evil effects of the system in India. When we consider China and Egypt and many other countries we shall see the same system, the same machine of capitalist-imperialism, at work exploiting other peoples.

We shall go back to our story. I have told you of the advanced stage of Indian cottage industries when the British came. With natural progress in the methods of production, and without any intervention from outside, it is probable that some time or other machine industry would have come to India. There was iron and coal in the country and, as we saw in England, these helped the new industrialism greatly, and indeed partly brought it about. Ultimately this would have happened in India also. There might has been some delay in this, owing to the chaotic political conditions. The British, however, intervened. They represented a country and a community which had already changed over to the new big machine production. One might think, therefore, that they would favour such a change in India also, and encourage that class in India which was most likely to bring it about. They did no such thing. Indeed, they did the very opposite of this. Treating India as a possible rival, they broke up her industries, and actually discouraged the growth of machine industry.

Thus we find a somewhat remarkable state of affairs in India. We find that the British, the most advanced people in Europe at the time, ally themselves in India with the most backward and conservative classes. They bolster up a dying feudal class; they create landlords; they support the hundreds of dependent Indian rulers in their semi-feudal states. They actually strengthen feudalism in India. Yet these British had been the pioneers in Europe of the middle class or bourgeois revolution which had given their Parliament power; they had also been the pioneers in the Industrial Revolution which had resulted in introducing industrial capitalism to the world. It was because of their lead in these matters that they went far ahead of their rivals and established a vast empire.

It is not difficult to understand why the British acted in this way in India. The whole basis of capitalism is cut-throat competition and exploitation, and imperialism is an advanced stage of this. So the British, having the power, killed their actual rivals and deliberately prevented the growth of other rivals. They could not possibly make friends with the masses, for the whole object of their presence in India was to exploit them. The interests of the exploiters and the exploited could never be the same. So they, the British, fell back on the relics of feudalism which India still possessed. These had little real strength left even when the British came; but they were propped up and given a small share in the exploitation of the country. This propping up could only give temporary relief to a class which had outlived its utility; when the props were removed they were sure to fall or adapt themselves to the new conditions. There were as many as seven hundred Indian states, big and small, depending on the goodwill of the British. You know some of these big States: Hyderabad, Kashmir, Mysore, Baroda, Gwalior, etc. But, curiously, most of the Indian rulers of these states are not descended from the old feudal nobility, just as most of the big zamindars have no very ancient traditions. There is one chief, however—the Maharana of Udaipur, the head of the Surya Vanshi, Rajputs of the race of the Sun, who can trace his lineage back to dim prehistoric days. Probably the only living person who can compete with him in this respect is the Mikado of Japan.

British rule also helped religious conservatism. This sounds strange, for the British claimed to profess Christianity, and yet their coming made Hinduism and Islam in India more rigid. To some extent this reaction was natural, as foreign invasion tends to make the religions and culture of the country protect themselves by rigidity. It was in this way that Hinduism had become rigid and caste had developed after the Muslim invasions. Now, both Hinduism and Islam reacted after this fashion. But, apart from this, the British Government in India actually—both deliberately and unconsciously—helped the conservative elements in the two religions.

The British were not interested in religion or in conversions; they were out to make money. They were afraid of interfering in any way in religious matters lest the people, in their anger, rose against them. So to avoid even the suspicion of interference, they went so far as actually to protect and help the country's religions, or rather the external forms of religion. The result often was that the outer form remained, but there was little inside it.

This fear of irritating the orthodox people made the government side with them in matters of reform. Thus the cause of reform was held up. An alien government can seldom introduce social reform, because every change it seeks to introduce is resented by the people. Hinduism and Hindu law were in many respects changing and progressive, though the progress had been remarkably slow in recent centuries. Hindu law itself is largely custom, and customs change and grow. This elasticity of the Hindu law disappeared under the British and gave place to rigid legal codes drawn up after consultation with the most orthodox people. Thus the growth of Hindu society, slow as it was, was stopped. The Muslims resented the new conditions even more, and retired into their shells.

A great deal of credit is taken by the British for the abolition of what is (rather incorrectly) called sati, the practice of a Hindu widow burning herself on the funeral pyre of her husband. They deserve some credit for this, but as a matter of fact the government only took action after many years of agitation by Indian reformers headed by Raja Ram Mohan Roy. Previous to them other rulers, and especially the Marathas, had forbidden it; the Portuguese Albuquerque had abolished the practice in Goa. It was put down by the British as a result of Indian agitation and Christian missionary endeavours. So far as I can remember, this was the only reform of religious significance which was brought about by the British Government.

~

The Dual Policy of the British Government

(*From* An Autobiography)

The Harijan movement was going on, guided by Gandhiji from Yeravda Prison and later from outside. There was a great agitation for removing the barriers to temple entry, and a Bill to that effect was introduced in the Legislative Assembly. And then the remarkable spectacle was witnessed of an outstanding leader of the Congress going from house to house in Delhi, visiting the members of the Assembly and canvassing for their votes for this Temple Entry Bill. Gandhiji himself sent an appeal through him to the Assembly members. And yet civil disobedience was still going on and people were going to prison, and the Assembly had been boycotted by the Congress and all our members had withdrawn from it. The rump that remained and the others who had filled the vacancies had distinguished themselves in this crisis by opposition to the Congress and support of the Government. A majority of them had helped the government to pass repressive legislation giving some permanence to the extraordinary provisions of the Ordinances. They had swallowed the Ottawa Pact, they had fed and feasted with the great ones in Delhi and Simla and London, and joined in the thank-offerings for British rule in India, and prayed for the success of what was called the ' Dual Policy ' in India.

I was amazed at Gandhiji's appeal, under the circumstances then existing, and even more so by the strenuous efforts of Rajagopalachariar, who, a few weeks before, had been the acting President of the Congress. Civil Disobedience, of course, suffered by these activities, but what hurt me more was the moral side. To me, for Gandhiji or any Congress leader to countenance such activities appeared immoral and almost a breach of faith with the large numbers of people in gaol or carrying on the struggle. But I knew that his way of looking at it was different.

The Government attitude to this Temple Entry Bill, then and subsequently, was very revealing. It put every possible difficulty in the way of its promoters, went on postponing it and encouraging opposition to it, and then finally declared its own opposition to it, and killed it. That, to a greater or lesser extent, has been its attitude to all measures of social reform in India, and on the plea of non-interference with religion, it has prevented social progress. But this, it need hardly be said, has not prevented it from criticising our social evils and encouraging others to do so. By a fluke, the Sarda Child Marriage Restraint Bill became law, but the subsequent history of this unhappy Act showed more than anything else how much averse to enforcing any such measure the Government was. The Government that could produce ordinances overnight, creating novel offences and providing for vicarious punishment, and could send scores of thousands of people to prison for breach of their provisions, apparently quailed at the prospect of enforcing one of its regular laws like the Sarda Act. The effect of the Act was first to increase tremendously the very evil it was intended to combat, for people rushed to take advantage of the intervening six months of grace which the Act very foolishly allowed. And then it was discovered that the Act was more or less of a joke and could be easily ignored without any steps being taken by Government. Not even the slightest attempt at propaganda was made officially, and most people in the villages never knew what the Act was. They heard distorted accounts of it from Hindu and Muslim village preachers, who themselves seldom knew the correct facts.

This extraordinary spirit of toleration of social evils in India which the British Government has shown is obviously not due to any partiality for them. It is true that they do not very much care about their removal, for these evils do not interfere with their business of governing India and exploiting her resources. There is also always the danger of irritating various people by proposing social reforms, and, having to face enough anger and irritation on the political plane, the British Government has no desire whatever to add to its troubles. But latterly the position has become worse from the point of view of the social reformer, for the British are becoming more and more the silent bulwarks of these evils. This is due to their close association with the most reactionary elements in India. As opposition to their rule increases they have to seek strange allies, and today the firmest champions of British rule in India are the extreme communalists and the religious reactionaries and obscurantists. The Muslim communal organizations are notoriously reactionary from every point of view political, economic, social. The Hindu Mahasabha rivals them, but it is left far behind in this backward-moving race by the Sanatanists, who combine religious obscurantism of an extreme type with fervent, or at any rate loudly expressed, loyalty to British rule.

If the British Government was quiescent and took no steps to popularise the Sarda Act and to enforce it, why did not the Congress or other non-official organizations carry on propaganda in favour of it? This question is often put by British and other foreign critics. So far as the Congress is concerned, it has been engaged during the last fifteen years, and especially since 1930, in a fierce life-and-death struggle for national freedom with the British rulers. The other organizations have no real strength or contact with the masses. Men and women of ideals and force of character and influence among the masses were drawn into the Congress and spent much of their time in British prisons.

Other organizations could seldom go beyond the passing of resolutions by select people who feared the mass touch. They functioned in a gentlemanly way or, like the All-India Women's Association, in a lady-like way, and the spirit of aggressive propaganda was not theirs. Besides, they too were paralysed by the terrible repression of all public activities by the Ordinances and the laws that followed them. Martial law may crush revolutionary activity, but at the same time it paralyses civilisation and most civilised activities.

But the real reason why the Congress and other non-official organizations cannot do much for social reform goes deeper. We suffer from the disease of nationalism, and that absorbs our attention and it will continue to do so till we get political freedom. As Bernard Shaw has said: "A conquered nation is like a man with cancer; he can think of nothing else.... There is indeed no greater curse to a nation than a nationalist movement, which is only the agonising symptom of a suppressed natural function. Conquered nations lose their place in the world's march because they can do nothing but strive to get rid of their nationalist movements by recovering their national liberty."

~

The Record of British Rule

(*From* An Autobiography)

What has been the record of British rule in India? I doubt if it is possible for any Indian or Englishman to take an objective and dispassionate view of this long record. And even if this were possible, it would be still more difficult to weigh and measure the psychological and other immaterial factors. We are told that British rule "has given to India that which throughout the centuries she never possessed, a government whose authority is unquestioned in any part of the subcontinent";[2] it has established the rule of law and a just and efficient administration; it has brought to India Western conceptions of parliamentary government and personal liberties; and "by transforming British India into a single unitary state it has engendered amongst Indians a sense of political unity" and thus fostered the first beginnings of nationalism.[3] That is the British case, and there is much truth in it, though the rule of law and personal liberties have not been evident for many years.

The Indian survey of this period lays stress on many other factors, and points out the injury, material and spiritual, that foreign rule has brought us. The viewpoint is so different that sometimes the very thing that is commended by the British is condemned by Indians. As Doctor Ananda Coomaraswamy writes: "One of the most remarkable features of British rule in India is that the greatest injuries inflicted upon the Indian people have the outward appearance of blessings."

---

[2] The quotations are from the Report of the Joint Parliamentary Committee on Indian Constitutional Reform (1934).

[3] Ibid.

As a matter of fact the changes that have taken place in India during the last century or more have been world changes common to most countries in the East and West. The growth of industrialism in Western Europe, and later on in the rest of the world, brought nationalism and the strong unitary state in its train everywhere. The British can take credit for having first opened India's window to the West and brought her one aspect of Western industrialism and science. But having done so they throttled the further industrial growth of the country till circumstances forced their hands. India was already the meeting-place of two cultures, the western Asiatic culture of Islam and the eastern, her own product, which spread to the Far East And now a third and more powerful impulse came from further west, and India became a focal point and a battle-ground for various old and new ideas. There can be no doubt that this third impulse would have triumphed and thus solved many of India's old problems, but the British, who had themselves helped in bringing it, tried to stop its further progress. They prevented our industrial growth, and thus delayed our political growth, and preserved all the out-of-date feudal and other relics they could find in the country. They even froze up our changing and to some extent progressing laws and customs at the stage they found them, and made it difficult for us to get out of their shackles. It was not with their goodwill or assistance that the bourgeoisie grew in India. But after introducing the railway and other products of industrialism they could not stop the wheel of change; they could only check it and slow it down, and this they did to their own manifest advantage.

"On this solid foundation the majestic structure of the Government of India rests, and it can be claimed with certainty that in the period which has elapsed since 1858 when the Crown assumed supremacy over all the territories of the East India Company, the educational and material progress of India has been greater than it was ever within her power to achieve during any other period of her long and chequered history."[4] This

---

[4] Report of the Joint Parliamentary Committee (1934).

statement is not so self-evident as it appears to be, and it has often been stated that literacy actually went down with the coming of British rule. But even if the statement was wholly true, it amounts to a comparison of the modern industrial age with past ages. In almost every country in the world the educational and material progress has been tremendous during the past century because of science and industrialism, and it may be said with assurance of any such country that progress of this kind "has been greater than was ever within her power to achieve during any other period of her long and chequered history" though perhaps that country's history may not be a long one in comparison with Indian history. Are we needlessly cantankerous and perverse if we suggest that some such technical progress would have come to us anyhow in this industrial age, and even without British rule? And, indeed, if we compare our lot with many other countries, may we not hazard the guess that such progress might have been greater, for we have had to contend against a stifling of that progress by the British themselves? Railways, telegraphs, telephones, wireless and the like are hardly tests of the goodness or beneficence of British rule. They were welcome and necessary, and because the British happened to be the agents who brought them first, we should be grateful to them. But even, these heralds of industrialism came to us primarily for the strengthening of British rule. They were the veins and arteries through which the nation's blood should have coursed, increasing its trade, carrying its produce, and bringing new life and wealth to its millions. It is true that in the long run some such result was likely, but they were designed and worked for another purpose to strengthen the imperial hold and to capture markets for British goods which they succeeded in achieving. I am all in favour of industrialisation and the latest methods of transport, but sometimes, as I rushed across the Indian plains, the railway, that life giver, has almost seemed to me like iron bands confining and imprisoning India.

The British conception of ruling India was the police conception of the State. The government's job was to protect the State and leave the rest to others. Their public finance dealt with military expenditure, police, civil administration, interest on debt. The economic needs of the citizens were not looked after, and were sacrificed to British interests. The cultural and other needs of the people, except for a tiny handful, were entirely neglected. The changing conceptions of public finance which brought free and universal education, improvement of public health, care of poor and feeble-minded, insurance of workers against illness, old age and unemployment, etc., in other countries, were almost entirely beyond the ken of the government. It could not indulge in these spending activities for its tax system was most regressive, taking a much larger proportion of small incomes than of the larger ones, and its expenditure on its protective and administrative functions was terribly heavy and swallowed up most of the revenue.

The outstanding feature of British rule was their concentration on everything that went to strengthen their political and economic hold on the country. Everything else was incidental. If they built up a powerful central government and an efficient police force, that was an achievement for which they can take credit, but the Indian people can hardly congratulate themselves on it. Unity is a good thing, but unity in subjection is hardly a thing to be proud of. The very strength of a despotic government may become a greater burden for a people; and a police force, no doubt useful in many ways, can be, and has been often enough, turned against the very people it is supposed to protect. Bertrand Russell, comparing modern civilisation with the old Greek, has recently written: "The only serious superiority of Greek civilisation as compared to ours was the inefficiency of the police, which enabled a larger proportion of decent people to escape."

Britain's supremacy in India brought us peace, and India was certainly in need of peace after the troubles and misfortunes that followed the break-up of the Moghal empire. Peace is a precious commodity, necessary for any progress, and it was welcome to us when it came. But even peace can be purchased at too great a price, and we can have the perfect peace of the grave, and the absolute safety of a cage or of prison. Or peace may be the sodden despair of men unable to better themselves. The peace which is imposed by an alien conqueror has hardly the restful and soothing qualities of the real article. War is a terrible thing and to be avoided, but it does encourage some virtues, which, according to William James, the psychologist, are: fidelity, cohesiveness, tenacity, heroism, conscience, education, inventiveness, economy, and physical health and vigour. Because of this, James sought for a moral equivalent of war which, without the horrors of war, would encourage these virtues in a community. Perhaps if he had learnt of non-cooperation and civil disobedience he would have found something after his own heart, a moral and peaceful equivalent of war.

~

Contradictions of British Rule in India: Ram Mohan Roy, The Press, Sir William Jones, English Education in Bengal

(*From* The Discovery of India)

Previous to British rule Bengal had been an outlying province of the Mughal Empire, important but still rather cut off from the centre. During the early mediaeval period many debased forms of worship and of Tantric philosophy and practices had flourished among the Hindus there. Then came many Hindu reform movements affecting social customs and laws and even changing somewhat the well-recognized rules of inheritance elsewhere. Chaitanya, a great scholar who became a man of faith and emotion, established a form of Vaishnavism, based on faith, and influenced greatly the people of Bengal. The Bengalis developed a curious mixture of high intellectual attainments and equally strong emotionalism. This tradition of loving faith and service of humanity was represented in Bengal in the second half of the nineteenth century by another remarkable man of saintly character, Ramakrishna Paramahansa; in his name an order of service was established which has an unequalled record in humanitarian relief and social work. Full of the ideal of the patient loving service of the Franciscans of old, and quiet unostentatious, efficient, rather like the Quakers, the members of the Ramakrishna

Mission carry on their hospitals and educational establishments and engage in relief work, whenever any calamity occurs, all over India and even outside.

Ramakrishna represented the old Indian tradition. Before him, in the eighteenth century, another towering personality had risen in Bengal, Raja Ram Mohan Roy, who was a new type combining in himself the old learning and the new. Deeply versed in Indian thought and philosophy, a scholar in Sanskrit, Persian, and Arabic, he was a product of the mixed Hindu-Moslem culture that was then dominant among the cultured classes of India. The coming of the British to India and their superiority in many ways led his curious and adventurous mind to find out what their cultural roots were. He learnt English but this was not enough; he learnt Greek, Latin, and Hebrew also to discover the sources of the religion and culture of the West. He was also attracted by science and the technical aspects of Western civilization, though at that time these technical changes were not so obvious as they subsequently became. Being of a philosophical and scholarly bent, Ram Mohan Roy inevitably went to the older literatures. Describing him, Monier-Williams, the Orientalist, has said that he was 'perhaps the first earnest-minded investigator of the science of Comparative Religion that the world has produced'; and yet, at the same time, he was anxious to modernize education and take it out of the grip of the old scholasticism. Even in those early days he was in favour of the scientific method, and he wrote to the Governor-General emphasizing the need for education in 'mathematics, natural philosophy, chemistry, anatomy, and other useful sciences.'

He was more than a scholar and an investigator; he was a reformer above all. Influenced in his early days by Islam and later, to some extent, by Christianity, he stuck nevertheless to the foundations of his own faith. But he tried to reform that faith and rid it of abuses and the evil practices that had become associated with it. It was largely because of his agitation for the abolition of sati that the British Government prohibited it. This sati, or the immolation of women on the funeral pyre of their husbands, was never widespread. But rare instances continued to occur among the upper classes. Probably the practice was brought to India originally by the Scytho-Tartars, among whom the custom prevailed of vassals and liegemen killing themselves on the death of their lord. In early Sanskrit literature the sati custom is denounced. Akbar tried hard to stop it, and the Marathas also were opposed to it.

Ram Mohan Roy was one of the founders of the Indian press. From 1780 onwards a number of newspapers had been published by Englishmen in India. These were usually very critical of the Government and led to conflict and the establishment of a strict censorship. Among the earliest champions of the freedom of the press in India were Englishmen and one of them, James Silk Buckingham, who is still remembered, was deported from the country. The first Indian-owned and edited newspaper was issued (in English) in 1818, and in the same year the Baptist missionaries of Serampore brought out a Bengali monthly and a weekly, the first periodicals published in an Indian language. Newspapers and periodicals in English and the Indian languages followed in quick succession in Calcutta, Madras, and Bombay.

Meanwhile the struggle for a free press had already begun, to continue with many ups and downs till today. The year 1818 also saw the birth of the famous Regulation III, which provided for the first time for detention without trial. This regulation is still in force today, and a number of people are kept in prison under this 126-year-old decree.

Ram Mohan Roy was associated with several newspapers. He brought out a bilingual, Bengali-English magazine, and later, desiring an all-India circulation, he published a weekly in Persian, which was recognized then as the language of the cultured classes all over India. But this came to grief soon after the enactment in 1823 of new measures for the control of the press. Ram Mohan and others protested vigorously against these measures and even addressed a petition to the King-in-Council in England.

Ram Mohan Roy's journalist activities were intimately connected with his reform movements. His synthetic and universalist points of view were resented by orthodox sections who also opposed many of the reforms he advocated. But he also had staunch supporters, among them the Tagore family which played an outstanding part later in the renaissance in Bengal. Ram Mohan went to England on behalf of the Delhi Emperor and died in Bristol in the early Thirties of the nineteenth century.

Ram Mohan Roy and others studied English privately. There were no English schools or colleges outside Calcutta and the Government's policy was definitely opposed to the teaching of English to Indians. In 1781, the Calcutta Madrasa was started by the Government in Calcutta for Arabic studies. In 1817, a group of Indians and Europeans started the Hindu College in Calcutta, now called the Presidency College. In 1791, a Sanskrit College was started in Benares. Probably in the second decade of the nineteenth century some missionary schools were teaching English. During the Twenties a school of thought arose in government circles in favour of the teaching of English, but this was opposed. However, as an experimental measure some English classes were attached to the Arabic school in Delhi and to some institutions in Calcutta. The final decision in favour of the teaching of English was embodied in Macaulay's Minute on Education of February, 1835. In 1857, the Universities of Calcutta, Madras and Bombay began their career.

~

Experience of Lathi Charges

(From An Autobiography*)*

The assault on Lala Lajpat Rai, and his subsequent death, increased the vigour of the demonstrations against the Simon Commission in the places which it subsequently visited. It was due in Lucknow, and the local Congress Committee made extensive preparations for its 'reception'. Huge processions, meetings, and demonstrations were organized many days in advance, both as propaganda and as rehearsals for the actual show. I went to

Lucknow, and was present at some of these. The success of these preliminary demonstrations, which were perfectly orderly and peaceful, evidently nettled the authorities, and they began to obstruct and issue orders against the taking out of processions in certain areas. It was in this connection that I had a new experience, and my body felt the baton and lathi blows of the police.

Processions had been prohibited, ostensibly to avoid any interference with the traffic. We decided to give no cause for complaint on this score, and arranged for small groups of sixteen, as far as I can remember, to go separately, along unfrequented routes to the meeting place. Technically, this was no doubt a breach of the order, for sixteen with a flag were a procession. I led one of the groups of sixteen and, after a big gap, came another such group under the leadership of my colleague, Govind Ballabh Pant. My group had gone perhaps about two hundred yards, the road was a deserted one, when we heard the clatter of horses' hoofs behind us. We looked back to find a bunch of mounted police, probably two or three dozen in number, bearing down upon us at a rapid pace. They were soon right upon us, and the impact of the horses broke up our little column of sixteen. The mounted policemen then started belabouring our volunteers with huge batons or truncheons and, instinctively, the volunteers sought refuge on the sidewalks, and some even entered the petty shops. They were pursued and beaten down. My own instinct had urged me to seek safety when I saw the horses charging down upon us; it was a discouraging sight. But then, I suppose, some other instinct held me to my place and I survived the first charge, which had been checked by the volunteers behind me. Suddenly I found myself alone in the middle of the road; a few yards away from me, in various directions, were the policemen beating down our volunteers. Automatically, I began moving slowly to the side of the road to be less conspicuous, but again I stopped and had a little argument with myself, and decided that it would be unbecoming for me to move away. All this was a matter of a few seconds only, but I have the clearest recollections of that conflict within me and the decision, prompted by my pride, I suppose, which could not tolerate the idea of my behaving like a coward. Yet the line between cowardice and courage was a thin one, and I might well have been on the other side. Hardly had I so decided, when I looked round to find that a mounted policeman was trotting up to me, brandishing his long new baton. I told him to go ahead, and turned my head away again in an instinctive effort to save the head and face. He gave me two resounding blows on the back. I felt stunned, and my body quivered all over but, to my surprise and satisfaction, I found that I was still standing. The police force was withdrawn soon after, and made to block the road in front of us. Our volunteers gathered together again, many of them bleeding and with split skulls, and we were joined by Pant and his lot, who had also been belaboured, and all of us sat down facing the police. So we sat for an hour or so, and it became dark. On the one side, various high officials gathered; on the other, large crowds began to assemble as the news spread. Ultimately, the officials agreed to allow us to go by our original route, and we went that way with the mounted policemen, who had charged us and belaboured us, going ahead of us as a kind of escort.

I have written about this petty incident in some detail because of its effect on me. The bodily pain I felt was quite forgotten in a feeling of exhilaration that I was physically strong enough to face and bear lathi blows. And a thing that surprised me was that right through the incident, even when I was being beaten, my mind was quite clear and I was consciously analysing my feelings. This rehearsal stood me in good stead the next morning, when a stiffer trial was in store for us. For the next morning was the time when the Simon Commission was due to arrive, and our great demonstration was going to take place.

My father was at Allahabad at the time, and I was afraid that the news of the assault on me, when he read about it in the next morning's papers, would upset him and the rest of the family. So I telephoned to him late in the evening to assure him that all was well, and that he should not worry. But he did worry and, finding it difficult to sleep over it, he decided at about midnight to come over to Lucknow. The last train had gone, and so he started by motorcar. He had some bad luck on the way, and it was nearly five in the morning by the time he had covered the journey of 146 miles and reached Lucknow, tired out and exhausted.

That was about the time when we were getting ready to go in procession to the station. The previous evening's incidents had the effect of rousing up Lucknow more than anything that we could have done, and even before the sun was out, vast numbers of people made their way to the station. Innumerable little processions came from various parts of the city, and from the Congress office started the main procession, consisting of several thousands, marching in fours. We were in this main procession. We were stopped by the police as we approached the station. There was a huge open space, about half a mile square, in front of the station (this has now been built over by the new station) and we were made to line up on one side of this maidan, and there our procession remained, making no attempt to push our way forward. The place was full of foot and mounted police, as well as the military. The crowd of sympathetic onlookers swelled up, and many of these persons managed to spread out in twos and threes in the open space. Suddenly we saw in the far distance a moving mass. They were two or three long lines of cavalry or mounted police, covering the entire area, galloping down towards us, and striking and riding down the numerous stragglers that dotted the maidan. That charge of galloping horsemen was a fine sight, but for the tragedies that were being enacted on the way, as harmless and very much surprised sightseers went under the horses' hoofs. Behind the charging lines these people lay on the ground, some still unable to move, others writhing in pain, and the whole appearance of that maidan was that of a battlefield. But we did not have much time for gazing on that scene or for reflections; the horsemen were soon upon us, and their front line clashed almost at a gallop with the massed ranks of our processionists. We held our ground, and, as we appeared to be unyielding, the horses had to pull up at the last moment and reared up on their hind legs with their front hoofs quivering in the air over our heads. And then began a beating of us, and battering with lathis and long batons both by the mounted and the foot police. It was a tremendous hammering, and the clearness of vision that I had had the evening before left me. All I knew was that I had to stay where I was, and must not yield or go back. I felt half blinded with the blows, and sometimes a dull anger seized me and a desire to hit out. I thought how easy it would be to pull down the police officer in front of me from his horse and to mount up myself, but long training and discipline held and I did not raise a hand, except to protect my face from a blow. Besides, I knew well enough that any aggression on our part would result in a ghastly tragedy, the firing and shooting down of large numbers of our men.

After what seemed a tremendous length of time, but was probably only a few minutes, our line began to yield slowly, step by step, without breaking up. This left me somewhat isolated, and more exposed at the sides. More blows came, and then I was suddenly lifted off my feet from behind and carried off, to my great annoyance. Some of my young colleagues, thinking that a dead-set was being made at me, had decided to protect me in this summary fashion.

Our processionists lined up again about a hundred feet behind our original line. The police also withdrew and stood in a line, fifty feet apart from us. So we remained, when the cause of all this trouble, the Simon Commission, secretly crept away from the station in the far distance, more than half a mile away. But, even so, they did not escape the back flags or demonstrators. Soon after, we came back in full procession to the Congress office, and there dispersed, and I went on to father, who was anxiously waiting for us.

Now that the excitement of the moment had passed, I felt pains all over my body and great fatigue. Almost every part of me seemed to ache, and I was covered with contused wounds and marks of blows. But fortunately I was not injured in any vital spot. Many of our companions were less fortunate, and were badly injured. Govind Ballabh Pant, who stood by me, offered a much bigger target, being six foot odd in height, and the injuries he received then have resulted in a painful and persistent malady which prevented him for a long time from straightening his back or leading an active life. I emerged with a somewhat greater conceit of my physical condition and powers of endurance. But the memory that endures with me, far more than that of the beating itself, is that of many of the faces of those policemen, and especially of the officers, who were attacking us. Most of the real beating and battering was done by European sergeants, the Indian rank and file were milder in their methods. And those faces, full of hate and blood lust, almost mad, with no trace of sympathy or touch of humanity! Probably the faces on our side just then were equally hateful to look at, and the fact that we were mostly passive did not fill our minds and hearts with love for our opponents, or add to the beauty of our countenances. And yet, we had no grievance against each other; no quarrel that was personal, no ill-will. We happened to represent, for the time being, strange and powerful forces which held us in thrall and cast us hither and thither, and, subtly gripping our minds and hearts, roused our desires and passions and made us their blind tools. Blindly we struggled, not knowing what we struggled for and whither we went. The excitement of action held us; but, as it passed, immediately the question arose: To what end was all this? To what end?

~

In Bareilly and Dehradun Gaols

(*From* An Autobiography)

... It was very noticeable that the treatment of political prisoners in 1932 and 1933 was worse than it had been two years earlier, in 1930. This could not have been due merely to the whims of individual officers, and the only reasonable inference seems to be that this was the deliberate policy of the Government. Even apart from political prisoners, the United Provinces Gaol Department had had the reputation in those years of being very much against anything that might savour of humanity. We had an interesting instance of this from an unimpeachable source. A distinguished gaol visitor, a gallant knight, not a rebel and a sedition-monger like us, but one whom the Government had delighted to honour, paid us a visit once in prison. He told us that some months earlier he had visited another gaol, and in his inspection note had described the gaoler as a "humane disciplinarian." The gaoler in question begged him not to say anything about his humanity, as this was at a discount in official circles. But the knight insisted, as he could not conceive that any harm would befall the gaoler because of his description. Result: soon after the gaoler was transferred to a distant and out-of-the-way place, which was in the nature of a punishment to him.

Some gaolers, who were considered to be particularly fierce and unscrupulous, were promoted and given titles. Graft is such a universal phenomenon in gaols that hardly any one keeps clear of it. But my own experience, and that of many of my friends, has been that the worst offenders among the gaol staff are usually those who pose as strict disciplinarians.

I have been fortunate in gaol and outside, and almost every one I have come across has given me courtesy and consideration, even when perhaps I did not deserve them. One incident in gaol, however, caused me and my people much pain. My mother, Kamala and Indira, my daughter, had gone to interview my brother-in-law, Ranjit Pandit, in the Allahabad District Gaol and, for no fault of theirs, they were insulted and hustled out by the gaoler. I was grieved when I learnt of this, and the reaction of the Provincial Government to it shocked me. To avoid the possibility of my mother being insulted by gaol officials, I decided to give up all interviews. For nearly seven months, while I was in Dehradun Gaol, I had no interview.

Prison Humours

Two of us were transferred together from the Bareilly District Gaol to the Dehra Dun Gaol—Govind Ballabh Pant and I. To avoid the possibility of a demonstration, we were not put on the train at Bareilly, but at a wayside station fifty miles out. We were taken secretly by motor car at night, and, after many months of seclusion, that drive through the cool night air was a rare delight.

Before we left Bareilly Gaol, a little incident took place which moved me then and is yet fresh in my memory. The Superintendent of Police of Bareilly, an Englishman, was present there, and, as I got into the car, he handed to me rather shyly a packet which he told me contained old German illustrated magazines. He said that he had heard that I was learning German and so he had brought these magazines for me. I had never met him before, nor have I seen him since. I do not even know his name. This spontaneous act of courtesy and the kindly thought that prompted it touched me and I felt very grateful to him.

During that long midnight drive I mused over the relations of Englishmen and Indians, of ruler and ruled, of official and nonofficial, of those in authority and those who have to obey. What a great gulf divided the two races, and how they distrusted and disliked each other. But more than the distrust and the dislike was the ignorance of each other, and, because of this, each side was a little afraid of the other and was constantly on its guard in the other's presence. To each, the other appeared as a sour-looking, unamiable creature, and neither realised that there was decency and kindliness behind the mask. As the rulers of the land, with enormous patronage at their command, the English had attracted to themselves crowds of cringing place hunters and opportunists, and they judged of India from these unsavoury specimens. The Indian saw the Englishman function only as an official with all the inhumanity of the machine and with all the passion of a vested interest trying to preserve itself. How different was the behaviour of a person acting as an individual and obeying his own impulses from his behaviour as an official or a unit in an army. The soldier, stiffening to attention, drops his humanity, and, acting as an automaton, shoots and kills inoffensive and harmless persons who have done him no ill. So also, I thought, the police officer who would hesitate to do an unkindness to an individual would, the day after, direct a lathi charge on innocent people. He would not think of himself as an individual then, nor will he consider as individuals those crowds whom he beats down or shoots.

As soon as one begins to think of the other side as a mass or a crowd, the human link seems to go. We forget that crowds also consist of individuals, of men and women and children, who love and hate and suffer.

An average Englishman, if he was frank, would probably confess that he knows some quite decent Indians, but they are exceptions, and as a whole Indians are a detestable crowd. The average Indian would admit that some Englishmen whom he knows were admirable, but, apart from these few, the English were an overbearing, brutal, and thoroughly bad lot. Curious how each person judges of the other race, not from the individual with whom he has come in contact, but from others about whom he knows very little or nothing at all.

Personally, I have been very fortunate and, almost invariably, I have received courtesy from my own countrymen as well as from the English. Even my gaolers and the policemen, who have arrested me or escorted me as a prisoner from place to place, have been kind to me, and much of the bitterness of conflict and the sting of gaol life has been toned down because of this human touch. It was not surprising that my own countrymen should treat me so, for I had gained a measure of notoriety and popularity among them. Even for Englishmen I was an individual and not merely one of the mass, and, I imagine, the fact that I had received my education in England, and especially my having been to an English public school, brought me nearer to them. Because of this, they could not help considering me as more or less civilised after their own pattern, however perverted my public activities appeared to be. Often I felt a little embarrassed and humiliated because of this special treatment when I compared my lot with that of most of my colleagues.

Despite all these advantages that I had, gaol was gaol, and the oppressive atmosphere of the place was sometimes almost unbearable. The very air of it was full of violence and meanness and graft and untruth; there was either cringing or cursing. A person who was at all sensitive was in a continuous state of tension. Trivial occurrences would upset one. A piece of bad news in a letter, some item in the newspaper, would make one almost ill with anxiety or anger for a while. Outside there was always relief in action, and various interests and activities produced an equilibrium of the mind and body. In prison there was no outlet and one felt bottled up and repressed, and, inevitably, one took one-sided and rather distorted views of happenings. Illness in gaol was particularly distressing.

And yet I managed to accustom myself to the gaol routine, and with physical exercise and fairly hard mental work, kept fit. Whatever the value of work and exercise might be outside, they are essential in gaol, for without them one is apt to go to pieces. I adhered to a strict timetable and, in order to keep up to the mark, I carried on with as many normal habits as I could, such as the daily shave (I was allowed a safety razor). I mention this minor matter because, as a rule, people gave it up and slacked in other ways. After a hard day's work, the evening found me pleasantly tired and sleep was welcomed.

And so the days passed, and the weeks and the months. But sometimes a month would stick terribly and would not end, or so it seemed. And sometimes I would feel bored and fed up and angry with almost everything and everybody with my companions in prison, with the gaol staff, with people outside for something they had done or not done, with the British Empire (but this was a permanent feeling), and above all with myself. I would become a bundle of nerves, very susceptible to various humours caused by gaol life. Fortunately I recovered soon from these humours.

Interview days were the red-letter days in gaol. How one longed for them and waited for them and counted the days! And after the excitement of the interview there was the inevitable reaction and a sense of emptiness and loneliness. If, as sometimes happened, the interview was not a success, because of some bad news which upset me, or some other reason, I would feel miserable afterwards.

There were gaol officials present of course at the interviews, but two or three times at Bareilly there was in addition a C.I.D. man present with paper and pencil, eagerly taking down almost every word of the conversation. I found this exceedingly irritating, and these interviews were complete failures.

And then I gave up these precious interviews because of the treatment my mother and wife had received in the course of an interview in the Allahabad Gaol and afterwards from the Government. For nearly seven months I had no interview. It was a dreary time for me, and when at the end of that period I decided to resume interviews and my people came to see me, I was almost intoxicated with the joy of it. My sister's little children also came to see me, and when a tiny one wanted to mount on my shoulder, as she used to do, it was more than my emotions could stand. That touch of home life, after the long yearning for human contacts, upset me.

When interviews stopped, the fortnightly letters from home or from some other gaol (for both my sisters were in prison) became all the more precious and eagerly expected. If the letter did not come on the appointed day I was worried. And yet when it did come, I almost hesitated to open it. I played about with it as one does with an assured pleasure, and at the back of my mind there was also a trace of fear lest the letter contain any news or reference which might annoy me. Letter writing and receiving in gaol were always serious incursions on a peaceful and unruffled existence. They produced an emotional state which was disturbing, and for a day or two afterwards one's mind wandered and it was difficult to concentrate on the day's work.

In Naini Prison and Bareilly Gaol I had several companions. In Dehradun there were three of us to begin with—Govind Ballabh Pant, Kunwar Anand Singh of Kashipur and I—but Pantji was discharged after a couple of months on the expiry of his six months. Two others joined us later. By the beginning of January 1933 all my companions had left me and I was alone. For nearly eight months, till my discharge at the end of August, I lived a solitary life in Dehradun Gaol with hardly any one to talk to, except some member of the gaol staff for a few minutes daily. This was not technically solitary confinement, but it was a near approach to it, and it was a dreary period for me. Fortunately I had resumed my interviews, and they brought some relief. As a special favour, I suppose, I was allowed to receive fresh flowers from outside and to keep a few photographs, and they cheered me greatly. Ordinarily, flowers and photographs are not permitted, and on several occasions I have not been allowed to receive the flowers that had been sent for me. Attempts to brighten up the cells were not encouraged, and I remember a superintendent of a gaol once objecting to the manner in which a companion of mine, whose cell was next to mine, had arranged his toilet articles. He was told that he must not make his cell look attractive and "luxurious ". The articles of luxury were: a toothbrush, toothpaste, fountain pen ink, a bottle of hair oil, a brush and comb, and perhaps one or two other little things.

One begins to appreciate the value of the little things of life in prison. One's belongings are so few and they cannot easily be added to or replaced, and one clings to them and gathers up odd bits of things which, in the world outside, would go to the waste paper basket. The property sense does not leave one even when there is nothing worthwhile to own and keep.

Sometimes a physical longing would come for the soft things of life- bodily comfort, pleasant surroundings, the company of friends, interesting conversation, games with children….A picture or a paragraph in a newspaper would bring the old days vividly before one, carefree days of youth, and a nostalgia would seize one, and the day would be passed in restlessness.

I used to spin a little daily, for I found some manual occupation soothing and a relief from too much intellectual work. My main occupation, however, was reading and writing. I could not have all the books I wanted, as there were restrictions and a censorship, and the censors were not always very competent for the job. Spengler's *Decline of the West* was held up because the title looked dangerous and seditious. But I must not complain, for I had, on the whole, a goodly variety of books. Again I seem to have been a favoured person, and many of my colleagues (A Class prisoners) had the greatest difficulty in getting books on current topics. In Benares Gaol, I was told, even the official White Paper, containing the British Government's constitutional proposals, was not allowed in, as it dealt with political matters. The only books that British officials heartily recommended were religious books or novels. It is wonderful how dear to the heart of the British Government is the subject of religion and how impartially it encourages all brands of it.

When the most ordinary civil liberties have been curtailed in India, it is hardly pertinent to talk of a prisoner's rights. And yet the subject is worthy of consideration. If a court of law sentences a person to imprisonment, does it follow that not only his body but also his mind should be incarcerated? Why should not the minds of prisoners be free even though their bodies are not? Those in charge of the prison administrations in India will no doubt be horrified at such a question, for their capacity for new ideas and sustained thought is usually limited. Censorship is bad enough at any time and is partisan and stupid. In India it deprives us of a great deal of modern literature and advanced journals and newspapers. The list of proscribed books is extensive and is frequently added to. To add to all this, the prisoner has to suffer a second and a separate censorship, and thus many books and newspapers that can be legally purchased and read outside the prison may not reach him.

Some time ago this question arose in the United States, in the famous Sing Sing Prison of New York, where some Communist newspapers had been banned. The feeling against Communists is very strong among the ruling classes in America, but in spite of this the prison authorities agreed that the inmates of the prison could receive any publication which they desired, including Communist newspapers and magazines. The sole exception made by the Warden was in the case of cartoons which he regarded as inflammatory.

It is a little absurd to discuss this question of freedom of mind in prison in India when, as it happens, the vast majority of the prisoners are not allowed any newspapers or writing materials. It is not a question of censorship but of total denial. Only A Class (or in Bengal, Division I) prisoners are allowed writing materials as a matter of course, and not even all these are allowed daily newspapers. The daily newspaper allowed is of the Government's choice. B and C Class prisoners, politicals and non-politicals, are not supposed to have writing materials. The former may sometimes get them as a very special privilege, which is frequently withdrawn. Probably the proportion of A Class prisoners to the others is one to a thousand, and they might well be excluded in considering the lot of prisoners in India. But it is well to remember that even these favoured A Class convicts have far less privileges in regard to books and newspapers than the ordinary prisoners in most civilised countries.

For the rest, the 999 in every thousand, two or three books are permitted at a time, but conditions are such that they cannot always take advantage of this privilege. Writing or the taking of notes of books read are dangerous pastimes in which they must not indulge. This deliberate discouragement of intellectual development is curious and revealing. From the point of view of reclaiming a prisoner and of making him a fit citizen, his mind should be approached and diverted, and he should be made literate and taught some craft. But this point of view has perhaps not struck the prison authorities in India. Certainly it has been conspicuous by its absence in the United Provinces. Recently attempts have been made to teach reading and writing to the boys and young men in prison, but they are wholly ineffective, and the men in charge of them have no competence. Sometimes it is said that convicts are averse to learning. My own experience has been the exact opposite, and I found many of them, who came to me for the purpose, to have a perfect passion for learning to read and write. We used to teach such convicts as came our way, and they worked hard; and sometimes when I woke up in the middle of the night I was surprised to find one or two of them sitting by a dim lantern inside their barrack, learning their lessons for the next day.

So I occupied myself with my books, going from one type of reading to another, but usually sticking to 'heavy' books. Novels made one feel mentally slack, and I did not read many of them. Sometimes I would weary of too much reading, and then I would take to writing. My historical series of letters to my daughter kept me occupied right through my two-year term, and they helped me very greatly to keep mentally fit. To some extent I lived through the past I was writing about and almost forgot about my gaol surroundings.

~

Communalism and Reaction

(From An Autobiography*)*

...The Aga Khan had emerged as the leader of the Muslims, and that fact alone showed that they still clung to their feudal traditions, for the Aga Khan was no bourgeois leader. He was an exceedingly wealthy prince and the religious head of a sect, and from the British point of view he was very much persona grata because of his close association with the British ruling classes. He was widely cultured, and lived mostly in Europe, the life of a wealthy English landed magnate and sportsman; he was thus far from being personally narrow-minded on communal or sectarian matters. His leadership of the Muslims meant the lining up of the Muslim landed classes as well as the growing bourgeoisie with the British Government; the communal problem was really secondary and was obviously stressed in the interests of the main objective. Sir Valentine Chirol tells us that the Aga Khan impressed upon Lord Minto, the Viceroy, "the Mahommedan view of the political situation created by the partition of Bengal, lest political concessions should be hastily made to the Hindus which would pave the way for the ascendency of a Hindu majority equally dangerous to the stability of British rule and to the interests of the Mahommedan minority whose loyalty was beyond dispute."

But behind this superficial lining up with the British Government other forces were working. Inevitably the new Muslim bourgeoisie was feeling more and more dissatisfied with existing conditions and was being drawn towards the nationalist movement. The Aga Khan himself had to take notice of this and to warn the British in characteristic language. He wrote in the Edinburgh Review of January 1914 (that is, long before the War) advising the Government to abandon the policy of separating Hindus from Muslims, and to rally the moderate of both creeds in a common camp so as to provide a counterpoise to the radical nationalist tendencies of young India both Hindu and Muslim. It was thus clear that he was far more interested in checking political change in India than in the communal interests of Muslims. But the Aga Khan or the British Government could not stop the inevitable drift of the Muslim bourgeoisie towards nationalism. The World War hastened the process, and as new leaders arose the Aga Khan seemed to retire into the background. Even Aligarh College changed its tone, and among the new leaders the most dynamic were the Ali Brothers, both products of Aligarh. Doctor M. A. Ansari, Moulana Abul Kalam Azad, and a number of other bourgeois leaders now began to play an important part in the political affairs of the Muslims. So also, on a more moderate scale, Mr. M. A. Jinnah. Gandhiji swept most of these leaders (not Mr. Jinnah) and the Muslims generally into his Noncooperation movement, and they played a leading part in the events of 1919–23.

Then came the reaction, and communal and backward elements, both among the Hindus and the Muslims, began to emerge from their enforced retirement. It was a slow process, but it was a continuous one. The Hindu Mahasabha for the first time assumed some prominence, chiefly because of the communal tension, but politically it could not make much impression on the Congress. The Muslim communal organizations were more successful in regaining some of their old prestige among the Muslim masses. Even so a very strong group of Muslim leaders remained throughout with the Congress. The British Government meanwhile gave every encouragement to the Muslim communal leaders who were politically thoroughly reactionary. Noting the success of these reactionaries, the Hindu Mahasabha began to compete with them in reaction, thereby hoping to win the goodwill of the Government. Many of the progressive elements in the Mahasabha were driven out or left of their own accord, and it inclined more and more towards the upper middle classes, and especially the creditor and banker class.

The communal politicians on both sides, who were interminably arguing about percentages of seats in legislatures, thought only in terms of patronage which influence in Government gives. It was a struggle for jobs for the middle-class intelligentsia. There were obviously not enough jobs to go round, and so the Hindu and Muslim communalists quarrelled about them, the former on the defensive, for they had most of the existing jobs, the latter always wanting more and more. Behind this struggle for jobs there was a much more important contest which was not exactly communal but which influenced the communal issue. On the whole the Hindus were, in the Punjab, Sind, and Bengal, the richer, creditor, urban class; the Muslims in these provinces were the poorer, debtor, rural class. The conflict between the two was therefore often economic, but it was always given a communal colouring. In recent months this has come out very prominently in the debates on various provincial bills for reducing the burden of rural debt, especially in the Punjab. The representatives of the Hindu Mahasabha have consistently opposed these measures and sided with the banker class.

The Hindu Mahasabha is always laying stress on its own irreproachable nationalism when it criticises Muslim communalism. That the Muslim organizations have shown themselves to be quite extraordinarily communal has been patent to everybody. The Mahasabha's communalism has not been so obvious, as it masquerades under a nationalist cloak. The test comes when a national and democratic solution happens to injure upper-class Hindu interests, and in this test the Mahasabha has repeatedly failed. The separation of Sind has been consistently opposed by them in the economic interests of a minority and against the declared wishes of the majority.

But the most extraordinary exhibition of anti-nationalism and reaction, both on the part of Muslim and Hindu communalists, took place at the Round Table Conferences. The British Government had insisted on nominating only definitely communal Muslims, and these, under the leadership of the Aga Khan, actually went to the length of allying themselves with the most reactionary and, from the point of view not only of India but of all progressive groups, the most dangerous elements in British public life. It was quite extraordinary to see the close association of the Aga Khan and his group with Lord Lloyd and his party. They went a step further, and made pacts with the representatives of the European Association and others at the R.T.C. This was very depressing, for this Association has been and is, in India, the stoutest and the most aggressive opponent of Indian freedom.

The Hindu Mahasabha delegates responded to this by demanding, especially in the Punjab, all manner of checks on freedom safeguards in the interests of the British. They tried to outbid the Muslims in their attempts to offer cooperation to the British Government, and, without gaining anything, damned their own case and betrayed the cause of freedom. The Muslims had at least spoken with dignity, the Hindu communalists did not even possess this.

The outstanding fact seems to me how, on both sides, the communal leaders represent a small upper class reactionary group, and how these people exploit and take advantage of the religious passions of the masses for their own ends. On both sides every effort is made to suppress and avoid the consideration of economic issues. Soon the time will come when these issues can no longer be suppressed, and then, no doubt, the communal leaders on both sides will echo the Aga Khan's warning of twenty years ago for the moderates to join hands in a common camp against radical tendencies. To some extent that is already evident, for however much the Hindu and Muslim communalists attack each other in public they cooperate in the Assembly and elsewhere in helping Government to pass reactionary measures. Ottawa was one of the links which brought the three together.

Meanwhile it is interesting to notice that the Aga Khan's close association with the extreme Right wing of the Conservative party continues. In October 1934 he was the guest of honour at the British Navy League dinner, at which Lord Lloyd presided, and he supported wholeheartedly the proposals for further strengthening the British Navy, which Lord Lloyd had made at the Bristol Conservative Conference. An Indian leader was thus so anxious about imperial defence and the safety of England that he wanted to go further in increasing British armaments than even Mr. Baldwin or the ' National' Government. Of course, this was all in the interest of peace.

The next month, in November 1934, it was reported that a film was privately shown in London, the object of which was "to link the Muslim world in lasting friendship with the British Crown". We were informed that the guests of honour on this occasion were the Aga Khan and Lord Lloyd. It would seem that the Aga Khan and Lord Lloyd have become almost as inseparably united two hearts that beat as one in imperial affairs, as Sir Tej Bahadur Sapru and Mr. M. R. Jayakar are in our national politics. And it is worth noticing that, during these months when the two were so frequently communing with each other, Lord Lloyd was leading a bitter and unrelenting attack on the official Conservative leadership and the National Government for their alleged weakness in giving too much to India.[5]

Latterly there has been an interesting development in the speeches and statements of some of the Muslim communal leaders. This has no real importance, but I doubt if many people think so, nevertheless it is significant of the mentality of communalism, and a great deal of prominence has been given to it. Stress has been laid on the ' Muslim nation ' in India, on 'Muslim culture' on the utter incompatibility of Hindu and Muslim 'cultures'. The inevitable deduction from this is (although it is not put baldly) that the British must remain in India for ever and ever to hold the scales and mediate between the two 'cultures'.

A few Hindu communal leaders think exactly on the same

---

[5] Recently a Council of some British peers and Indian Muslims has been formed to cement and further the union of these extreme reactionary elements.

lines, with this difference, however, that they hope that being in a majority, their brand of 'culture ' will ultimately prevail.

Hindu and Muslim 'cultures' and the 'Muslim nation': how these words open out fascinating vistas of past history and present and future speculation! The Muslim nation in India, a nation within a nation, and not even compact, but vague, spread out, indeterminate. Politically, the idea is absurd, economically it is fantastic; it is hardly worth considering. And yet it helps us a little to understand the mentality behind it. Some such separate and unmixable 'nations' existed together in the Middle Ages and afterwards. In the Constantinople of the early days of the Ottoman Sultans each such 'nation' lived separately and had a measure of autonomy- Latin Christians, Orthodox Christians, Jews, etc. This was the beginning of extraterritoriality which, in more recent times, became such a nightmare to many eastern countries. To talk of a 'Muslim nation', therefore, means that there is no nation at all but a religious bond; it means that no nation in the modern sense must be allowed to grow; it means that modern civilisation should be discarded and we should go back to the medieval ways; it means either autocratic government or a foreign government; it means, finally, just nothing at all except an emotional state of mind and a conscious or unconscious desire not to face realities, especially economic realities. Emotions have a way of upsetting logic, and we may not ignore them simply because they seem so unreasonable. But this idea of a Muslim nation is the figment of a few imaginations only, and, but for the publicity given to it by the Press, few people would have heard of it. And even if many people believed in it, it would still vanish at the touch of reality.

~

Struggle

(From An Autobiography*)*

...In thinking over the troubles and conflicts of the world, I forgot to some extent my own personal and national troubles. I would even feel buoyant occasionally at the fact that I was alive at this great revolutionary period of the world's history. Perhaps I might also have to play some little part in my own corner of the world in the great changes that were to come. At other times I would find the atmosphere of conflict and violence all over the world very depressing. Worse still was the sight of intelligent men and women who had become so accustomed to human degradation and slavery that their minds were too coarsened to resent suffering and poverty and inhumanity. Noisy vulgarity and organized humbug flourished in this stifling moral atmosphere, and good men were silent. The triumph of Hitler and the Brown Terror that followed was a great shock, though I consoled myself that it could only be temporary. One almost had the feeling of the futility of human endeavour. The machine went on blindly, what could a little cog in it do?

But still the communist philosophy of life gave me comfort and hope. How was it to be applied to India? We had not solved yet the problem of political freedom, and the nationalistic outlook filled our minds. Were we to jump to economic freedom at the same time or take them in turn, however short the interval might be? World events as well as happenings in India were forcing the social issue to the front, and it seemed that political freedom could no longer be separated from it.

The policy of the British Government in India had resulted in ranging the socially reactionary classes in opposition to political independence. That was inevitable, and I welcomed the clearer demarcation of the various classes and groups in India. But was this fact appreciated by others? Apparently not by many. It was true that there were a handful of orthodox Communists in some of the big cities and they were hostile to, and bitterly critical of, the national movement. The organized Labour movement, especially in Bombay and, to a lesser extent, in Calcutta, was also socialistic in a loose kind of way, but it was broken up into bits and suffering from the depression. Vague communistic and socialist ideas had spread among the intelligentsia, even among intelligent government officials. The younger men and women of the

Congress, who used to read Bryce on Democracies and Morley and Keith and Mazzini, were now reading, when they could get them, books on socialism and communism and Russia. The Meerut Conspiracy Case had helped greatly in directing people's minds to these new ideas, and the world crisis had compelled attention. Everywhere there was in evidence a new spirit of enquiry, a questioning, and a challenge to existing institutions. The general direction of the mental wind was obvious, but still it was a gentle breeze, unsure of itself. Some people flirted with Fascist ideas. A clear and definite ideology was lacking. Nationalism still was the dominating thought.

It seemed clear to me that nationalism would remain the outstanding urge, till some measure of political freedom was attained. Because of this the Congress had been, and was still (apart from certain Labour circles), the most advanced organization in India, as it was far the most powerful. During the past thirteen years, under Gandhiji's leadership, it had produced a wonderful awakening of the masses and, in spite of its vague bourgeois ideology, it had served a revolutionary purpose. It had not exhausted its utility yet, and was not likely to do so till the nationalist urge gave place to a social one. Future progress, both ideological and in action, must therefore be largely associated with the Congress, though other avenues could also be used.

To desert the Congress seemed to me thus to cut oneself adrift from the vital urge of the nation, to blunt the most powerful weapon we had, and perhaps to waste energy in ineffective adventurism. And yet, was the Congress, constituted as it was, ever likely to adopt a really radical social solution? If such an issue was placed before it, the result was bound to be to split it into two or more parts, or at least to drive away large sections from it. That in itself was not undesirable or unwelcome if the issues became clearer and a strongly-knit group, either a majority or minority in the Congress, stood for a radical social programme.

But Congress at present meant Gandhiji. What would he do? Ideologically he was sometimes amazingly backward, and yet in action he had been the greatest revolutionary of recent times in

India. He was a unique personality, and it was impossible to judge him by the usual standards, or even to apply the ordinary canons of logic to him. But because he was a revolutionary at bottom and was pledged to political independence for India, he was bound to play an uncompromising role till that independence was achieved. And in this very process he would release tremendous mass energies and would himself, I half hoped, advance step by step towards the social goal.

The orthodox Communists in India and outside have for many years past attacked Gandhiji and the Congress bitterly, and imputed all manner of base motives to the Congress leaders. Many of their theoretical criticisms of Congress ideology were able and pointed, and subsequent events partly justified them. Some of the earlier Communist analyses of the general Indian political situation turned out to be remarkably correct. But as soon as they leave their general principles and enter into details, and especially when they consider the role of the Congress, they go hopelessly astray. One of the reasons for the weakness in numbers as well as influence of the Communists in India is that, instead of spreading a scientific knowledge of communism and trying to convert people's minds to it, they have largely concentrated on abuse of others. This has reacted on them and done them great injury. Most of them are used to working in labour areas, where a few slogans are usually enough to win over the workers. But mere slogans are not enough for the intellectual, and they have not realised that in India today the middle-class intellectual is the most revolutionary force. Almost in spite of the orthodox Communists, many intellectuals have been drawn to communism, but even so there is a gulf between them.

According to the Communists, the objective of the Congress leaders has been to bring mass pressure on the government in order to obtain industrial and commercial concessions in the interests of Indian capitalists and zamindars. The task of the Congress is "to harness the economic and political discontent of the peasantry, the lower middle-class and the industrial working-class to the chariot of the mill-owners and financiers of Bombay, Ahmedabad and

Calcutta." The Indian capitalists are supposed to sit behind the scenes and issue orders to the Congress Working Committee first to organize a mass movement and, when it becomes too vast and dangerous, to suspend it or sidetrack it. Further, that the Congress leaders really do not want the British to go away, as they are required to control and exploit a starving population, and the Indian middle class do not feel themselves equal to this.

It is surprising that able Communists should believe this fantastic analysis, but believing this as they apparently do, it is not surprising that they should fail so remarkably in India. Their basic error seems to be that they judge the Indian National Movement from European Labour standards, and used as they are to the repeated betrayals of the labour movement by the labour leaders, they apply the analogy to India. The Indian National Movement is obviously not a labour or proletarian movement. It is a bourgeois movement, as its very name implies, and its objective so far has been, not a change of the social order, but political independence. This objective may be criticised as not far-reaching enough, and nationalism itself may be condemned as out of date. But accepting the fundamental basis of the movement, it is absurd to say that the leaders betray the masses because they do not try to upset the land system or the capitalist system. They never claimed to do so. Some people in the Congress, and they are a growing number, want to change the land system and the capitalist system, but they cannot speak in the name of the Congress.

It is true that the Indian capitalist classes (not the big zamindars and taluqadars) have profited greatly by the national movement because of British and other foreign boycotts, and the push given to swadeshi. This was inevitable, as every national movement encourages home industries and preaches boycotts. As a matter of fact, the Bombay mill industry in a body, during the continuance of civil disobedience and when we were preaching the boycott of British goods, had the temerity to conclude a pact with Lancashire. From the point of view of the Congress, this was a gross betrayal of the national cause, and it was characterised as such. The representative of the Bombay mill owners in the

Assembly also consistently ran down the Congress and 'extremists ' while most of us were in gaol.

The part that many capitalist elements have played in India during the past few years has been scandalous, even from the Congress and nationalist viewpoint. Ottawa may have benefited, temporarily, some small groups, but it was bad in the interest of Indian industry as a whole, and made it even more subservient to British capital and industry. It was harmful to the masses, and it was negotiated while our struggle was being carried on, and many thousands were in prison. Every Dominion wrung out the hardest terms from England, but India had the privilege of making almost a gift to her. During the last few years also, financial adventurers have trafficked in gold and silver at India's expense.

As for the big zamindars and taluqadars, they ranged themselves completely against the Congress in the Round Table Conference, and they openly and aggressively declared themselves on the side of the Government right through civil disobedience. It was with their help that Government passed repressive legislation in various provinces embodying the Ordinances. And in the United Provinces Council the great majority of the zamindar members voted against the release of civil disobedience prisoners.

The idea that Gandhiji was forced to launch seemingly aggressive movements in 1921 and 1930 because of mass pressure is also absolutely wrong. Mass stirrings there were, of course, but on both occasions it was Gandhiji who forced the pace. In 1921 he carried the Congress almost single-handed, and plunged it into noncooperation. In 1930 it would have been quite impossible to have any aggressive and effective direct action movement if he had resisted it in any way.

It is very unfortunate that foolish and ill-informed criticisms of a personal nature are made, because they divert attention from the real issues.

To attack Gandhiji's bona fides is to injure oneself and one's own cause, for to the millions of India he stands as the embodiment of truth, and anyone who knows him at all realises the passionate earnestness with which he is always seeking to do right.

Communists in India have associated with the industrial workers of the big towns. They have little knowledge of, or contact with, the rural areas. The industrial workers, important as they are, and likely to be more so in the future, must take second place before the peasants, for the problem of today in India is the problem of the peasantry. Congress workers, on the other hand, have spread all over these rural areas and, in the ordinary course, the Congress must develop into a vast peasant organization. Peasants are seldom revolutionary after their immediate objective is attained, and it is likely that sometime in the future the usual problem of city versus village and industrial worker versus peasant will rise in India also.

~

The Karachi Resolution: 1931

The Karachi Congress resolution on Fundamental Rights and Economic Programme, as varied by the All-India Congress Committee in its meeting held in Bombay on 6, 7, and 8 August, 1931, runs as follows:

This Congress is of opinion that to enable the masses to appreciate what 'Swaraj,' as conceived by the Congress, will mean to them, it is desirable to state the position of the Congress in a manner easily understood by them. In order to end the exploitation of the masses, political freedom must include real economic freedom of the starving millions. The Congress therefore declares that any constitution which may be agreed to on its behalf should provide, or enable the Swaraj Government to provide, the following:

Fundamental Rights and Duties

(i) Every citizen of India has the right of free expression of opinion, the right of free association and combination, and the right to assemble peacefully and without arms, for a purpose not opposed to law or morality.

(ii) Every citizen shall enjoy freedom of conscience and the right freely to profess and practise his religion, subject to public order and morality.

(iii) The culture, language and script of the minorities and of the different linguistic areas shall be protected.

(iv) All citizens are equal before the law, irrespective of religion, caste, creed or sex.

(v) No disability attaches to any citizen by reason of his or her religion, caste, creed or sex, in regard to public employment, office of power or honour, and in the exercise of any trade or calling.

(vi) All citizens have equal rights and duties in regard to wells, tanks, roads, schools and places of public resort, maintained out of state or local funds, or dedicated by private persons for the use of the general public.

(vii) Every citizen has the right to keep and bear arms, in accordance with regulations and reservations made in that behalf.

(viii) No person shall be deprived of his liberty, nor shall his dwelling or property be entered, sequestered, or confiscated, save in accordance with law.

(ix) The State shall observe neutrality in regard to all religions.

(x) The franchise shall be on the basis of universal adult suffrage.

(xi) The State shall provide for free and compulsory primary education.

(xii) The State shall confer no titles.

(xiii) There shall be no capital punishment.

(xiv) Every citizen is free to move throughout India and to stay and settle in any part thereof, to acquire property and to follow any trade or calling, and to be treated equally with regard to legal prosecution or protection in all parts of India.

Labour

2. (*a*) The organization of economic life must conform to the principle of justice, to the end that it may secure a decent standard of living.

(*b*) The State shall safeguard the interests of industrial workers and shall secure for them, by suitable legislation and in other ways, a living wage, healthy conditions of work, limited hours of labour, suitable machinery for the settlement of disputes between employers and workmen, and protection against the economic consequences of old age, sickness and unemployment.

3. Labour to be freed from serfdom and conditions bordering on serfdom.
4. Protection of women workers, and especially, adequate provision for leave during maternity period.
5. Children of school-going age shall not be employed in mines and factories.
6. Peasants and workers shall have the right to form unions to protect their interest.

Taxation and Expenditure

7. The system of land tenure and revenue and rent shall be reformed and an equitable adjustment made of the burden on agricultural land, immediately giving relief to the smaller peasantry, by a substantial reduction of agricultural rent and revenue now paid by them, and in case of uneconomic holdings, exempting them from rent, so long as necessary, with such relief as may be just and necessary to holders of small estates affected by such exemption or reduction in rent, and to the same end, imposing a graded tax on net incomes from land above a reasonable minimum.
8. Death duties on a graduated scale shall be levied on property above a fixed minimum.
9. There shall be a drastic reduction of military expenditure so as to bring it down to at least one half of the present scale.
10. Expenditure and salaries in civil departments shall be largely reduced. No servant of the state, other than specially employed experts and the like, shall be paid above a certain fixed figure, which should not ordinarily exceed Rs. 500 per month.

11. No duty shall be levied on salt manufactured in India.

Economic and Social Programme

12. The State shall protect indigenous cloth; and for this purpose pursue the policy of exclusion of foreign cloth and foreign yarn from the country and adopt such other measures as may be found necessary. The State shall also protect other indigenous industries, when necessary, against foreign competition.
13. Intoxicating drinks and drugs shall be totally prohibited, except for medicinal purposes.
14. Currency and exchange shall be regulated in the national interest.
15. The State shall own or control key industries and services, mineral resources, railways, waterways, shipping and other means of public transport.
16. Relief of agricultural indebtedness and control of usury—direct and indirect.
17. The State shall provide for the military training of citizens so as to organize a means of national defence apart from the regular military forces.

~

Earthquake[6]

(*From* An Autobiography)

...The city of Monghyr was the last place in our tour. We had wandered a good deal and gone almost up to the frontier of Nepal, and we had seen many harrowing sights. We had become used to ruins and destruction on a vast scale. And yet when we saw Monghyr and the absolute destruction of this rich city, we gasped and shivered at the horror of it. I can never forget that terrible sight.

---

[6] The 1934 Bihar–Nepal earthquake occurred on 15 January and caused widespread damage in northern Bihar and in Nepal.

All over the earthquake areas there was a very painful absence of self-help among the residents, both in the cities and villages. Probably the middle classes in the cities were the worst offenders in this respect. They all waited for somebody to take action and help them, either the government or the non-official relief agencies. Others who offered their services thought that work meant ordering people about. Part of this feeling of helplessness was no doubt due to the nervous collapse brought about by the terror of the earthquake, and it must have gradually lessened.

In marked contrast with this was the energy and capacity of the large numbers of relief workers who poured in from other parts of Behar and other provinces. It was wonderful to see the spirit of efficient service of these young men and women and, in spite of the fact that a host of separate relief organizations were working, there was a great deal of co-operation between them.

In Monghyr I indulged in a theatrical gesture to give a push to the self-help movement for digging and removing the debris. I did so with some hesitation, but it turned out to be a success. All the leaders of the relief organizations went out with spades and baskets and did a good day's digging, and we brought out the corpse of a little girl. I left Monghyr that day, but the digging went on and many local people took it up with very good results.

Of all the non-official relief organizations the Central Relief Committee, of which Rajendra Prasad was the head, was by far the most important. This was by no means a purely Congress organization, and it developed into an all-India body representing various groups and the donors. It had, however, the great advantage of having the Congress organization in the rural areas at its disposal. In no province in India, except Gujarat and some districts of the United Provinces, were the Congress workers more in touch with the peasants. In fact the workers themselves came largely from the peasantry; Behar is pre-eminently the peasant province of India and even its middle classes are closely allied to the peasantry. Sometimes when, as Congress Secretary, I went to inspect the Behar Provincial Congress Committee's office, I criticised in vigorous language what I considered was their inefficiency and general slackness in keeping office. There was a tendency to sit rather than stand, to lie down rather than sit. The office was one of the barest I had seen, for they would try to carry on without many of the usual office accessories. Yet, in spite of my criticism of the office, I knew well that from the Congress point of view the province was one of the most earnest and devoted in the country. Congress made no show there, but it had the solid backing of the peasantry. Even in the All India Congress Committee the Behar members seldom took up an aggressive attitude in any matter. They seemed to be a little surprised at finding themselves there. But in both the Civil Disobedience movements Behar put up a splendid record. Even in the subsequent individual civil disobedience, it did well.

The Relief Committee availed itself of this fine organization to reach the peasantry. In the rural areas no other agency, not even the government, could be so helpful. And the head of both the Relief Committee and the Behar Congress organization was Rajendra Babu, the unquestioned leader of Behar. Looking like a peasant, a typical son of the soil of Behar, he is not impressive at first sight till one notices his keen frank eyes and his earnest look. One does not forget that look or those eyes, for through them truth looks at you and there is no doubting them. Peasant-like, he is perhaps a little limited in outlook, somewhat unsophisticated from the point of view of the modern world, but his outstanding ability, his perfect straightness, his energy, and his devotion to the cause of Indian freedom are qualities which have made him loved not only in his own province but throughout India. No one in any province in India occupies quite that universally acknowledged position of leadership as Rajendra Babu does in Behar. Few others, if any, can be said to have imbibed more thoroughly the real message of Gandhiji.

It was fortunate that a man like him was available for the leadership of the relief-work in Behar, and it was faith in him that drew a vast sum of money from all over India. Weak in health, he threw himself into the work of relief. He overworked himself, for he became the centre of all activity and everybody turned to him for advice.

During my tour in the earthquake areas, or just before going there, I read with a great shock Gandhiji's statement to the effect that the earthquake had been a punishment for the sin of untouchability. This was a staggering remark and I welcomed and wholly agreed with Rabindra Nath Tagore's answer to it. Anything more opposed to the scientific outlook it would be difficult to imagine. Perhaps even science will not be absolutely dogmatic today about the effect of emotional states and psychic occurrences on matter. A mental shock may result in indigestion or something worse to the person concerned. But to suggest that a human custom or failing had its reactions on the movements of the earth's crust is an astounding thing. The idea of sin and divine wrath and man's relative importance in the affairs of the universe take us back a few hundred years, when the Inquisition flourished in Europe and burned Giordano Bruno for his scientific heresy and sent many a witch to the stake! Even in the eighteenth century in America leading Boston divines attributed earthquakes in Massachusetts to the impiety of lightning rods.

And if the earthquake was a divine punishment for sin, how are we to discover for which sin we are being punished? For, alas! we have many sins to atone for. Each person can have his pet explanation; we may have been punished for submitting to alien domination, or for putting up with an unjust social system. The Maharaja of Durbhanga, the owner of enormous estates, was, financially, one of the major sufferers from the earthquake. We might as well say that this was a judgment on the zamindari system. That would be nearer the mark than to suggest that the more or less innocent people of Behar were being made to suffer vicariously for the sins of untouchability of the people of South India. Why did not the earthquake visit the land of untouchability itself? Or the British Government might call the calamity a divine punishment for civil disobedience, for, as a matter of fact, North Behar, which suffered most from the earthquake, took a leading part in the freedom movement.

We can go on speculating indefinitely in this manner. And then, of course, the question arises, why we should interfere with the workings of Providence or try to lessen the effect of its divine decrees by our humane efforts. And we begin to wonder why Providence has played this cruel joke on us: to make us full of imperfections, to surround us with snares and pitfalls, to create a miserable and cruel world, to make the tiger and the lamb, and then to punish us.

"When the stars threw down their spears
And water'd heaven with their tears,
Dare he laugh his work to see?
Dare he who made the lamb make thee?"

On my last night in Patna I sat up till very late with many friends and comrades who had gathered there from various provinces to offer their services for relief work. The U.P. was well represented and some of our chosen men were there. We discussed a problem that was troubling us: how far must we allow ourselves to be involved in earthquake relief? That meant, to that extent at least, a withdrawal from political work. Relief work was very exacting and we could not take it up casually. Absorption in it might well involve a long period of absence from the active political sphere, and that was bound to have a bad effect politically on our province. Although there were many in the Congress fold, the people who make a difference were always limited in number and could ill be spared. And yet the call of the earthquake could not be ignored. For my part I had no intention of devoting myself exclusively to relief work. I felt that there would be no lack of people for that; there were few for more risky activities.

~

A Visit to Gandhi Ji

(From An Autobiography*)*

Recently there has been an artistic awakening, led by the brilliant Tagore family, and its influence is already apparent all over India. But how can any art flourish widely when the people of the country are hampered and restricted and suppressed at every turn and live in an atmosphere of fear?

In Bombay I met many friends and comrades, some only recently out of prison. The socialistic element was strong there, and there was much resentment at recent happenings in the upper ranks of the Congress. Gandhiji was severely criticised for his metaphysical outlook applied to politics. With much of the criticism I was in agreement, but I was quite clear that, situated as we were, we had little choice in the matter and had to carry on. Any attempt to withdraw civil disobedience would have brought no relief to us, for the government's offensive would continue and all effective work would inevitably lead to prison. Our national movement had arrived at a stage when it had to be suppressed by government, or it would impose its will on the British Government. This meant that it had arrived at a stage when it was always likely to be declared illegal and, as a movement, it could not go back even if civil disobedience was withdrawn. The continuance of disobedience made little difference in practice, but it was an act of moral defiance which had value. It was easier to spread new ideas during a struggle than it would be when the struggle was wound-up for the time being, and demoralisation ensued. The only alternative to the struggle was a compromising attitude to the British authority and constitutional action in the councils.

It was a difficult position, and the choice was not an easy one. I appreciated the mental conflicts of my colleagues, for I had myself had to face them. But I found there, as I have found elsewhere in India, some people who wanted to make high socialistic doctrine a refuge for inaction. It was a little irritating to find people, who did little themselves, criticise others who had shouldered the burden in the heat and dust of the fray as reactionaries. These parlour socialists are especially hard on Gandhiji as the arch-reactionary, and advance arguments which in logic, leave little to be desired. But the little fact remains that this 'reactionary' knows India, understands India, almost is peasant India, and has shaken up India as no so-called revolutionary has done. Even his latest Harijan activities have gently but irresistibly undermined orthodox Hinduism and shaken it to its foundations. The whole tribe of the Orthodox have ranged themselves against him, and consider him their most dangerous enemy, although he continues to treat them with all gentleness and courtesy. In his own peculiar way he has a knack of releasing powerful forces which spread out, like ripples on the water's surface, and affect millions. Reactionary or revolutionary, he has changed the face of India, given pride and character to a cringing and demoralised people, built up strength and consciousness in the masses, and made the Indian problem a world problem. Quite apart from the objectives aimed at and its metaphysical implications, the method of non-violent noncooperation or civil resistance is a unique and powerful contribution of his to India and the world, and there can be no doubt that it has been peculiarly suited to Indian conditions.

I think it is right that we should encourage honest criticism, and have as much public discussion of our problems as possible. It is unfortunate that Gandhiji's dominating position has to some extent prevented this discussion. There was always a tendency to rely on him and to leave the decision to him. This is obviously wrong, and the nation can only advance by reasoned acceptance of objectives and methods, and a cooperation and discipline based on them and not on blind obedience. No one, however great he may be, should be above criticism.

But when criticism becomes a mere refuge for inaction there is something wrong with it. For socialists to indulge in this kind of thing is to invite condemnation from the public, for the masses judge by acts. "He who denies the sharp tasks of today," says Lenin, "in the name of dreams about soft tasks of the future becomes an opportunist. Theoretically it means to fail to base oneself on the developments now going on in real life, to detach oneself from them in the name of dreams."

Socialists and communists in India are largely nurtured on

literature dealing with the industrial proletariat. In some selected areas, like Bombay or near Calcutta, large numbers of factory workers abound, but for the rest India remains agricultural, and the Indian problem cannot be disposed of, or treated effectively in terms of the industrial workers. Nationalism and rural economy are the dominating considerations, and European socialism seldom deals with these. Pre-war conditions in Russia were a much nearer approach to India, but there again the most extraordinary and unusual occurrences took place, and it is absurd to expect a repetition of these anywhere else. I do believe that the philosophy of communism helps us to understand and analyse existing conditions in any country, and further indicates the road to future progress. But it is doing violence and injustice to that philosophy to apply it blindfold and without due regard to facts and conditions.

Life is anyhow a complex affair, and the conflicts and contradictions of life sometimes make one despair a little. It is not surprising that people should differ, or even that comrades with a common approach to problems should draw different conclusions. But a person who tries to hide his own weakness in high-sounding phrases and noble principles is apt to be suspect. A person who tries to save himself from prison by giving undertakings and assurances to the government, or by other dubious conduct, and then has the temerity to criticise others, is likely to injure the cause he espouses.

Bombay being a vast cosmopolitan city had all manner of people. One prominent citizen, however, showed a perfectly remarkable catholicity in his political, economic, social and religious outlook. As a Labour leader, he was a socialist; in politics generally he called himself a Democrat; he was a favourite of the Hindu Sabha and he promised to protect old religious and social customs and prevent the legislature from interfering; at election time he became the nominee of the Sanatanists, those high priests at the shrine of the ancient mysteries. Not finding this varied and diverting career exhausting enough, he utilised his superfluous energy in criticising Congress and condemning Gandhiji as reactionary. In cooperation with a few others he started a Congress Democratic Party, which incidentally had nothing to do with democracy, and was connected with Congress only in so far as it attacked that august body. Searching for fresh fields to conquer, he then attended the Geneva Labour Conference as a Labour delegate. One might almost think that he was qualifying for the Prime Ministership of a 'National' Government after the English fashion.

Few people can have had the advantage of such a varied outlook and activities. And yet among the critics of the Congress there were many who had experimented in various fields, and who kept a finger in many a pie. A few of these called themselves socialists, and they gave a bad name to socialism.

~

The Last Phase: Nationalism Versus Imperialism, Helplessness of the Middle Classes, Gandhi Comes

(*From* The Discovery of India)

What could we do? How could we pull India out of this quagmire of poverty and defeatism which sucked her in? Not for a few years of excitement and agony and suspense, but for long generations our people had offered their 'blood and toil, tears and sweat.' And this process had eaten its way deep into the body and soul of India, poisoning every aspect of our corporate life, like that fell disease which consumes the tissues of the lungs and kills slowly but inevitably. Sometimes we thought that some swifter and more obvious process, resembling cholera or the bubonic plague, would have been better; but that was a passing thought, for adventurism leads nowhere, and the quack treatment of deep-seated diseases does not yield results.

And then Gandhi came. He was like a powerful current of fresh air that made us stretch ourselves and take deep breaths; like a beam of light that pierced the darkness and removed the scales from our eyes; like a whirlwind that upset many things, but most of all the working of people's minds. He did not descend from the top; he seemed to emerge from the millions of India, speaking their language and incessantly drawing attention to them and their appalling condition. Get off the backs of these peasants and workers, he told us, all you who live by their exploitation; get rid of the system that produces this poverty and misery. Political freedom took new shape then and acquired a new content. Much that he said we only partially accepted or sometimes did not accept at all. But all this was secondary. The essence of his teaching was fearlessness and truth, and action allied to these, always keeping the welfare of the masses in view. The greatest gift for an individual or a nation, so we had been told in our ancient books, was abhaya (fearlessness), not merely bodily courage but the absence of fear from the mind. Janaka and Yajnavalka had said, at the dawn of our history, that it was the function of the leaders of a people to make them fearless. But the dominant impulse in India under British rule was that of fear—pervasive, oppressing, strangling fear; fear of the army, the police, the widespread secret service; fear of the official class; fear of laws meant to suppress and of prison; fear of the landlord's agent; fear of the moneylender; fear of unemployment and starvation, which were always on the threshold. It was against this all-pervading fear that Gandhi's quiet and determined voice was raised: Be not afraid. Was it so simple as all that? Not quite. And yet fear builds its phantoms which are more fearsome than reality itself, and reality, when calmly analysed and its consequences willingly accepted, loses much of its terror.

So, suddenly, as it were, that black pall of fear was lifted from the people's shoulders, not wholly of course, but to an amazing degree. As fear is a close companion to falsehood, so truth follows fearlessness. The Indian people did not become much more truthful than they were, nor did they change their essential nature overnight; nevertheless a sea of change was visible as the need for falsehood and furtive behaviour lessened. It was a psychological change, almost as if some expert in psychoanalytical methods had probed deep into the patient's past, found out the origins of his complexes, exposed them to his view, and thus rid him of that burden.

There was that psychological reaction also, a feeling of shame at our long submission to an alien rule that had degraded and humiliated us, and a desire to submit no longer whatever the consequences might be.

We did not grow much more truthful perhaps than we had been previously, but Gandhi was always there as a symbol of uncompromising truth to pull us up and shame us into truth. What is truth? I do not know for certain, and perhaps our truths are relative and absolute truth is beyond us. Different persons may and do take different views of truth, and each individual is powerfully influenced by his own background, training, and impulses. So also Gandhi. But truth is at least for an individual what he himself feels and knows to be true. According to this definition I do not know of any person who holds to the truth as Gandhi does. That is a dangerous quality in a politician, for he speaks out his mind and even lets the public see its changing phases.

Gandhi influenced millions of people in India in varying degrees. Some changed the whole texture of their lives, others were only partly affected, or the effect wore off; and yet not quite, for some part of it could not be wholly shaken off. Different people reacted differently and each give his own answer to this question. Some might well say almost in the words of Alcibiades: 'Besides, when we listen to anyone else talking, however eloquent he is, we don't really care a damn what he says; but when we listen to you, or to someone else repeating what you've said, even if he puts it ever so badly, and never mind whether the person who is listening is man, woman, or child, we're absolutely staggered and bewitched. And speaking for myself, gentlemen, if I wasn't afraid you'd tell me I was completely bottled, I'd swear on oath what an extraordinary effect his words have had on me—and still do, if it comes to that. For the moment I hear him speak I am smitten by a kind of sacred rage, worse than any Corybant, and my heart jumps into my mouth and the tears start into my eyes—Oh, and not only me, but lots of other men.

'And there is one thing I've never felt with anybody else—not the kind of thing you would expect to find in me, either—and that is a sense of shame. Socrates is the only man in the world that can make me feel ashamed. Because there's no getting away from it, I know I ought to do the things he tells me to; and yet the moment I'm out of his sight I don't care what I do to keep in with the mob. So I dash off like a runaway slave, and keep out of his way as long as I can: and the next time I meet him I remember all that I had to admit the time before, and naturally I feel ashamed....

'Yes, I have heard Pericles and all the other great orators, and very eloquent I thought they were; but they never affected me like that; they never turned my whole soul upside down and left me feeling as if I were the lowest of the low; but this latter day Maryas, here, has often left me in such a state of mind that I've felt I simply couldn't go on living the way I did....

'Only I've been bitten by something much more poisonous than a snake; in fact, mine is the most painful kind of bite there is. I've been bitten in the heart, or the mind or whatever you like to call it...'[7]

[7] From *The Five Dialogues of Plato*, Everyman's Library.

Religion and Spirituality

Coconada and M. Mohamad Ali

(From An Autobiography*)*

In December 1923 the annual session of the Congress was held at Coconada in the South. Maulana Mohamad Ali was the President and, as was his wont, he delivered an enormously long presidential address. But it was an interesting one. He traced the growth of political and communal feeling among the Moslems and showed how the famous Moslem deputation to the Viceroy in 1908, under the leadership of the Aga Khan, which led to the first official declaration in favour of separate electorates, was a command performance and had been engineered by the Government itself.

Mohamad Ali induced me, much against my will, to accept the All India Congress secretaryship for his year of presidentship. I had no desire to accept executive responsibility, when I was not clear about future policy. But I could not resist Mohamad Ali, and both of us felt that some other secretary might not be able to work as harmoniously with the new President as I could. He had strong likes and dislikes, and I was fortunate enough to be included in his 'likes'. A bond of affection and mutual appreciation tied us to each other. He was deeply and, as I considered, most irrationally religious, and I was not, but I was attracted by his earnestness, his overflowing energy and keen intelligence. He had a nimble wit, but sometimes his devastating sarcasm hurt, and he lost many a friend thereby. It was quite impossible for him to keep a clever remark to himself, whatever the consequences might be.

We got on well together during his year of office, though we had many little points of difference. I introduced in our A.I.C.C. office a practice of addressing all our members by their names only, without any prefixes or suffixes, honorific titles and the like. There are so many of these in India- Mahatma, Maulana, Pandit, Shaikh, Syed, Munshi, Moulvi, and latterly Sriyut and Shri, and, of course, Mr and Esquire and they are so abundantly and often unnecessarily used that I wanted to set a good example. But I was not to have my way. Mohamed Ali sent me a frantic telegram directing me as president to revert to our old practice and, in particular, always to address Gandhiji as Mahatma.

Another frequent subject for argument between us was the Almighty. Mohamed Ali had an extraordinary way of bringing in some reference to God even in Congress resolutions, either by way of expressing gratitude or some kind of prayer. I used to protest, and then he would shout at me for my irreligion. And yet, curiously enough, he would tell me later that he was quite sure that I was fundamentally religious, in spite of my superficial behaviour or my declarations to the contrary. I have often wondered how much truth there was in his statement. Perhaps it depends on what is meant by religion and religious.

I avoided discussing this subject of religion with him, because I knew we would only irritate each other, and I might hurt him. It is always a difficult subject to discuss with convinced believers of any creed. With most Moslems it is probably an even harder matter for discussion, since no latitude of thought is officially permitted to them. Ideologically, theirs is a straight and narrow path, and the believer must not swerve to the right or the left. Hindus are somewhat different, though not always so. In practice they may be very orthodox; they may, and do, indulge in the most out-of-date, reactionary and even pernicious customs, and yet they will usually be prepared to discuss the most radical ideas about religion. I imagine the modern Arya Samajists have not, as a rule, this wide intellectual approach. Like the Moslems, they follow their own straight and narrow path. There is a certain philosophical tradition among the intelligent Hindus, which, though it does not affect practice, does make a difference to the ideological approach to a religious question. Partly, I suppose, this is due to the wide and often conflicting variety of opinions and customs that are included in the Hindu fold. It has, indeed, often been remarked that Hinduism is hardly a religion in the usual sense of the word. And yet, what amazing tenacity it has got, what tremendous power of survival! One may even be a professing atheist as the old Hindu philosopher, Charvaka, was and yet no one dare say that he has ceased to be a Hindu. Hinduism clings on to its children, almost despite them. A Brahman I was born, and a Brahman I seem to remain whatever I might say or do in regard to religion or social custom. To the Indian world I am 'Pandit' so and so, in spite of my desire not to have this or any other honorific title attached to my name. I remember meeting a Turkish scholar once in Switzerland, to whom I had sent previously a letter of introduction in which I had been referred to as 'Pandit Jawaharlal Nehru'. He was surprised and a little disappointed to see me for, as he told me, the 'Pandit' had led him to expect a reverend and scholarly gentleman of advanced years.

So Mohamad Ali and I did not discuss religion. But he did not possess the virtue of silence, and some years later (I think this was in 1925 or early in 1926) he could not repress himself on this subject any more. He burst out one day, as I was visiting him in his house in Delhi, and said that he insisted on discussing religion with me. I tried to dissuade him, pointing out that our veiwpoints were very different, and we were not likely to make much impression on each other. But he was not going to be diverted. "We must have it out," he said. " I suppose you think that I am a fanatic. Well, I am going to show you that I am not." He told me that he had studied the subject of religion deeply and extensively. He pointed out shelves full of books on various religions, especially Islam and Christianity, and including some modern books like H. G. Wells's *God, the Invisible King*. During the long years of his wartime internment, he had gone through the Quran repeatedly, and consulted all the commentaries on it. As a result of this study he found out, so he told me, that about 97 per cent, of what was contained in the Quran was entirely reasonable, and could be justified even apart from the Quran. The remaining 3 per cent was not prima facie acceptable to his reason. But was it more likely that the Quran, which was obviously right in regard to 97 per cent, was also right in regard to the remaining 3 per cent, than that his feeble reasoning faculty was right and the Quran wrong? He came to the conclusion that the chances were heavily in favour of the Quran, and so he accepted it as 100 per cent correct.

The logic of this argument was not obvious, but I had no wish to argue. What followed really surprised me. Mohamad Ali said that he was quite certain that if any one read the Quran with an open and receptive mind, he would be convinced of its truth. He knew (he added) that Bapu (Gandhiji) had read it carefully, and he must, therefore, have been convinced of the truth of Islam. But his pride of heart had kept him from declaring this. After his year of presidentship, Mohamad Ali gradually drifted away from the Congress, or, perhaps, as he would have put it, the Congress drifted away from him. The process was a slow one, and he continued to attend Congress and A.I.C.C. meetings, and take vigorous part in them for several years more. But the rift widened, estrangement grew. Perhaps no particular individual or individuals were to blame for this; it was an inevitable result of certain objective conditions in the country. But it was an unfortunate result, which hurt many of us. For, whatever the differences on the communal question might have been, there were very few differences on the political issue. He was devoted to the idea of Indian independence. And because of this common political outlook, it was always possible to come to some mutually satisfactory arrangement with him on the communal issue. There was nothing in common, politically, between him and the reactionaries who pose as the champions of communal interests.

It was a misfortune for India that he left the country for Europe in the summer of 1928. A great effort was then made to solve the communal problem, and it came very near success. If Mohamad Ali had been here then, it is just conceivable that matters would have shaped differently. But by the time he came back the break had already taken place and, inevitably, he found himself on the other side.

Two years later, in 1930, when large numbers of our people were in prison and the Civil Disobedience movement was in full swing, Mohamad Ali ignored the Congress decision, and attended the Round Table Conference. I was hurt by his going. I believe that in his own heart he was unhappy about it, and there is enough evidence of this in his activities in London. He felt that his real place was in the fight in India, not in the futile conference chamber in London. And if he had returned to his country he would, I feel sure, have joined that struggle. Physically, he was a doomed man, and for years past the grip of disease was tightening upon him. In London his overwhelming anxiety to achieve, to do something worthwhile, when rest and treatment was what he needed, hastened his end. The news of his death came to me in Naini Prison as a blow.

I met him for the last time on the occasion of the Lahore Congress in December 1929. He was not pleased with some parts of my presidential address, and he criticised it vigorously. He saw that the Congress was going ahead, and becoming politically more aggressive. He was aggressive enough himself, and, being so, he disliked taking a backseat and allowing others to be in the front. He gave me solemn warning: "I warn you, Jawahar, that your present colleagues will desert you. They will leave you in the lurch in a crisis. Your own Congressmen will send you to the gallows." A dismal prophecy! The Coconada Congress, held in December 1923, had a special interest for me, because the foundations of an all-India volunteer organization, the Hindustani Seva Dal, were laid there.

There had been no lack of volunteer organizations even before, both for organizational work and for gaol-going. But there was little discipline, little cohesion. Dr. N. S. Hardiker conceived the idea of having a well-disciplined all-India corps trained to do national work under the general guidance of the Congress. He pressed me to cooperate with him in this, and I gladly did so, for the idea appealed to me. The beginnings were made at Coconada. We were surprised to find later how much opposition there was to the Seva Dal among leading Congressmen. Some said that this was a dangerous departure, as it meant introducing a military element in the Congress, and the military arm might overpower the civil authority! Others seemed to think that the only discipline necessary was for the volunteer to obey orders issued from above, and for the rest it was hardly desirable for volunteers even to walk in step. At the back of the mind of some was the notion that the idea of having trained and drilled volunteers was somehow inconsistent with the Congress principle of nonviolence. Hardiker, however, devoted himself to this task, and by the patient labour of years he demonstrated how much more efficient and even nonviolent our trained volunteers could be.

Soon after my return from Coconada, in January 1924, I had a new kind of experience in Allahabad. I write from memory, and I am likely to get mixed up about dates. But I think that was the year of the Kumbh, or the Ardh-Kumbh, the great bathing mela held on the banks of the Ganges at Allahabad. Vast numbers of pilgrims usually turn up, and most of them bathe at the confluence of the Ganges and the Jumna the Triveni, it is called, as the mythical Saraswati is also supposed to join the other two. The Ganges riverbed is about a mile wide, but in winter the river shrinks and leaves a wide expanse of sand exposed, which is very useful for the camps of the pilgrims. Within this riverbed, the Ganges frequently changes its course. In 1924 the current of the Ganges was such that it was undoubtedly dangerous for crowds to bathe at the Triveni. With certain precautions, and the control of the numbers bathing at a time, the danger could be greatly lessened.

I was not at all interested in this question, as I did not propose to acquire merit by bathing in the river on the auspicious days. But I noticed in the Press that a controversy was going on between Pandit Madan Mohan Malaviya and the Provincial Government, the latter (or the local authorities) having issued orders prohibiting all bathing at the junction of the rivers. This was objected to by Malaviyaji, as, from the religious point of view, the whole point was to bathe at that confluence. The Government was perfectly justified in taking precautions to prevent accidents and possible serious loss of life, but, as usual, it set about its work in the most wooden and irritating way possible.

On the big day of the Kumbh, I went down to the river early in the morning to see the mela, with no intention of bathing. On arrival at the river bank, I learnt that Malaviyaji had sent some kind of polite ultimatum to the District Magistrate, asking him for permission to bathe at the Triveni. Malaviyaji was agitated, and the atmosphere was tense. The Magistrate refused permission. Thereupon Malaviyaji decided to offer Satyagraha, and, accompanied by about two hundred others, he marched towards the junction of the rivers. I was interested in these developments and, on the spur of the moment, joined the Satyagraha band. A tremendous barrier had been erected right across the open space, to keep away people from the confluence. When we reached this high palisade, we were stopped by the police, and a ladder we had was taken away from us. Being nonviolent Satyagrahis, we sat down peacefully on the sands near the palisade. And there we sat for the whole morning and part of the afternoon. Hour after hour went by, the sun became stronger, the sand hotter, and all of us hungrier. Foot and mounted police stood by on both sides of us. I think the regular cavalry was also there. Most of us grew impatient, and said that something should be done. I believe the authorities also grew impatient, and decided to force the pace. Some order was given to the cavalry, who mounted their horses. It struck me (I do not know if I was right) that they were going to charge us and drive us away in this fashion. I did not fancy the idea of being chased by mounted troopers, and, anyhow, I was fed up with sitting there. So I suggested to those sitting near me that we might as well cross over the palisade, and I mounted it. Immediately scores of others did likewise, and some even pulled out a few stakes, thus making a passageway. Somebody gave me a national flag, and I stuck it on top of the palisade, where I continued to sit. I grew rather excited, and thoroughly enjoyed myself, watching the people clambering up or going through and the mounted troopers trying to push them away. I must say that the cavalry did their work as harmlessly as possible. They waved about their wooden staffs, and pushed people with them, but refrained from causing much injury. Faint memories of revolutionary barricades came to me.

At last I got down on the other side and, feeling very hot after my exertions, decided to have a dip in the Ganges. On coming back, I was amazed to find that Malaviyaji and many others were still sitting on the other side of the palisade as before. But the mounted troopers and the foot police now stood shoulder to shoulder between the Satyagrahis and the palisade. So I went (having got out by a roundabout way) and sat down again near Malaviyaji. For some time we sat on, and I noticed that Malaviyaji was greatly agitated; he seemed to be trying to control some strong emotion. Suddenly, without a hint to any one, he dived in the most extraordinary way through the policemen and the horses. For any one, that would have been a surprising dive, but for an old and physically weak person like Malaviyaji, it was astounding. Anyhow, we all followed him; we all dived. After some effort to keep us back the cavalry and the police did not interfere. A little later they were withdrawn.

We half expected some proceedings to be taken against us by the Government, but nothing of the kind happened. Government probably did not wish to take any steps against Malaviyaji, and so the smaller fry got off too.

~

What Is Religion?

(From An Autobiography*)*

Our peaceful and monotonous routine in gaol was suddenly upset in the middle of September 1932 by a bombshell. News came that Gandhiji had decided to "fast unto death" in disapproval of the separate electorates given by Mr. Ramsay MacDonald's Communal Award to the Depressed Classes. What a capacity he had to give shocks to people! Suddenly all manner of ideas rushed into my head; all kinds of possibilities and contingencies rose up before me and upset my equilibrium completely. For two days I was in darkness with no light to show the way out, my heart sinking when I thought of some results of Gandhiji's action. The personal aspect was powerful enough, and I thought with anguish that I might not see him again. It was over a year ago that I had seen him last on board ship on the way to England. Was that going to be my last sight of him?

And then I felt annoyed with him for choosing a side issue for his final sacrifice- just a question of electorate. What would be the result on our freedom movement? Would not the larger issues fade into the background, for the time being at least? And if he attained his immediate object and got a joint electorate for the Depressed Classes, would not that result in a reaction and a feeling that something has been achieved and nothing more need be done for a while? And was not his action a recognition, and in part an acceptance, of the Communal Award and the general scheme of things as sponsored by the Government? Was this consistent with Non-Cooperation and Civil Disobedience? After so much sacrifice and brave endeavour, was our movement to tail off into something insignificant?

I felt angry with him at his religious and sentimental approach to a political question, and his frequent references to God in connection with it. He even seemed to suggest that God had indicated the very date of the fast. What a terrible example to set!

If Bapu died! What would India be like then? And how would her politics run? There seemed to be a dreary and dismal future ahead, and despair seized my heart when I thought of it.

So I thought and thought, and confusion reigned in my head, and anger and hopelessness, and love for him who was the cause of this upheaval. I hardly knew what to do, and I was irritable and short-tempered with everybody, and most of all with myself.

And then a strange thing happened to me. I had quite an emotional crisis, and at the end of it I felt calmer and the future seemed not so dark. Bapu had a curious knack of doing the right thing at the psychological moment, and it might be that his action—impossible to justify—as it was from my point of view would lead to great results, not only in the narrow field in which it was confined, but in the wider aspects of our national struggle. And even if Bapu died our struggle for freedom would go on. So whatever happened, one must keep ready and fit for it. Having made up my mind to face even Gandhiji's death without flinching, I felt calm and collected and ready to face the world and all it might offer.

Then came news of the tremendous upheaval all over the country, a magic wave of enthusiasm running through Hindu society, and untouchability appeared to be doomed. What a magician, I thought, was this little man sitting in Yeravda Prison, and how well he knew how to pull the strings that move people's hearts!

A telegram from him reached me. It was the first message I had received from him since my conviction, and it did me good to hear from him after that long interval. In this telegram he said:

> During all these days of agony you have been before mind's eye. I am most anxious to know your opinion. You know how I value your opinion. Saw Indu (and) Sarup's children. Indu looked happy and in possession of more flesh. Doing very well. Wire reply. Love.

It was extraordinary, and yet it was characteristic of him, that in the agony of his fast and in the midst of his many preoccupations, he should refer to the visit of my daughter and my sister's children to him, and even mention that Indira had put on flesh! (My sister was also in prison then and all these children were at school in Poona.) He never forgets the seemingly little things in life which really mean so much.

News also came to me just then that some settlement had been reached over the electorate issue. The superintendent of the gaol was good enough to allow me to send an answer to Gandhiji, and I sent him the following telegram:

> Your telegram and brief news that some settlement reached filled me with relief and joy. First news of your decision to fast caused mental agony and confusion, but ultimately optimism triumphed and I regained peace of mind. No sacrifice too great for suppressed downtrodden classes. Freedom must be judged by freedom of lowest but feel danger of other issues obscuring only goal. Am unable to judge from religious view point. Danger your methods being exploited by others but how can I presume to advise a magician. Love.

A 'pact ' was signed by various people gathered in Poona, and with unusual speed the British Prime Minister accepted it and varied his previous award accordingly, and the fast was broken. I disliked such pacts and agreements greatly, but I welcomed the Poona Pact apart from its contents.

The excitement was over and we reverted to our gaol routine. News of the Harijan movement and of Gandhiji's activities from prison came to us, and I was not very happy about it. There was no doubt that a tremendous push had been given to the movement to end untouchability and raise the unhappy depressed classes, not so much by the pact as by the crusading enthusiasm created all over the country. That was to be welcomed. But it was equally obvious that civil disobedience had suffered. The country's attention had been diverted to other issues, and many Congress workers had turned to the Harijan cause. Probably most of these people wanted an excuse to revert to safer activities which did not involve the risk of gaol going or, worse still, lathi blows and confiscations of property. That was natural, and it was not fair to expect all the thousands of our workers to keep always ready for intense suffering and the breakup and destruction of their homes. But still it was painful to watch this slow decay of our great movement. Civil disobedience was, however, still going on, and occasionally there were mass demonstrations like the Calcutta Congress in March-April 1933. Gandhiji was in Yeravda Prison, but he had been given certain privileges to meet people and issue directions for the Harijan movements. Somehow this took away from the sting of his being in prison. All this depressed me.

Many months later, early in May 1933, Gandhiji began his twenty-one-day fast. The first news of this had again come as a shock to me, but I accepted it as an inevitable occurrence and schooled myself to it. Indeed, I was irritated that people should urge him to give it up, after he had made up his mind and declared it to the public. For me the fast was an incomprehensible thing and, if I had been asked before the decision had been taken, I would certainly have spoken strongly against it. But I attached great value to Gandhiji's word, and it seemed to me wrong for anyone to try to make him break it, in a personal matter which, to him, was of supreme importance. So, unhappy as I was, I put up with it.

A few days before beginning his fast he wrote to me, a typical letter which moved me very much. As he asked for a reply, I sent him the following telegram:

> Your letter. What can I say about matters I do not understand? I feel lost in strange country where you are the only familiar landmark and I try to grope my way in dark but I stumble. Whatever happens my love and thoughts will be with you.

I had struggled against my utter disapproval of his act and my desire not to hurt him. I felt, however, that I had not sent him a cheerful message, and now that he was bent on undergoing his terrible ordeal, which might even end in his death, I ought to cheer him up as much as I could. Little things make a difference psychologically, and he would have to strain every nerve to survive. I felt also that we should accept whatever happened, even his death, if unhappily it should occur, with a stout heart. So I sent him another telegram:

> Now that you are launched on your great enterprise may I send you again love and greetings and assure you that I feel more clearly now that whatever happens it is well and whatever happens you win.

He survived the fast. On the first day of it he was discharged from prison, and on his advice Civil Disobedience was suspended for six weeks.

Again I watched the emotional upheaval of the country during the fast, and I wondered more and more if this was the right method in politics. It seemed to be sheer revivalism, and clear thinking had not a ghost of a chance against it. All India, or most of it, stared reverently at the Mahatma and expected him to perform miracle after miracle and put an end to untouchability and get swaraj and so on and did precious little itself! And Gandhiji did not encourage others to think; his insistence was only on purity and sacrifice. I felt that I was drifting further and further away from him mentally, in spite of my strong emotional attachment to him. Often enough he was guided in his political activities by an unerring instinct. He had the flair for action, but was the way of faith the right way to train a nation? It might pay for a short while, but in the long run?

And I could not understand how he could accept, as he seemed to do, the present social order, which was based on violence and conflict. Within me also conflict raged, and I was torn between rival loyalties. I knew that there was trouble ahead for me, when the enforced protection of gaol was removed. I felt lonely and homeless, and India, to whom I had given my love and for whom I had laboured, seemed a strange and bewildering land to me. Was it my fault that I could not enter into the spirit and ways of thinking of my countrymen? Even with my closest associates I felt that an invisible barrier came between us and, unhappy at being unable to overcome it, I shrank back into my shell. The old world seemed to envelop them, the old world of past ideologies, hopes and desires. The new world was yet far distant.

> "Wandering between two worlds, one dead,
> The other powerless to be born,
> With nowhere yet to rest his head."

India is supposed to be a religious country above everything else, and Hindu and Moslem and Sikh and others take pride in their faiths and testify to their truth by breaking heads. The spectacle of what is called

religion, or at any rate organized religion, in India and elsewhere has filled me with horror, and I have frequently condemned it and wished to make a clean sweep of it. Almost always it seems to stand for blind belief and reaction, dogma and bigotry, superstition and exploitation, and the preservation of vested interests. And yet I knew well that there was something else in it, something which supplied a deep inner craving of human beings. How else could it have been the tremendous power it has been and brought peace and comfort to innumerable tortured souls? Was that peace merely the shelter of blind belief and absence of questioning, the calm that comes from being safe in harbour, protected from the storms of the open sea, or was it something more? In some cases certainly it was something more.

But organized religion, whatever its past may have been, today is very largely an empty form devoid of real content. Mr. G. K. Chesterton has compared it (not his own particular brand of religion, but others!) to a fossil which is the form of an animal or organism from which all its own organic substance has entirely disappeared, but which has kept its shape, because it has been filled up by some totally different substance. And even where something of value still remains, it is enveloped by other and harmful contents.

That seems to have happened in our Eastern religions as well as in the Western. The Church of England is perhaps the most obvious example of a religion which is not a religion in any real sense of the word. Partly that applies to all organized Protestantism, but the Church of England has probably gone further because it has long been a State political department.[1]

---

[1] In India the Church of England has been almost indistinguishable from the Government. The officially paid (out of Indian revenues) priests and chaplains are the symbols of the imperial power just as the higher services are. The Church has been, on the whole, a conservative and

Many of its votaries are undoubtedly of the highest character, but it is remarkable how that Church has served the purposes of British imperialism and given both capitalism and imperialism a moral and Christian covering. It has sought to justify, from the highest ethical standards, British predatory policy in Asia and Africa, and given that extraordinary and enviable feeling of being always in the right to the English. Whether the Church has helped in producing this attitude of smug rectitude or is itself a product of it, I do not know. Other less favoured countries on the Continent of Europe and in America often accuse the English of hypocrisy. *Perfide Albion* is an old taunt but the accusation is probably the outcome of envy at British success, and certainly no other imperialist Power can afford to throw stones at England,

---

reactionary force in Indian politics and generally opposed to reform or advance. The average missionary is usually wholly ignorant of India's past history and culture and does not take the slightest trouble to find out what it was or is. He is more interested in pointing out the sins and failings of the heathen. Of course, there have been many fine exceptions. India does not possess a more devoted friend than Charlie Andrews, whose abounding love and spirit of service and overflowing friendliness it is a joy to have. The Christa Seva Sangh of Poona contains some fine Englishmen, whose religion has led them to understand and serve and not to patronize, and who have devoted themselves with all their great gifts to a selfless service of the Indian people. There are many other English churchmen whose memory is treasured in India.

The Archbishop of Canterbury, speaking in the House of Lords on 12 December, 1934, referred to the preamble of the Montagu-Chelmsford reforms of 191 9 and said that "he sometimes thought the great declaration had been somewhat hastily made, and supposed that it was one of the hasty, generous gestures after the War, but the goal set could not be withdrawn." It is worthy of note that the head of the English Church should take such an exceedingly conservative view of Indian politics. A step, which was considered wholly insufficient by Indian opinion and which, because of this, led to non-cooperation and all its consequences, is considered by the Archbishop as "hasty and generous/' It is a comforting doctrine from the point of view of the English ruling classes, and, no doubt, this conviction of their own generosity, even to the point of rashness, must produce a righteous glow of satisfaction.

for its own record is equally shady. No nation that is consciously hypocritical could have the reserves of strength that the British have repeatedly shown, and the brand of 'religion' which they have adopted has apparently helped them in this by blunting their moral susceptibilities where their own interests were concerned. Other peoples and nations have often behaved far worse than the British have done, but they have never succeeded, quite to the same extent, in making a virtue of what profited them. All of us find it remarkably easy to spot the mote in the other's eye and overlook the beam in our own, but perhaps the British excel at the performance.[2]

Protestantism tried to adapt itself to new conditions and wanted to have the best of both worlds. It succeeded remarkably so far as this world was concerned, but from the religious point of view it fell, as an organized religion, between two stools, and religion gradually gave place to sentimentality and big business. Roman Catholicism escaped this fate, as it stuck on to the old stool, and, so long as that stool holds, it will flourish. Today it seems to be the only living religion, in the restricted sense of the word, in the West. A Roman Catholic friend sent me in prison many books on Catholicism and Papal Encyclicals and I read them with interest. Studying them, I realised the hold it had on such large numbers of people. It offered, as Islam and popular Hinduism offer, a safe anchorage from doubt and mental conflict, an assurance of a future life which will make up for the deficiencies of this life.

---

[2] A recent instance of how the Church of England indirectly influences politics in India has come to my notice. At a provincial conference of the U.P. Indian Christians held at Cawnpore on the 7 November, 1934, the Chairman of the Reception Committee, Mr. E. V. David, said: "As Christians we are bound by our religion to loyalty to the King, who is the Defender of our Faith." Inevitably that meant support of British imperialism in India. Mr. David further expressed his sympathies with some of the views of the 'die hard' Conservative elements in England in regard to the I.C.S., the police, and the whole proposed constitution, which, according to them, might endanger Christian missions in India.

I am afraid it is impossible for me to seek harbourage in this way. I prefer the open sea, with all its storms and tempests. Nor am I greatly interested in the afterlife, in what happens after death. I find the problems of this life sufficiently absorbing to fill my mind. The traditional Chinese outlook, fundamentally ethical and yet irreligious or tinged with religious scepticism, has an appeal for me, though in its application to life I may not agree. It is the Tao, the path to be followed and the way of life that interests me; how to understand life, not to reject it but to accept it, to conform to it and to improve it. But the usual religious outlook does not concern itself with this world. It seems to me to be the enemy of clear thought, for it is based not only on the acceptance, without demur, of certain fixed and unalterable theories and dogmas, but also on sentiment and emotion and passion. It is far removed from what I consider spiritual and things of the spirit, and it deliberately or unconsciously shuts its eyes to reality lest reality may not fit in with preconceived notions. It is narrow and intolerant of other opinions and ideas; it is self-centred and egotistic, and it often allows itself to be exploited by self-seekers and opportunists.

This does not mean that men of religion have not been and are not still often of the highest moral and spiritual type. But it does mean that the religious outlook does not help, and even hinders, the moral and spiritual progress of a people, if morality and spirituality are to be judged by this world's standards, and not by the hereafter. Usually religion becomes an asocial quest for God or the Absolute, and the religious man is concerned far more with his own salvation than with the good of society. The mystic tries to rid himself of self, and in the process usually becomes obsessed with it. Moral standards have no relation to social needs, but are based on a highly metaphysical doctrine of sin. And organized religion invariably becomes a vested interest and thus inevitably a reactionary force opposing change and progress.

It is well known that the Christian church in the early days did not help the slaves to improve their social status. The slaves became the feudal serfs of the Middle Ages of Europe because of economic conditions. The attitude of the Church, as late as two hundred years ago (in 1727), was well exemplified in a letter written by the Bishop of London to the slave owners of the southern colonies of America.[3]

"Christianity," wrote the Bishop," and the embracing of the gospel does not make the least alteration in Civil property or in any of the duties which belong to civil relations; but in all these respects it continues Persons just in the same State as it found them. The Freedom which Christianity gives is Freedom from the bondage of Sin and Satan and from the Dominion of Men's Lusts and Passions and inordinate Desires; but as to their outward condition, whatever that was before, whether bond or free, their being baptised and becoming Christians makes no manner of change in them."

No organized religion today will express itself in this outspoken manner, but essentially its attitude to property and the existing social order will be the same.

Words are well known to be, by themselves, very imperfect means of communication, and are often understood in a variety of ways. No word perhaps in any language is more likely to be interpreted in different ways by different people as the word 'religion' (or the corresponding words in other languages).

Probably to no two persons will the same complex of ideas and images arise on hearing or reading this word. Among these ideas and images may be those of rites and ceremonial, of sacred books, of a community of people, of certain dogmas, of morals, reverence, love, fear, hatred, charity, sacrifice, asceticism, fasting, feasting, prayer, ancient history, marriage, death, the next world, of riots and the breaking of heads, and so on. Apart from the tremendous confusion caused by this immense variety of images and interpretations, almost invariably there will be a strong emotional response which will make dispassionate consideration impossible. The word 'religion' has lost all precise significance

[3] This letter is quoted in Reinhold Niebuhr's *Moral Man and Immoral Society* (p. 78), a book which is exceedingly interesting and stimulating.

(if it ever had it) and only causes confusion and gives rise to interminable debate and argument, when often enough entirely different meanings are attached to it. It would be far better if it was dropped from use altogether and other words with more limited meanings were used instead, such as: theology, philosophy, morals, ethics, spirituality, metaphysics, duty, ceremonial, etc. Even these words are vague enough, but they have a much more limited range than 'religion.' A great advantage would be that these words have not yet attached to themselves, to the same extent, the passions and emotions that surround and envelop the word 'religion.'

What then is religion (to use the word in spite of its obvious disadvantages)? Probably it consists of the inner development of the individual, the evolution of his consciousness in a certain direction which is considered good. What that direction is will again be a matter for debate. But, as far as I understand it, religion lays stress on this inner change and considers outward change as but the projection of this inner development. There can be no doubt that this inner development powerfully influences the outer environment. But it is equally obvious that the outer environment powerfully influences the inner development. Both act and interact on each other. It is a commonplace that in the modern industrial West outward development has far outstripped the inner, but it does not follow, as many people in the East appear to imagine, that because we are industrially backward and our external development has been slow, therefore our inner evolution has been greater. That is one of the delusions with which we try to comfort ourselves and try to overcome our feeling of inferiority. It may be that individuals can rise above circumstances and environment and reach great inner heights. But for large groups and nations a certain measure of external development is essential before the inner evolution can take place. A man who is the victim of economic circumstances, and who is hedged and restricted by the struggle to live, can very rarely achieve inner consciousness of any high degree. A class that is downtrodden and exploited can never progress inwardly. A nation which is politically and economically subject to another and hedged and circumscribed and exploited can never achieve inner growth. Thus even for inner development external freedom and a suitable environment become necessary. In the attempt to gain this outer freedom and to change the environment so as to remove all hindrances to inner development, it is desirable that the means should be such as not to defeat the real object in view. I take it that when Gandhiji says that the means are more important than the end, he has something of this kind in view. But the means should be such as lead to the end, otherwise they are wasted effort, and they might even result in even greater degradation, both outer and inner.

"No man can live without religion," Gandhiji has written somewhere. "There are some who in the egotism of their reason declare that they have nothing to do with religion. But that is like a man saying that he breathes, but that he has no nose." Again he says: "My devotion to truth has drawn me into the field of politics; and I can say without the slightest hesitation, and yet in all humility, that those who say that religion has nothing to do with politics do not know what religion means." Perhaps it would have been more correct if he had said that most of these people who want to exclude religion from life and politics mean by that word 'religion' something very different from what he means. It is obvious that he is using it in a sense probably moral and ethical more than any other, different from that of the critics of religion. This use of the same word with different meanings makes mutual comprehension still more difficult.

A very modern definition of religion, with which the men of religion will not agree, is that of Professor John Dewey. According to him, religion is "whatever introduces genuine perspective into the piecemeal and shifting episodes of existence"; or again "any activity pursued in behalf of an ideal end against obstacles, and in spite of threats of personal loss, because of conviction of its general and enduring value, is religious in quality." If this is religion, then surely no one can have the slightest objection to it.

Romain Rolland also has stretched religion to mean something which will probably horrify the orthodox of organized religions. In his *Life of Ramkrishna*, he says:

> "... many souls who are or who believe they are free from all religious belief, but who in reality live immersed in a state of superrational consciousness, which they term Socialism, Communism, Humanitarianism, Nationalism and even Rationalism. It is the quality of thought and not its object which determines its source and allows us to decide whether or not it emanates from religion. If it turns fearlessly towards the search for truth at all costs with single-minded sincerity prepared for any sacrifice, I should call it religious; for it presupposes faith in an end to human effort higher than the life of existing society, and even higher than the life of humanity as a whole. Scepticism itself, when it proceeds from vigorous natures true to the core, when it is an expression of strength and not of weakness, joins in the march of the Grand Army of the religious Soul."

I cannot presume to fulfil the conditions laid down by Romain Rolland, but on these terms I am prepared to be a humble camp-follower of the Grand Army.

~

What Is Hinduism?

(From The Discovery of India*)*

The word 'Hindu' does not occur at all in our ancient literature. The first reference to it in an Indian book is, I am told, in a Tantrik work of the eighth century B.C., where 'Hindu' means a people and not the followers of a particular religion. But it is clear that the word is a very old one, as it occurs in the Avesta and in old Persian. It was used then and for a thousand years or more later by the peoples of western and central Asia for India, or rather for the people living on the other side of the Indus river. The word is clearly derived from Sindhu, the old, as well as the present, Indian name for the Indus. From this Sindhu came the words Hindu and Hindustan, as well as Indus and India.

The famous Chinese pilgrim I-tsing, who came to India in the seventh century B.C., writes in his record of travels that the 'northern tribes', that is the people of Central Asia, called India 'Hindu' (Hsin-tu) but, he adds, 'this is not at all a common name... and the most suitable name for India is the Noble Land (Aryadesha).' The use of the word 'Hindu' in connection with a particular religion is of very late occurrence.

The old inclusive term for religion in India was Arya dharma. Dharma really means something more than religion. It is from a root word which means, to hold together; it is the inmost constitution of a thing, the law of its inner being. It is an ethical concept which includes the moral code, righteousness, and the whole range of man's duties and responsibilities. Arya dharma would include all the faiths (Vedic and non-Vedic) that originated in India; it was used by Buddhists and Jains as well as by those who accepted the Vedas. Buddha always called his way to salvation the 'Aryan Path'.

The expression Vedic dharma was also used in ancient times to signify more particularly and exclusively all those philosophies, moral teachings, ritual and practices, which were supposed to derive from the Vedas. Thus all those who acknowledged the general authority of the Vedas could be said to belong to the Vedic dharma.

Sanatana dharma, meaning the ancient religion, could be applied to any of the ancient Indian faiths (including Buddhism and Jainism), but the expression has been more or less monopolized today by some orthodox sections among the Hindus who claim to follow the ancient faith.

Buddhism and Jainism were certainly not Hinduism or even the Vedic dharma. Yet they arose in India and were integral parts of Indian life, culture and philosophy. A Buddhist or Jain in India is a hundred per cent product of Indian thought and culture, yet neither is a Hindu by faith. It is, therefore, entirely misleading to refer to Indian culture as Hindu culture. In later ages this culture was greatly influenced by the impact of Islam, and yet it remained basically and distinctively Indian. Today it is experiencing in a hundred ways the powerful effect of the industrial civilization, which rose in the west, and it is difficult to say with any precision what the outcome will be.

Hinduism, as a faith, is vague, amorphous, many-sided, all things to all men. It is hardly possible to define it, or indeed to say definitely whether it is a religion or not, in the usual sense of the word. In its present form, and even in the past, it embraces many beliefs and practices, from the highest to the lowest, often opposed to or contradicting each other. Its essential spirit seems to be to live and let live. Mahatma Gandhi has attempted to define it: 'If I were asked to define the Hindu creed, I should simply say: Search after truth through nonviolent means. A man may not believe in God and still call himself a Hindu. Hindu-ism is a relentless pursuit after truth ... Hinduism is the religion of truth. Truth is God. Denial of God we have known. Denial of truth we have not known. Truth and nonviolence', so says Gandhi; but many eminent and undoubted Hindus say that nonviolence, as Gandhi understands it, is no essential part of the Hindu creed. We thus have truth left by itself as the distinguishing mark of Hinduism. That, of course, is no definition at all.

It is, therefore, incorrect and undesirable to use 'Hindu' or 'Hinduism' for Indian culture, even with reference to the distant past, although the various aspects of thought, as embodied in ancient writings, were the dominant expression of that culture. Much more is it incorrect to use those terms, in that sense, today. So long as the old faith and philosophy were chiefly a way of life and an outlook on the world, they were largely synonymous with Indian culture; but when a more rigid religion developed, with all manner of ritual and ceremonial, it became something more and at the same time something much less than that composite culture. A Christian or a Moslem could, and often did, adapt himself to the Indian way of life and culture, and yet remained in faith an orthodox Christian or Moslem. He had Indianized himself and become an Indian without changing his religion.

The correct word for 'Indian', as applied to country or culture or the historical continuity of our varying traditions, is

'Hindi', from 'Hind', a shortened form of Hindustan. Hind is still commonly used for India. In the countries of Western Asia, in Iran and Turkey, in Iraq, Afghanistan, Egypt, and elsewhere, India has always been referred to, and is still called: Hind; and everything Indian is called 'Hindi'. 'Hindi' has nothing to do with religion, and a Moslem or Christian Indian is as much a Hindi as a person who follows Hinduism as a religion. Americans who call all Indians Hindus are not far wrong; they would be perfectly correct if they used the word 'Hindi'. Unfortunately, the word 'Hindi' has become associated in India with a particular script—the devanagri script of Sanskrit—and so it has become difficult to use it in its larger and more natural significance. Perhaps when present-day controversies subside we may revert to its original and more satisfying use. Todayy, the word 'Hindustani' is used for Indian; it is, of course, derived from Hindustan. But this is too much of a mouthful and it has no such historical and cultural associations as 'Hindi' has. It would certainly appear odd to refer to ancient periods of Indian culture as 'Hindustani'.

Whatever the word we may use, Indian or Hindi or Hindustani, for our cultural tradition, we see in the past that some inner urge towards synthesis, derived essentially from the Indian philosophic outlook, was the dominant feature of Indian cultural, and even racial, development. Each incursion of foreign elements was a challenge to this culture, but it was met successfully by a new synthesis and a process of absorption. This was also a process of rejuvenation and new blooms of culture arose out of it, the background and essential basis, however, remaining much the same.

~

The Acceptance and the Negation of Life

(From The Discovery of India*)*

As a man grows to maturity he is not entirely engrossed in, or satisfied with, the external objective world. He seeks also some inner meaning, some psychological and physical satisfactions. So also with peoples and civilizations as they mature and grow adult. Every civilization and every people exhibit these parallel streams of an external life and an internal life. When they meet or keep close to each other, there is an equilibrium and stability. When they diverge conflict arises and the crises that torture the mind and spirit.

We see from the period of the Rig Veda hymns onwards the development of both these streams of life and thought. The early ones are full of the external world, of the beauty and mystery of nature, of joy in life and an overflowing vitality. The gods and goddesses, like those of Olympus, are very human; they are supposed to come down and mix with men and women; there is no hard and fast line dividing the two. Then thought comes and the spirit of inquiry and the mystery of a transcendental world deepens. Life still continues in abundant measure, but there is also a turning away from its outward manifestations and a spirit of detachment grows as the eyes are turned to things invisible, which cannot be seen or heard or felt in the ordinary way. What is the object of it all? Is there a purpose in the universe? And, if so, how can man's life be put in harmony with it? Can we bring about a harmonious relation between the visible and invisible worlds, and thus find out the right conduct of life?

So we find in India, as elsewhere, these two streams of thought and action—the acceptance of life and the abstention from it—developing side by side, with the emphasis on the one or the other varying in different periods. Yet the basic background of that culture was not one of other-worldliness or world-worthlessness. Even when, in philosophical language, it discussed the world as maya, or what is popularly believed to be illusion, that very conception was not an absolute one but relative to what was thought of as ultimate reality (something like Plato's shadow of reality), and it took the world as it is and tried to live its life and enjoy its manifold beauty. Probably Semitic culture, as exemplified in many religions that emerged from it, and certainly early Christianity, was far more other-worldly. T. E. Lawrence says that 'the common base of all Semitic creeds, winners or losers, was the ever present idea of world-worthlessness.' And this often led to an alternation of self-indulgence and self-denial.

In India we find during every period when her civilization bloomed an intense joy in life and nature, a pleasure in the act of living, the development of art and music and literature and song and dancing and painting and the theatre, and even a highly sophisticated inquiry into sex relations. It is inconceivable that a culture or view of life based on other-worldliness or world-worthlessness could have produced all these manifestations of vigorous and varied life. Indeed it should be obvious that any culture that was basically other-worldly could not have carried on for thousands of years.

Yet some people have thought that Indian thought and culture represent essentially the principle of life negation and not of life affirmation. Both principles are, I suppose, present in varying degrees in all the old religions and cultures. But I should have thought that Indian culture, taken as a whole, never emphasized the negation of life, though some of its philosophies did so; it seems to have done so much less than Christianity. Buddhism and Jainism rather emphasized the abstention from life, and in certain periods of Indian history there was a running away from life on a big scale, as, for instance, when large numbers of people joined the Buddhist Viharas or monasteries. What the reason for this was I do not know. Equally, or more, significant instances can be found during the Middle Ages in Europe when a wide-spread belief existed that the world was coming to an end. Perhaps the ideas of renunciation and life-negation are caused or emphasized by a feeling of frustration due to political and economic factors.

Buddhism, in spite of its theoretical approach, or rather approaches, for there are several, as a matter of fact avoids extremes; its is the doctrine of the golden mean, the middle path. Even the idea of Nirvana was very far from being a kind of nothingness, as it is sometimes supposed to be; it was a positive condition, but because it was beyond the range of human thought negative terms were used to describe it. If Buddhism, a typical product of Indian thought and culture, had merely been a doctrine of life negation or denial, it would surely have had some such effect on the hundreds of millions who profess it. Yet, as a matter of fact, the Buddhist countries are full of evidence to the contrary, and the Chinese people are an outstanding example of what affirmation of life can be.

The confusion seems to have arisen from the fact that Indian thought was always laying stress on the ultimate purpose of life. It could never forget the transcendent element in its makeup; and so, while affirming life to the full, it refused to become a victim and a slave of life. Indulge in right action with all your strength and energy, it said, but keep above it, and do not worry much about the results of such action. Thus it taught detachment in life and action, not abstention from them. This idea of detachment runs through Indian thought and philosophy, as it does through most other philosophies. It is another way of saying that a right balance and equilibrium should be kept between the visible and invisible worlds, for if there is too much attachment to action in the visible world, the other world is forgotten and fades away, and action itself becomes without ultimate purpose.

There is an emphasis on truth, a dependence on it, a passion for it, in these early adventures of the Indian mind. Dogma or revelation are passed by as something for lesser minds which cannot rise above them. The approach was one of experiment based on personal experience. That experience, when it dealt with the invisible world, was, like all emotional and psychic experiences, different from the experience of the visible, external world. It seemed to go out of the three-dimensional world we know into some different and vaster realm, and was thus difficult to describe in terms of three dimensions. What that experience was, and whether it was a vision or realization of some aspects of truth and reality, or was merely a phantasm of the imagination, I do not know. Probably it was often self-delusion. What interests me more is the approach, which was not authoritarian or dogmatic but was an attempt to discover for oneself what lay behind the external aspect of life.

It must be remembered that the business of philosophy in India was not confined to a few philosophers or highbrows. Philosophy was an essential part of the religion of the masses; it percolated to them in some attenuated form and created that philosophic outlook which became nearly as common in India as it is in China. That philosophy was for some a deep and intricate attempt to know the causes and laws of all phenomena, the search for the ultimate purpose of life, and the attempt to find an organic unity in life's many contradictions. But for many it was a much simpler affair, which yet gave them some sense of purpose, of cause and effect, and endowed them with courage to face trial and misfortune and not lose their gaiety and composure. 'The ancient wisdom of China and India, the Tao or the True Path,' wrote Tagore to Dr. Tai Chit-tao, 'was the pursuit of complete-ness, the blending of life's diverse work with the joy of living.' Something of that wisdom impressed itself even upon the illiterate and ignorant masses, and we have seen how the Chinese people, after seven years of horrible war, have not lost the anchor of their faith or the gaiety of their minds. In India our trial has been more drawn out, and poverty and uttermost misery have long been the inseparable companions of our people. And yet they still laugh and sing and dance and do not lose hope.

~

Orthodox of All Religions Unite![4]

Some years ago I happened to be in Benares and as I was driving through the narrow city streets, my car was held up by a crowd. A procession was passing through and, apart from the processionists, there were many sightseers and little boys intent on sharing in the fun. Crowds interest me and I got down from the car to find out what was afoot. The procession was certainly an interesting one and it had certain unique features. We saw Brahmans, the most

[4] Almora District Jail, 23 August 1935. Published in *Modern Review,* December 1935, pp. 625-631.

orthodox of their kind, with all manner of caste marks proudly displayed on their foreheads, marching shoulder to shoulder with bearded moulvies; the priests from the ghats fraternized with the mullahs from the mosques, and one of the standards they carried in triumph bore the flaming device: 'Hindu Mussalman *Ekta Ki Jai*'—Victory to Hindu-Muslim Unity! Very gratifying, we thought. But still what was all this about?

We soon found out from their cries and the many other standards they carried. This was a joint protest by the orthodox of both religions against the Sarda Act (or perhaps it was a Bill at the time) which prohibited marriages of girls under fourteen. The pious and the holy of both faiths had joined ranks and hands to declare that they would not submit to this outrage on their deepest convictions and most cherished rights. Were they going to be bullied by the threats of so-called reformers into giving up their right to marry child-wives? Never! Law or no law they would continue to marry little immature girls for was not post-puberty marriage a sin?—and thus enhance the glory of religion. Had not a noted Vaidya (physician) of Benares stated that in order to proclaim his adherence to the ancient dharma and his abhorrence of newfangled notions like the Sarda Act, he, even he, although he was round about sixty years of age, would marry afresh a girl under the prescribed legal age? Faith and religion had built up their great structures on the sacrifice of their votaries. Surely the movement against the Sarda Act would not lack its martyrs.

We mixed with the crowd and marched along for some distance by the side of the procession. Devadas Gandhi[5] was with me and some Benares friends and soon we were recognized by the processionists. They did not welcome us or shower greetings on us, and I am afraid we did not encourage them to do so. Our looks and attire separated us from the ranks of the faithful—we had neither beards nor caste marks—and we carried on an irreverent

[5] M.K. Gandhi's youngest son, a prominent journalist for the *Hindustan Times*. Interestingly, his wife, Lakshmi, was only fifteen when they fell in love, but they waited four years to marry.

and somewhat aggressive commentary on the procession and its sponsors. Offensive slogans were hurled at us and there was some jostling about. Just then the procession arrived at the Town Hall and for some reason or other started stone-throwing. A bright young person thereupon pulled some crackers and this had an extraordinary effect on the serried ranks of the orthodox. Evidently thinking that the police or the military had opened fire, they dispersed and vanished with exceeding rapidity. A few crackers were enough to put the procession to flight, but not even a cracker was required to make the British Government in India surrender on this issue. A little shouting, in which oddly enough the Muslims took the leading share, was enough to kill and bury the Sarda Act. It was feeble enough at birth with all manner of provisions which hindered its enforcement and then it gave six months' grace which resulted in a spate of child marriages. And then, after the six months were over? Nothing happened; child marriages continued as before and government and magistrates looked the other way while the Sarda Act was torn to shreds and cast to the dogs. In some instances the person who ventured to bring a breach to a court himself got into trouble for his pains and was fined. True, in one instance a Punjab villager who had given his ten-year daughter in marriage and deliberately broken the provisions of the Sarda Act despite warning was sentenced to one month's imprisonment. But this error on the part of the magistrate was soon rectified by the Punjab Government who hastened to send a telegram ordering the release of the offender against the Act. (This case has been taken from Miss E.F. Rathbone's interesting little book, *Child Marriage*)

What were we doing all this time? We were in prison. For six years now we have been mostly in prison, sometimes as many as sixty or seventy thousand at a time. Outside, a strict censorship prevailed, meetings were forbidden and an attempt to enter a rural area was almost certain to lead to prison, if not worse. The various emergency laws and denial of civil liberties were certainly not aimed at preventing support of the Sarda Act. But in effect they left the field clear to the opponents of that measure. And the government in its distress at having to combat a great political movement directed against it, sought allies in the most reactionary of religious and social bigots. To obtain their goodwill the Sarda Act was sat upon, extinguished. 'Hindu Mussalman *Ekta Ki Jai*'—Victory to Hindu-Muslim Unity!

The Muslims deserve their full share in this victory. Most of us had thought that the child-wife evil was largely confined to Hindus. But whatever the early disproportion might have been, Muslims were evidently determined not to be outdistanced in this matter as in others, by Hindus. So while on the one hand they claimed more seats in the councils, more jobs as policemen, deputy collectors, tahsildars, chaprasis and the like, they hurried on with the work of increasing their child-wives. From the most noted taluqdars in Oudh to the humble workers, they all joined in this endeavour, till at last the 1931 census proclaimed that victory had come to them. The report of the Age of Consent Committee[6] had previously prepared us to revise our previous opinion but the census went much further than had been expected. It told us that Muslims had actually surpassed the Hindus in the proportion of their child-wives. In Assam "Muslims have now far the largest proportion of child-wives in all the early age groups;" in Behar and Orissa the census tells us that "whereas the proportion of Hindu girl-wives (including widows) below the age of ten has increased since 1921 from 105 to 160, among Muslims it has increased from 76 to 202." Truly a triumph for the Sarda Act and the government that is supposed to enforce it.

Lest it be said that our enlightened Indian states lag behind on this issue, the Government of Mysore has recently made its position clear. A venturesome member sought to introduce a Child Marriage Restraint Bill, on the lines of the Sarda Act, in the Mysore Council. The motion was stoutly opposed by a Dewan Bahadur on behalf of the Muslims. The government generously permitted the official members to vote as they liked, but, oddly

[6] The Age of Consent Committee was appointed by the Government of India on 25 June, 1928 and its report was published on 26 August, 1929.

enough, the entire official bloc, including two European members, voted against the motion and with their votes helped to defeat it. Religion was again saved.

This instance of the Sarda Act was a revealing one, for it showed that all the shouting about Hindu-Muslim friction and disunity was exaggerated and, in any event, misdirected. That there was such friction nobody could deny, but it was the outcome not so much of religious differences as of economic distress, unemployment, and a race for jobs, which put on a sanctified garb and in the name of religion deluded and excited the masses. If the difference had been essentially religious, one would have thought that the orthodox of the two faiths would be the farthest removed from each other and the most hostile to each other's pretensions. As a matter of fact they combine frequently enough to combat any movement of reform, social, economic, political. Both look upon the person who wants to change the existing order in any way as the real enemy; both cling desperately and rather pathetically to the British Government, for instinctively they realise that they are in the same boat with it.

Nearly twenty two years ago, before the War, in January, 1914, the Aga Khan wrote an article in the *Edinburgh Review* on the Indian situation. He advised the government to abandon the policy of separating Hindus from Muslims and to rally the moderate of both creeds in a common camp so as to provide a counterpoise to the radical nationalist tendencies of young India, both Hindu and Muslim. In those days extremism was confined to nationalism and did not go beyond the political plane. Even so the Aga Khan sensed that the vital division lay not along religious lines but along political—between those who more or less stood for British domination in India and others who desired to end it. That nationalist issue still dominates the field and is likely to do so as long as India remains politically unfree. But today other issues have also assumed prominence—social and economic. If radical political change was feared by the moderate and socially backward elements, much more are they terrified by the prospect of social and economic change. Indeed it is the fear of the latter that has reacted on the political issue and made many a so-called advanced politician retrace his steps. He has in some cases become frankly a reactionary in politics, or a camouflaged reactionary like the communalists, or an open champion of his class interests and vested rights, like the big zamindars and taluqdars and industrialists.

I have no doubt that this process will continue and will lead to the toning down of communal and religious animosities, to Hindu-Muslim unity of a kind. The communalists of various groups, in spite of their mutual hostility, will embrace each other like long lost brothers and swear fealty in a new joint campaign against those who are out for radical change, politically or socially or economically. The new alignment will be a healthier one and the issues will be clearer. The indications towards some such grouping are already visible, though they will take some time to develop.

Sir Mohammad Iqbal, the champion of the solidarity of Islam, is in cordial agreement with orthodox Hindus in some of their most reactionary demands. He writes: "I very much appreciate the orthodox Hindus demand for protection against religious reformers in the new constitution. Indeed this demand ought to have been first made by the Muslims." He further explains that "the encouragement in India of religious adventurers on the ground of modern liberalism tends to make people more and more indifferent to religion and will eventually completely eliminate the important factor of religion from the life of the Indian community. The Indian mind will then seek some other substitute for religion which is likely to be nothing less than the form of atheistic materialism which has appeared in Russia."

This fear of communism has driven many liberals and other middle groups in Europe to fascism and reaction. Even the old enemies, the Jesuits and the Freemasons, have covered up their bitter hostility of two hundred years to face the common enemy. In India communism and socialism are understood by relatively very few persons and most people who shout loudest against them are supremely ignorant about them. But they are influenced partly instinctively because of their vested interests, and partly because of the propaganda on the part of the government, which always stresses the religious issue.

Sir Mohammad Iqbal's argument, however, takes us very much further than merely anti-communism or anti-socialism and it is worthwhile examining it in some detail. His position on this issue of suppression of all reformers, is, it should be remembered, almost the same as that of the Sanatanist Hindus. And even a party which presumes to call itself democratic or nationalist (or perhaps some other name—it is difficult to keep pace with the periodic transformations of half a dozen worthy gentlemen in western India)—declared recently in its programme that it was opposed to all legislative interference[7] with religious rights and customs. In India this covers a wide field and there are few departments of life which cannot be connected with religion. Not to interfere with them legislatively is a mild way of saying that the orthodox may continue in every way as before and no changes will be permitted.

~

Religion, Philosophy and Science

(From The Discovery of India*)*

Truth as ultimate reality, if such there is, must be eternal, imperishable, unchanging. But that infinite, eternal and unchanging truth cannot be apprehended in its fullness by the finite mind of man which can only grasp, at most, some small aspect of it limited by time and space, and by the state of development of that mind and the prevailing ideology of the period. As the mind develops and enlarges its scope, as ideologies change and new symbols are used to express that truth, new aspects of it come to light, though the core of it may yet be the same. And so, truth has

---

[7] The Democratic Swaraj Party, at a meeting held at Akola on 1 August, 1935, passed a resolution advocating a policy "of non-interference by legislatures in religious matters."

ever to be sought and renewed, reshaped, and developed, so that, as understood by man, it might keep in line with the growth of his thought and the development of human life. Only then does it become a living truth for humanity, supplying the essential need for which it craves, and offering guidance in the present and for the future.

But if some one aspect of the truth has been petrified by dogma in a past age, it ceases to grow and develop and adapt itself to the changing needs of humanity; other aspects of it remain hidden and it fails to answer the urgent questions of a succeeding age. It is no longer dynamic but static, no longer a life-giving impulse but dead thought and ceremonial and a hindrance to the growth of the mind and of humanity. Indeed, it is probably not even understood to the extent it was understood in that past age when it grew up and was clothed in the language and symbols of that age. For its context is different in a later age, the mental climate has changed, new social habits and customs have grown up, and it is often difficult to understand the sense, much less the spirit, of that ancient writing. Moreover, as Aurobindo Ghose has pointed out, every truth, however true in itself, yet taken apart from others which at once limit and complete it, becomes a snare to bind the intellect and a misleading dogma; for in reality each is one thread of a complex weft and no thread must be taken apart from the weft.

Religions have helped greatly in the development of humanity. They have laid down values and standards and have pointed out principles for the guidance of human life. But with all the good they have done, they have also tried to imprison truth in set forms and dogmas, and encouraged ceremonials and practices which soon lose all their original meaning and become mere routine. While impressing upon man the awe and mystery of the unknown that surrounds him on all sides, they have discouraged him from trying to understand not only the unknown but what might come in the way of social effort. Instead of encouraging curiosity and thought, they have preached a philosophy of submission to nature, to established churches, to the prevailing social order, and to everything that is. The belief in a supernatural agency which ordains everything has led to a certain irresponsibility on the social plane, and emotion and sentimentality have taken the place of reasoned thought and inquiry. Religion, though it has undoubtedly brought comfort to innumerable human beings and stabilized society by its values, has checked the tendency to change and progress inherent in human society.

Philosophy has avoided many of these pitfalls and encouraged thought and inquiry. But it has usually lived in its ivory tower cut off from life and its day-to-day problems, concentrating on ultimate purposes and failing to link them with the life of man. Logic and reason were its guides and they took it far in many directions, but that logic was too much the product of the mind and unconcerned with fact.

Science ignored the ultimate purposes and looked at fact alone. It made the world jump forward with a leap, built up a glittering civilization, opened up innumerable avenues for the growth of knowledge, and added to the power of man to such an extent that for the first time it was possible to conceive that man could triumph over and shape his physical environment. Man became almost a geological force, changing the face of the planet earth chemically, physically, and in many other ways. Yet when this sorry scheme of things entirely seemed to be in his grasp, to mould it nearer to the heart's desire, there was some essential lack and some vital element was missing. There was no knowledge of ultimate purposes and not even an understanding of the immediate purpose, for science had told us nothing about any purpose in life. Nor did man, so powerful in his control of nature, have the power to control himself, and the monster he had created ran amok. Perhaps new developments in biology, psychology, and similar sciences, and the interpretation of biology and physics, may help man to understand and control himself more than he has done in the past. Or, before any such advances influence human life sufficiently, man may destroy the civilization he has built and have to start anew.

There is no visible limit to the advance of science, if it is given the chance to advance. Yet it may be that the scientific method of observation is not always applicable to all the varieties of human experience and cannot cross the uncharted ocean that surrounds us. With the help of philosophy it may go a little further and venture even on these high seas. And when both science and philosophy fail us, we shall have to rely on such other powers of apprehension as we may possess. For there appears to be a definite stopping place beyond which reason, as the mind is at present constituted, cannot go. 'La derniere demarche de la raison,' says Pascal, 'c'est de connaitre qu'il y a une infinite de choses qui la surpassent. Elle est bien faible si elle ne va jusque-la.'[8]

Realizing these limitations of reason and scientific method, we have still to hold on to them with all our strength, for without that firm basis and background we can have no grip on any kind of truth or reality. It is better to understand a part of truth and apply it to our lives, than to understand nothing at all and flounder helplessly in a vain attempt to pierce the mystery of existence. The applications of science are inevitable and unavoidable for all countries and peoples today. But something more than its application is necessary. It is the scientific approach, the adventurous and yet critical temper of science, the search for truth and new knowledge, the refusal to accept anything without testing and trial, the capacity to change previous conclusions in the face of new evidence, the reliance on observed fact and not on preconceived theory, the hard discipline of the mind—all this is necessary, not merely for the application of science but for life itself and the solution of its many problems. Too many scientists today, who swear by science, forget all about it outside their particular spheres. The scientific approach and temper are, or should be, a way of life, a process of thinking, a method of acting and associating with our fellow men. That is a large order and undoubtedly very few of us, if any at all, can function in this way

[8] Roughly translated, 'The last step of reason is to know that there is an infinity of things that surpass it. Reason is very weak if it cannot go there.'

with even partial success. But this criticism applies in equal or even greater measure to all the injunctions which philosophy and religion have laid upon us. The scientific temper points out the way along which man should travel. It is the temper of a free man. We live in a scientific age, so we are told, but there is little evidence of this temper in the people anywhere or even in their leaders.

Science deals with the domain of positive knowledge but the temper which it should produce goes beyond that domain. The ultimate purposes of man may be said to be to gain knowledge, to realize truth, to appreciate goodness and beauty. The scientific method of objective inquiry is not applicable to all these, and much that is vital in life seems to lie beyond its scope—the sensitiveness to art and poetry, the emotion that beauty produces, the inner recognition of goodness. The botanist and zoologist may never experience the charm and beauty of nature; the sociologist may be wholly lacking in love for humanity. But even when we go to the regions beyond the reach of the scientific method and visit the mountain tops where philosophy dwells and high emotions fill us, or gaze at the immensity beyond, that approach and temper are still necessary.

Very different is the method of religion. Concerned as it is principally with the regions beyond the reach of objective inquiry, it relies on emotion and intuition. And then it applies this method to everything in life, even to those things which are capable of intellectual inquiry and observation: Organized religion, allying itself to theology and often more concerned with its vested interests than with things of the spirit, encourages a temper which is the very opposite to that of science. It produces narrowness and intolerance, credulity and superstition, emotionalism and irrationalism. It tends to close and limit the mind of man, and to produce a temper of a dependent, unfree person.

Even if God did not exist, it would be necessary to invent Him, so Voltaire said—'si Dieu n'existait pas, il faudrait l'inventer.' Perhaps that is true, and indeed the mind of man has always been trying to fashion some such mental image or conception which grew with the mind's growth. But there is something also in the reverse proposition: even if God exists, it may be desirable not to look up to Him or to rely upon Him. Too much dependence on supernatural factors may lead, and has often led, to a loss of self-reliance in man and to a blunting of his capacity and creative ability. And yet some faith seems necessary in things of the spirit which are beyond the scope of our physical world, some reliance on moral, spiritual, and idealistic conceptions, or else we have no anchorage, no objectives or purpose in life. Whether we believe in God or not, it is impossible not to believe in something, whether we call it a creative life-giving force or vital energy inherent in matter which gives it its capacity for self-movement and change and growth, or by some other name, something that is as real, though elusive, as life is real when contrasted with death. Whether we are conscious of it or not most of us worship at the invisible altar of some unknown god and offer sacrifices to it—some ideal, personal, national or international; some distant objective that draws us on, though reason itself may find little substance in it; some vague conception of a perfect man and a better world. Perfection may be impossible of attainment, but the demon in us, some vital force, urges us on and we tread that path from generation to generation.

As knowledge advances, the domain of religion, in the narrow sense of the word, shrinks. The more we understand life and nature, the less we look for supernatural causes. Whatever we can understand and control ceases to be a mystery. The processes of agriculture, the food we eat, the clothes we wear, our social relations, were all at one time under the dominion of religion and its high priests. Gradually they have passed out of its control and become subjects for scientific study. Yet much of this is still powerfully affected by religious beliefs and the superstitions that accompany them. The final mysteries still remain far beyond the reach of the human mind and are likely to continue to remain so. But so many of life's mysteries are capable of and await solution, that an obsession with the final mystery seems hardly necessary or justified. Life still offers not only the loveliness of the world but also the exciting adventure of fresh and never ceasing discoveries, of new panoramas opening out and new ways of living, adding to its fullness and ever making it richer and more complete.

It is therefore with the temper and approach of science, allied to philosophy, and with reverence for all that lies beyond, that we must face life. Thus we may develop an integral vision of life which embraces in its wide scope the past and the present, with all their heights and depths, and look with serenity towards the future. The depths are there and cannot be ignored, and always by the side of the loveliness that surrounds us is the misery of the world. Man's journey through life is an odd mixture of joy and sorrow; thus only can he learn and advance. The travail of the soul is a tragic and lonely business.

External events and their consequences affect us powerfully, and yet the greatest shocks come to our minds through inner fears and conflicts. While we advance on the external plane, as we must if we are to survive, we have also to win peace with ourselves and between ourselves and our environment, a peace which brings satisfaction not only to our physical and material needs but also to those inner imaginative urges and adventurous spirits that have distinguished man ever since he started on his troubled journey in the realms of thought and action. Whether that journey has any ultimate purpose or not we do not know, but it has its compensations, and it points to many a nearer objective which appears attainable and which may again become the starting point for a fresh advance.

Science has dominated the western world and everyone there pays tribute to it, and yet the west is still far from having developed the real temper of science. It has still to bring the spirit and the flesh into creative harmony. In India in many obvious ways we have a greater distance to travel. And yet there may be fewer major obstructions on our way, for the essential basis of Indian thought for ages past, though not its later manifestations, fits in with the scientific temper and approach, as well as with internationalism. It is based on a fearless search for truth, on the solidarity of man, even on the divinity of everything living, and on the free and cooperative development of the individual and the species, ever to greater freedom and higher stages of human growth.

~

On Religion

(From Glimpses of World History*)*

...What, then, is one to do with religion? For some people religion means the other world: heaven, paradise or whatever it may be called. In the hope of going to heaven they are religious or do certain things. This reminds me of the child who behaves in the hope of being rewarded with a jam puff or jalebi! If the child is always thinking of the jam puff or the jalebi, you would not say that it had been properly trained, would you? Much less would you approve of boys and girls who did everything for the sake of jam puffs and the like. What, then, shall we say of grownup persons who think and act in this way? For, after all, there is no essential difference between the jam puff and the idea of paradise. We are all more or less selfish. But we try to train up our children so that they may become as unselfish as possible. At any rate, our ideals should be wholly unselfish, so that we may try to live up to them.

We all desire to achieve, to see the result of our actions. That is natural. But what do we aim at? Are we concerned with ourselves only or with the larger good—the good of society, of our country, or of humanity? After all, this larger good will include us also. Some days ago, I think, I gave you a Sanskrit verse in one of my letters. This stated that the individual should be sacrificed for the family, the family for the community, and the community for the country. I shall give you the translation of another verse from Sanskrit. This is from the *Bhagavata*. It runs thus: "I desire not the supreme state of bliss with its eight perfections, nor the cessation of rebirth. May I take up the sorrow of all creatures who suffer and enter into them so that they may be made free from grief."

One religious man says this, and another says that. And, often enough, each one of them considers the other a fool or a knave. Who is right? As they talk of things which cannot be seen or proved, it is difficult to settle the argument. But it seems rather presumptuous of both of them to talk with certainty of such matters and to break each other's heads over them. Most of us are narrow-minded and not very wise. Can we presume to imagine that we know the whole truth and to force this down the throat of our neighbour? It may be we are right. It may be that our neighbour is also right. If you see a flower on a tree, you do not call it the tree. If another person sees the leaf only, and yet another the trunk, each has seen part of the tree only. How foolish it would be for each one of them to say that the tree was the flower only or the leaf or the trunk, and to fight over this!

I am afraid the next world does not interest me. My mind is full of what I should do in this world, and if I see my way clearly here, I am content. If my duty here is clear to me, I do not trouble myself about any other world.

As you grow up, you will meet all kinds of people: religious people, anti-religious people, and people who do not care either way. There are big churches and religious organizations possessing great wealth and power, sometimes using them for good purposes, sometimes for bad. You will meet very fine and noble people who are religious, and knaves and scoundrels who, under the cloak of religion, rob and defraud others. And you will have to think about these matters and decide for yourself. One can learn much from others, but everything worthwhile one has to find out or experience oneself. There are some questions which each person has to answer for himself or herself.

Do not be in a hurry to decide. Before you can decide anything big or vital you will have to train yourself and educate yourself to do so. It is right that people should think for themselves and decide for themselves, but they must have the ability to decide. You would not ask a newborn babe to decide anything! And there are many people who, though grown in years, are almost like newborn babes so far as their minds are concerned.

January 20, 1931

~

Jesus and Christianity

(*From* Glimpses of World History)

...The story of Christ or Jesus, as his name was, is given in the New Testament of the Bible, and you know something about it. In these accounts given in the Gospels little is said about his youth. He was born at Nazareth, he preached in Galilee, and he came to Jerusalem when he was over thirty. Soon after he was tried and sentenced by the Roman governor, Pontius Pilate. It is not clear what Jesus did or where he went before he started his preaching. All over Central Asia, in Kashmir and Ladakh and Tibet and even farther north, there is still a strong belief that Jesus or Isa travelled about there. Some people believe that he visited India also. It is not possible to say anything with certainty, and indeed most authorities who have studied the life of Jesus do not believe that Jesus came to India or Central Asia. But there is nothing inherently improbable in his having done so. In those days the great universities of India, specially Takshashila in the north-west, attracted earnest students from distant countries, and Jesus might well have come there in quest of knowledge. In many respects the teaching of Jesus is so similar to Gautama's teaching that it seems highly probable that he was fully acquainted with it. But Buddhism was sufficiently known in other countries, and Jesus could well have known of it without coming to India.

Religions, as every schoolgirl knows, have led to conflict and bitter struggles. But it is interesting to watch the beginnings of the world religions and to compare them. There is so much that is similar in their outlook and their teaching that one wonders why people should be foolish enough to quarrel about details and unessentials. But the early teachings are added to and distorted till it is difficult to recognize them; and the place of the teacher is taken by narrow-minded and intolerant bigots. Often enough religion has served as a handmaiden to politics and imperialism....

...As Christianity grew, violent disputes arose about the divinity of Jesus. You will remember my telling you how Gautama the Buddha, who claimed no divinity, came to be worshipped as a god and as an avatar. Similarly, Jesus claimed no divinity. His repeated statements that he was the son of God and the son of man do not necessarily mean any divine or superhuman claim. But human beings like to make gods of their great men, whom, having deified, they refrain from following! Six hundred years later the Prophet Mohammad started another great religion, but, profiting perhaps by these instances, he stated clearly and repeatedly that he was human, and not divine.

So, instead of understanding and following the teachings of Jesus, the Christians argued and quarrelled about the nature of Jesus' divinity and about the Trinity. They called each other heretics and persecuted each other and cut each other's heads off. There was a great and violent controversy at one time among different Christian sects over a certain diphthong. One party said that the word *Homo-ousion* should be used in a prayer; the other wanted *Homoi-ousion*—this difference had reference to the divinity of Jesus. Over this diphthong fierce war was raged and large numbers of people were slaughtered.

These internal disputes took place as the Church grew in power. They have continued between various Christian sects till quite recent times in the West.

You may be surprised to learn that Christianity came to India long before it went to England or western Europe, and when even in Rome it was a despised and proscribed sect. Within 100 years or so of the death of Jesus, Christian missionaries came to South India by sea. They were received courteously and permitted to preach their new faith. They converted a large number of people, and their descendants have lived there, with varying fortunes, to this day. Most of them belong to old Christian sects which have ceased to exist in Europe. Some of these have their headquarters now in Asia Minor.

Christianity is politically the dominant religion today, because it is the religion of the dominant peoples of Europe. But it is strange to think of the rebel Jesus preaching nonviolence and ahimsa and a revolt against the social order, and then to compare him with his loud-voiced followers of today, with their imperialism and armaments and wars and worship of wealth. The Sermon on the Mount and modern European and American Christianity—how amazingly dissimilar they are! It is not surprising that many people should think that Bapu is far nearer to Christ's teaching than most of his so-called followers in the West today.

~

The Upanishads

(From The Discovery of India*)*

The Upanishads are instinct with a spirit of inquiry, of mental adventure, of a passion for finding out the truth about things. The search for this truth is, of course, not by the objective methods of modern science, yet there is an element of the scientific method in the approach. No dogma is allowed to come in the way. There is much that is trivial and without any meaning or relevance for us today. The emphasis is essentially on self-realization, on knowledge of the individual self and the absolute self, both of which are said to be the same in essence. The objective external world is not considered unreal but real in a relative sense, an aspect of the inner reality.

There are many ambiguities in the Upanishads and different interpretations have been made. But that is a matter for the philosopher or scholar. The general tendency is towards monism and the whole approach is evidently intended to lessen the differences that must have existed then, leading to fierce debate. It is the way of synthesis. Interest in magic and such like supernatural knowledge is sternly discouraged, and ritual and ceremonies without enlightenment are said to be in vain—'those engaged in them, considering themselves men of understanding and learned, stagger along aimlessly like blind men led by the blind, and fail to reach the goal.' Even the Vedas are treated as the lower knowledge; the higher one being that of the inner mind. There is a warning given against philosophical learning without discipline of conduct. And there is a continuous attempt to harmonize social activity with spiritual adventure. The duties and obligations imposed by life were to be carried out, but in a spirit of detachment.

Probably the ethic of individual perfection was overemphasized and hence the social outlook suffered. 'There is nothing higher than the person,' say the Upanishads. Society must have been considered as stabilized and hence the mind of man was continually thinking of individual perfection, and in quest of this it wandered about in the heavens and in the innermost recesses of the heart. This old Indian approach was not a narrow nationalistic one, though there must have been a feeling that India was the hub of the world, just as China and Greece and Rome have felt at various times. 'The whole world of mortals is an interdependent organism,' says the Mahabharata.

The metaphysical aspects of the questions considered in the Upanishads are difficult for me to grasp, but I am impressed by this approach to a problem which has so often been shrouded by dogma and blind belief. It was the philosophical approach and not the religious one. I like the vigour of the thought, the questioning, the rationalistic background. The form is terse, often of question and answer between pupil and teacher, and it has been suggested that the Upanishads were some kind of lecture notes made by the teacher or taken down by his disciples. Professor F.W. Thomas in 'The Legacy of India' says: 'What gives to the Upanishads their unique quality and unfailing human appeal is an earnest sincerity of tone, as of friends conferring upon matters of deep concern.' And C. Rajagopalachari thus eloquently speaks of them: 'The spacious imagination, the majestic sweep of thought, and the almost reckless spirit of exploration with which, urged by the compelling thirst for truth, the Upanishad teachers and pupils dig into the "open secret" of the universe, make this most ancient of the world's holy books still the most modern and most satisfying.'

The dominating characteristic of the Upanishads is the dependence on truth. 'Truth wins ever, not falsehood. With truth is paved the road to the Divine.' And the famous invocation is for light and understanding: 'Lead me from the unreal to the real! Lead me from darkness to light! Lead me from death to immortality.'

Again and again the restless mind peeps out, ever seeking, ever questioning: 'At whose behest doth mind light on its perch? At whose command doth life, the first, proceed? At whose behest do men send forth this speech? What god, indeed, directed eye and ear?' And again: 'Why cannot the wind remain still? Why has the human mind no rest? Why, and in search of what, does the water run out and cannot stop its flow even for a moment?' It is the adventure of man that is continually calling and there is no resting on the way and no end of the journey. In the Aitereya Brahmana there is a hymn about this long endless journey which we must undertake, and every verse ends with the refrain: Charaiveti, charaiveti—'Hence, O traveller, march along, march along!'

There is no humility about all this quest, the humility before an all-powerful deity, so often associated with religion. It is the triumph of mind over the environment. 'My body will be reduced to ashes and my breath will join the restless and deathless air, but not I and my deeds. O mind, remember this always, remember this.' In a morning prayer the sun is addressed thus: 'O sun of refulgent glory, I am the same person as makes thee what thou art!' What superb confidence!

What is the soul? It cannot be described or defined except negatively: 'It is not this, not this.' Or, in a way, positively: 'That thou art!' The individual soul is like a spark thrown out and reabsorbed by the blazing fire of the absolute soul. 'As fire, though one, entering the world, takes a separate form according to whatever it burns, so does the inner Self within all things become different, according to whatever it enters, yet itself is without form.' This realization that all things have that same essence removes the barriers which separate us from them and produces a sense of unity with humanity and nature, a unity which underlies the diversity and manifoldness of the external world. 'Who knoweth all things are Self; for him what grief existeth, what delusion, when (once) he gazeth on the oneness?' 'Aye, whoso seeth all things in that Self, and Self in everything; from That he'll no more hide.'

It is interesting to compare and contrast the intense individualism and exclusiveness of the Indo-Aryans with this all-embracing approach, which overrides all barriers of caste and class and every other external and internal difference. This latter is a kind of metaphysical democracy. 'He who sees the one spirit in all, and all in the one spirit, henceforth can look with contempt on no creature.' Though this was theory only, there can be no doubt that it must have affected life and produced that atmosphere of tolerance and reasonableness, that acceptance of freethought in matters of faith, that desire and capacity to live and let live, which are dominant features of Indian culture, as they are of the Chinese. There was no totalitarianism in religion or culture, and they indicate an old and wise civilization with inexhaustible mental reserves.

There is a question in the Upanishads to which a very curious and yet significant answer is given. 'The question is: "What is this universe? From what does it arise? Into what does it go?" And the answer is: "In freedom it rises, in freedom it rests, and into freedom it melts away." 'What exactly this means I am unable to understand, except that the authors of the Upanishads were passionately attached to the idea of freedom and wanted to see everything in terms of it. Swami Vivekananda was always emphasizing this aspect.

It is not easy for us, even imaginatively, to transplant ourselves to this distant period and enter the mental climate of that day. The form of writing itself is something that we are unused to, odd looking, difficult to translate, and the background of life is utterly different. We take for granted so many things today because we are used to them, although they are curious and unreasonable enough. But what we are not used to at all is much more difficult to appreciate or understand. In spite of all these difficulties and almost insuperable barriers, the message of the Upanishads has found willing and eager listeners throughout Indian history and has powerfully moulded the national mind and character. 'There is no important form of Hindu thought, heterodox Buddhism included, which is not rooted in the Upanishads,' says Bloomfield.

Early Indian thought penetrated to Greece, through Iran, and influenced some thinkers and philosophers there. Much later, Plotinus came to the east to study Iranian and Indian philosophy and was especially influenced by the mystic element in the Upanishads. From Plotinus many of these ideas are said to have gone to St Augustine, and through him influenced the Christianity of the day.[9]

The rediscovery by Europe, during the past century and a half, of Indian philosophy created a powerful impression on European philosophers and thinkers. Schopenhauer, the pessimist, is often quoted in this connection. 'From every sentence (of the Upanishads) deep, original and sublime thoughts arise, and the whole is pervaded by a high and holy and earnest spirit....In the whole world there is no study ... so beneficial and so elevating as that of the Upanishads....(They) are products of the highest wisdom....It is destined sooner or later to become the faith of the people.' And again: 'The study of the Upanishads has been the solace of my life, it will be the solace of my death.' Writing on this, Max Muller says: 'Schopenhauer was the last man to write at random, or to allow himself to go into ecstasies over so-called mystic and inarticulate thought. And I am neither afraid nor ashamed to say that I share his enthusiasm for the Vedanta,

[9] Romain Rolland has given a long Note (as an appendix to his book on Vivekananda), 'On the Hellenic-Christian Mysticism of the First Centuries and its Relationship to Hindu Mysticism.' He points out that 'a hundred facts testify to how great an extent the East was mingled with Hellenic thought during the second century of our era.'

and feel indebted to it for much that has been helpful to me in my passage through life.' In another place Max Muller says: 'The Upanishads are the... sources of... the Vedanta philosophy, a system in which human speculation seems to me to have reached its very acme.' 'I spend my happiest hours in reading Vedantic books. They are to me like the light of the morning, like the pure air of the mountains—so simple, so true, if once understood.'

But perhaps the most eloquent tribute to the Upanishads and to the later book, the Bhagavad Gita, was paid by A.E. (G. W. Russell) the Irish poet: 'Goethe, Wordsworth, Emerson and Thoreau among moderns have something of this vitality and wisdom, but we can find all they have said and much more in the grand sacred books of the East. The Bhagavad Gita and the Upanishads contain such godlike fullness of wisdom on all things that I feel the authors must have looked with calm remembrance back through a thousand passionate lives, full of feverish strife for and with shadows, ere they could have written with such certainty of things which the soul feels to be sure.'[10]

The Advantages and Disadvantages of an Individualistic Philosophy

There is, in the Upanishads, a continual emphasis on the fitness of the body and clarity of the mind, on the discipline of both body and mind, before effective progress can be made. The acquisition of knowledge, or any achievement, requires restraint, self-suffering, self-sacrifice. This idea of some kind of penance, tapasya, is inherent in Indian thought, both among the thinkers at the top and the unread masses below. It is present today as it was present some thousands of years ago, and it is necessary to

[10] There is an odd and interesting passage in one of the Upanishads (the Chhandogya): 'The sun never sets nor rises. When people think to themselves the sun is setting lie only changes about after reaching the end of the day, and makes night below and day to what is on the other side. Then when people think he rises in the morning, he only shifts himself about after reaching the end of the night, and makes day below and night to what is on the other side. In fact he never does set at all.'

appreciate it in order to understand the psychology underlying the mass movements which have convulsed India under Gandhiji's leadership.

It is obvious that the ideas of the authors of the Upanishads, the rarefied mental atmosphere in which they moved, were confined to a small body of the elect who were capable of under-standing them. They were entirely beyond the comprehension of the vast mass of the people. A creative minority is always small in numbers but, if it is in tune with the majority, and is always trying to pull the latter up and make it advance, so that the gap between the two is lessened, a stable and progressive culture results. Without that creative minority a civilization must inevitably decay. But it may also decay if the bond between a creative minority and the majority is broken and there is a loss of social unity in society as a whole, and ultimately that minority itself loses its creativeness and becomes barren and sterile; or else it gives place to another creative or vital force which society throws up."

It is difficult for me, as for most others, to visualize the period of the Upanishads and to analyse the various forces that were at play. I imagine, however, that in spite of the vast mental and cultural difference between the small thinking minority and the unthinking masses, there was a bond between them or, at any rate, there was no obvious gulf. The graded society in which they lived had its mental gradation also and these were accepted and provided for. This led to some kind of social harmony and conflicts were avoided. Even the new thought of the Upanishads was interpreted for popular purposes so as to fit in with popular prejudices and superstitions, thereby losing much of its essential meaning. The graded social structure was not touched; it was preserved. The conception of monism became transformed into one of monotheism for religious purposes, and even lower forms of belief and worship were not only tolerated but encouraged, as suited to a particular stage of development.

Thus the ideology of the Upanishads did not permeate to any marked extent to the masses and the intellectual separation between the creative minority and the majority became more marked. In course of time this led to new movements—a powerful wave of materialistic philosophy, agnosticism, atheism. Out of this again grew Buddhism and Jainism, and the famous Sanskrit epics, the Ramayana and the Mahabharata, wherein yet another attempt was made to bring about a synthesis between rival creeds and ways of thought. The creative energy of the people, or of the creative minority, is very evident during these periods, and again there appears to be a bond between that minority and the majority. On the whole they pull together.

~

Buddha's Teaching

(From The Discovery of India*)*

Behind these political and economic revolutions that were changing the face of India, there was the ferment of Buddhism and its impact on old-established faiths and its quarrels with vested interests in religion. Far more than the debates and arguments, of which India has always been so enamoured, the personality of a tremendous and radiant being had impressed the people and his memory was fresh in their minds. His message, old and yet very new and original for those immersed in metaphysical subtleties, captured the imagination of the intellectuals; it went deep down into the hearts of the people. 'Go unto all lands,' had said the Buddha to his disciples, 'and preach this gospel. Tell them that the poor and the lowly, the rich and the high, are all one, and that all castes unite in this religion as do the rivers in the sea.' His message was one of universal benevolence, of love for all. For 'Never in this world does hatred cease by hatred; hatred ceases by love.' And 'Let a man overcome anger by kindness, evil by good.'

It was an ideal of righteousness and self-discipline. 'One may overcome a thousand men in battle, but he who conquers himself is the greatest victor.' 'Not by birth, but by his conduct alone, does a man become a low-caste or a Brahmin.' Even a sinner is not to be condemned, for 'who would willingly use hard speech to those who have done a sinful deed, strewing salt, as it were, upon the wound of their fault?' Victory itself over another leads to unhappy consequences—'Victory breeds hatred, for the conquered is unhappy.'

All this he preached without any religious sanction or any reference to God or another world. He relies on reason and logic and experience and asks people to seek the truth in their own minds. He is reported to have said: 'One must not accept my law from reverence, but first try it as gold is tried by fire.' Ignorance of truth was the cause of all misery. Whether there is a God or an Absolute or not, he does not say. He neither affirms nor denies. Where knowledge is not possible we must suspend judgment. In answer to a question, Buddha is reported to have said: 'If by the absolute is meant something out of relation to all known things, its existence cannot be established by any known reasoning. How can we know that anything unrelated to other things exists at all? The whole universe, as we know it, is a system of relations: we know nothing that is, or can be, unrelated.' So we must limit ourselves to what we can perceive and about which we can have definite knowledge.

So also Buddha gives no clear answer about the existence of the soul. He does not deny it and he does not affirm it. He refuses to discuss this question, which is very remarkable, for the Indian mind of his day was full of the individual soul and the absolute soul, of monism and monotheism and other metaphysical hypotheses. But Buddha set his mind against all forms of metaphysics. He does, however, believe in the permanence of a natural law, of universal causation, of each successive state being determined by pre-existing conditions, of virtue and happiness and vice and suffering being organically related.

We use terms and descriptions in this world of experience and say 'it is' or 'it is not.' Yet neither may be correct when we go behind the superficial aspect of things, and our language may be inadequate to describe what is actually happening. Truth may lie somewhere in the middle of 'is' and 'is not' or beyond them. The river flows continuously and appears to be the same from moment to moment, yet the waters are ever changing. So also fire. The flame keeps glowing and even maintains its shape and form, yet it is never the same flame and it changes every instant. So everything continually changes and life in all its forms is a stream of becoming. Reality is not something that is permanent and unchanging, but rather a kind of radiant energy, a thing of forces and movements, a succession of sequences. The idea of time is just a notion abstracted by mere usage, from this or that event.' We cannot say that one thing is the cause of something else for there is no core of permanent being which changes. The essence of a thing is its immanent law of relation to other so-called things. Our bodies and our souls change from moment to moment; they cease to be, and something else, like them and yet different, appears and then passes off. In a sense we are dying all the time and being reborn and this succession gives the appearance of an unbroken identity. It is 'the continuity of an ever-changing identity.' Everything is flux, movement, change.

All this is difficult for our minds to grasp, used as we are to set methods of thinking and of interpreting physical phenomena. Yet it is remarkable how near this philosophy of the Buddha brings us to some of the concepts of modern physics and modern philosophic thought.

Buddha's method was one of psychological analysis and, again, it is surprising to find how deep was his insight into this latest of modern sciences. Man's life was considered and examined without any reference to a permanent self, for even if such a self exists, it is beyond our comprehension. The mind was looked upon as part of the body, a composite of mental forces. The individual thus becomes a bundle of mental states, the self is just a stream of ideas. 'All that we are is the result of what we have thought.'

There is an emphasis on the pain and suffering of life, and the 'Four Noble Truths' which Buddha enunciated deal with this suffering, its cause, the possibility of ending it, and the way to do it. Speaking to his disciples, he is reported to have said: 'and while ye experienced this (sorrow) through long ages, more tears have flowed from you and have been shed by you, while ye strayed and wandered on this pilgrimage (of life), and sorrowed and wept, because that was your portion which ye abhorred, and that which ye loved was not your portion, than all the water which is in the four great oceans.'

Through an ending of this state of suffering is reached 'Nirvana.' As to what Nirvana is, people differ, for it is impossible to describe a transcendental state in our inadequate language and in terms of the concepts of our limited minds. Some say it is just extinction, a blowing out. And yet Buddha is reported to have denied this and to have indicated that it was an intense kind of activity. It was the extinction of false desire, and not just annihilation, but it cannot be described by us except in negative terms.

Buddha's way was the middle path, between the extremes of self-indulgence and self-mortification. From his own experience of mortification of the body, he said that a person who has lost his strength cannot progress along the right path. This middle path was the Aryan eightfold path: right beliefs, right aspirations, right speech, right conduct, right mode of livelihood, right effort, right-mindedness, and right rapture. It is all a question of self-development, not grace. And if a person succeeds in developing along these lines and conquers himself, there can be no defeat for him: 'Not even a god can change into defeat the victory of a man who has vanquished himself.'

Buddha told his disciples what he thought they could understand and live up to. His teaching was not meant to be a full explanation of everything, a complete revelation of all that is. Once, it is said, he took some dry leaves in his hand and asked his favourite disciple, Ananda, to tell him whether there were any other leaves besides those in his hand. Ananda replied: 'The leaves of autumn are falling on all sides, and there are more of them than can be numbered.' Then said the Buddha: 'In like manner I have given you a handful of truths, but besides these there are many thousands of other truths, more than can be numbered.'

Culture, Literature and Science

What Is Culture?

(Speech delivered at the inauguration of the Indian Council for Cultural Relations, New Delhi, 9 April, 1950)

I have come here with pleasure, because I have always looked forward to furthering the cause of India's cultural association, not only with the neighbouring countries to the East and West but with the wider world outside. It is not a question of merely wanting such cultural association or considering it good; it is rather a question of the necessity of the situation which is bound to worsen if nothing is done to prevent it. I earnestly hope that formation of the Indian Council of Cultural Relations will lead to a better understanding between our people and the peoples of other countries.

There is a great deal of confusion in my mind and I shall state quite frankly what it is. All kinds of basic questions crop up from what is going on in the world around us. Nations, individuals and groups talk of understanding one another and it seems an obvious thing that people should try to understand one another and to learn from one another. Yet, when I look through the pages of history or study current events, I sometimes find that people who know one another most, quarrel most. Countries, which are next door to one another in Europe or in Asia, somehow seem to rub one another up the wrong way, though they know one another very thoroughly. Thus, knowledge, by itself, does not lead to greater cooperation or friendship. This is not a new thing. Even the long pages of history show that. Has there been something wrong in individual nations or in the approach to this question? Or is it something else that has not worked as it should have done?

When we talk of cultural relations, the question that immediately arises in my mind is—what exactly is the 'culture' that people talk so much about? When I was younger in years, I remember reading about German 'kultur' and of the attempts of the German people to spread it by conquest and other means. There was a big war to spread this 'kultur' and to resist it. Every country and every individual seem to have their peculiar idea of culture. When there is talk about cultural relations—although it is very good in theory—what actually happens is that those peculiar ideas come into conflict and instead of leading to friendship they lead to more estrangement. It is a basic question—what is culture? And I am certainly not competent to give you a definition of it because I have not found one.

One can see each nation and each separate civilization developing its own culture that had its roots in generations hundreds and thousands of years ago. One sees these nations being intimately moulded by the impulse that initially starts a civilization going on its long path. That conception is by other conceptions and one sees action and interaction these varying conceptions. There is, I suppose, no culture in the world which is absolutely pristine, pure and unaffected by any other culture. It simply cannot be, just as nobody can say that he belongs one hundred per cent to a particular racial type, because in the course of hundreds and thousands of years unmistakable changes and mixtures have occurred.

So, culture is bound to get a little mixed up, even though the basic element of a particular national culture remains dominant. If that kind of thing goes on peacefully, there is no harm in it. But it often leads to conflicts. It sometimes leads a group to fear that their culture is being overwhelmed by what they consider to be an outside or alien influence. Then they draw themselves into a shell which isolates them and prevents their thoughts and ideas going out. That is an unhealthy situation, because in any matter and much

> **more so in what might be called a matter, stagnation is the worst possible thing. Culture, if it has any value, must have a certain depth. It must also have a certain dynamic character.**

After all, culture depends on a vast number of factors. If we leave out what might be called the basic mould that was given to it in the early stages of a nation's or a people's growth, it is affected by geography, by climate and by all of other factors. The culture of Arabia is intimately governed by the geography and the deserts of Arabia because it there. Obviously, the culture of India in the old days was affected greatly, as we see in our own literature, by the Himalayan forests and the great rivers of India among other things, a natural growth from the soil. Of the various domains of culture like architecture, music and literature, any two may mix together, as they often did and produce a happy combination. But where there is an attempt to improve something or the other which does not naturally grow and mould itself without uprooting itself, conflict inevitably arises. Then also comes something which to my mind is basically opposed to all ideas of culture. And that is the isolation of the mind and the deliberate shutting up of the mind to other influences. My own view of India's history is that we can almost measure the growth and the advance of India and the decline of India by relating them to periods when India had her mind open to the outside world and when she wanted to close it up. The more she closed it up, the more static she became. Life, whether of the individual, group, nation or society, is essentially a dynamic, changing, growing thing. Whatever stops that dynamic growth also injures it and undermines it.

We have had great religions and they have had an enormous effect on humanity. Yet, if I may say so with all respect and without meaning any ill to any person, those very religions, in the measure that they made the mind of man static, dogmatic and bigoted, have had, to my mind, an evil effect. The things they said may be good but when it is claimed that the last word has been said, society becomes static.

The individual human being or race or nation must necessarily have a certain depth and certain roots somewhere. They do not count for much unless they have roots in the past, which past is after all the accumulation of generations of experience and some type of wisdom. It is essential that you have that. Otherwise you become just pale copies of something which has no real meaning to you as an individual or as a group. On the other hand, one cannot live in roots alone. Even roots wither unless they come out in the sun and the free air. Only then can the roots give you sustenance. Only then can there be a branching out and a flowering. How, then are you to balance these two essential factors? It is very difficult, because some people think a great deal about the flowers and the leaves on the branches, forgetting that they only flourish because there is a stout root to sustain them. Others think so much of the roots that no flowers or leaves or branches are left; there is only a thick stem somewhere. So, the question is how one is to achieve a balance.

Does culture mean some inner growth in the man? Of course, it must. Does it mean the way he behaves to others? Certainly it must. Does it mean the capacity to understand the person? I suppose so. Does it mean the capacity to make yourself understood by the other person? I suppose so. It means all that. A person who cannot understand another's veiwpoint is to that extent limited in mind and culture, because nobody, perhaps, barring some very extraordinary human beings, can presume to have the fullest knowledge and wisdom. The other party or the other group may also have some inkling of knowledge or wisdom or truth and if we shut our minds to that then we not only deprive ourselves of it but we cultivate an attitude of mind which, I would say, is opposed to that of a cultured man. The cultured mind, rooted in itself, should have its doors and windows open. It should have the capacity to understand the other's veiwpoint fully even though it cannot always agree with it. The question of agreement or disagreement only arises when you understand a thing. Otherwise, it is blind negation which is not a cultured approach to any question.

I should like to use another word—science. What is a scientific approach to life's problems? I suppose it is one of examining everything, of seeking truth by trial and error and by experiment, of never saying that this must be so but trying to understand why it is so and, if one is convinced of it, of accepting it, of having the capacity to change one's notions the moment some other proof is forthcoming, of having an open mind, which tries to imbibe the truth wherever it is found. If that is culture, how far is it represented in the modern world and in the nations of today? Obviously, if it was represented more than it is, many of our problems, national and international, would be far easier to solve.

Almost every country in the world believes that it has some special dispensation from Providence, that it is of the chosen people or race and that others, whether they are good or bad are somewhat inferior creatures. It is extraordinary how this kind of feeling persists in all nations of the East as well as of the West without exception. The nations of the East are strongly entrenched in their own ideas and convictions and sometimes in their own sense of superiority about certain matters. Anyhow, in the course of the last two or three hundred years, they have received many knocks on the head and they have been humiliated, they have been debased and they have been exploited. And so, in spite of their feeling that they were superior in many ways, they were forced to admit that they could be knocked about and exploited. To some extent, this brought a sense of realism to them. There was also an attempt to escape from reality by saying that it was sad that we were not so advanced in material and technical things but that these were after all superficial things; nevertheless, we were superior in essential things, in spiritual things, in moral values. I have no doubt that spiritual things and moral values are ultimately more important than other things but the way one finds escape in the thought that one is spiritually superior, simply because one is inferior in a material and physical sense, is surprising. It does not follow by any means. It is an escape from facing up to the causes of one's degradation.

Nationalism, of course, is a curious phenomenon which at a certain stage in a country's history gives life, growth, strength and unity but, at the same time, it has a tendency to limit one, because one thinks of one's country as something different from the rest of the world. The perspective changes and one is continuously thinking of one's own struggles and virtues and failings to the exclusion of other thoughts. The result is that the same nationalism, which is the symbol of growth for a people, becomes a symbol of the cessation of that growth in the mind. Nationalism, when it becomes successful, sometimes goes on spreading in an aggressive way and becomes a danger internationally. Whatever line of thought you follow, you arrive at the conclusion that some kind of balance must be found. Otherwise something that was good can turn into evil. Culture, which is essentially good, becomes not only static but aggressive and something that breeds conflict and hatred when looked at from a wrong point of view. How you are to find a balance, I do not know. Apart from the political and economic problems of the age, perhaps, that is the greatest problem today, because behind it there is a tremendous conflict in the spirit of man and a tremendous search for something which it cannot find. We turn to economic theories because they have an undoubted importance. It is folly to talk of culture or even of God when human beings starve and die. Before one can talk about anything else one must provide the normal essentials of life to human beings. That is where economics comes in. Human beings today are not in the mood to tolerate this suffering and starvation and inequality when they see that the burden is not equally shared. Others profit while they only bear the burden.

We have inevitably to deal with these problems in economic and other ways but I do think that behind it all there is a tremendous psychological problem in the minds of the people. It may be that some people think about it consciously and deliberately and others rather unconsciously and dimly but that this conflict exists in the spirit of man today is certain. How it will be resolved, I do not know. One thing that troubles me is this: people who understand one another more and more begin often enough to quarrel more and more. Nevertheless, it does not follow from this that we should not try to understand one another. That would amount to limiting oneself completely and that is something which really cannot be done in the context of the modern world. Therefore, it becomes essential that we try to understand one another in the right way. The right way is important. The right approach is the friendly approach, important, because a friendly approach brings a friendly response. I have not the shadow of a doubt that it is a fundamental rule of human life that, if the approach is good, the response is good. If the approach is bad, the response is likely to be bad, too. So, if we approach our fellow human beings or countries in a friendly way, with our minds and hearts open and prepared to accept whatever good comes to them—and that does not mean surrendering something that we consider of essential value to truth or to our own genius—then we shall be led not only towards understanding but the right type of understanding.

So, I shall leave you to determine what culture and wisdom really are. We grow in learning, in knowledge and in experience, till we have such an enormous accumulation of them that it becomes impossible to know exactly where we stand. We are overwhelmed by all this and, at the same time, somehow or other we have a feeling that all these put together do not necessarily represent a growth in the wisdom of the human race. I have a feeling that perhaps some people who did not have all the advantages of modern life and modern science were essentially wiser than most of us are. Whether or not we shall be able in later times to combine all this knowledge, scientific growth and betterment of the human species with true wisdom, I do not know. It is a race between various forces. I am reminded of the saying of a very wise man who was a famous Greek poet:

> What else is Wisdom? What of man's endeavour or God's high grace, so lovely and so great?
> To stand from fear set free, to breathe and wait,
> To hold a hand uplifted over Hate,
> And shall not Loveliness be loved for ever?

~

Foreword to *Rajatarangini*[1]

Nearly four years ago, when we were both together in Naini Central Prison, Ranjit Pandit told me of his intention to translate Kalhana's *Rajatarangini.* I warmly encouraged him to do so and saw the beginnings of this undertaking. We came out of prison and went back later and so, in and out, and mostly in, we have spent the last four years. But we were kept in different gaols and many high walls and iron gates separated us, and I was unable to follow the progress of the translation. It turned out to be a much vaster undertaking than I had imagined and I was glad that the translator persevered with his work in spite of the difficulties and delays inseparable from a residence in gaol.

It was Ranjit Pandit's wish, in those early days when he began the translation, that it should be introduced to the public by a preface or a foreword from my father, Pandit Motilal Nehru. Indeed, one of the reasons which led him to translate this ancient story of our old homeland was to enable my father to read it, for he knew no Sanskrit. But that was not to be, and now I am told that, in his absence, the duty of writing that foreword devolves upon me. I must play the substitute however poorly qualified I may be for the task.

It is for scholars and learned men to appraise and judge this translation. That is not my task. I feel a little overwhelmed by the ability, learning and tremendous industry that Ranjit Pandit has put into this work. It was a work worth doing. Nearly half a century ago, Mr S.P. Pandit[2] wrote of the *Rajatarangini* that it was "the only work hitherto discovered in India having any pretensions to be considered as a history." Such a book must necessarily have importance for every student of old Indian history and culture.

---

[1] Dehra Dun District Jail, 28 June 1934. J.N. Papers, N.M.M.L. R.S. Pandit's translation of *Rajatarangini* was first published in 1955. The book is an analysis of the dynasties which ruled Kashmir from the earliest period when Gonanda ruled as a vassal of the Pandavas to Kalhana's time, i.e., 1149 A.D.

[2] (1840–1894); a distinguished Sanskrit scholar and editor of Sanskrit works.

It is a history and it is a poem, though the two perhaps go ill together, and in a translation especially we have to suffer for this combination. For we cannot appreciate the music of the poetry, the charm of Kalhana's noble and melodious language, if only the inexactitude and the extravagant conceits remain. The translator has preferred a literal rendering, sometimes even at the cost of grace of language, and I think he has chosen rightly, for in a work of this kind exactitude is necessary.

Written eight hundred years ago, the story is supposed to cover thousands of years, but the early part is brief and vague, and sometimes fanciful, and it is only in the later periods, approaching Kalhana's own times, that we see a close-up and have a detailed account. It is a story of medieval times and often enough it is not a pleasant story. There is too much of palace intrigue and murder and treason and civil war and tyranny. It is the story of autocracy, and military oligarchy here as in Byzantium or elsewhere. In the main it is a story of the kings and royal families and the nobility, not of the common folk—indeed the very name is the 'River of Kings'.

And yet Kalhana's book is something far more than a record of kings' doings. It is a rich storehouse of information, political, social and to some extent economic. We see the panoply of the middle ages, the feudal knights in glittering armour, quixotic chivalry and disgusting cruelty, loyalty unto death and senseless treachery; we read of royal amours and intrigues and of fighting and militant and adulterous queens. Women seem to play quite an important part, not only behind the scenes but in the councils and the fields as leaders and soldiers.

Sometimes we get intimate glimpses of human relations and human feelings, of love and hatred, of faith and passion. We read of Suyya's[3] engineering feats and irrigation works; of Lalitaditya's[4]

---

[3] In the reign of Avantivarman (855–883 A.D.) Suyya regulated the course of the river Vitastha with a view to improve the drainage of the valley.

[4] (c 700–736 A.D.); a celebrated king of Kashmir who took the city of Kanauj and extended his conquests to the far south.

distant wars of conquest in far countries; of Meghavahana's[5] curious attempt to spread nonviolence also by conquest; of the building of temples and monasteries and their destruction by unbelievers and iconoclasts who confiscated the temple treasures. And then there were famines and floods and great fires which decimated the population and reduced the survivors to misery.

It was a time when the old economic system was decaying, the old order was changing in Kashmir as it was in the rest of India. Kashmir had been the meeting-ground of the different cultures of Asia, the western Greco-Roman and Iranian and the eastern Mongolian; but essentially it was a part of India and the inheritor of Indo-Aryan traditions. And as the economic structure collapsed it shook up the old Indo-Aryan polity and weakened it and made it an easy prey to internal commotion and foreign conquest. Flashes of old Indo-Aryan ideals come out but they are already out of date under the changing conditions. Warlords march up and down and make havoc of the people. Popular risings take place—Kalhana describes Kashmir as "a country which delighted in insurrection!"—and they are exploited by military leaders and adventurers to their own advantage. We reach the end of that period of decay which ultimately ushered in the Muslim conquest of India. Yet Kashmir was strong enough because of its mountain fastnesses to withstand and repulse Mahmud of Ghazni, the great conqueror, who made a habit of raiding India to fill his coffers and build up an empire in Central Asia.[6] It was nearly two hundred years after Kalhana wrote his history that Kashmir submitted to Muslim rule, and even then it was not by external conquest but by a local revolution headed by a Muslim official of the last Hindu ruler, Queen Kota.[7]

---

[5] Meghavahana's conquest was motivated by the imposition of ahimsa upon other kings.

[6] He undertook seventeen expeditions to India during the years 1000 to 1026.

[7] The widow of Udaiyana Deva, the last ruler of Kashmir, was overthrown by her minister, Shah Mirza. The latter ascended the throne in 1346 a.d.

I have read this story of olden times with interest because I am a lover of Kashmir and all its entrancing beauty; because, perhaps, deep down within me and almost forgotten by me, there is something which stirs at the call of the old homeland from where we came long, long ago; and because I cannot answer that call as I would, I have to content myself with dreams and fantasies, and I revisit the glorious valley girt by the Himalayan snows through books and cold print. As I write this my vision is limited by high walls that seem to close in upon me and envelop me and the heat of the plains oppresses me. But Kalhana has enabled me to overstep these walls and forget the summer heat, and to visit that land of the Sun God "where realizing that the land created by his father is unable to bear the heat, the hot-rayed sun honours it by bearing himself with softness in summer," where dawn first appears with a golden radiance on the eternal snows and, in the evening, "the daylight renders homage to the peaks of the towering mountains," where in the valley below, the lazy sleepy Vitastha[8] winds slowly through smiling fields and richly-laden fruit trees, and creeps under the lordly chenars, and passes through still lakes covered with lotus blooms, and then wakes up and rushes down the gorges to the plains of the Punjab below. Man has sunk low there in his poverty but nature remains cruel and unfeeling, yet soft and smiling to the eye and the senses. "The joy of plunging into the Ganga is not known to those who reside in the sandy deserts," writes Kalhana; how can the dwellers in the plains know of the joys of the mountains, and especially of this jewel of Asia, situated in the heart of that mighty continent?

The translator has used, as he should, the scholar's method of transcription for Sanskrit names and words. He must forgive me if, being a layman, I do not fancy this, and so, with all apologies to the International Congress of Orientalists, I propose to continue to write Sanskrit and Krishna and not Samskrta or Krsna. I do not like an old friend to develop an alien look, and what seem to be

[8] The Jhelum.

five consonants all in a bunch are decidedly foreign and strange-looking to me.

It is not for me to congratulate the translator, who is both my brother-in-law and a dear comrade, but I should like to commend especially his valuable notes and appendices.

~

The Epics: History, Tradition and Myth

(From The Discovery of India*)*

The two great epics of ancient India—the Ramayana and the Mahabharata—probably took shape in the course of several hundred years, and even subsequently additions were made to them. They deal with the early days of the Indo-Aryans, their conquests and civil wars, when they were expanding and consolidating themselves, but they were composed and compiled later. I do not know of any books anywhere which have exercised such a continuous and pervasive influence on the mass mind as these two. Dating back to a remote antiquity, they are still a living force in the life of the Indian people. Not in the original Sanskrit, except for a few intellectuals, but in translations and adaptations, and in those innumerable ways in which tradition and legend spread and become a part of the texture of a people's life. They represent the typical Indian method of catering all together for various degrees of cultural development, from the highest intellectual to the simple unread and untaught villager. They make us understand somewhat the secret of the old Indians in holding together a variegated society divided up in many ways and graded in castes, in harmonizing their discords, and giving them a common background of heroic tradition and ethical living. Deliberately they tried to build up a unity of outlook among the people, which was to survive and overshadow all diversity.

Among the earliest memories of my childhood are the stories from these epics told to me by my mother or the older ladies of the house, just as a child in Europe or America might listen to fairy tales or stories of adventure. There was for me both adventure and the fairy element in them. And then I used to be taken every year to the popular open air performances where the Ramayana story was enacted and vast crowds came to see it and join in the processions. It was all very crude, but that did not matter, for everyone knew the story by heart and it was carnival time.

In this way Indian mythology and old tradition crept into my mind and got mixed up with all manner of other creatures of the imagination. I do not think I ever attached very much importance to these stories as factually true, and I even criticized the magical and supernatural element in them. But they were just as imaginatively true for me as were the stories from the Arabian Nights or the *Panchatantra*, that storehouse of animal tales from which Western Asia and Europe have drawn so much.[9] As I grew up other pictures crowded into my mind: fairy stories, both Indian and European, tales from Greek mythology, the story of Joan of Arc, Alice in Wonderland, and many stories of Akbar and Birbal, Sherlock Holmes, King Arthur and his Knights, the Rani of Jhansi, the young heroine of the Indian Mutiny, and tales of Rajput chivalry and heroism. These and many others filled my mind in strange confusion, but always there was the background of Indian mythology which I had imbibed in my earliest years.

---

[9] The story of the innumerable translations and adaptations of the *Panchatantra* into Asiatic and European languages is a long, intricate, and fascinating one. The first known translation was from Sanskrit into Pahlavi in the middle of the sixth century A.C. at the instance of Khusrau Anushirwan, Emperor of Persia. Soon after (c. 570 A.C.) a Syrian translation appeared, and later on an Arabic one. In the eleventh century new translations appeared in Syrian, Arabic, and Persian, the last named becoming famous as the story of 'Kalia Daman.' It was through these translations that the *Panchatantra* readied Europe. There was a Greek translation from the Syrian at the end of the eleventh century, and a little later a Hebrew translation. In the fifteenth and sixteenth centuries a number of translations and adaptations appeared in Latin, Italian, Spanish, German, Swedish, Danish, Dutch Icelandic, French, English, Hungarian, Turkish, and a number of Slav languages. Thus the stories of the *Panchatantra* merged into Asiatic and European literatures.

If it was so with me, in spite of the diverse influences that worked on my mind, I realized how much more must old mythology and tradition work on the minds of others and, especially, the unread masses of our people. That influence is a good influence both culturally and ethically, and I would hate to destroy or throw away all the beauty and imaginative symbolism that these stories and allegories contain.

Indian mythology is not confined to the epics; it goes back to the Vedic period and appears in many forms and garbs in Sanskrit literature. The poets and the dramatists take full advantage of it and build their stories and lovely fancies round it. The Ashoka tree is said to burst into flower when touched by the foot of a beautiful woman. We read of the adventures of Kama, the god of love, and his wife, Rati (or rapture), with their friend Vasanta, the god of spring. Greatly daring, Kama shoots his flowery arrow at Shiva himself and is reduced to ashes by the fire that flashed out of Shiva's third eye. But he survives as Ananga, the bodiless one.

Most of the myths and stories are heroic in conception and teach adherence to truth and the pledged word, whatever the consequences, faithfulness unto death and even beyond, courage, good works and sacrifice for the common good. Sometimes the story is pure myth, or else it is a mixture of fact and myth, an exaggerated account of some incident that tradition preserved. Facts and fiction are so interwoven together as to be inseparable, and this amalgam becomes an imagined history, which may not tell us exactly what happened but does tell us something that is equally important—what people believed had taken place, what they thought their heroic ancestors were capable of, and what ideals inspired them. So, whether fact or fiction, it became a living element in their lives, ever pulling them up from the drudgery and ugliness of their everyday existence to higher realms, ever pointing towards the path of endeavour and right living, even though the ideal might be far off and difficult to reach.

Goethe is reported to have condemned those who said that the old Roman stories of heroism, of Lucretia and others, were spurious and false. Anything, he said, that was essentially false and spurious could only be absurd and unfruitful and never beautiful and inspiring, and that 'if the Romans were great enough to invent things like that, we at least should be great enough to believe them.'

Thus this imagined history, mixture of fact and fiction, or sometimes only fiction, becomes symbolically true and tells us of the minds and hearts and purposes of the people of that particular epoch. It is true also in the sense that it becomes the basis for thought and action, for future history. The whole conception of history in ancient India was influenced by the speculative and ethical trends of philosophy and religion. Little importance was attached to the writing of a chronicle or the compilation of a bare record of events. What those people were more concerned with was the effect and influence of human events and actions on human conduct. Like the Greeks, they were strongly imaginative and artistic and they gave rein to this artistry and imagination in dealing with past events, intent as they were on drawing some moral and lesson from them for future behaviour. Unlike the Greeks, and unlike the Chinese and the Arabs, Indians in the past were not historians. This was very unfortunate and it has made it difficult for us now to fix dates or make up an accurate chronology. Events run into each other, overlap and produce an enormous confusion. Only very gradually are patient scholars today discovering the clues to the maze of Indian history. There is really only one old book, Kalhana's *Rajatarangini*, a history of Kashmir written in the twelfth century B.C., which may be considered as history. For the rest we have to go to the imagined history of the epics and other books, to some contemporary records, to inscriptions, to artistic and architectural remains, to coins, and to the large body of Sanskrit literature, for occasional hints; also, of course, to the many records of foreign travellers who came to India, notably Greeks and Chinese, and, during a later period, Arabs. This lack of historical sense did not affect the masses, for as elsewhere and more so than elsewhere, they built up their view of the past from the traditional accounts and myth and story that were handed to them from generation to generation. This imagined history and mixture of fact and legend became widely known and gave to the people a strong and abiding cultural background. But the ignoring of history had evil consequences which we pursue still. It produced a vagueness of outlook, divorced from life as it is, a credulity, a woolliness of the mind where fact was concerned. That mind was not at all woolly in the far more difficult, but inevitably vaguer and more indefinite, realms of philosophy; it was both analytic and synthetic, often very critical, sometimes sceptical. But where fact was concerned, it was uncritical, because, perhaps, it did not attach much importance to fact as such. The impact of science and the modern world have brought a greater appreciation of facts, a more critical faculty, a weighing of evidence, a refusal to accept tradition merely because it is tradition. Many competent historians are at work now, but they often err on the other side and their work is more a meticulous chronicle of facts than living history. But even today it is strange how we suddenly become overwhelmed by tradition, and the critical faculties of even intelligent men cease to function. This may partly be due to the nationalism that consumes us in our present subject state. Only when we are politically and economically free will the mind function normally and critically.

~

The Mahabharata

(*From* The Discovery of India)

It is difficult to date the epics. They deal with remote periods when the Aryans were still in the process of settling down and consolidating themselves in India. Evidently many authors have written them or added to them in successive periods. The Ramayana is an epic poem with a certain unity of treatment; the Mahabharata is a vast and miscellaneous collection of ancient lore. Both must have taken shape in the pre-Buddhist period, though additions were no doubt made later.

Michelet, the French historian, writing in 1864, with special reference to the Ramayana, says: 'Whoever has done or willed too much let him drink from this deep cup a long draught of life and youth.... Everything is narrow in the west—Greece is small and I stifle; Judea is dry and I pant. Let me look towards lofty Asia and the profound East for a little while. There lies my great poem, as vast as the Indian Ocean, blessed, gilded with the sun, the book of divine harmony wherein is no dissonance. A serene peace reigns there, and in the midst of conflict an infinite sweetness, a boundless fraternity, which spreads over all living things, an ocean (without bottom or bound) of love, of pity, of clemency.'

Great as the Ramayana is as an epic poem, and loved by the people, it is really the *Mahabharata* that is one of the outstanding books of the world. It is a colossal work, an encyclopaedia of tradition and legend, and political and social institutions of ancient India. For a decade or more a host of competent Indian scholars have been engaged in critically examining and collating the various available texts, with a view to publishing an authorized edition. Some parts have been issued by them but the work is still incomplete and is proceeding. It is interesting to note that even in these days of total and horrible war, Russian oriental scholars have produced a Russian translation of the Mahabharata.

Probably this was the period when foreign elements were coming into India and bringing their customs with them. Many of these customs were unlike those of the Aryans, and so a curious mixture of opposing ideas and customs is observable. There was no polyandry among the Aryans, and yet one of the leading heroines of the Mahabharata story is the common wife of five brothers. Gradually the absorption of the earlier indigenous elements as well as of newcomers was taking place, and the Vedic religion was being modified accordingly. It was beginning to take that all-inclusive form which led to modern Hinduism.

This was possible, as the basic approach seems to have been that there could be no monopoly in truth, and there were many ways of seeing it and approaching it. So all kinds of different and even contradictory beliefs were tolerated.

In the *Mahabharata* a very definite attempt has been made to emphasize the fundamental unity of India, or Bharatvarsha as it was called, from Bharat, the legendary founder of the race. An earlier name was Aryavarta, the land of the Aryas, but this was confined to Northern India up to the Vindhya mountains in Central India. The Aryans had probably not spread beyond that mountain range at that period. The Ramayana story is one of Aryan expansion to the south. The great civil war, which occurred later, described in the Mahabharata, is vaguely supposed to have taken place about the fourteenth century B.C. That war was for the overlordship of India (or possibly of northern India), and it marks the beginning of the conception of India as a whole, of Bharatvarsha. In this conception a large part of modern Afghanistan, then called Gandhara (from which the name of the present city of Kandahar), which was considered an integral part of the country was included. Indeed the queen of the principal ruler was named Gandhari, the lady from Gandhara. Dilli or Delhi, not the modern city but ancient cities situated near the modern site, named Hastinapur and Indraprastha, becomes the metropolis of India.

Sister Nivedita (Margaret Noble), writing about the *Mahabharata,* has pointed out: 'The foreign reader…is at once struck by two features: in the first place its unity in complexity; and, in the second, its constant efforts to impress on its hearers the idea of a single centralized India, with a heroic tradition of her own as formative and uniting impulse.'[10]

The *Mahabharata* contains the Krishna legends and the famous poem, the *Bhagavad Gita.* Even apart from the philosophy of the Gita, it lays stress on ethical and moral principles in statecraft and in life generally. Without this foundation of dharma there is no true happiness and society cannot hold together. The aim is social welfare, not the welfare of a particular group only but of the

---

[10] I have taken this quotation from Sir S. Radhakrishnan's *Indian Philosophy*. I am indebted to Radhakrishnan for other quotations and much else in this and other chapters.

whole world, for 'the entire world of mortals is a self-dependent organism.' Yet dharma itself is relative and depends on the times and the conditions prevailing, apart from some basic principles, such as adherence to truth, nonviolence, etc. These principles endure and do not change, but otherwise dharma, that amalgam of duties and responsibilities, changes with the changing age. The emphasis on nonviolence, here and elsewhere, is interesting, for no obvious contradiction appears to be noticed between this and fighting for a righteous cause. The whole epic centres round a great war. Evidently the conception of ahimsa, nonviolence, had a great deal to do with the motive, the absence of the violent mental approach, self-discipline and control of anger and hatred, rather than the physical abstention from violent action, when this became necessary and inevitable.

The *Mahabharata* is a rich storehouse in which we can discover all manner of precious things. It is full of a varied, abundant and bubbling life, something far removed from that other aspect of Indian thought which emphasized asceticism and negation. It is not merely a book of moral precepts though there is plenty of ethics and morality in it. The teaching of the *Mahabharata* has been summed up in the phrase: 'Thou shalt not do to others what is disagreeable to thyself.' There is an emphasis on social welfare and this is noteworthy, for the tendency of the Indian mind is supposed to be in favour of individual perfection rather than social welfare. It says: 'Whatever is not conducive to social welfare, or what ye are likely to be ashamed of, never do.' Again: 'Truth, self-control, asceticism, generosity, non-violence, constancy in virtue—these are the means of success, not caste or family.' 'Virtue is better than immortality and life.' 'True joy entails suffering.' There is a dig at the seeker after wealth: 'The silkworm dies of its wealth.' And, finally, the injunction so typical of a living and advancing people; 'Discontent is the spur of progress.'

There is in the *Mahabharata* the polytheism of the Vedas, the monism of the Upanishads, and deisms, and dualisms, and monotheism. The outlook is still creative and more or less rationalistic, and the feeling of exclusiveness is yet limited. Caste is not rigid. There was still a feeling of confidence, but as external forces invaded and challenged the security of the old order, that confidence lessened somewhat and a demand for greater uniformity arose in order to produce internal unity and strength. New taboos grew up. The eating of beef, previously countenanced, is later absolutely prohibited. In the *Mahabharata* there are references to beef or veal being offered to honoured guests.

~

Literature in Hindi and in Other Languages[11]

Once, at an informal discussion, I had said that in the last forty or fifty years, among our provincial languages, Bengali, Marathi and Gujarati had progressed more than Hindi. This statement upset some Hindi writers and they were annoyed with me. I had absolutely no intention of saying anything against the richness of Hindi, but perhaps my meaning was not clear and it might have been misunderstood by some. Later I learnt that many who knew more than I did, held the same opinion. So I am being bold enough to write about this.

I was not thinking of ancient Hindi literature. I am also aware that there has been an awakening and progress in modern Hindi literature. What I meant was that among our provincial languages this awakening first took place in Bengali, then in Marathi and Gujarati and only later in Hindi. Because of this, initially Bengali, Marathi and Gujarati progressed a little ahead. Why is this awakening in all languages taking place? There are various reasons, but the primary one is the influx of new ideas. The literature, culture and political condition of any country are closely knit. It was perhaps the English poet Milton who had

[11] Almora District Jail, 29 July, 1935. J.N. Papers, N.M.M.L. Original in Hindi.

written somewhere that if shown the language of any country, without knowing anything else about it, he could tell the type of country it was, free or subject, civilized or uncivilized, strong or weak, brave or timid.

With the decline of our country, our literatures also deteriorated and remained in this condition for a long time. But they began to make progress with the rise of national consciousness. This started first in Bengal. New ideas poured in mostly from Europe and they infused a new life. Our political associations conducted all their work in English. Besides this, their influence filtered into the provincial languages—first Bengali, then Marathi and Gujarati, followed by Hindi. Hindi lagged behind, not because of its ancient literature but because of the late development of political consciousness in Hindi speaking areas. Besides, as there was no proper communication between the languages, we could not take early advantage of the awakening in other regions.

We should benefit by this experience and establish some relationship among all the languages of the country. Men of letters should form an association and meet occasionally. Then, instead of fostering competition and rivalry, there will be harmony among them and they can help in each other's progress. Ideas will spread fast throughout the country and there will be a growing sense of unity. I have learnt that some attempt is being made to initiate this, but I do not know much about it.

I cherish the hope that such an Indian literary association will include all the languages of India. Hindi and Urdu are not just sister languages, but are two facets of the same body. They have to be merged. Bengali, Marathi and Gujarati are younger sisters of Hindi. The languages of the south are the oldest in our country. Apart from these, other sundry languages should be included in the association. I would even recommend that English be granted a place. It is not one of our languages but it is of considerable importance in the life of our country. It has become a kind of foster language.

There can be considerable disagreement in such an association, especially on the question of script. Some day we will have to resolve such issues but at the moment it cannot be done, and any effort to do so will result in a lot of heart-burning. On the question of script, the first major step in my opinion would be to decide on a common script for Hindi, Marathi and Gujarati. It can only be achieved by mutual understanding and cooperation. There is hardly any scope for the least bit of coercion.

I am absolutely certain that Hindi or Hindustani should be our national language and it will be so, even though there are two scripts. I also know this—that the major languages of our provinces will make considerable progress and that we should promote them. There is no clash between their advancement and that of adopting Hindi as the national language. Those who in their fervour try to create a conflict will harm both.

Our litterateurs should also maintain contact with the literature of the world and participate in international literary organizations. Without this we cannot rank among the progressive nations of the world. We have to admit that in this modern age, there is an influx of new ideas from America and Europe. Without an understanding of them we cannot confront the present-day world. The primary thing this modern age teaches us is that the world is one and cannot be fragmented and those who wish to remain separate will lag behind.

A number of us should learn foreign languages. They will be the windows through which we can look at the world and through which sunlight and fresh air will come in. Many of us know English and we should take advantage of this as this language is constantly expanding. It is mainly because of the United States—the wealthiest and the most powerful nation at present. But a mere knowledge of English is not enough, and this has resulted in our being often deceived. We have begun to see the world through English eyes, not realising that they are biased. Despite our political struggle against the British rule, we remain slaves of British thought. It is only their books that we read, their newspapers and the news communicated by them that we obtain. This does have a strong effect on us. If we read French, German and Russian books or newspapers we would realise that there is more to the world besides the English and we would not give disproportionate importance to them. It is therefore imperative that some of our boys and girls learn foreign languages other than English, specially French, German, Russian and Spanish (which is spoken all over South America). It would also be worthwhile for some of our people to learn Japanese and Chinese. There are still quite a few people knowing Persian in our country.

In Europe it is presumed that an educated person knows at least two or three languages; and this is often the case. It will be a little more difficult for us, and not many can learn foreign languages. It would therefore be better if well-known books in foreign languages are translated into Hindi. This seems all the more necessary, if we desire to understand the current trend of thoughts in the world. Such books are very few at present and even those are not well translated. Our translators—especially those employed in newspapers—make literal translations, rarely concerning themselves with the inner meaning of words and phrases. Those who love words know that every word has life, a soul and a history and this makes it difficult to explain, let alone translate. Our university students bravely go on translating in a hurried manner, unthinkingly—words are just plucked out of the dictionary and thrust in. This turns the throbbing, pulsating and lively word into a lifeless corpse and that which had sense becomes meaningless. This massacre of the innocent causes sorrow.

~

Time in Prison: The Urge to Action

(From *The Discovery of India*)

...The real problems for me remain problems of individual and social life, of harmonious living, of a proper balancing of an individual's inner and outer life, of an adjustment of the relations between individuals and between groups, of a continuous becoming something better and higher of social development, of the ceaseless adventure of man. In the solution of these problems the way of observation and precise knowledge and deliberate reasoning, according to the method of science, must be followed. This method may not always be applicable in our quest of truth, for art and poetry and certain psychic experiences seem to belong to a different order of things and to elude the objective methods of science. Let us, therefore, not rule out intuition and other methods of sensing truth and reality. They are necessary even for the purposes of science. But always we must hold to our anchor of precise objective knowledge tested by reason, and even more so by experiment and practice, and always we must beware of losing ourselves in a sea of speculation unconnected with the day-to-day problems of life and the needs of men and women. A living philosophy must answer the problems of today.

> **It may be that we of this modern age, who so pride ourselves on the achievements of our times, are prisoners of our age, just as the ancients and the men and women of medieval times were prisoners of their respective ages. We may delude ourselves, as others have done before us, that our way of looking at things is the only right way, leading to truth. We cannot escape from that prison or get rid entirely of that illusion, if illusion it is.**

Yet I am convinced that the methods and approach of science have revolutionized human life more than anything else in the long course of history, and have opened doors and avenues of further and even more radical change, leading up to the very portals of what has long been considered the unknown. The technical achievements of science are obvious enough: its capacity to transform an economy of scarcity into one of abundance is evident, its invasion of many problems which have so far been the monopoly of philosophy is becoming more pronounced.

Space-time and the quantum theory utterly changed the picture of the physical world. More recent researches into the nature of matter, the structure of the atom, the transmutation of the elements, and the transformation of electricity and light, either into the other, have carried human knowledge much further. Man no longer sees nature as something apart and distinct from himself. Human destiny appears to become a part of nature's rhythmic energy.

All this upheaval of thought, due to the advance of science, has led scientists into a new region, verging on the metaphysical. They draw different and often contradictory conclusions. Some see in it a new unity, the antithesis of chance. Others, like Bertrand Russell, say, 'Academic philosophers ever since the time of Parmenides have believed the world is unity. The most fundamental of my beliefs is that this is rubbish.' Or again, 'Man is the product of causes which had no prevision of the end they were achieving; his origin, his growth, his hopes and fears, his loves and beliefs are but the outcome of accidental collocations of atoms.' And yet the latest developments in physics have gone a long way to demonstrate a fundamental unity in nature. 'The belief that all things are made of a single substance is as old as thought itself; but ours is the generation which, first of all in history, is able to receive the unity of nature, not as a baseless dogma or a hopeless aspiration, but a principle of science based on proof as sharp and clear as anything which is known.'[12]

Old as this belief is in Asia and Europe, it is interesting to compare some of the latest conclusions of science with the fundamental ideas underlying the Advaita Vedantic theory. These ideas were that the universe is made of one substance whose form is perpetually changing, and further that the sum-total of energies remains always the same. Also that 'the explanations of things are to be found within their own nature, and that no external beings or existences are required to explain what is going on in the universe,' with its corollary of a self-evolving universe.

It does not very much matter to science what these vague

[12] Karl K. Darrow. *The Renaissance of Physics* (New York, 1936), 301.

speculations lead to, for meanwhile it forges ahead in a hundred directions, in its own precise experimental way of observation, widening the bounds of the charted region of knowledge, and changing human life in the process. Science may be on the verge of discovering vital mysteries, which yet may elude it. Still it will go on along its appointed path, for there is no end to its journeying. Ignoring for the moment the 'why?' of philosophy, science will go on asking 'how?', and as it finds this out it gives greater content and meaning to life, and perhaps takes us some way to answering the 'why?'.

Or, perhaps, we cannot cross that barrier, and the mysterious will continue to remain the mysterious, and life with all its changes will still remain a bundle of good and evil, a succession of conflicts, a curious combination of incompatible and mutually hostile urges.

Or again, perhaps, the very progress of science, unconnected with and isolated from moral discipline and ethical considerations, will lead to the concentration of power and the terrible instruments of destruction which it has made, in the hands of evil and selfish men, seeking the domination of others—and thus to the destruction of its own great achievements. Something of this kind we see happening now, and behind this war there lies this internal conflict of the spirit of man.

How amazing is this spirit of man! In spite of innumerable failings, man, throughout the ages, has sacrificed his life and all he held dear for an ideal, for truth, for faith, for country and honour. That ideal may change, but that capacity for self-sacrifice continues, and, because of that, much may be forgiven to man, and it is impossible to lose hope for him. In the midst of disaster, he has not lost his dignity or his faith in the values he cherished. Plaything of nature's mighty forces, less than a speck of dust in this vast universe, he has hurled defiance at the elemental powers, and with his mind, cradle of revolution, sought to master them. Whatever gods there be, there is something godlike in man, as there is also something of the devil in him.

The future is dark, uncertain. But we can see part of the way leading to it and can tread it with firm steps, remembering that nothing that can happen is likely to overcome the spirit of man which has survived so many perils; remembering also that life, for all its ills, has joy and beauty, and that we can always wander, if we know how to, in the enchanted woods of nature.

'What else is wisdom? What of man's endeavour
Or God's high grace, so lovely and so great?
To stand from fear set free, to breathe and wait;
To hold a hand uplifted over Hate;
And shall not Loveliness be loved for ever?[13]

~

Supporting Writers and Poets

(From D.S. Rao's Five Decades: A Short History of Sahitya Akademi*)*

My dear Krishna,

I wonder if you know the case of Nirala, a Hindi poet of Allahabad. He has done good work, in the past and even now sometimes writes well in his lucid moments. Often he is not lucid at all. His old books are popular and some, I believe, are text-books. But, in his folly or extremity, he has sold all those books for a song to various publishers getting just 25 or 30 or 50 rupees for a book. The whole copyright was supposed to be sold. Publishers have made large sums of money and continue to make it and he gets nothing for it and practically starves. This is a scandalous case of a publisher exploiting a writer shamelessly. Personally I think that, even in strict law, this kind of arrangement might be capable of being challenged.

Anyhow, this leads me to say that our Akadamy should immediately think about an amendment of the copyright law. Some attempts were made, I remember, by me a year or two ago and I wrote to our Law Ministry, but nothing much came of it. I think you might collect material for this and prepare a note.

---

[13] Chorus from The Bacchae of Euripides. Gilbert Murray's translation.

Meanwhile, Nirala deserves some financial help. It is no good giving the help to him directly because he gives it away to others immediately. In fact, he gives away his clothes, his last shirt and everything. Mahadevi Verma and some others in Allahabad of a Literary Association there try to look after him and give him some money too. I think we should arrange to pay Rs.100/- a month for him and this money should be sent to Mahadevi Verma.

This might well be out of the fund which the Education Ministry has for such purposes. Will you please mention this case to Maulana Saheb and, if he agrees, his Ministry can process it.

You can get more particulars about Nirala from Mahadevi Verma.

Yours sincerely,
Jawaharlal Nehru

Shri Krishna Kripalini
Secretary, Sahitya Akadami
55/1 Ferozeshah Road
New Delhi

~

The Spirit of Science

(Speech at the opening ceremony of the Fuel Research Institute, Digwadih, 22 April, 1950)

In the course of less than four months, we have put up, declared open or are going to declare open three national laboratories. I suppose before this year is out some more national laboratories will also be started. This is a great venture testifying to the faith which our scientists and, I hope, our Government have in science. I suppose the putting up of fine and attractive buildings does some service to science; nevertheless, buildings do not make science as Dr Raman has often reminded us. It is human beings who make science, not bricks and mortar. Properly equipped buildings, however, help the human being to work efficiently. It is, therefore, desirable to have these fine laboratories for trained persons to work in and for persons to be trained for future work.

You, Sir, referred to the spirit of science. I wonder what exactly that spirit is and to what extent we agree or differ in our ideas of it. Is science, as is often supposed, a handmaiden to industry? It certainly wants to help industry, though not merely for the sake of helping industry but also because it wants to create work for the nation, so that people may have better living conditions and greater opportunities for growth. That I suppose will be agreed to but there is something more to it. What ultimately does science represent?

You, Sir, just referred to scientists declaring war on nature. May I put it in a different way? We seek the cooperation of nature, we seek to uncover the secrets of nature, to understand them and to utilize them for the benefit of humanity. The active principle of science is discovery. Now, what is, if I may ask, the active principle of a social framework or society? Usually, it stands for conservatism, remaining where we are, not changing and carrying on, though, of course, with some improvement and further additions. Nevertheless, it is a principle of continuity rather than of change. So, we come up against a certain inherent conflict in society between the coexisting principles of continuity and of conservatism and the scientific principle of discovery which brings about change and challenges that continuity. So the scientific worker, although he is praised and patted on the back, is, nevertheless, not wholly approved of, because he conies and upsets the status quo of things. Normally speaking, science seldom really has the facilities that it deserves except when some misfortune comes to a country in the shape of war. Then everything has to be set aside and science has its way, even though it is for an evil purpose.

It is interesting to see this conflict between the normal conservatism of a static society and the normal revolutionary tendency of the scientist's discovery which often changes the basis of that society. It changes living conditions and the conditions that govern human life and human survival.

I take it that most people who talk glibly of science, including our great industrialists, think of science merely as a kind of handmaiden to make their work easier. And so it is. Of course, it does make their work easier. It adds to the wealth of the nation and betters conditions. All this science does do. But surely science is something more than that. The history of science shows that it does not simply better the old. It sometimes upsets the old. It does not merely add new truths to the old ones but sometimes the new truth it discovers disintegrates *some* part of the old truths and thereby upsets the way of men's thinking and the way of their lives. Science, therefore, does not merely repeat the old in better ways or add to the old but creates something that is new to the world and to human consciousness.

If we pursue this line of thought, what exactly does the spirit of science mean? It means many things. It means not only accepting the fresh truth that science may bring, not only improving the old but being prepared to upset the old if it goes against that spirit. It also means not being tied down to something that is old because it is old, because we have carried on with it but being able to accept its disintegration; it means not being tied down to a social fabric or an industrial fabric or an economic fabric if it goes against the new discovery.

Whatever they may say, most countries normally do not like to change. The human being is essentially a conservative animal. He is used to certain ways of life and anyone trying to change them meets with his disapproval. Nevertheless, change comes and people have to adapt themselves to it; they have done so in the past. All countries, as I said, are normally conservative. But I imagine that our country is more than normally conservative. It is for this reason that I venture to place these thoughts before you. I find a curious hiatus in people's thinking. I find it even in the thinking of scientists who praise science and practise it in the laboratory but discard the ways of science, its method of approach and the spirit of science in everything else they do in life. They become completely unscientific. If we approach science in the proper way, it does some good and there is no doubt that it will always do some good. It teaches us new ways of doing things. Perhaps, it improves our conditions of industrial life but the basic thing that science should do is to teach us to think straight, to act straight and not to be afraid of discarding anything or of accepting anything, provided there are sufficient reasons for doing so. I should like our country to understand and appreciate that idea all the more, because in the realm of thought our country in the past has, in a sense, been singularly free and it has not hesitated to look down the deep well of truth whatever it might contain. Nevertheless, in spite of such a free mind, our country encumbered itself to such an extent in matters of social practice that its growth was hindered and is hindered in a hundred ways even today. Our customs are just ways of looking at little things that govern our lives and have no significant meaning. Even then, these customs come in our way. Now that we have attained independence, there is naturally a resurgence of all kinds of new forces, both good and bad: good forces are, of course, liberated by a sense of freedom but along with them there are also a number of forces which, under the guise of what people call culture, narrow our minds and our outlook. These forces are essentially a restriction and denial of any real kind of culture. Culture is the widening of the mind and of the spirit. It is never a narrowing of the mind or a restriction of the human spirit or of the country's spirit. Therefore, if we look at science in the real way and if we think of these research institutes and laboratories in a fundamental sense, then they are something more than just little ways of improving things and of finding out how this or that should be done. Of course, we have to do that, too. But these institutes must gradually affect our minds, not only the minds of the young men and young women who would work here but also the mind of others, more specially the minds of the rising generation, so that the nation may imbibe the spirit of science and be prepared to accept the new truth, even though it has to discard something of the old. Only then will this approach to science bear true fruit. It is because we attach importance to these research institutes that we have ventured to ask you, Sir, Mr President, to take the trouble to come all the way here to open this third of our great national laboratories and we are very grateful to you that you have taken the trouble to do so. I am sure that your visit here and the visits of the many distinguished scientists will prove a blessing to this institute. Besides, it will help to draw people's attention not only to the external applications and implications of science but to its real value which lies in widening the spirit of man and thereby bettering humanity at large.

BOOK II

ON NEHRU

EDITOR'S NOTE

This section comprises memories and assessments of Nehru by his contemporaries, or near contemporaries. The intention here is not to present academic or critical analyses of the man and his achievements or otherwise—that is a task for a different book, different people. The effort here, a necessary one at this time, is to remind ourselves why Nehru matters—indeed, why he *should* matter—and why he was and is regarded as a remarkable mind and leader, even by those who cannot, by any stretch of the imagination, be called his followers or admirers.

Nehru on Nehru

From *An Autobiography*

... It was true that I had achieved, almost accidentally as it were, an unusual degree of popularity with the masses; I was appreciated by the intelligentsia; and to young men and women I was a bit of a hero, and a halo of romance seemed to surround me in their eyes. Songs had been written about me, and the most impossible and ridiculous legends had grown up. Even my opponents had often put in a good word for me and patronisingly admitted that I was not lacking in competence or in good faith.

Only a saint, perhaps, or an inhuman monster could survive all this, unscathed and unaffected, and I can place myself in neither of these categories. It went to my head, intoxicated me a little, and gave me confidence and strength. I became (I imagine so, for it is a difficult task to look at oneself from outside) just a little bit autocratic in my ways, just a shade dictatorial. And yet I do not think that my conceit increased markedly. I had a fair measure of my abilities, I thought, and I was by no means humble about them. But I knew well enough that there was nothing at all remarkable about them, and I was very conscious of my failings. A habit of introspection probably helped me to retain my balance and view many happenings connected with myself in a detached manner. Experience of public life showed me that popularity was often the handmaiden of undesirable persons; it was certainly not an invariable sign of virtue or intelligence. Was I popular then because of my failings or my accomplishments? Why indeed was I popular?

Not because of intellectual attainments, for they were not

extraordinary, and, in any event, they do not make for popularity. Not because of so-called sacrifices, for it is patent that hundreds and thousands in our own day in India have suffered infinitely more, even to the point of the last sacrifice. My reputation as a hero is entirely a bogus one, and I do not feel at all heroic, and generally the heroic attitude or the dramatic pose in life strikes me as silly. As for romance, I should say that I am the least romantic of individuals. It is true that I have some physical and mental courage, but the background of that is probably pride: personal, group, and national, and a reluctance to be coerced into anything.

I had no satisfactory answer to my question. Then I proceeded along a different line of inquiry. I found that one of the most persistent legends about my father and myself was to the effect that we used to send our linen weekly from India to a Paris laundry. We have repeatedly contradicted this, but the legend persists. Anything more fantastic and absurd it is difficult for me to imagine, and if anyone is foolish enough to indulge in this wasteful snobbery, I should have thought he would get a special mention for being a prize fool.

Another equally persistent legend, often repeated in spite of denial, is that I was at school with the Prince of Wales. The story goes on to say that when the Prince came to India in 1921 he asked for me; I was then in gaol. As a matter of fact, I was not only not at school with him, but I have never had the advantage of meeting him or speaking to him.

I do not mean to imply that my reputation or popularity, such as they are, depend on these or similar legends. They may have a more secure foundation, but there is no doubt that the super structure has a thick covering of snobbery, as is evidenced by these stories. At any rate, there is the idea of mixing in high society and living a life of luxury and then renouncing it all, and renunciation has always appealed to the Indian mind. As a basis for a reputation this does not at all appeal to me. I prefer the active virtues to the passive ones, and renunciation and sacrifice for their own sakes have little appeal for me. I do value them from another point of view, that of mental and spiritual training just as a simple and regular life is necessary for the athlete to keep in good physical condition. And the capacity for endurance and perseverance in spite of hard knocks is essential for those who wish to dabble in great undertakings. But I have no liking or attraction for the ascetic view of life, the negation of life, the terrified abstention from its joys and sensations. I have not consciously renounced anything that I really valued; but then values change.

The question that my friend had asked me still remained unanswered: did I not feel proud of this hero worship of the crowd? I disliked it and wanted to run away from it, and yet I had got used to it, and when it was wholly absent, I rather missed it. Neither way brought satisfaction, but, on the whole, the crowd had filled some inner need of mine. The notion that I could influence them and move them to action gave me a sense of authority over their minds and hearts; and this satisfied, to some extent, my will to power. On their part, they exercised a subtle tyranny over me, for their confidence and affection moved inner depths within me and evoked emotional responses. Individualist as I was, sometimes the barriers of individuality seemed to melt away, and I felt that it would be better to be accursed with these unhappy people than to be saved alone. But the barriers were too solid to disappear, and I peeped over them with wondering eyes at this phenomenon which I failed to understand.

Conceit, like fat on the human body, grows imperceptibly, layer upon layer, and the person whom it affects is unconscious of the daily accretion. Fortunately the hard knocks of a mad world tone it down or even squash it completely, and there has been no lack of these hard knocks for us in India during recent years. The school of life has been a difficult one for us, and suffering is a hard taskmaster.

I have been fortunate in another respect also- the possession of family members and friends and comrades, who have helped me to retain a proper perspective and not to lose my mental equilibrium. Public functions, addresses by municipalities and local boards and other public bodies, processions and the like, used to be a great strain on my nerves and my sense of humour and reality. The most extravagant and pompous language would be used, and everybody would look so solemn and pious that I felt an almost uncontrollable desire to laugh, or to stick out my tongue, or stand on my head, just for the pleasure of shocking and watching the reactions on the faces at that august assembly! Fortunately for my reputation and for the sober respectability of public life in India, I have suppressed this mad desire and usually behaved with due propriety. But not always. Sometimes there has been an exhibition on my part in a crowded meeting, or more often in processions, which I find extraordinarily trying. I have suddenly left a procession, arranged in our honour, and disappeared in the crowd, leaving my wife or some other person to carry on, perched up in a car or carriage, with that procession.

This continuous effort to suppress one's feelings and behave in public is a bit of a strain, and the usual result is that one puts on a glum and solid look on public occasions. Perhaps because of this I was once described in an article in a Hindu magazine as resembling a Hindu widow! I must say that, much as I admire Hindu widows of the old type, this gave me a shock. The author evidently meant to praise me for some qualities as he thought I possessed a spirit of gentle resignation and renunciation and a smileless devotion to work. I had hoped that I possessed and, indeed, I wish that Hindu widows would possess more active and aggressive qualities and the capacity for humour and laughter. Gandhiji once told an interviewer that if he had not had the gift of humour he might have committed suicide, or something to this effect. I would not presume to go so far, but life certainly would have been almost intolerable for me but for the humour and light touches that some people gave to it.

My very popularity and the brave addresses that came my way, full (as is, indeed, the custom of all such addresses in India) of choice and flowery language and extravagant conceits, became subjects for raillery in the circle of my family and intimate friends. The high-sounding and pompous words and titles that were often used for all those prominent in the national movement, were picked out by my wife and sisters and others and bandied about irreverently. I was addressed as Bharat Bhushan 'Jewel of India' Tyagamurti 'O Embodiment of Sacrifice'; and this lighthearted treatment soothed me, and the tension of those solemn public gatherings, where I had to remain on my best behaviour, gradually relaxed. Even my little daughter joined in the game. Only my mother insisted on taking me seriously, and she never wholly approved of any sarcasm or raillery at the expense of her darling boy. Father was amused; he had a way of quietly expressing his deep understanding and sympathy.

But all these shouting crowds, and dull and wearying public functions, and interminable arguments, and the dust and tumble of politics touched me on the surface only, though sometimes the touch was sharp and pointed. My real conflict lay within me, a conflict of ideas, desires and loyalties, of subconscious depths struggling with outer circumstances, of an inner hunger unsatisfied. I became a battleground, where various forces struggled for mastery. I sought an escape from this; I tried to find harmony and equilibrium, and in this attempt I rushed into action. That gave me some peace; outer conflict relieved the strain of the inner struggle.

Why am I writing all this sitting here in prison? The quest is still the same, in prison or outside, and I write down my past feelings and experiences in the hope that this may bring me some peace and psychic satisfaction.

~

...Indeed, I often wonder if I represent any one at all, and I am inclined to think that I do not, though many have kindly and friendly feelings towards me. I have become a queer mixture of the East and West, out of place everywhere, at home nowhere. Perhaps my thoughts and approach to life are more akin to what is called Western than Eastern, but India clings to me, as she does to all her children, in innumerable ways; and behind me lie, somewhere in the subconscious, racial memories of a hundred, or whatever the number may be, generations of Brahmans. I cannot get rid of either that past inheritance or my recent acquisitions.

They are both part of me, and, though they help me in both the East and the West, they also create in me a feeling of spiritual loneliness not only in public activities but in life itself. I am a stranger and alien in the West. I cannot be of it. But in my own country also, sometimes, I have an exile's feeling.

The distant mountains seem easy of access and climbing, the top beckons, but, as one approaches, difficulties appear, and the higher one goes the more laborious becomes the journey and the summit recedes into the clouds. Yet the climbing is worth the effort and has its own joy and satisfaction. Perhaps it is the struggle that gives value to life, not so much the ultimate result. Often it is difficult to know which is the right path; it is easier sometimes to know what is not right, and to avoid that is something after all. If I may quote, with all humility, the last words of the great Socrates: "I know not what death is—it may be a good thing, and I am not afraid of it. But I do know that it is a bad thing to desert one's past, and I prefer what may be good to what I know to be bad."

~

We Want No Caesars

(Nehru writing as 'Chanakya' on Nehru)

Rashtrapati Jawaharlal ki Jai. The Rashtrapati looked up as he passed swiftly through the waiting crowds, his hands went up and were joined together in salute, and his pale hard face was lit up by a smile. It was a warm personal smile and the people who saw it responded to it immediately and smiled and cheered in return.

The smile passed away and again the face became stern and sad, impassive in the midst of the emotion that it had roused in the multitude. Almost it seemed that the smile and the gesture accompanying it had little reality behind them; they were just tricks of the trade to gain the goodwill of the crowds whose darling he had become. Was it so?

Watch him again. There is a great procession and tens of thousands of persons surround his car and cheer him in an ecstasy of abandonment. He stands on the seat of the car, balancing himself rather well, straight and seemingly tall, like a god, serene and unmoved by the seething multitude. Suddenly there is that smile again, or even a merry laugh, and the tension seems to break and the crowd laughs with him, not knowing what it is laughing at. He is godlike no longer but a human being claiming kinship and comradeship with the thousands who surround him and the crowd feels happy and friendly and takes him to its heart. But the smile is gone and the pale stern face is there again.

Is all this natural or the carefully thought out trickery of the public man? Perhaps it is both and long habit has become second nature now. The most effective pose is one in which there seems to be least of posing, and Jawaharlal has learnt well to act without the paint and powder of the actor. With his seeming carelessness and insouciance, he performs on the public stage with consummate artistry. Whither is this going to lead him and the country? What is he aiming at with all his apparent want of aim? What lies behind that mask of his, what desires, what will to power, what insatiate longings?

These questions would be interesting in any event, for Jawaharlal is a personality which compels interest and attention. But they have a vital significance for us, for he is bound up with the present in India, and probably the future, and he has the power in him to do great good to India or great injury. We must therefore seek answers to these questions.

For nearly two years now he has been President of the Congress and some people imagine that he is just a camp follower in the Working Committee of the Congress, suppressed or kept in check by others. And yet steadily and persistently he goes on increasing his personal prestige and influence both with the masses and with all manner of groups and people. He goes to the peasant and the worker, to the zamindar and the capitalist, to the merchant and the peddler, to the brahmin and the untouchable, to the Muslim, the Sikh, the Christian and the Jew, to all who make up the great variety of Indian life. To all these he speaks in a slightly different language, ever seeking to win them over to his side. With an energy that is astonishing at his age, he has rushed about across this vast land of India, and everywhere he has received the most extraordinary of popular welcomes. From the far north to Cape Comorin he has gone like some triumphant Caesar passing by, leaving a trail of glory and a legend behind him. Is all this for him just a passing fancy which amuses him, or some deep design, or the play of some force which he himself does not know? Is it his will to power, of which he speaks in his autobiography, that is driving him from crowd to crowd and making him whisper to himself:

> "I drew these tides of men into my hands
> and wrote my will across the sky in stars."

What if the fancy turn? Men like Jawaharlal, with all their capacity for great and good work, are unsafe in democracy. He calls himself a democrat and a socialist, and no doubt he does so in all earnestness, but every psychologist knows that the mind is ultimately a slave to the heart and logic can always be made to fit in with the desires and irrepressible urges of a person.

> **A little twist and Jawaharlal might turn a dictator sweeping aside the paraphernalia of a slow-moving democracy. He might still use the language and slogans of democracy and socialism, but we all know how fascism has fattened on this language and then cast it away as useless lumber.**

Jawaharlal is certainly not a fascist, not only by conviction but by temperament. He is far too much of an aristocrat for the crudity and vulgarity of fascism. His very face and voice tell us that:

> "Private faces in public places
> are better and nicer than
> public faces in private places."

The fascist face is a public face and it is not a pleasant face in public or private. Jawaharlal's face as well as his voice are definitely private. There is no mistaking that even in a crowd, and his voice at public meetings is an intimate voice which seems to speak to individuals separately in a matter-of-fact homely way. One wonders as one hears it or sees that sensitive face what lies behind them, what thoughts and desires, what strange complexes and repressions, what passions suppressed and turned to energy, what longings which he dare not acknowledge even to himself. The train of thought holds him in public speech, but at other times his looks betray him, for his mind wanders away to strange fields and fancies, and he forgets for a moment his companion and holds inaudible converse with the creatures of his brain. Does he think of the human contacts he has missed in his life's journey, hard and tempestuous as it has been; does he long for them? Or does he dream of the future of his fashioning and of the conflicts and triumphs that he would fain have? He must know well that there is no resting by the way in the path he has chosen, and even triumph itself means greater burdens. As Lawrence said to the Arabs: "There could be no rest-houses for revolt, no dividend of joy paid out." Joy may not be for him, but something greater than joy may be his, if fate and fortune are kind—the fulfilment of a life purpose.

Jawaharlal cannot become a fascist. And yet he has all the makings of a dictator in him- vast popularity, a strong will directed to a well-defined purpose, energy, pride, organizational capacity, ability, hardness, and, with all his love of the crowd, an intolerance of others and a certain contempt for the weak and the inefficient. His flashes of temper are well known and even when they are controlled, the curling of the lips betrays him. His over-mastering desire to get things done, to sweep away what he dislikes and build anew, will hardly brook for long the slow processes of democracy. He may keep the husk but he will see to it that it bends to his will. In normal times he would be just an efficient and successful executive, but in this revolutionary epoch, Caesarism is always at the door, and is it not possible that Jawaharlal might fancy himself as a Caesar?

Therein lies danger for Jawaharlal and for India. For it is not through Caesarism that India will attain freedom, and though she may prosper a little under a benevolent and efficient despotism, she will remain stunted and the day of the emancipation of her people will be delayed.

For two consecutive years Jawaharlal has been President of the Congress and in some ways he has made himself so indispensable that there are many who suggest that he should be elected for a third term. But a greater disservice to India and even to Jawaharlal can hardly be done.

By electing him a third time we shall exalt one man at the cost of the Congress and make the people think in terms of Caesarism. We shall encourage in Jawaharlal the wrong tendencies and increase his conceit and pride. He will become convinced that only he can bear this burden or tackle India's problems.

Let us remember that, in spite of his apparent indifference to office, he has managed to hold important offices in the Congress for the last seventeen years. He must imagine that he is indispensable, and no man must be allowed to think so. India cannot afford to have him as President of the Congress for a third year in succession.

There is a personal reason also for this. In spite of his brave talk, Jawaharlal is obviously tired and stale and he will progressively deteriorate if he continues as President. He cannot rest, for he who rides a tiger cannot dismount. But we can at least prevent him from going astray and from mental deterioration under too heavy burdens and responsibilities. We have a right to expect good work from him in the future. Let us not spoil that and spoil him by too much adulation and praise. His conceit is already formidable. It must be checked. We want no Caesars.

(Nehru himself added the following note to this article later):

5 October 1931. J.N. Papers, N.M.M.L

"This article was written by Jawaharlal Nehru, but it was published anonymously in The Modern Review *of Calcutta, November 1937. 'Rashtrapati' is a Sanskrit word meaning Head of the State.*

The title is popularly used for President of the Indian National Congress. Chanakya was a famous Minister of Chandragupta, who built an empire in north India in the fourth century B.C., soon after Alexander's raid on India. Chanakya is the prototype of Machiavelli."

India and the World on Nehru

'Jawahar will be My Successor'[1]

Mahatma Gandhi

In the background of this speech is the CWC resolution passed in its meeting on 30 December, 1941. The British government had announced India's participation in World War II, without consulting the Indian leaders, and more importantly without committing itself to India's independence after the war. There was widespread resentment and the people were restive with the 'individual satyagraha'. The Bardoli resolution reflected the popular mood and Congress's response to it. The resolution also sought to finetune the 'doctrinaire insistence on nonviolence' both for the Congress party and the future government of India. Nehru was supposed to be main brain behind this resolution and defended it vigorously at the Wardha meeting of AICC in January 1942, sharply attacking its opponents. So sharp was Nehru's attack on absolute reliance on nonviolence even as an instrument of state policy, that it left Rajendra Prasad quite 'upset' as noted by Gandhiji in this speech.

Given this context, the following speech of Gandhiji containing his unequivocal declaration—'Jawahar will be my successor'—and also his confidence—'Once I am gone, he will do what I am doing now. Then he will speak my language too'—becomes most significant and poignant.

~

[1] Extract from Gandhiji's speech to the AICC session, 25 January, 1942 from the *Collected Works of Mahatma Gandhi* Vol. 81 (New Delhi: Publications Division, 1942), 432-434.

I wish to stop you from dividing the house by seeking a vote on this resolution. I do not want the Congress to look ridiculous in the eyes of the world. We have not a clean slate to write on. Our leaders have taken a step which has produced worldwide reactions. To alter the resolution out of shape is to ignore these. It would be unwise to change the policy adopted by the Working Committee. It will make the Congress appear ridiculous before the world. The world has a right to expect that the Working Committee's policy will be endorsed by the AICC. We have no valid grounds to alter it. To those who want to catch up with me and introduce a new resolution for preserving ahimsa, I would say: 'Yes, it does bring you credit. If you have chewed and digested ahimsa, I shall follow in your footsteps and so will Maulana Saheb. But I see no such evidence in you. If you bring another resolution merely to retain my leadership, it will be a foolish step. In fact, it will amount to violence. Therefore you should accept this resolution, however imperfect it may be.'

Do not please go away with the idea that there is a rift in the Congress lute. As Maulana Saheb has said, the Working Committee has functioned like members of a happy family. Somebody suggested that Pandit Jawaharlal and I were estranged. This is baseless. Jawaharlal has been resisting me ever since he fell into my net. You cannot divide water by repeatedly striking it with a stick. It is just as difficult to divide us. I have always said that not Rajaji, nor Sardar Vallabhbhai, but Jawaharlal will be my successor. He says whatever is uppermost in his mind, but he always does what I want. When I am gone he will do what I am doing now. Then he will speak my language too. After all he was born in this land. Every day he learns some new thing. He fights with me because I am there. Whom will he fight when I am gone? And who will suffer his fighting? Ultimately, he will have to speak my language. Even if this does not happen, I would at least die with this faith.

There is another reason why this resolution should be supported. (By chance this resolution has) become a mirror of the Congress in which all groups can see themselves. I can see my own reflection, and so can Rajendra Babu, Badshah Khan, Sardar and the rest. Those who have spent a lifetime in cursing the Government as also those who wish to compromise with the Government can see their own reflections in this mirror.

Maulana Saheb has not properly described how this resolution was framed. This is not the resolution as drafted by Jawaharlal. His draft has been materially amended. Rajaji also had a hand in revising it. People have an erroneous impression about Jawaharlal that he never budges from his views. Today at least he cannot get that certificate. He argues vehemently, but when the time for action arrives, he can make considerable compromises. This resolution is a product of a general consensus. The views of all the members of the Working Committee are reflected in this resolution. Like khichri it contains pulses, rice, salt, chilli and spices. Maulana Saheb has already explained the different points of view within the Working Committee. We have many groups amongst us. One is represented by Jawaharlal. His opposition to participation in the war effort is almost as strong as mine, though his reasons are different. He will not concede that he has retraced his steps in consenting to this resolution. But he himself will agree that the Rajaji group can take a different view of this resolution. The original draft had left no room for Rajaji and his followers to function. Rajaji would like to participate in the war effort if the Government accepted the conditions laid down by the Congress. So he has opened a tiny window for himself. Through this window Rajaji will try to pull Jawahar towards him and Jawahar will pull in the opposite direction. It is no longer open to the Government and the Congress critics to say that the Congress has banged the door against negotiation on the doctrinaire ground of nonviolence. The resolution throws on the Government the entire burden of wooing the Congress by meeting its legitimate demands and securing its participation in the war effort.

That nothing much is to be expected from the Government is probably too true. Only the resolution puts the Congress right with the expectant world by debunking the criticism that the

Congress is an organization of doctrinaires. And since there is a party in the Congress ready to welcome an honourable offer that will satisfy the rigidest test, it is as well that the resolution has accommodated this party. It has to be seen which group ultimately pulls the others. Whichever group wins, how can it harm us? We need have no objection.

Although different points of view have thus been accommodated in this resolution, it is not open to the charge of duplicity. It seeks to give an opportunity to different points of view to influence one another. This is how I understand it. Jawahar, Rajaji, Rajendra Babu as well as a man like me have each some elbow room in this resolution.

How does this resolution leave scope for Rajendra Babu? We have contemplated some step for the future, which upsets him. But we are not here to decide what we shall do in the future. When India becomes free, the resolution says, we can defend ourselves with arms. If we wish to help China and Russia, the resolution leaves us free to do so. We have no ill will against the Britishers, and for that matter against Germans, Italians or Japanese. How then can we have an ill will against China and Russia? The Russians have created a brave new thing. But I have my doubts as to how long they can defend their freedom in this manner. Experience tells us that any great work founded on force does not last. The Chinese sail in the same boat with us. It is a vast country and I am proud of it. I would like all these nations to be at peace with one another. If China seeks to defend herself with arms, she will have to become like Japan. She will have to do everything that Hitler and Mussolini are doing. I would like to think that when the occasion arises India would defend herself through nonviolence and thus be a messenger of peace to the whole world. Jawahar will also then work for it—not for war. Rajendra Babu can therefore support this resolution. As a political [weapon] nonviolence is no small thing; it can bring about all these results.

~

New Leaders and Their Different Ideologies

Bhagat Singh

Bhagat Singh (1907–1931), a socialist and a revolutionary, was executed by the British government in 1931, when he was just twenty-three. He remains an icon of modern Indian history and a heroic figure of the Indian freedom struggle. He was also an astonishingly mature and deeply political thinker, although in popular discourse today, he is only a young man who went to the gallows fearlessly. His remarkable mind has been eclipsed.

Also, in the popular imagination, Bhagat Singh and Subhash Chandra Bose are clubbed together as revolutionaries, 'men of action' who shared the same ideology and often presented as the polar opposites of Jawaharlal Nehru. This article, originally published as 'Naye Netaaon ke Alag Alag Vichar' *in the July 1928 issue of the journal* Kirti, *shows us just how wrong this notion is.*

~

After the failure of the non-cooperation movement,[2] the Indian people had lost hope. Communal conflict between Hindus and Muslims wiped out the little resolve that still remained. But once a sense of awakening has come upon a nation, it cannot remain asleep for long. In just a few days, the public is back on its feet and ready for battle. Today, India is full of life and vigour again; it is awake. We may not see clear signs of a great mass movement, but the ground is certainly being prepared for it. Many new leaders with a modern sensibility are emerging. Young leaders are at the forefront this time, and youth movements are

---

[2] The non-cooperation movement began in 1920, after the Jallianwala Bagh massacre. Led by Mahatma Gandhi, it was an immensely successful non-violent resistance movement; public transportation and British-manufactured goods were boycotted, and many Indians returned official honours and titles and resigned from positions in the civil and military institutions of the British Indian government. In February 1922, Gandhi called off the movement after a police station was attacked and burnt down by protestors in Chauri Chaura.

proliferating. Only young leaders are commanding the attention of patriotic-minded Indians. Even the tallest veteran leaders are being left behind.

The leaders who have gained prominence this time are the venerable Subhash Chandra Bose of Bengal and the eminent Pandit Jawaharlal Nehru. These are the two leaders who appear to be rising above all others in India and involving themselves in youth movements in particular. They are both uncompromising champions of Indian independence; both intelligent and genuine patriots. And yet, their ideologies are as different as night and day. One is believed to be a devotee and proponent of India's ancient culture and the other a committed follower of western civilization. If one is regarded as tender-hearted and sensitive, the other is spoken of as a quintessential revolutionary. Our attempt in this essay will be to present their respective ideologies before the public, so that people understand the difference between the two and make up their own minds.

But before we examine the ideas of these two leaders, it is important to mention another who is a champion of independence just as they are, and is also a prominent figure in certain youth movements. Sadhu Vaswani may not be as well known as the leading lights of the Congress, he may not occupy a special place in the country's political arena, yet his influence is apparent among the youth, who will shape the country's future. The organization Sadhu Vaswani founded—Bharat Yuva Sangh—has a particular hold on young Indians. Vaswani's ideology can be summed up in a single phrase: Back to the Vedas. This call was first given by the Arya Samaj. It is based on the belief that the Almighty has poured all the knowledge of the world into the Vedas. No progress is possible beyond them. Therefore, the world has not and cannot achieve anything greater than the wonders our very own India had achieved in the ancient past! So that is the entire faith of people like Vaswani. Which is why he says:

> 'Up until now, our politics has either considered Mezzini and Voltaire as its ideals, or it has sought inspiration from Lenin and

Tolstoy. This, when they should know that they have far greater ideals in our ancient rishis ...'

Vawani is convinced that once upon a time, our country had reached the final summit of development and today there is no reason for us to move forward at all; we only need to go back to the past.

Vaswani is a poet. Everything about his ideology is poetic. He is also a great practitioner of religious dharma. He wants to establish 'Shakti-dharma'. He says, 'At this time we need shakti—power—more than ever. He does not use the word 'shakti' only for India. He sees the word as the path and means to a kind of Devi, a special godhead. Like a very emotional poet he tells us:

> 'For in solitude have I communicated with her, our admired Bharat Mata and my aching head has heard voices saying—"The day of freedom is not far off." Sometimes indeed a strange feeling visits me and I say to myself: Holy, holy is Hindustan. For still is she under the protection of her mighty Rishis and their beauty is around us, but we behold it not.'

It must be the poet's lament that makes him declare, over and over like a man deranged or distracted: 'Our mother is the greatest. She is the mightiest. No one alive can vanquish her!' In this fashion, driven purely by emotion, he ends up saying things like this: 'Our national movement must become a purifying mass movement, if it is to fulfil its destiny without falling into class war, one of the dangers of Bolshevism.'

He believes that all one needs to do is to say—'Go among the poor, go to the villages, give them free medicines'—and our mission is accomplished. He's a romantic poet. His poetry can offer no special purpose, it can only excite the heart a little. In fact, he has no vision to offer, except great noise about our ancient civilization. He gives nothing to young minds. His only aim is to fill every heart with plain emotion. He has obvious influence among the youth, and it is growing. His ideas are regressive and patchy, as we've seen above. Such ideas have no direct connection with politics, and yet they have a significant effect. Mainly because it is the youth who are the future, and it is among them that such ideas are being propagated.

Let us now return to Subhash Chandra Bose and Jawaharlal Nehru. During the last three months, they have both chaired many conferences and put their thoughts and ideas before people. The government considers Subhash Babu a member of the group that is committed to overthrowing it, for which reason it had charged and imprisoned him under the Bengal Act. Upon his release, he was chosen as the leader of the Extremist group [of the Congress]. He espouses Purna Swaraj [complete independence], and argued for this in his presidential address at the Maharashtra session [of the Congress].

Pandit Jawaharlal Nehru is the son of the Swaraj Party leader Motilal Nehru. He is a barrister, and a very learned man. He has travelled to Russia and other countries. He is also a leader of the Extremist group, and it was due to his efforts, and those of his fellow leaders, that the resolution for Purna Swaraj was passed and adopted at the Madras session. Before this, he had spoken emphatically in favour of Purna Swaraj at the Amritsar session.

And yet, the two leaders are poles apart in their thinking. Reading the transcripts of their speeches at the Amritsar and Maharashtra sessions, this difference was apparent to us. But the difference became clear as daylight after a speech delivered in Bombay. Pandit Nehru was chairing the conference and Subhash Bose made a speech. He is a very emotional Bengali. He began his address with the statement that India has a special message for the world. It has a lesson in spirituality for humanity. And then he launched into his speech like a man in the grip of disorienting emotion—'Behold the Taj Mahal on a moonlit night and think of the vision of that heart that imagined it. Recall that a Bengali novelist has written that "our flowing tears hardened into stone within us". Bose also declares that we should return to the Vedas. In his Poona [Congress session] address, he had expounded on 'nationalism' and said that internationalists criticize nationalism as narrow, chauvinistic ideology, but that this is a mistake. Indian nationalist thought, according to him, is nothing of the kind.

It is not chauvinistic. It is not born of self-interest, and it is not oppressive, because at its root is the philosophy of *Satyam Shivam Sundaram*—Truth is bountiful and beautiful.

The same old romanticism. Pure emotionalism. And [like Vaswani], Bose too has great faith in his ancient past. He sees only greatness in this ancient era. In his thinking, there's nothing new in the system of panchayati raj, or the rule of the people, which he says is very old in India. He goes so far as to say that Communism isn't new to India either. Anyway, that day in Bombay, he went on long and hard about India's special message for the world.

Pandit Jawaharlal Nehru, like many others, holds an entirely different view: 'Every country thinks it has a special message for the world. England has arrogated to itself the right to teach the world culture. I don't see anything special that belongs to my country alone. But Subhash Babu has great belief in such things.' Nehru also says, 'Every youth must rebel. Not only in the political sphere, but in social, economic and religious spheres also. I have not much use for any man who comes and tells me that such and such thing is said in the Koran. Everything unreasonable must be discarded, even if they find authority for it in the Vedas and the Koran.'

These are the thoughts of a true revolutionary, while Subhash Chandra's are the thoughts of someone who wants to replace one regime with another. One man thinks our old systems are very superior; the other man believes we should rebel against these systems. Yet the latter is called emotional, sensitive, and the former a transformative revolutionary! At one point Pandit Nehru says:

> 'To those who still fondly cherish old ideas and are striving to bring back the conditions which prevailed in Arabia 1300 years ago or in the vedic age in India, I say that it is inconceivable that you can bring back the hoary past. The world of reality will not retrace its steps, the world of imagination may remain stationary.'

This is why he feels it is necessary to revolt.

Subhash Babu supports Purna Swaraj, complete independence,

because the British are people of the West and we are of the East. Pandit ji's position is that we need to establish our own rule so that we can change the entire social structure. This is why we must have complete and absolute independence.

Subhash Babu is in sympathy with labour, the working class, and wants to improve their condition. Pandit ji wants to bring in a revolution and change the existing system altogether. Subhash Chandra is emotional and romantic—he is giving the young food for their hearts, and only their hearts. The other man is an epochal change-maker who is fuelling not just the heart but also the mind:

> 'They should aim at Swaraj for the masses based on Socialism. That was a revolutionary change which they could not bring about without revolutionary methods ... Mere reform or gradual repairing of the existing machinery could not achieve the real, proper Swaraj for the general masses.'

Subhash Babu feels the need to focus on national politics only as long as it is necessary to safeguard and promote India's position in world politics. But Pandit ji has freed himself of the narrow confines of plain nationalism and emerged into an open field.

Now the ideas of the [two] leaders are before us. Which way should we incline? One Punjabi newspaper has heaped praise upon Subhash Chandra and said of Pandit ji and others that such rebels destroy themselves beating their heads against stone. We must of course remember that Punjab has always been a rather emotional province. People's passions here rise very quickly and just as quickly subside, like foam.

Subhash Chandra doesn't appear to be providing any intellectual nourishment, only food for the heart. The need of the hour now is for the youth of Punjab to understand and strengthen revolutionary ideas. At this time, Punjab needs food for the mind, and this can only be found with Pandit Jawaharlal Nehru. This does not mean we should become his blind followers. But as far as ideas are concerned, the young people of Punjab should align themselves with him, so that they can know the true meaning of revolution, realize the need for a revolution in India, understand the significance of revolution in the world at large, and so on. Through serious thought and analysis, the youth should bring clarity and conviction to their ideas, so that even in times of very little hope, times of disillusionment and defeat, they should not lose direction, stand tall and strong against a hostile world and not give up. This is how the public will achieve the goal of revolution.

Translated by Speaking Tiger

~

Maulana Azad on Nehru[3]

Maulana Abul Kalam Azad

Nehru and Maulana Abul Kalam Azad (1888–1958) were fellow freedom fighters and good friends but in 1946, on the question of an alliance with the Unionist Party in Punjab, they had differences. Some people also actively worked to spoil relations between them. After a few more disagreements and reasoned debate however, Nehru admitted to his short-sightedness and made peace.

~

The position was specially difficult in the Punjab. It was a Muslim majority province but no party had a clear majority. The Muslim members were divided between the Unionist Party and the Muslim League. I held discussions with both the groups. The League, as I have said, declined my invitation under instructions from Mr Jinnah. I was however able to carry out negotiations in a way which gave the Unionist Party the opportunity of forming the Ministry with the support of the Congress. The Governor was personally inclined in favour of the Muslim League but he found that he had no option but to invite Khizir Hayat Khan the leader of the Unionist Party to form the Government.

---

[3] Abul Kalam Azad, *India wins Freedom: The Complete Version,* 137–140.

This was the first time that Congress had come into the Government in the Punjab. This was a development which had till then been regarded as almost impossible. Political circles throughout the country declared that I had shown great skill and statesmanship in the negotiations which led to the formation of the Punjab Ministry. Independent members throughout the country congratulated me in unqualified terms. The *National Herald* which is the organ of the UP Congress congratulated me on the manner in which I had solved the complex and difficult problem of the Punjab, and went so far as to say that my handling of the situation was one of the clearest examples of statesmanship and skill in negotiation exhibited by any Congress leader.

I was pleased by this response in the country but there was one thing which also saddened me. From the very beginning of my activities in the Congress, Jawaharlal and I had been the best of friends. We had always seen eye to eye and leaned on one another for support. The question of any rivalry or jealousy between us had never arisen and I thought would never arise. In fact my friendship with the family began from the days of Pandit Motilal Nehru. In the beginning, I had looked on Jawaharlal as a brother's son and he had regarded me as his father's friend.

Jawaharlal is by nature warm-hearted and generous and personal jealousies never entered into his mind. Some of his relations and friends did not however like his cordial relations with me and sought to create difficulties and jealousies between us. Jawaharlal is however very vain and cannot stand that anybody else should receive greater support or admiration than he. Jawaharlal has also a weakness for theoretical considerations and they took advantage of this to turn him against me. They spoke to him and said that the alliance of Congress with the Unionist Party was in principle wrong. They argued that the Muslim League was a mass organisation and the Congress should have formed a coalition with the Muslim League and not with the Unionist Party in the Punjab, This was the line which the Communists had adopted openly. Jawaharlal was partially influenced by their views and may have thought that I was sacrificing leftist principles in forming a coalition with the Unionist Party.

Those who wanted to create a division between Jawaharlal and me also kept on telling him that the praise showered on me was a reflection on other Congress leaders including him. If his own paper, The *National Herald,* should speak so highly of me, the result would be that soon I would achieve an unrivalled position in the Congress organisation.

I do not know how far these persuasions had any effect on Jawaharlal's mind but during the meeting of the Congress Working Committee at Bombay, I found that he began to oppose my line of action on almost every item. Jawaharlal took the line that the policy I had adopted in the Punjab was not correct. He even said that I had brought down the prestige of the Congress. I was both surprised and sorry to hear this. What I had done in the Punjab was to put Congress into the Government in spite of the fact that the Governor had been working for installing a Muslim League Ministry. Through my endeavours, the Muslim League had been isolated and Congress, though it was a minority, had become the decisive factor in Punjab affairs. Khizir Hayat Khan was the Chief Minister through Congress support and he had naturally come under its influence.

Jawaharlal held that the participation of the Congress in the Government without being the majority party was not right. This would force the Congress to enter into compromises and perhaps make it resile from its principles. I denied that there was any risk of the Congress giving up its principles but at the same time made it dear that if the Working Committee did not approve of my decision in Lahore, it could adopt any new policy it liked. Congress had not given any guarantee of remaining in office and could come out whenever it chose.

Gandhiji came out strongly in support of my views. He said that though Congress was in a minority in the Punjab, it had secured a decisive voice in the formation and working of the Ministry through my negotiations. He held that there could be no better solution from the Congress point of view and he was against any change in the decision I had taken. When Gandhiji expressed himself in categorical terms, all other members of the Working Committee supported me and Jawaharlal had to acquiesce.

The next question which came up before the Working Committee was that of negotiations with the Cabinet Mission. Till now whenever there had been any negotiation with the Government, the Congress President had represented the organisation. When Stafford Cripps came in 1942, Jawaharlal had himself proposed that I should be the sole negotiator on behalf of Congress. In the Simla Conference I was again the sole representative and even Gandhiji did not participate. This time however Jawaharlal adopted a different attitude. He proposed that the discussions with the Cabinet Mission should be conducted by a small subcommittee of the Working Committee and not a single representative.

His proposal surprised me. I had never thought that Jawaharlal would raise any such question. I however felt that the question of confidence was involved and therefore opposed him. I pointed out that till now, the Congress President had been the sole representative of the organisation and I saw no reason for a change. If the Working Committee felt that a change in procedure was necessary, it certainly had the right to carry it out but I would not be a party to such a decision. In fact I would regard this as a reduction in the functions of the President of the Congress.

Here again Gandhiji supported me. He said clearly that he saw no reason for a change. If the Congress President could be the sole representative in the discussions with Cripps and Wavell, he did not see why there should be a change now. If a Committee was now appointed to negotiate with the Cabinet Mission the inference would be that there was lack of confidence in the Congress President. Experience had also shown that there could be no better representative of the Congress than its President. The appointment of a Committee at this stage would therefore not help but result in confusion among Congress rank and file and the general public.

The Working Committee accepted Gandhiji's advice and

again appointed the President as the sole representative of the Congress. Jawaharlal perhaps felt that the matter had gone too far and left a bad impression on me. As was my usual practice, I was staying with Bhulabhai Desai. Jawaharlal came to me early next morning and with great affection and sincerity assured me that his proposal did not for a moment indicate any lack of confidence in my leadership. His only purpose had been to strengthen my hands, as he felt that I could better carry the negotiations if some of my colleagues were associated with me. He admitted frankly that his reading had been wrong and he desired that we should forget the whole episode. I was pleased by his frank talk. He and I have been the best of friends and it had hurt me that there should be any difference between us.

~

Leader of Our Legions[4]

Vallabhbhai Patel

'Sardar' Vallabhbhai Patel (1875–1950) played a leading role in India's Independence movement as part of the Indian National Congress and guided its integration into a united, independent nation. He was India's first Home Minister and Deputy Prime Minister, as part of Nehru's cabinet. While the two leaders frequently disagreed on many issues, publicly and privately, they had immense respect for each other's contributions to Indian social and political life, as the extract below shows.

~

Jawaharlal and I have been fellow-members of the Congress, soldiers in the struggle for freedom, colleagues in the Congress Working Committee and other bodies of the Congress, devoted followers of the Great Master who has unhappily left us to battle with grave problems without his guidance, and co-sharers in the great and onerous burden of administration of this vast country.

---

[4] From *Nehru Abhinandan Granth*, 14 October 1949.

Having known each other in such intimate and varied fields of activity we have naturally grown fond of each other; our mutual affection has increased as years have advanced, and it is difficult for people to imagine how much we miss each other when we are apart and unable to take counsel together in order to resolve our problems and difficulties. This familiarity, nearness, intimacy and brotherly affection make it difficult for me to sum him up for public appreciation, but, then, the idol of the nation, the leader of the people, the Prime Minister of the country, and the hero of the masses, whose noble record and great achievements are an open book, hardly needs any commendation from me.

A clean and resolute fighter, he always fought hard and straight against the foreign government. Having received the baptism of fire in his early thirties as an organizer of the peasants' movement in the U.P., he imbibed to the full the knowledge of the art and science of nonviolent warfare. His ardent emotionalism and his hatred of injustice and oppression converted him into a crusader in the war against poverty, and with an instinctive sympathy for the poor he threw himself heart and soul into the struggle for the amelioration of the lot of the peasantry. His sphere of activities widened, and he soon blossomed forth into a silent organizer of the great institution to which we all dedicated ourselves as an instrument of our emancipation. Gifted with idealism of a high order, a devotee of beauty and art in life, and equipped with an infinite capacity to magnetize and inspire others and a personality which would be remarkable in any gathering of the world's foremost men, Jawaharlal has gone from strength to strength as a political leader. His trip to foreign countries, necessitated by the ailment of his wife, raised his conception of Indian nationalism to an ethereal international plane. That was the beginning of that international phase of his life and character which has throughout been noticeable in his approach to internal and world problems. Ever since, Jawaharlal has never looked back. He has grown in stature both in India and abroad. The sincerity of his convictions, the breadth of his outlook, the clarity of his vision, and the purity of his emotions—all these have brought to him the homage of millions in this country and outside.

It was, therefore, in the fitness of things that in the twilight preceding the dawn of independence he should have been our leading light, and that when India was faced with crisis after crisis, following the achievement of our freedom, he should have been the upholder of our faith and the leader of our legions. No one knows better than myself how much he has laboured for his country in the last two years of our difficult existence. I have seen him age quickly during that period, on account of the worries of the high office that he holds and the tremendous responsibilities that he wields. He has never spared himself in the cause of the refugees who have seldom knocked at his door without redress. In the councils of the Commonwealth his has been a most notable contribution; on the world's stage he has played a very remarkable part. Yet, with all this he has maintained that original youthful look, that balanced poise, that sense of perspective and that sang-froid and *bonhomie* which are the results of a disciplined philosophy and trained intellect.

It is obviously impossible to do justice to his great and pre-eminent personality in these few considered words. The versatility of his character and attainments at once defy delineation. His thoughts have sometimes a depth which it is not easy to fathom, but underlying them all is a transparent sincerity and a robustness of youth which endear him to every one without distinction of caste and creed, race or religion.

It is to this priceless possession of a free India that we pay homage today on the occasion of the diamond jubilee of his birth. May he secure greater and greater triumphs in the cause of his country and in the pursuit of his ideals!

~

My Discovery of Jawaharlal[5]

Aruna Asaf Ali

Aruna Asaf Ali (1909–1996) was an Indian independence activist who famously hoisted the Indian national flag at the Gowalia Tank maidan in Bombay during the Quit India Movement in 1942. She became Delhi's first mayor in 1958 and received the Bharat Ratna posthumously in 1997. In the essay below, Ali throws light on how, despite constant criticism from both sides of the political spectrum, Nehru always engaged with his critics and was steadfast in his commitment to social as well as economic equality.

~

In an article contributed to the *Asia* magazine of June 1936, Jawaharlal Nehru said:

> It is curious how one cannot resist the tendency to give an anthropomorphic form to a country. Such is the force of habit and early associations. India becomes Bharat Mata, Mother India, a beautiful lady, very old but very youthful in appearance, sad-eyed and forlorn, cruelly treated by aliens and outsiders, and calling upon her children to protect her.

Adopting this image, one might say that during the two decades from 1869 to 1889, Mother India gave birth to a remarkable brood of sons and daughters who would deliver her from foreign thralldom.

Consider the roll of honour (and the list is by no means exhaustive): 1869, Mohandas Karamchand Gandhi; 1875, Vallabhbhai Patel; 1878, C. Rajagopalachari; 1879, Sarojini Naidu; 1880, M.A. Ansari; 1882, Subramania Bharati and Bidhan Chandra Roy; 1883, Vinayak Damodar Savarkar; 1884, Rajendra Prasad; 1886, Rameshwari Nehru and Muthulakshmi Reddi; 1887, S. Satyamurti and Govind Ballabh Pant; 1888, Maulana

[5] From the *Jawaharlal Nehru: Centenary Volume*, ed. Sheila Dikshit, K. Natwar Singh, G. Parthasarathi, H.Y. Sharada Prasad, S. Gopal and Ravinder Kumar (New Delhi: Oxford University Press, 1989).

Azad, S. Radhakrishnan and M. Asaf Ali; 1889, Jawaharlal Nehru and Acharya Narendra Deva.

This stellar cluster reminds me of another passage by Jawaharlal Nehru. He wrote in *Glimpses of World History* about 'how, in the lives of nations, periods of brilliant life come and go. For a while they brighten up everything and enable the men and women of that period and country to create things of beauty. People seem to become inspired.' The Gandhi-Nehru years were such a period in India's history. I have often remarked to friends that my greatest good fortune was to have been born when I was born ... so that I grew up when the country was aglow with the light radiated by Mahatma Gandhi and Jawaharlal Nehru; and to have married the man whom I married—it was Asaf Saheb who broadened my mental horizons beyond the English literature which had been my only enthusiastic interest as a convent educated student.

I have been asked many a time, specially by young persons, when I first met Jawaharlal. It will be more accurate to speak of the first occasion when I saw him.

It was early in the winter of 1928, in Delhi. I was nineteen at the time. Asaf and I, who had married a few weeks earlier, in September, were invited to dinner by Brijlal Nehru and his wife Rameshwari at their residence on Clive Road (now Tyagaraja Marg). Brijlal, a nephew of Motilal Nehru, wanted us to meet his uncle and his cousin, Jawaharlal, who were on a visit to Delhi and were staying with him.

Though my husband was of the same age as Jawaharlal, he was equally well acquainted with Motilal Nehru and was a practising lawyer, unlike Jawaharlal who never developed a serious interest in the profession in which his father had attained high fame and wealth. Asaf often met Motilal Nehru, whom he esteemed as a towering senior both in public life and in the legal profession. This was the background to the 'Establishment Nehru' of Delhi inviting us to meet his seditious clansmen from Allahabad.

As we waited for Jawaharlal's return from a speaking tour of some Punjab towns, the conversation was mainly between Motilal

Nehru and my husband because they were temperamentally akin in their political views, both favouring participation in the legislatures to advance the national cause. Suddenly Motilalji stopped in the middle of the conversation to enquire, 'Chhote saab aagaye?' and instructed the domestics to keep hot water ready for the young master's bath.

At last Jawaharlal burst in, all covered with dust. He barely glanced in our direction as he went quickly in for a wash and change. He must have thought it was the usual evening gathering of some of the capital's Anglicised elite who were his cousin's colleagues and friends.

I was introduced to Jawaharlal on his joining us for dinner, and was dazzled by the first close view of him. Jawaharlal looked me up and down with amused curiosity. I might well have struck him as a dolled-up slip of a girl, destined to decorate drawing rooms. It was with very little comprehension that I followed the conversation during and after dinner.

In spite of acquiring some political knowledge from reading and talks with my husband, I was hardly prepared for following the proceedings at the Congress session in December 1929 at Lahore which I attended. Jawaharlal's election as Congress President earlier that year, when he was only forty, made him one of the youngest to hold the office.

The Lahore Congress was a thrilling spectacle. Jawaharlal, smartly dressed in a black sherwani, rode to the venue of the session on a magnificent white horse at the head of the presidential procession. He looked every inch the knight errant of the Freedom Movement. Some of us gathered roses and narcissi and presented them to the youthful and winsome Rashtrapati. (That was how the Congress President was referred to till India became a sovereign republic with the head of the state designated as Rashtrapati.)

On the last day of the year 1929, at the approach of midnight, Mahatma Gandhi moved a resolution at the Lahore Congress defining the Congress objective as complete independence, as opposed to Dominion Status. It was adopted amidst deafening applause. The next morning, on New Year's Day 1930, Jawaharlal unfurled the national flag on the bank of the river Ravi. As the tricolour fluttered in the breeze, the poet's lines coursed through my mind:

> Bliss was it in that dawn to be alive,
> But to be young was very heaven.

The Independence resolution authorized the Congress leadership to forge the sanctions, through civil disobedience, for realizing the objective. Gandhiji decided to base the Civil Disobedience Movement on nonpayment of the tax on salt. It was a tax which even the poorest had to pay even though salt was a basic need and a free gift of nature. I went through my baptism of fire during the Salt Satyagraha, and was imprisoned in 1930 and again in 1932. In 1941 I courted arrest during the Individual Satyagraha which was launched in protest against India being dragged, as a colony, into Britain's war that was claimed to be in defence of democracy. During these years I was a typical desh sevika or a volunteer in the national cause, complying unquestioningly with the calls given by the Congress Working Committee from time to time. It was in 1942, after the All India Congress Committee adopted the Quit India resolution in Bombay, and the British authorities rounded up all Congress leaders at one fell swoop in the early hours of 9 August, that I first exercised my own political judgment. I was not sure whether Mahatma Gandhi and Jawaharlal Nehru would approve, but I adopted as my guideline Gandhiji's injunction: 'Do or die'.

Maulana Azad was to have hoisted the national flag at the Gowalia Tank maidan in Bombay on the morning of 9 August. Instead, he was under arrest and—as I found when I accompanied my husband, who was arrested along with other members of the Working Committee, in a police taxi to Victoria Terminus—on his way to an unknown destination. After the train left I decided on an impulse that I would go to the Gowalia Tank Maidan and announce to the people the arrest of the leaders. The police ordered the crowd to disperse. Not wanting the flag to remain unfurled, I rushed up to the dais in a defiant mood, quickly pulled the string to unfurl the flag and told the gathering about the arrest of the national leaders. Few knew my identity. Some thought that the girl with plaited hair was a college student from Delhi. Hardly had the flag been unfurled when the police lobbed tear gas shells into the crowd. The assembled men and women ran helter skelter with tears streaming from their eyes. Among them was Indira Gandhi, though I was not aware of it at the time. 'I had my first experience of a tear-gas attack at the flag-hoisting ceremony,' she recalls in *Remembered Moments.*

The experience of that morning made me decide that I would not once again tamely enter jail by offering satyagraha. The people were indignant and roused at the arrest of the leaders, and the indignation should find organized expression in such a forceful manner that the alien rulers would have no option but to quit India. This was also the feeling of several other delegates who had come to the All India Congress Committee meeting. These comprised Congress socialists mainly, but included several Gandhians like R.R. Diwakar and Sucheta Kripalani. We all felt that the savage repression let loose by the British occupation forces against the spontaneous protest at the arrest of the national leaders should be channelized into organized resistance, on the lines of the underground movement of the partisans of freedom in Nazi-occupied Europe. I told myself that our action was in consonance with the spirit of the Quit India resolution which called for 'a mass struggle on nonviolent lines on the widest possible scale' and which also said: 'A time may come when it may not be possible to issue instructions or for instructions to reach our people. When this happens, every man and woman who is participating in this movement must function for himself or herself within the four corners of the general instructions issued. Every Indian who desires freedom and strives for it must be his own guide.'

Both on the underground Congress Radio and in our illegally circulated literature, we were careful to draw a distinction between planned dislocation of Britain's imperialist war effort, on the one hand, and senseless destruction—as by latter-day terrorists—of lives and property. It is remarkable that though some lily-white Gandhians, more loyal to nonviolence than the Mahatma, turned up their noses at us during and after the Quit India movement, neither Gandhiji nor Jawaharlal Nehru disowned us.

When I emerged from underground life early in 1946 following cancellation of the warrant for my arrest, I was bewildered by the spectacle of Congress leaders negotiating with the British rulers to enter the Viceroy's Executive Council in the company of the Muslim League. It seemed to me a betrayal of the cause for which they had given the best years of their lives, for which we of the younger generation had fought in the Quit India movement. My association with socialist colleagues had radicalized my outlook on social and economic problems. I could not see how the Congress could bring about any fundamental change within the structure of the British colonial establishment. Then came the final blow: acceptance of the subcontinent's partition as the price of independence, because of the Hindu-Muslim riots which swept northern India following the Muslim League's 'direct action' in Calcutta in August 1946. I felt dazed, as Jawaharlal and many others must have felt when Gandhiji terminated the Non-Cooperation Movement of the 1920s following an outbreak of mob violence at Chauri Chaura. I would take my doubts and my criticism to Jawaharlal. He found time, in the midst of the political drama in which he was a principal actor, to hear me patiently and to explain the compulsions of the situation as he saw them.

I also gave public expression to my anguish in a series of articles in *Janata,* the weekly founded and edited by Edatata Narayanan.

These outpourings of mine, in which I raised many questions without even attempting to answer them, were trenchantly critical of the Congress leadership. Yet, when Achyut Patwardhan arranged for the publication of the articles in book form in 1947, Jawaharlal contributed a Foreword which was not only generous to me personally but showed his extraordinary capacity for sympathetic understanding of those who differed from him. It was also a testament of his faith in the capabilities of Indian womanhood. He wrote:

> Among the many strange things that have happened in India during this quarter of a century, perhaps the most notable is the emergence of Indian womanhood. Large numbers of Indian women have played an important role in our struggle for freedom. Many of them have stood out by their ability, capacity for organization and self-sacrifice for a cause. Some of them can be ranked very high in any assembly of women all over the world. This fact, more than any other, demonstrates the renaissance of the Indian people and the strong foundations on which we have built our movement for freedom.

I would take to Jawaharlal not only my doubts and questions about a transfer of power negotiated with the British rulers on the basis of India's partition, but the polarization in international relations after the Second World War. I could understand Winston Churchill's anti-Sovietism, but why did Indian socialists seem to echo his Iron Curtain speech at Fulton? Was the Soviet Union a vast prisonhouse as its detractors alleged?

Jawaharlal advised me to go to Soviet Russia and see for myself. But before that, he said, I would do well to spend some time in London, study the history of the socialist and communist movements at the British Museum library, and discuss the subject with persons like V. K. Krishna Menon and his friends of the British Left.

I did not know at the time that, in advising me to visit Russia, Jawaharlal wanted me to go through the same kind of education that he had envisaged for his daughter. It was many years later that I found in the *Selected Works of Jawaharlal Nehru* his letter of 9 July 1941 in which he tells Indira:

> I had hoped that after your formal education at a university was completed, you might supplement it by some travel in various countries….I wanted you to go to Russia to see things there for yourself….Then with this background of mental training and a

> wider culture I expected you to return to India and discover the fascinating thing that is India.

Early in 1950 I applied for an entry visa for my first visit to the Soviet Union. It took quite some time coming. Jawaharlal, refusing to be provoked by the rude things that were being said about him and Gandhiji at that time by Soviet commentators, had sent Dr Radhakrishnan to Moscow as India's second ambassador. Krishna Menon was our High Commissioner in London. Both Dr Radhakrishnan and Krishna Menon tried to help expedite the visa, but what clinched the issue appears to have been Jayaprakash Narayan's reference, at a Socialist Party convention in Madras, to my criticism of the socialists for their dilution of Marxism.

I sailed from England to Leningrad in the company of D.N. Pritt, the noted British jurist and Marxist, and his wife Maria Frances. I was greatly impressed by much of what I saw in the Soviet Union—the eradication of destitution and reduction in disparities, the equal participation of women in all sectors of post-war reconstruction, and the care lavished on children and their education. But I did not hesitate to tell academicians A.M. Dyakov and Balabushevich, who were assigned to act as my intellectual guides, that the Soviets were quite wrong in their negative assessment of Mahatma Gandhi and of Jawaharlal Nehru.

The soundness of Jawaharlal's judgment in sending Dr Radhakrishnan to Moscow was soon vindicated. The philosopher-statesman's patient and persuasive presentations of India's position, and the Indian Government's peace-oriented initiatives in relation to the Korean War and other issues convinced the Soviet authorities that our foreign policy was truly independent and non-aligned. A token of the changed perception was Stalin's gesture in receiving Dr Radhakrishnan for a discussion. When Stalin died in March 1953, I met Jawaharlal who agreed in the course of our talk that it would be appropriate for him as Prime Minister to make a reference in Parliament to the late Soviet leader who was a symbol of his country's heroic resistance to Hitler's aggression. Parliament adjourned for the day after Jawaharlal's tribute.

Jawaharlal's kind and friendly attitude to me during these years was in spite of my identifying myself with the Leftist criticism of the Congress and of his government. I did not realize at the time that if Jawaharlal was a prisoner of conservative forces—a potential Lenin fallen among Kerenskys, as I used to describe him—we of the Left were ourselves substantially to blame. We deserted him instead of strengthening the Congress Left. The communists, who had alienated themselves from the national mainstream by their People's War policy and opposition to the Quit India struggle, swung to the other extreme and refused for several years to acknowledge that India became politically independent in August 1946.

Even the non-communist Left, unfortunately, chose to be doctrinaire. I remember Jawaharlal telling me that it was not proper for the Congress Socialist Party (C.S.P.) to have contested the municipal election in Bombay as a distinct party with its own flag, against Congress candidates. He wanted the socialists to function, as they used to, as a group within the Congress. When objection was raised by some Congress leaders to dual membership, Jawaharlal asked me to advise the socialists to function as part of the Congress. Gandhiji, too, wanted the socialists to stay with the Congress. I expressed my objection and reiterated his advice. Maulana Azad was of the same view.

Had we socialists heeded this advice when the Congress imposed a ban on dual membership in its new 1948 constitution, we could have strengthened Jawaharlal's hands within the Congress against the Rightists. With the senior Congress leaders approaching old age, we socialists could well have acquired decisive influence in the party in a few years. But the C.S.P. decided to leave the parent body, imagining that we could offer a socialist alternative to the Congress. By doing so, the socialists weakened both themselves and Jawaharlal.

How greatly we socialists overrated our influence was to be demonstrated soon. Following the decision to leave the Congress, Narendra Deva and twelve other members resigned from the United Provinces Assembly to which they had been elected in

1946 on the Congress ticket. The socialists could not win any of these seats in the by-elections that followed.

The exit of the socialists from the Congress led to such developments as the election of Purushottamdas Tandon as Congress President in September 1950, defeating J.B. Kripalani whom Jawaharlal preferred. Another negative consequence of Rightist dominance was the dropping of the Hindu Code Bill from the Congress manifesto for the first general elections of 1951–2. It is a different matter that in his own constituency of Allahabad East, when his principal rival, Prabhudutt Brahmachari, offered to withdraw from the contest if the Prime Minister would agree to drop the proposed legislation, Jawaharlal spurned the offer and fought the election on the very issue of improving women's status through codification and reform of Hindu law.

The last great opportunity of forging an alliance of the Left with progressive forces in the Congress was thrown away in 1953 when Jayaprakash Narayan laid down rigid preconditions instead of responding positively to Jawaharlal's invitation to him to join the government. There was no reason for Jawaharlal making this generous overture except to hasten the country's progress towards socialism, since the Congress party enjoyed a massive majority in the Lok Sabha.

Another example of the broad-mindedness of Jawaharlal and the Congress of those days was their asking me to stand for election as the first Mayor of Delhi. The party position in the Municipal Corporation of Delhi was such that the Jana Sangh would have been able to get its nominee elected unless the Congress and the communist members joined hands. I was at that time no longer a member of the Communist Party which I had joined a few years earlier, and was engaged in the constructive work of the Bharat Sevak Samaj. As I was acceptable to both the Congress and the communist groups, Jawaharlal and the then Home Minister, Govind Ballabh Pant, asked me to contest the election. This resulted in my election as Mayor.

In the late 1950s, Rightist forces within and outside the Congress became vocal in their criticism of the Nehru government's policies of nationalization and radical land reforms. Several of us who were known as 'Nehru Socialists' now became convinced of the need to strengthen Jawaharlal's hands if the country was not to slide back to the pre-1947 scenario of landlords and capitalists thriving under foreign patronage. It was in order to explain Jawaharlal's policies and gather support among the intelligentsia that the weekly news magazine *Link* was established in 1958. The founding editor was Edatata Narayanan, whom I had come to know during the Quit India struggle when he gave up his position as assistant editor of *The Hindustan Times* to join the underground resistance. *Link* was intended to articulate the need to combine patriotism with the impulse for social justice, and to strengthen the bonds of friendship between India and the socialist world.

Within a couple of years, when the occupation of a considerable extent of Indian territory on the northern border by the forces of Communist China was disclosed, Jawaharlal became vulnerable to criticism. And after the humiliating reverses suffered by India in the hostilities that broke out towards the close of 1962, the attacks on Jawaharlal became virulent—V.K. Krishna Menon serving as a proxy for those who wanted to see the removal of Jawaharlal from power.

The attack now came from two sides. Gunning for him from the Right were those who wanted India to line up with the West. Citing the Chinese invasion as proof of the failure of Nehru's foreign policy, they hoped that if Nehru could be toppled on the sensitive issue of military reverses, his domestic policies aimed at land redistribution and public ownership of key industries could also be reversed. On the other side, an influential section in the yet undivided Communist Party attacked Nehru for allowing himself to be dragged into hostilities with a socialist neighbour.

Those of us who saw in steadfast adherence to Nehru's policies the only hope for the survival and strengthening of India as a free nation determined to achieve socialism, felt the need for a daily newspaper, published from the capital, which would counter the tendentious campaign launched against Jawaharlal. The dedicated efforts of Dr A.V. Baliga, the famed surgeon of Bombay who donated his fabulous earnings to humanitarian and public causes, resulted in the launching of *Patriot* within six months of the trauma suffered by the country in the autumn of 1962. It owed not a little to the encouragement and support received from many other friends including Feroze Gandhi, V.K. Krishna Menon and K.D. Malviya. It was Feroze Gandhi who advised me to make a request to Jawaharlal for the allotment, to the United India Periodicals which had launched *Link,* of the plot of land on which Link House now stands. Without Link House, the launching of *Patriot* would have been impossible. Even with the building and the rental income from it, I have often had occasion to recall the warning sounded by Jawaharlal when I informed him of our *Patriot* project, about the formidable financial difficulties of running a daily newspaper. He spoke from his own experience of *National Herald,* which he had founded in Lucknow in 1938. Moreover, there is a difference between the two. Jawaharlal's *National Herald* was linked to a militant anti-British political movement which the newspaper supported and from which, in turn, it drew support. When *Patriot* was launched we had hoped to strengthen, and in turn to derive strength from, a broadly based people's movement to actualize the vision of a free India in which the fruits of development would reach the toiling masses. This expectation has been belied. The cruel hand of death claimed both Dr Baliga and Jawaharlal Nehru soon after, within a year of our launching the newspaper. Subsequently, owing to the fragmentation of progressive forces, the course of economic and social development has increasingly taken an elitist bent. It has widened economic disparities, making a mockery of Jawaharlal's vision.

I try to derive consolation from the adage that it is darkest before a new dawn. It is for the younger generation to relight the torch of Jawaharlal's vision and to correct the course of development. Persons of my generation can but remind today's young people of the India of Gandhiji's and Jawaharlal's dreams. An opportunity to do this came my way when friends connected with the Nehru Memorial Library asked me to write about Jawaharlal's contribution to the reawakening of Indian women. Being no scholar or writer of books, I undertook the task with diffidence. But after I discovered in Shri G.N.S. Raghavan a person who could share the burden and provide the kind of collaboration I needed, the task turned into an intellectually exhilarating discovery of Jawaharlal Nehru—the development of his radiant personality and the maturing of his view of life. This discovery I have attempted to share with others in *Private Face of a Public Person,* a little book which is in the nature of a prelude to the main work on the resurgence of Indian women.

There is a sense in which our discovery of a person becomes complete only after he or she has passed out of our time and entered history. This has been true of my comprehension of Jawaharlal's life and work. My understanding of him is now the richer for the rereading of his speeches and writings and the reliving, while writing the books, of the golden moments of the Freedom Struggle and of my association with him.

Jawaharlal himself summed up in a few sentences his profoundly humanist vision of development in the course of the first Azad Memorial Lecture which he delivered in 1959 (brought out by the Indian Council for Cultural Relations in book form under the title *India Today and Tomorrow*). He said:

> Poverty is a degradation, and the obvious reaction is to get rid of it. To talk of freedom in poverty is almost a contradiction in terms. But too much wealth and affluence, whether in an individual or a society, has also its attendant evils which are becoming evident. The mere piling up of material riches may lead to an emptiness in the inner life of man. There is a danger that socialism, while leading to affluence and even equitable distribution, may still miss some of the significant features of life. It is largely for this reason that stress becomes necessary on the individual.

These words have proved prophetic. Today, leaders of political thought all over the world have come to realize both the truths, namely that poverty is a social crime and that material wealth must go hand in hand with compassion and tolerance. It is a measure of Jawaharlal's rich contribution that his counsel is of continuing relevance to the world's successive generations.

~

Nehru and Indian Science

Baldev Singh[1]

Baldev Singh (1902–1961) was an Indian independence movement leader and the first Defence Minister of India. In the following essay, he details how Nehru was instrumental in setting up the foundations for scientific research in India.

~

Independence gave Nehru the opportunity to translate into action his already formed conviction that science was crucial to the solution of India's needs and problems. In 1937, at his instance, the Congress Working Committee had called on the Congress governments to appoint committees of experts to devise a machinery for planning. As Chairman of the National Planning Committee (1938), he had interacted with scientists like Meghnad Saha, P.C. Mahalanobis and others. Nehru's conviction is best described in his message to the silver jubilee session (1938) of the Indian Science Congress:

> Though I have long been a slave driven in a chariot of Indian politics, with little leisure for other thoughts, my mind has often wandered to the days when as a student I haunted the laboratories of that home of science, Cambridge. And though circumstances made me part company with science, my thoughts turned to it with longing. In later years, through devious processes, I arrived again at science, when I realized that science was not only a pleasant diversion and abstraction, but was of the very texture of life, without which our modern world would vanish

[1] From *Jawaharlal Nehru on Science: Speeches Delivered at the Annual Sessions of the Indian Science Congress* (1986).

> away. Politics led me to economics and this led me inevitably to science and the scientific approach to all our problems and to life itself. It was science alone that could solve these problems of hunger and poverty, of insanitation and illiteracy, of superstition and deadening custom and tradition, of vast resources running to waste, of a rich country inhabited by starving people.

The scientific community recognized Nehru's enlightened approach and honoured him by electing him to preside over the thirty-fourth session of the Indian Science Congress (1947), when he was Vice President of the Interim Government.

The origins of organized scientific and industrial research in India are to be ascribed to the compulsions of the Second World War. The Board of Scientific and Industrial Research was established in 1940 and the Council of Scientific and Industrial Research (C.S.I.R.) in 1942. Early in 1945 the Government of India sent a deputation of scientists led by Dr S.S. Bhatnagar to visit scientific institutions in the United Kingdom, the United States of America and Canada. Simultaneously, the Government invited Professor A.V. Hill, Nobel Laureate and Secretary of the Royal Society of Great Britain, to visit India, report on the state of Indian science and make recommendations for its future organization. A comprehensive review of the scientific research activities in the universities, research institutes, government departments, defence establishments and industrial firms was carried out by the Industrial Research Planning Committee under the chairmanship of R.K. Shanmukham Chetty. The committee concluded that 'the present research activity in India does not represent even the bare minimum, whether judged by international standards or the actual requirements of the country in her present state of industrial development.' The committee made recommendations for setting up a National Research Council for the direction and control of scientific and industrial research and the establishment of research institutes in various disciplines. The Board of Scientific and Industrial Research formed 'specialized committees' to draw up plans for setting up the

National Physical and Chemical Laboratories and other research institutes. At this stage, the structuring of Indian scientific and industrial research appears to have been deeply influenced by the British institutions, scientists and the Royal Society.

In his presidential address at the thirty-fourth session of the Indian Science Congress in 1947, Nehru declared: 'We are intensely interested in scientific development in India and shall do everything in our power to encourage scientific research. We should like to tap all the scientific talent in the country and to give it opportunities for growth and service to the community.' The occasion when distinguished scientists from India and overseas were present was utilized to lay the foundation stone of India's first national laboratory, the National Physical Laboratory (4 January, 1947). Nehru observed, 'In the turmoil of the present, what seemed to me far more important and essential was laying the foundation of the great development of India.'

Commenting on the memoranda submitted to him by the Commander-in-Chief and the Defence Member, Nehru drew up a comprehensive note (3 February, 1947) outlining the role of science in defence. He wrote: 'Modern defence as well as modern industry require scientific research both on a broad basis and in highly specialized ways. Even more than before, war is controlled by the latest scientific inventions and devices.'

At this stage, it would be useful to describe briefly Nehru's contribution to various facets of the country's scientific activity.

In his speech while laying the foundation stone of the National Physical Laboratory, Nehru observed: 'What comes in the way of rapid development in India is not so much lack of money as lack of trained personnel.' Following this he drafted a note (11 February, 1947) giving his views and suggestions on 'The Need for a Scientific Manpower Committee' for circulation to members of the government. He noted that such a committee had been set up in the United Kingdom, where scientific training was much more developed and organized. He quoted Dr Homi Bhabha, who had estimated that 'about 1 per cent or less of our scientific manpower is being utilized at present, though even that is not properly organized.' Nehru considered the training of scientists and the utilization of scientific talents 'a first priority in all our schemes of development'. The Scientific Manpower Committee was set up in April 1947 and became the precursor of the National Register for Scientific and Technical Personnel, under the Council of Scientific and Industrial Research. A scientists' pool was later formed to attract Indian scientists who were abroad and provide them short-term placement on return.

In January 1945, a high-level committee had been established with Nalini Ranjan Sarkar as chairman and several Indian and British scientists, educationists, industrialists and administrators as members 'to consider the establishment of high-grade technical institutes in India, possibly on the lines of the Massachusetts Institute of Technology, to ensure an adequate supply of technical personnel to meet the demands of the administrative services and industrial development'. Post-war problems, the consequences of Partition and scarcity of resources intervened, and it was only in March 1952 that Nehru laid the foundation stone of the first of four Institutes of Technology at Kharagpur, at a site which had served as a detention camp during the Freedom Movement. Nehru declared that 'these are the bases on which New India will be built.' In 1956 he delivered the first convocation address of the institute and said that 'there was something wrong if we put up this very expensive Institute and train people and then do not utilize their services.' In March 1959, he laid the foundation stone of the second Institute of Technology in Bombay, established with the assistance of the Soviet Union and UNESCO. Pointing to the crucial importance of trained personnel, he said, 'Among the many things that are being done in India today, the establishment of these great institutes of technical training and knowledge is perhaps the most important, not only for the present, but even more so for the, future.'

As mentioned earlier, the need for a well-staffed and equipped central research organization at the outbreak of the Second World War in 1939 had resulted in the setting up of the Board of Scientific and Industrial Research (B.S.I.R.) in 1940 with Dr

S.S. Bhatnagar as Director. In 1941, the government created an Industrial Research Fund for the 'purposes of fostering industrial development in the country' with an annual grant of Rs 10 lakhs for a period of five years. The Council of Scientific and Industrial Research (C.S.I.R.) was established as a registered society to implement the objectives of the Industrial Research Fund.

In the first three or four years after its establishment, the Council was mainly engaged in problems related to war. However, plans were prepared by expert committees for the establishment of national physical and chemical laboratories and institutes for research in metallurgy, fuels, glass, roads and buildings. The funding of research in the universities and other academic institutions was undertaken through a number of committees of the Board of Scientific and Industrial Research. The Industrial Research Planning Committee under Sir R.K. Shanmukham Chetty submitted its report in 1945.

In 1944, following Professor A.V. Hill's[1] recommendations, a separate Department of Planning and Development was created under Sir Ardeshir Dalai, who had presided over the twenty-eighth session of the Indian Science Congress at Banaras in 1941. The C.S.I.R. was transferred to his portfolio. The advent of the Interim Government in September 1946 resulted in C. Rajagopalachari becoming the President of the C.S.I.R.

Nehru was aware of these developments. While laying the foundation stone of the National Physical Laboratory, he said, 'I have been watching and reading about these schemes of various types of laboratories being set up in various parts of India and have also to some extent scrutinized other vast schemes.' When the Cabinet of the first National Government was announced in August 1947, scientific research was included as a new portfolio with Prime Minister Nehru himself assuming its charge. On 23 August, 1947, at a meeting attended by several ministers, secretaries and others, Nehru discussed the future organization

[1] English physiologist, a Nobel laureate, credited as the founder of the disciplines of biophysics and operations research.

of scientific research: 'It is necessary to ensure for scientific research as much coordination and encouragement as possible. Without proper coordination, there is bound to be considerable overlapping and waste.' He concluded, 'It is conceivable that the Prime Minister could function as Chairman of the Council [C.S.I.R.], while there could be a Vice Chairman who may be concerned with its administrative functioning.' Presiding over his first meeting of the governing body of the C.S.I.R. on 25 August, 1947, he said, 'I wished to associate myself with the Council in my individual capacity since I am interested in its work, and also in my official capacity to show what importance the new government attaches to scientific development in India.'

By the middle 1950s, besides the National Physical and National Chemical Laboratories, several other central laboratories, dealing with research on electro-chemistry, fuels, glass and ceramics, instruments, electronics, engineering, marine chemicals, food, drugs, medicinal and botanical plants and leather technology had come up, as had a regional laboratory. Nehru took every opportunity to visit these laboratories, meet the younger scientists and speak to them on their role in improving the lot of India's millions. He warned scientists against any dilution in the quality of their research. He also hoped that the location of laboratories in different parts of the country would help to spread the scientific temper throughout the land.

In the sixteen years of Nehru's presidentship of the C.S.I.R., seventeen national laboratories were established. Nehru also visited, met and addressed scientists of various other research institutes such as the Indian Institute of Science, Bangalore, the Indian Statistical Institute, Calcutta, the Bose Research Institute, Calcutta, the Haffkine Institute, Bombay, and the Department of Chemical Technology, Bombay. He also associated himself with the research effort of organizations in the private industrial sector, notably the J.K. Institute of Applied Physics, Allahabad, the J.K. Institute of Radiology, Kanpur, the CIBA Research Centre, Bombay, the M.R.F. Research Centre, Madras, and the Ahmedabad Textile Industries Research Institute, Ahmedabad.

In the field of atomic energy, India owes its initiatives to Dr Homi Bhabha who, as early as 12 March, 1944 (seventeen months before the dropping of the first atom bomb at Hiroshima), sent a proposal to the trustees of the Sir Dorabji Tata Trust for the setting up of an institute of fundamental research. He wrote, 'When nuclear energy has been successfully applied for power production, in say a couple of decades from now, India will not have to look abroad for its experts but will find them ready at hand.' At his instance, in January 1946 the Board of Scientific and Industrial Research appointed an Atomic Energy Research Committee under his chairmanship.

Nehru looked at atomic energy in its future perspective and said: 'Probably in another ten or fifteen years, practical applications of atomic energy will be made. This would mean a great revolution upsetting economic theories and structures. This revolution caused by atomic energy can either destroy civilization or take it up to higher levels' (13 November, 1945). In his presidential address to the Indian Science Congress, he said, 'We shall develop it, I hope in cooperation with the rest of the world and for peaceful purposes.' Following discussions at the Science Congress he wrote to the Viceroy, Lord Wavell, and recorded a note to the Cabinet recommending state ownership of the mineral resources of India, particularly minerals bearing uranium and thorium.

In June 1947, the Government of India and the C.S.I.R. constituted a nine-member Board of Research in Atomic Energy, with Homi Bhabha as chairman, to take overall charge of planning, financing and organization of research and development in atomic energy and the control, utilization and export of related raw materials. In April 1948, Nehru placed the Atomic Energy Bill before the Constituent Assembly, which sought to give powers to the Atomic Energy Board to carry out atomic research in a non-public and secret way, coordinate research in its domain and cooperate with other countries and agencies. The Atomic Energy Commission was set up on 10 August 1948, in the Department of Scientific Research under Nehru's direct charge. In 1954, the government considered it expedient to create a separate Department of Atomic Energy directly under the Prime Minister with Homi Bhabha as Secretary.

These regulations enabled the government fully to control the exploitation and export of monazite sands from Kerala. In 1950 a company, the Indian Rare Earths Ltd., was established to separate rare earths from monazite sand and further process it to thorium and uranium salts. Nehru inaugurated the factory in 1952 and recalled his early association with the negotiations with a French concern. He announced plans for the erection of a medium-sized reactor for producing atomic energy, and said, 'The Government of India attach great importance to the development of atomic energy, because atomic energy will make a very important contribution to the world's resources of power for industrial use and social use in the future.'

In January 1957, Nehru performed the opening of the Atomic Energy Establishment at Trombay and visited the first swimming pool type reactor. He christened it Apsara and referred to the help received in the construction of the Canada-India reactor and the continuous cooperation with the atomic energy establishments of the United Kingdom, the United States and France. In 1959, he visited the Atomic Energy Establishment, the Canada-India Reactor, the Apsara and the Tata Institute of Fundamental Research. He was again there in 1960 to see the Zerlina reactor, designed, engineered and constructed by Indian engineers and was duly informed of its reaching criticality in January 1961. In 1962, the Atomic Energy Act was further amended to give the Commission and Department total responsibility for planning, research, design and development, including the erection of atomic reactors and power generation for peaceful purposes.

Addressing a conference of scientists on the development of atomic energy for peaceful purposes in November 1954, Nehru made a comprehensive survey of the international developments of atomic and hydrogen bombs. He stressed the need for state control and development of atomic energy from the angles of both investment and state policy. Greatly concerned at the misuse of atomic energy for military purposes and at the suggestion of Bertrand Russell, Nehru asked Dr D.S. Kothari to make an objective study, with the materials available, of the consequences of the use of nuclear, thermonuclear and other weapons of mass destruction. This resulted in the publication in 1957 of the book, *Nuclear Explosions and their Effects,* for which Nehru wrote a foreword.

Nehru believed that atomic energy would be the harbinger of a revolution in the social, economic and political life of the world. Laying the foundation stone of the Tata Institute of Fundamental Research on 1 January, 1954, Nehru remarked: 'We have heard of various major revolutions in human history—the American Revolution, the French, the Russian, the Chinese. These stand out. But, obviously, a far bigger revolution than all these put together was the Industrial Revolution, which changed the face of things in this world; and a big or bigger revolution may be the one brought about by gradual command over atomic or nuclear energy.'

Arising out of the work of the Atomic Energy Commission, two other developments of significance took place. At the recommendation of the Atomic Energy Commission, the Government of India set up the Electronics Committee under Homi Bhabha's chairmanship in 1963 to review the entire field of electronic components and equipment with regard to research, development and production and advise on the quickest and most economical way for national self-sufficiency in the field. Tragically, neither Nehru nor Bhabha was alive when the committee submitted its report in 1966. The other development was in regard to the setting up of an Indian National Committee for Space Research (INCOSPAR) in 1962 and the establishment of a Rocket Launching Facility at Thumba (TERLS). Both committees developed into independent commissions and departments modelled on the pattern of the Atomic Energy Commission.

While Nehru was directly in charge of the C.S.I.R. and

the Department of Atomic Energy, he was interested in the development and policy formulation of a number of other areas.

In the early 1940s, defence science activities were confined to ordnance laboratories at Kanpur and units at Calcutta, Bombay, Bangalore and Lahore, with some metallurgical research at Tatanagar. In his 26 para note to the Cabinet on defence policy (referred to earlier) Nehru dealt in detail with the role of scientific research, technical manpower, industrial strength, atomic energy and the modernization of weapons.

In February 1948, Nehru discussed with Bhabha his report on atomic energy research and wrote to the Defence Minister, then Sardar Baldev Singh: 'The future belongs to those who produce atomic energy. That is going to be the chief, noted power of the future. Of course, Defence is intimately concerned with this.' He then referred to Bhabha's suggestion of having a Scientific Adviser for the Defence Ministry. Specifically he considered it 'far better for a real first rate man to come here from time to time to advise us, together with two good men from India.' Bhabha was to be one of them. This resulted in the invitation to Professor P.M.S. Blackett to become Visiting Adviser in regard to the Defence Science Organization and the appointment of Dr D. S. Kothari as Scientific Adviser to the Defence Minister (12 July, 1948).

In April 1958, Nehru addressed scientists of the Defence Science Organization and outlined the factors that constituted the country's real defence. Opening the Second Defence Exhibition later the same year, Nehru said, 'We in India, whether on the military, naval or air side or the civilian side, have to catch up with this modern science and modern technology. There is no other hope for us.' Stressing the importance of the indigenous development of defence equipment at the Defence Production Conference (31 August, 1959), he 'regarded a country dependent on imported weapons as a second-rate country.' He again emphasized the need for self-sufficiency in his speech at the Defence Science Laboratory (13 April 1960) and said: 'It is better to produce and have a second-class weapon than to rely on a first-class weapon which you do not produce and get from outside. We cannot be up to date in science and technology by relying on outsiders who supplied us.'

The Imperial (later Indian) Council of Agricultural Research was the earliest organization of scientific research in the country. Nehru recognized agriculture as the base of India's economy. He associated himself with functions of the Indian Council of Agricultural Research and visited many of its institutes.

The areas of medicine and health claimed his special attention. Discussing the problems of health and medicine at the Health Minister's Conference, he stressed the importance of looking to public health and prevention of disease rather than to an individual's problem with health. He recalled the glorious days of the Indian systems of medicine when their influence had spread to far-away countries. Even without accepting the basic premises of the Indian systems in their entirety, it would be desirable to integrate some of the excellent remedies into the modern system, after subjecting them to scientific testing. In his address to the Association of Surgeons (30 December, 1960) he referred to the high costs of medicine and surgery which put them beyond the means of the poor and proposed the introduction of state regulation of medicine for the benefit of the community. Speaking at the silver jubilee celebrations of the Medical Council of India (13 February, 1959), he expressed concern at the falling standards in teaching and research in medicine and health. In particular, he was distressed at the resistance of doctors to serving in villages and remote hill areas. Small hospitals in villages were more important than big hospitals in a few cities and district towns. The growth of the population posed a problem for economic and social development and he felt that the medical profession should concern itself with family limitation, planned parenthood and birth control.

In his speeches at the opening ceremony of the Central Drug Research Institute, Lucknow, and at the state-owned Hindustan Antibiotics, Pimpri, he hoped that research into and production of drugs could be divorced from market exploitation. This important sphere of public interest should be state-controlled and when possible, owned by the state. His last address on the subject of health was at the second convocation of the All India Institute of Medical Sciences, New Delhi (15 April 1964). He complimented the institute on caring not so much for quantity as quality, but he went on to say, 'One thing that troubles me in spite of such fine institutes as this one, there are vast areas in this country, vast numbers in rural areas, where the benefits of modern medicine do not reach.'

Nehru was a major influence in diverse scientific and socio-scientific fields. He helped to steer their activities into the mainstream of development. In his address to the Board of Irrigation and Power, he spoke of the environmental problems of deforestation, waterlogging and flood control. He would have no hesitation in inviting the best of foreign experts to handle large irrigation and power projects rather than risk leaving them in inexperienced Indian hands. He cautioned against the growing tendency towards 'giganticism' in undertaking large projects which took time and large investments; smaller power and irrigation projects brought quicker social and economic returns.

'In his address to the Aeronautical Society, he recalled his witnessing an aeronautical exhibition in Frankfurt in 1910 and hoped that his association with the society would create a mental atmosphere in favour of newer forms of endeavour. Inaugurating an Aero-Club, he commended gliding as giving air sense to boys and girls.

Nehru gave encouragement to the Indian Standards Institutions, pioneering the introduction of decimal coinage and piloting the legislation on a metric system of weights and measures. In 1959, he moved the Indian Statistical Institute Bill in the Lok Sabha which gave the organization the status of an 'Institution of National Importance' and ensured its autonomy in functioning.

Nehru was also associated actively with the work of United Nations agencies and bodies in India such as UNESCO, W.H.O.,

ECAFE, F.A.O., UNICEF and the United Nations Atomic Energy Commission.

Nothing sums up Nehru's faith in science better than the Scientific Policy Resolution of the Government of India which was tabled in the Lok Sabha on 13 March, 1958. The resolution acknowledged the role of science and technology in national prosperity, and the social and cultural advancement of the people. Through the resolution, the government undertook 'to foster, promote and sustain, by all appropriate means, the cultivation of science and scientific research in all its aspects—pure, applied and educational; to ensure that the creative talent of men and women is encouraged and finds full scope in scientific activity; and in general to secure for the people of the country all the benefits that can accrue from the acquisition and application of scientific knowledge.' To implement the policy, Nehru appointed a Scientific Advisory Committee to the Cabinet. It is a measure of the support and encouragement to science and technology provided by the government under Nehru that the expenditure on scientific research and science based activities increased from Rs 1.10 crores in 1948–9 to Rs 85.06 crores in 1965–6. The stock of scientific and technical personnel rose fourfold, from 188,000 in 1950 to 731,500 in 1965.

In the chapter entitled 'Religion, Philosophy and Science' in *The Discovery of India,* Nehru wrote, 'The scientific approach and temper are, or should be, a way of life, a process of thinking, a method of acting and associating with one's fellow men.' He was critical of scientists 'who swear by science, but forget all about it outside their particular spheres.' At the opening of the National Physical Laboratory in 1950, he advised scientists to 'think of science as a method or approach to life and life's problems in general'. Addressing the Conference of Scientists and Educationists in August 1962, Nehru remarked: 'So far as we are concerned, we are definitely committed both by our general planning approach and more particularly by what we have said about science to encouraging science and technology—encouraging it not only in its various technical fields but in all that lies behind it, the scientific temper, the scientific approach to life's problems. Unless we function more and more according to the scientific temper, the advance we make may not be wholly good, because science is not merely training to do a job but a training to think in a particular way.'

As Prime Minister, Nehru made it a point to inaugurate and participate in the annual sessions of the Indian Science Congress. The only exceptions were in 1948, 1961 and 1964. Other scientific institutions also received his encouragement. In his speech while laying the foundation stone for the National Institute of Sciences (19 April 1948) he observed: 'There is no other way except the way of science ultimately for the development of human life and institutions. This is the scientific approach to life's problems.' Addressing the anniversary meeting of the same institute on 20 January, 1959, Nehru asked scientists to think in terms of humanity, as 'we are still producing not very desirable human beings.' Speaking at a meeting of the organization in 1962, after the Chinese aggression against India, he said: 'Science has given so much power... that war today is simple folly. It does not even seek to solve the question we have to face, when we can get everything that we want through peaceful methods.' Nehru appreciated the role of working scientists in helping the advancement of science and was elected the first President of the Association of Scientific Workers of India. He addressed their annual general meetings during the sessions of the Indian Science Congress.

Besides maintaining close personal contact with top Indian scientists, he took every opportunity during his journeys abroad to visit scientific institutions and meet scientists. Among eminent scientists with whom he had a close relationship were Albert Einstein, Bertrand Russell, Henry Dale, Alexander Fleming, A.V. Hill, Frederic Joliot-Curie, Niels Bohr, J.D. Bernal, J.B.S. Haldane and P.M.S. Blackett.

This article cannot be better ended than by recalling a portion of Nehru's address to the 1955 session of the Indian Science Congress. 'I myself, am not bound by dogmas and am always prepared to admit my mistakes and rectify them. I believe that such an approach is nearer to what may be called the scientific approach, and in that sense I consider myself having a scientific temperament, although I cannot claim to be a scientist.'

~

Nehru, Press and Parliament

Nikhil Chakravartty[2]

Nikhil Chakravartty (1913–1998) was an important journalist in post-Independence India. In 1959, he set up the India Press Agency and immediately broke the story on the espionage activities of the then Prime Minister's personal assistant, M.O. Mathai. He was also the founder-editor of the respected current affairs weekly Mainstream *and fought for press freedom and against Rajiv Gandhi's Anti-Defamation Bill between 1975–77. In the following essay Chakravartty recalls how Nehru considered the Fourth Estate as a 'partner in nation-building', and was committed to the freedom of the Press. He held regular press conferences 'where questions were answered readily and with informality, creating a bond of friendly understanding between head of the executive and members of the Press.'*

~

It is a forbidding task to write about Jawaharlal Nehru. Millions have seen and heard him. In his eventful lifespan he wrote millions of words and spoke many more millions. Twenty-five years have elapsed since his death and yet he is remembered even by those who have never seen him. In fact, with the passing of years, Jawaharlal Nehru emerges as even more significant and more relevant for our time. When a mountain recedes into the distance, its majesty comes out in full measure.

In his lifetime, Nehru had many critics, but he faced them always with dignity and never with any rancour. His life was one of intense political involvement. Most of the time he was the principal actor on the political scene. But there was never an occasion

[2] From *Jawaharlal Nehru: Centenary Volume.*

when he maligned or abused an opponent within his party or an adversary outside. He might have had many failings, but nobody, not even his bitterest critic, could accuse him of pettiness.

What is of supreme importance to note is that all his actions and policies were guided by an independent understanding of the forces at work in the world around him. Over the years he had painstakingly cultivated an understanding of the interplay of world forces. In this endeavour, Nehru always tried to take a holistic, long-term view and sought to relate it to day-to-day developments. In this attempt at integration, the input did not consist only of mere political events and calculations but included developments in science, philosophy and social change.

For him, politics was never the mundane practice of the power game: it had a wider connotation, as he always took into account the urges and interests of the broad mass of humanity both at home and the world over. Hence his constant endeavour to keep in view the moral dimension of politics instead of regarding power as an end in itself. From this angle, he never hesitated to acknowledge his own shortcomings.

While he could legitimately claim that through planning his government was laying the foundations of industrialization, thereby creating the wherewithal for India emerging as a modern state, capable of defending its hard-earned independence,

> **Nehru was conscious, till the end, that the economic development that took place under his guidance had not eliminated the scourge of poverty for millions, nor overcome the widening gap of disparity between the affluent and the underprivileged. Not once did he indulge in any slogan-mongering to obscure the realities.**

Nehru was a great communicator in the best sense of the term. All true democrats have to be. One of the most significant features of our Freedom Struggle was that it was essentially based on awakening the consciousness of the millions. We did not, in the final analysis, win our freedom by engineering a military coup or by seeking the help of any foreign agency, but by instilling into our unarmed masses the consciousness that they must shed all fear of the foreign power and recognize that the Raj could be ended by the united strength of the Indian people. To bring about this consciousness, the leadership of our national struggle adopted some of the most imaginative techniques of mass communication. By making the people realize that foreign rule rested on fear, and freedom from fear would lead to freedom from foreign rule, the national leadership built up an invincible strength. The imperial power was itself overpowered as mass consciousness moved to a higher and higher level.

It was no accident that some of our foremost leaders were editors of journals. Tilak edited *Kesari,* Mahatma Gandhi edited *Young India* and *Harijan,* and Nehru edited *Independent* and later founded *The National Herald.* Many other leaders put forward their points of view through newspapers. The Press in those days was an important auxiliary force of the Freedom Struggle. This led to the growth of partisanship in journals—an attitude of 'My country right or wrong'—but it also ensured deep national commitment on the part of those who worked in newspapers.

This tradition of regarding the Press as a respected ally in the Freedom Struggle was sought to be maintained after Independence. It was, however, difficult to do so, because circumstances changed: the transfer of ownership of British-owned newspapers to Indian hands took place while the tradition of national service was fast fading out in the afterglow of Independence.

Nehru tried his best to sustain that tradition even under the altered conditions.

Those who had the privilege of watching Jawaharlal Nehru as Prime Minister—as I did for over a decade before Nehru passed away—can relate many instances of his unfailing care and consideration in treating the Fourth Estate as a partner in nation-building; and also his commitment to the freedom of the Press as an essential component of our democracy. For Nehru, this was the continuation of the tradition of our Freedom Struggle, and not just a manifestation of Anglo-Saxon liberalism.

Nehru's Press conferences, held with religious regularity, developed into a truly great institution of our democracy. They were always a memorable experience. The questions were answered readily and with informality, creating a bond of friendly understanding between head of the executive and members of the Press. Issues demanding serious attention to governmental policies were handled with precision and without equivocation. The occasional quick repartee to a pompous question was heartily enjoyed by all. There never was a barrier between the government on the one side and the Press on the other, as one notices very often nowadays. Rather, it always turned out to be the most fruitful interaction, evoking mutual respect. Behind it all one could discern Nehru's anxiety to maintain and develop a close rapport between the political leadership and the Press, which he cherished as one of the proud legacies of the Freedom Struggle.

Journalists who served during the years of Nehru's stewardship had no two opinions about his commitment to the freedom of the Press. Even those in the Press who were the severest critics of his policies, internal or foreign, ungrudgingly acknowledged this commitment of his. And as the lights went out in some of our neighbouring countries, we could understand all the more poignantly the strength of that commitment. In the very year when the Constitution was promulgated, 1950, Jawaharlal Nehru, in an address to the All India Newspaper Editors' Conference in New Delhi, presented what might rightly be called his credo on the subject:

> To my mind, the freedom of the Press is not just a slogan from the larger point of view, but it is an essential attribute of the democratic process. I have no doubt that even if the Government dislikes the liberties taken by the Press and considers them dangerous, it is wrong to interfere with the freedom of the Press. By imposing restrictions you do not change anything; you merely suppress the public manifestation of certain things,

> thereby causing the idea and thought underlying them to spread further. Therefore, I would rather have a completely free Press with all the dangers involved in the wrong use of that freedom than a suppressed or regulated press.

Four years later, addressing the same organization, he declared: 'I do not wish to come in the way, legislatively or otherwise, of the widest criticism or even condemnation of governmental policy.' In the twenty-five years since Nehru's death, no leader of government has ventured to give such a categoric pledge.

When a leader makes such a commitment, the community of journalists should have no hesitation in accepting from him the injunction to undertake corresponding obligations as well. It was only because Nehru offered such an unequivocal guarantee of Press freedom that the journalists of India never questioned his admonitions. In his 1954 speech to the All India Newspaper Editors' Conference, Nehru asserted, 'So far as I am concerned I am prepared to lose every election in India but to give no quarter to communalism or casteism.' And he exhorted the Press to join him in the crusade against communalism. The words he used were not flamboyant but direct and deeply felt: 'We have our evil side and our good side. But I am quite sure that there is a very great deal of the good side in the Indian people, and if we appeal to it we shall always get the right response. If our newspapers keep this in view and appeal to the good side, they will help in the emotional integration of India. They will thus do a great service. Let us think not only of our past common heritage, but of the India that we are building up which will also be a common heritage of all of us. I would submit to the editors that through this service to the people they will ultimately be serving themselves also.'

Not only in his denunciation of casteism and communalism, but in his detestation of vulgarity he was equally emphatic:

'I have often wondered whether freedom of expression implies all kinds of vulgar and obscene approaches. My idea of freedom does not include them. Degradation of public taste is terrible. We have to oppose it.'

Jawaharlal Nehru was never condescending towards media practitioners, as he tried to carry forward the bond that had been forged during the Freedom Struggle between the political leadership and the Press. It was a common identity between peers. He never spoke to journalists from a high pedestal, but he had a remarkable way of showing up their vulnerability. Here is a devastating passage: 'To some extent, politicians and newspapermen or journalists have much in common. Both presume to talk too much, write too much, and deliver homilies; both require no qualifications at all for their jobs!' The politician and the newspaperman, if he has the gift of expression, get going. Whether there is any content behind that expression is totally immaterial. No political leader could more effectively divest the journalist of his conceit.

Time and again Jawaharlal Nehru spoke of the need to pause, ponder and think. In 1952 he said: 'Normally a politician or a newspaperman has few lucid moments, because he functions from day to day, hour to hour, and minute to minute. He does not have the time to think. That is the fault of our present-day civilization. Not only newspapermen and politicians but others too are gradually being drawn into the whirlpool of incessant activity without thinking.' He comes back to the same theme a couple of years later: 'Of the dominating features of the age we live in, one of the most noticeable is that people are gradually losing the art of thinking. They often take other people's opinion for granted. They are regimented, not only in states that are called totalitarian but in other countries also, by the conditions they live in. They are not allowed to think, and the person who does not fit in with the majority opinion has a very unfortunate time of it. There is no law against him, but the facts are against him. In this matter the newspapers can perform a very valuable service, although newspapers too inevitably have become more like pocket digests than something that will enable people to think.'

It is not difficult to guess how Nehru would have felt about present-day television—a readymade capsule of 'quickies' for men and women in a hurry to gulp down.

Nehru's capacity to share thoughts, instead of delivering homilies from the pulpit, brought out the greatness of the man. He never lectured, he explained. The letters which he wrote to Chief Ministers every fortnight, almost without interruption up to 1960, constituted a unique experiment at political education through correspondence, covering all the major topics of the day, national and international. Their tone was never that of hectoring leader, but was marked by an implicit informality—a style which has become virtually extinct in our political life today.

Not only in his dealings with the Press, but in other spheres of democratic activity also, Jawaharlal Nehru went out of his way to establish enduring conventions. One such institution was Parliament. The Opposition in his time was smaller in number than today, and yet Nehru had the wisdom and foresight to provide it with more opportunities of expression than its numerical strength would warrant. For he realized that no democracy in our country, with its multidimensional problems, would succeed without the willing consent of all. It was not brute majority but genuine consensus that could make democracy a functioning reality in this country.

When I came to Delhi thirty-seven years ago, it was a proud privilege to watch the proceedings of the two Houses from the Press gallery. Down below, one would see a fairly large number of members even if the debate was on some unimportant subject. At every major debate the House was nearly full. What was equally worth noting was that Jawaharlal Nehru, as Leader of the House, was almost always present in the House. Sometimes attending to his files, but certainly listening to the ongoing debate. Rarely would the Leader of the Opposition speak without Nehru himself being present.

Under Nehru, senior party leaders kept an eye on the performance of newcomers, spotting talent and enabling them to rise in the parliamentary hierarchy. And on the Treasury Benches, a promising newcomer making a hit as a competent parliamentarian would find himself or herself being considered for a ministerial berth. I distinctly remember an occasion when such talent-spotting took place before our very eyes. It was one of those lean days when the budget demand of the Ministry of Irrigation was being discussed. An independent member, rather nondescript, was speaking. It was a thin house. But within a few minutes Prime Minister Nehru got up and requested the Speaker to grant more time to the member who was on his feet. By the time the member sat down, after having had his full say, I told a colleague in the Press gallery that this Member of Parliament would soon be made a minister. My colleague dismissed the idea. At the next reshuffle a few weeks later, the Member of Parliament did indeed become the Minister in charge of irrigation. He was Dr K.L. Rao, the distinguished engineer.

Nehru went out of his way to reiterate that the basis of parliamentary functioning was mutual respect among members. They might belong to different parties, but within the precincts of Parliament, each and every member carried the same status and was entitled to the same courtesy. There was no such thing as a ruling party member commanding higher status than one not belonging to that party. So far as the dignity of the House and the exercise of mutual respect were concerned, Nehru set the model as Leader of the House. With him present, abuse and name-calling were unthinkable. No Member of Parliament could be called a liar, as happened recently in the Lok Sabha.

Never a pontiff but a persuader, Nehru sought interaction even in his dealings with the masses. His capacity to listen was as remarkable as his eloquence. The well-known expert on mass communication, Wilbur Schramm, describes his encounter with Nehru thus: 'This was on an afternoon and he was relaxed, happy. He said, "By the way, what is this mass communication? I do not think I understand it very well." And I said, "But, Mr Prime Minister, you are the chief mass communicator of India." I mentioned the crowds of hundreds of thousands, the books and the broadcasts. He threw back his head and laughed.

“Oh, that!” he said. “I guess I do know something about it.” He poked fun at the electronic system, the loudspeakers that would not work or go out before half of his long speeches were over. Then he said something that I never forgot. He said, “This will help us to talk together.” And I will remember it all my life—This will help us to *talk together.*’

~

The Nehru Legacy in Planning

Sukhamoy Chakravarty[3]

Sukhamoy Chakravarty (1934–1990) was an Indian economist who, along with Prasanta Chandra Mahalanobis, was a key architect of the Five-Year plans of India. In the following essay Chakravarty outlines Nehru's commitment to democratic planning, i.e. recognizing the complimentary roles of the state and the private sector in bringing economic growth for all.

~

On the occasion of the Nehru centenary, I should like to address myself to defining the nature of the Nehru legacy in planning, especially in the context of problems currently facing our country.

Planning is not the most favoured word today as it was four decades ago. The market is supposed to unleash human productive potential. It has been argued repeatedly in recent years that planning is synonymous with *etatism* and that it stifles initiative. ‘Take the state off our backs’ is the cry of powerful sections of neoconservatives in the West. To a lesser extent, the same voice is heard in India. While a deep-seated sense of respect still prevents people from attributing all the deficiencies of the actual experience of Indian planning to Nehru's design, there is no doubt that, if pressed, Nehru will not escape criticism in this area.

---

[3] From *Jawaharlal Nehru: Centenary Volume.*

It is a fact, however, that Nehru's adoption of a planned pattern of economic and social development for India was deep and pervasive. But it was not based on a doctrinaire philosophy of history. What he understood by a planned economy was a regime where things could be made to happen through foresight, goodwill and cooperation. In contrast, in a market economy things just happen. It may be that sometimes in a market economy, things go very well indeed but then there come large periods when things stagnate and misery grows.

This is the law of alternation of 'good times' with 'bad', of 'boom' and 'bust', which economists have not been able to comprehend fully as yet.

Nehru was not a professional economist but he had read history and had read it with great interest as his remarkable book, *Glimpses of World History*, shows. He was well aware that nineteenth century capitalism had unleashed vast productive forces, but he was also aware that it had caused massive dislocation in the accepted ways of life along with considerable suffering imposed on labouring men.

He was impressed by the Russian Revolution as opening a new phase in human history. He visited the Union of Soviet Socialist Republics in the late 1920s and wrote a series of articles, most of which were published in *The Hindu* during April and May 1928. These were later republished in book form. He felt that there were very important lessons to be drawn from the Soviet experience for structurally backward countries when they try to develop.

His admiration for certain aspects of Soviet economic development notwithstanding, it would be inaccurate to attribute this influence alone as the major intellectual reason behind his opting for planning. It may be recalled that there were certain aspects of Nehru's economic approach which can be traced back to Ranade and to the example that had been furnished in the then State of Mysore by M. Visvesvaraya, who had deep affinity for Ranade's thinking.

Furthermore, there was the role of Gandhiji's ideas which Nehru could not accept but it was not something that he could reject either. Deep empathy for the way an Indian peasant feels, so characteristic of Gandhiji's thought, was not part of Nehru's intuitive feelings. But a broad egalitarian approach, where peasants would not be excluded from the results of the growth process, was part of Nehru's approach to planning. He never dreamt of 'squeezing the peasant' as the indispensable basis for India's industrialization, which he undoubtedly believed to be the key to the long-term growth and stability of the Indian economy, including agriculture.

Despite favouring private initiative in many areas such as agriculture, science, etc., it is also clear that at no stage of his life did Nehru adopt a free market philosophy of economics and politics. His commitment to planning as a rational mode of conflict resolution remained with him till the last days of his life.

Nehru defined his strategy of planned development as a judicious mixture of two types of institutional motive force: public and private. He recognized the crucial role that the state had to play in formulating a programme of structural transformation of our society. But he never displayed a liking for 'statism' as such. Hence, his repeated emphasis that planning must be carried out in a democratic environment. It may be recalled that the first five-year plan was launched after India had adopted in its Constitution a system of governance based on universal adult suffrage, a bold decision as seen by many of his countrymen, which owes a lot to Nehru's commitment to democracy.

Nehru's commitment to planning went a long way beyond the mere articulation of a broad philosophy. Democratic economic planning in a backward economy certainly raises many paradoxes. Sometimes, over-impressed by these paradoxes, learned scholars have denounced it as a sheer impossibility and have recommended authoritarian modes of government to facilitate the task of so-called primary accumulation. Even those who have otherwise differed in proposing a 'basic needs' approach have not always denounced authoritarianism. Nehru never thought along these lines and was willing to put up with some of the slowness which our democratic system displays because, like Gandhiji, he believed that ends and means cannot be dissociated. Nehru was well aware that there were major problems which were involved in such an ambitious undertaking. Hence, he approached the Indian intelligentsia as well as like-minded scholars abroad for suggestions and clarifications. He found some resonance to his ideas in P.C. Mahalanobis, V.K.R.V. Rao and Homi Bhabha among others.

The strategy of overall development which Nehru worked with the help of Mahalanobis was a major exercise in terms of scope and conceptual articulation. I have discussed it at some length in my recent book, *Development Planning: The Indian Experience.* This exercise, of which the *Draft Second Five-Year Plan* is possibly the most concrete embodiment, gave the overall frame for investment allocation, while Bhabha concentrated on building up a modern scientific base to which Nehru attached great importance. As stated already, Nehru was of the opinion that without industrialization, India's age-old backwardness could not be removed.

Was Nehru right in this perception? In some basic sense the answer is 'yes'. His adoption of a heavy-industry oriented model of industrialization in the second five-year plan was criticized by many economists who believed in the 'textiles first' strategy for a backward country. They have criticized him for ignoring export possibilities. I cannot accept the indictments they have passed with such confidence. I believe that, given our resource endowments of coal and iron ore, and industrial experience in steel-making in Mysore State and more notably represented by the Tatas, steel was an appropriate sector for India to develop during the late 1950s. Primary product exports had limited prospects, then and now. The Nehru-Mahalanobis strategy envisaged export substitution through initial investment in steel and subsequent growth in engineering exports. It is unfortunate that this transition has not yet taken place. But then one should look carefully into our record of implementation, which involves unconscionable delays as well as failure to carry out modernization in proper time.

Looking back over the entire period of 1950-65, I cannot,

however, help feeling that agriculture was somewhat neglected not by intention but because of the acceptance of certain facile assumptions. Institutional changes were supposed to bring about profound changes in agriculture without checking carefully whether such changes were in fact taking place at all at the grassroots level. While the first phase of land reform was carried out, the second and more important phase of 'land to the tillers' was left unfulfilled, which was part of the Congress approach to the problem for land reform. When, subsequently, technological changes were introduced to boost lagging agricultural production, the gains were accordingly very unequally appropriated by different regions and by the social strata. Nehru, it should be recalled, attached great importance to the restructuring of agrarian relationships, as he was well aware of the conditions prevailing in Uttar Pradesh, a predominantly zamindari area. Why, then, did he not push decisively in this direction? Thus, to me, it appears as a major default which has led to a more difficult situation, especially because of changed demographic conditions. Perhaps historians can throw more light on this. Despite this basic limitation, the first three five-year plans broke the grip of stagnation on Indian economy and society. It is also possible to maintain that, but for adverse international developments, the trajectory of growth chalked out by the three plans could have done much to transform the quality of our life. As things turned out, however, adverse external developments during the mid-1960s after Nehru's passing away brought about a change in intellectual outlook along with a strengthening of certain vested interests.

Deficiencies in regard to production have continued side by side with less than appropriate distribution of the benefits of such development as has taken place. The logic of planning in a mixed economy in the earlier stages of development required a much greater degree of discipline, both in terms of restraints on consumption, especially conspicuous consumption, and in terms of the efficiency of directing investment flows into sectors such as wage goods sectors. The organizational framework devised to deal with problems of growth accompanied by a better distribution of incomes has turned out to be extremely inadequate in relation to our needs. While public investment has played an important part in stepping up production in many areas as well as in maintaining a buoyant level of demand, the role of the public sector has not been that of a commanding height as Nehru had originally envisaged. A major issue of contemporary development is how best to activate and mobilize resources through better management of our public enterprises.

I do not share the belief that 'privatization' of existing public assets is our answer to the resource problem; nor do I believe that the public sector is the principal instrument of resource mobilization. After all, the public sector in an economy such as ours has also a very important role to play in spearheading technical change. Without utilizing modern science and technology in productivity of overall resource use, we shall not be able to overcome the lagging productivity growth which our economy demonstrates. The public sector has a very major potential in this respect, but our signalling mechanisms are extremely deficient.

There is no doubt that as a result of nearly four decades of planning, the country has registered significant progress in industrial diversification, increased levels of agricultural production due to the initiative taken by Shri C. Subramaniam and others, and a higher skill composition of the working population. But it is also unfortunately quite evident that these benefits of the growth process have been unevenly spread. If we try to analyse the reasons for these deficiencies, we are ultimately led to the conclusion that we have made many political compromises which go against the logic of development. We have also not resisted in recent years the growth of the consumerist subculture which ill suits a country with so much unemployment and under-employment. In other words, we have failed to mobilize enough resources, human and material, to cope with our pressing problems and relied increasingly on softerzz options.

In recent years, many observers have discerned a shift away from the strategy of self-reliant growth. Is this an optical illusion or is there a substantive reality behind it? If it is the latter, it would appear that Nehru's policy is being altered in a significant way. Our balance of payments is currently under considerable pressure, a fact not unknown to the general public. Our debt-service ratio which used to be very modest, is now pretty high and rising. The number of foreign collaboration agreements has been increasing fast. All this would suggest a shift. But there are two compensating considerations which must be carefully evaluated before we can come to a conclusion as to whether the Nehruvian strategy has been altered. First, if recent attempts at opening up the economy are aimed at inducting new technology which will strengthen the growth of our productive forces, departure from the Nehruvian path may be less than what it appears at first sight. However, if they are aimed at modernization of consumption at a faster rate rather than modernization of production of basic commodities, such a departure would indeed have occurred. Further, if foreign borrowing is being resorted to to meet a budgetary gap in rupee terms, there would appear to be a serious default on the resource mobilization front. Current debates in the country should be increasingly focused on these critical issues, because if true and unchecked, they would imply serious distortions in our economy and polity.

It is difficult to deny that the process of resource mobilization for equitable development in a society such as ours is a very difficult one. But it does not follow that it is therefore any less pressing. Indeed, it is no exaggeration to say that we shall only be compounding our own difficulties by not taking the right decision right now. Here clearly the need to raise the domestic savings rate, especially public savings, is a pressing problem and so is the need to finance it on an equitable basis. Nehru was acutely conscious of the need for speedy development and the advantages of an equitable distribution of incomes and assets for maintaining a socio-political environment where the legitimacy of government will be beyond question. His concern for legitimacy was so great that he never believed in a mere technocratic solution to our problems even though he firmly believed, as we have noted, that science and technology had a lot to offer us in ensuring a better future.

India today is in many ways a very different place from what it was when the planning process was initiated. So is the contemporary world. We have achieved significant success, but there is a lot that remains undone. Has planning lost out in importance compared with a market economy for India when there is a strong trend in some parts of the world to get away from planning? I do not think so. It is, however, clear that the current trend makes it essential for India to be far more innovative in forging new links and relationships, but this by itself does not negate the case for planning. This is because India is a large and varied country, with a dense and fast-growing population, no longer terribly well endowed with natural resources which are greatly in world demand. The amount of rent that we can extract from the rest of the world because of specific factor endowments is very limited. That implies that we have to manage our internal resources now efficiently, not only in a myopic sense, but also in terms of a long-term sustainable rate of development, taking the ecological pressures into account.

Planning today implies above all three things: to make adequate provision for the future, the yet unborn generations; to take better care of the poorer sections of our society, including lagging regions, especially in eastern and central India; and to help facilitate much greater induction of socially relevant technology. None of these is likely to be done by a market system. At least, there is nothing in economic theory or economic history, including the recent history of east Asia, which would suggest otherwise.

This may well require that our planning may have to be far more strategic in character, also more decentralized in some respects, and more efficient in terms of designs for implementation.

All this would, of course, require far greater attention to be paid to the development of our human skill base, the ability to cope with newly emerging situations and to a change in attitude regarding work norms. But a broad sense of a social concern which transcends a mere acquisitive mentality that a narrow reliance on the market mechanism fosters has to be generated.

After all, planning requires a broad measure of public consensus. It is in forging a new consensus that the planning process has a very important role to play.

Nehru's legacy in planning is very valuable because he viewed planning as a societal response, modulated through our historic experience of both colonial subjugation and a long feudal past.

This is a legacy which we will do well to preserve and deepen in the context of the closing decade of the twentieth century.

~

Growing Up in the Nehru Era

Kartar Singh Duggal[4]

Kartar Singh Duggal (1917–2012) was an Indian writer who wrote in Punjabi, Urdu, Hindi, and English. He served as the director of All India Radio, and was awarded the Padma Bhushan in 1988 and the Sahitya Akademi Fellowship in 2007. In the following essay he recalls the consummate statesmanship of Nehru, how he deeply cared for his countrymen and was pained to see crowds resorting to physical violence. In a particularly startling incident, Duggal recalls how, in the wake of the Partition, Nehru physically grappled with rioters looting shops near Connaught Place, eventually supplying the police forces with courage to overpower the mob.

~

Let me first recapitulate some of the glimpses of Pandit Jawaharlal Nehru indelibly etched on my memory.

His autobiography had just been published. Given my fondness for Panditji, I acquired a copy first thing, retired to a secluded corner and started reading it; skipping even my meals,

[4] From *Jawaharlal Nehru: Centenary Volume.*

I was absorbed in it till late in the evening. It was the same story the next day and then another day until I had read the book from cover to cover. It was like reading the scriptures.

The Congress had decided to participate in the provincial elections as provided in the India Act of 1935. Jawaharlal undertook a whirlwind tour of the country. During his visit to Rawalpindi, he was to address a public meeting in the Municipal Gardens. The arrangements for his reception were to be seen to be believed. The roads were swept, the streets were scrubbed, festive arches were erected, and banners and bunting fluttered all over the route. The city folk made a beeline for the venue of the rally: Hindus, Muslims and Sikhs. The villagers trudged miles and miles on foot or trekked on ponies or bullock carts. The Municipal Gardens swarmed with a mass of humanity. It was time for him to arrive, but Jawaharlal was nowhere. Then came word that his plane was late. But the people had to hear him. They wouldn't budge an inch. They waited and waited until eventually his plane was sighted in the blue sky. The crowds started shouting: *'Inquilab Zindabad, Bharat Mata Ki Jai, Jawaharlal Nehru Zindabad!'* The slogan-shouting and singing of patriotic songs continued until Panditji's motorcade arrived on the scene. The moment the people had a glimpse of their beloved leader, they surged in a frenzy towards him in a massive wave. It was a herculean task hewing a path for him to the dais. As he appeared on the stage, the slogan-shouting started again, rending the sky. It went on and on. And then Panditji raised his arms. As if a curtain had dropped, there was pin drop silence all over. Not a bird fluttered. That was Nehru's magic.

When, in the course of his speech, he made an appeal for funds, the audience vied with one another showering stacks of currency notes and bags of coins on the stage. The womenfolk would not be left behind. They pulled out their ornaments, rings, bangles, lockets and necklaces and piled them at his feet. The dais was literally littered with offerings. And all this happened at a stone's throw from the biggest imperial cantonment in British India.

When Independence came, it brought its own problems in its trail.

The most immediate was the communal flare-up. Both sides of the border with Pakistan were riven with strife. There was rioting in Noakhali, Punjab and Bihar and then it travelled to Delhi. One evening, having finished my work in Broadcasting House, I decided to walk back home. As I reached the Regal Building on Parliament Street, I was stopped. Across the park, the rioters were shouting slogans, breaking open the shops and ransacking them. The police watched as helpless spectators; at best they stopped traffic at various lanes leading to Connaught Place. Stranded, I didn't know how long I was going to witness this unsavoury spectacle, when suddenly the continuous whistling of an escort vehicle was heard, followed by a car. It was the Prime Minister. The moment he arrived, Panditji started grappling with the rioters. He would slap one and shout at another. He snatched back stolen property and restored it to the shops. Seeing the Prime Minister on the spot, the police, too, went into action. Soon the rioters were overpowered. Then Panditji climbed onto the hood of a car parked nearby and started admonishing the rowdy elements. 'The eyes of the whole world are on you,' he said, 'you should know what you are doing…'

No less formidable was the task of rehabilitating millions of refugees who had been hounded out of their hearths and homes from across the border. Shelterless and jobless, they swarmed into the refugee camps dotted all over the border in the east and the west.

I remember a meeting Panditji came to address at Ferozepur, a town in Punjab, in 1948. Not fewer than four lakh people had turned up to hear him. They had come from remote towns and from villages on the border where they lived under the shadow of aggression. They all came to have a glimpse of their leader who had got for them their country's freedom. Halfway through his speech, some people turned up with a flag and started shouting anti-establishment slogans. Panditji asked them to sit down and not disturb the meeting. They did not pay heed. The next time they raised a slogan, the audience was enraged and there was a scuffle. Panditji was frantically asking them to sit down and listen to him. The agitators, however, seemed to be bent on making trouble. At this, the police began wielding their lathis. His countrymen being beaten up with sticks in front of him was not a sight Panditji relished. He ordered the police to stop the lathi charge and withdraw. Now the agitators tried to avenge themselves on the police and trouble flared up once again. Panditji roared at the police. It pained him to see the people being beaten up and manhandled. He tried to reach the spot, but was held back physically by a senior police official. And then there was firing. Utter chaos prevailed. Nehru shouted at the top of his voice. It is said that more than one person had lost his life in the scuffle. And within a few minutes the rowdy elements were overpowered. A miracle was performed. Panditji made that large audience of four lakh people sit down again and listen to him. He started by narrating to them a fable and then at a convenient point when the audience had calmed down and was completely settled, he picked up the thread of his speech. And the address went on for not less than an hour.

No less irksome was the impatience of the enthusiasts of Hindi to have it adopted as the official language. They had the support of political stalwarts. They were most overbearing in the Ministry of Information and Broadcasting which was under Sardar Patel's charge. The complexion of broadcast language underwent a severe change. The arrogance of the newly appointed Hindi producers was such that they would reject or rewrite good enough broadcast scripts and make them unintelligible to the common listener. Panditji had to broadcast on some occasion. The Prime Minister's Office asked us to prepare a Hindi version of his English speech sent to us in advance. The responsibility for translation of the Prime Minister's speech was entrusted to the seniormost Hindi expert on the staff. After the Prime Minister had recorded his talk in English, the Hindi version was placed before him. Panditji had hardly read the first paragraph when he flared up, 'Yeh kaunsi zaban hai?' (What language is this?). Saying this, he threw the script away and placing the original in English before him, he started recording the Hindi version.

As a broadcaster, my most unforgettable experience of covering the Prime Minister was in 1958 when Panditji visited Jabalpur. I was then in charge of the Bhopal station of All India Radio. Jabalpur being in my jurisdiction, I decided to lead the A.I.R. team, more out of my devotion for Panditji than anything else. The Prime Minister participated in not fewer than six functions in one day, including the launching of MAN, a vehicle manufactured for the defence forces with foreign collaboration.

The last function of the day was the inauguration of a maternity and child welfare home named after Kamala Nehru. It was already late in the evening. Panditji was unduly delayed. It was his sixth public function that A.I.R. was covering. I was sitting close to the dais. As he arrived, Panditji did away with all the formalities and went straight to the microphone. For a moment, it seemed that he had forgotten what function he was participating in. He asked the organizers what it was about in a whisper. When he was told that it was the Kamala Nehru Maternity & Child Welfare Centre, a tender memory seemed suddenly to have overtaken him. He appeared to have switched back several decades. He stood speechless for a while and then with misty eyes came down the dais without uttering a word. The inauguration ceremony was over.

On 27 May, 1964, I was busy working in my office in Akashvani Bhawan on the fourth floor when a colleague came and said, 'He is sinking, Prime Minister Nehru.' And then he added, 'Maybe he has already gone.' The pen dropped from my hand as I heard it. Speechless, I came out of my room and walked up to the staircase landing from where one could see the national flag hoisted on Parliament House. The flag was still there, fluttering as usual. Gazing at the flag, I started composing these verses in Punjabi:

Don't you die,
Let me die instead,
Don't you die.

Don't you die,
She can die instead,
Don't you die.

Don't you die,
They can die instead,
Don't you die.

Don't you die,
At what price can one buy your life?
Don't you die.

Don't you die,
How long is it since Ramu came to live with us?
Don't you die."

As the last line was on my lips, I found the national flag being lowered over Parliament House.

Panditji had an ineffable charm that worked on the youth of my generation. And he possessed it most unmistakably until his passing away.

I have written a great deal—novels and short stories, poetry and plays, literary essays and criticism, and won considerable acclaim. But I believe that my best writing is my autobiography entitled *Kis Peh Khohlon Ganthri*. And I must acknowledge that I conceived it on the pattern of Jawaharlal's autobiography. It is more the story of my times than the story of my person.

Nehru belonged to the people. And he went to them again and again. They were his tonic. The dead stone walls of Delhi could not imprison him.

He was back among the people every time he had an opportunity. He has said: 'I go out and see masses of people, my people, your people and derive inspiration from them. There is something dynamic and something growing within them, and I grow with them.' After the setback he suffered in Bhubaneswar, all sorts of stories became current about his health, especially in the foreign press. K.A. Abbas met Panditji and suggested that he should appear on television a couple of times during a month. It would be reassuring, he thought. 'In that case,' reacted Panditji spontaneously, 'Why can't I address one or two public meetings every month?' The people indeed invigorated him.

And yet it was not that Nehru never had a hostile audience. There were occasions when odd splinter groups came prepared to interrupt and disrupt his meetings and cause confusion. Many a time, he walked into the camp of his staunchest critics and seldom failed to win them over with the fire of his courage, the transparency of his heart, his deep humanism, his sense of fair play and his dedication to democratic ways. He was the most handsome man amongst the world leaders of his time, and his charm was disarming. His buoyant spirit, his vivid enthusiasm, his intellectual tolerance, his deep insights made his critics helpless. Never one to compromise on basic principles, he had a largeness of heart and width of vision that enabled him to see the other man's point of view. He had flexibility of approach, and resilience in action. He was a strong disciplinarian in his public meetings. He wanted all arrangements to be flawless—the public address system to be perfect, the seating arrangements to be proper. He would stand no stray noises, no unnecessary movements.

Nehru was no orator in the accepted sense. He did not have a premeditated beginning or end for his speech. He did not make any conscious attempt to build up effect. He just thought aloud. He took his audience along to the recesses of his thoughts. It was the stream-of-consciousness technique. He wandered from subject to subject, seemed to be rambling and yet came back to the point unerringly. And every time he came out with something new, something fresh, something which had not occurred to his audience before...

...He evolved, over the years, a happy synthesis of Hindi and Urdu, the language of the people. It was in this language that he spoke to his countrymen about the complex problems facing them as also about commonplace matters of everyday importance. He took liberties with syntax and evolved new patterns, but he always succeeded in creating the desired effect, in underlining his point and reaching his audience unerringly.

Nehru developed this art in his own way. He talked to people, the sort of talking we have on radio—direct, intimate, free from the tyranny of the written word. Nehru spoke either in Hindusthani or in English. When he spoke in Hindusthani, it is said, he thought in English, and then translated himself into Hindusthani simultaneously. It may not be untrue. We have it on Maulana Azad's evidence that during his prison days, Jawaharlal would sometimes talk in his sleep in English.

Jawaharlal Nehru's spirit was indomitable. He feared nobody and he had malice for none. His public speeches averaged a duration of ninety minutes. He talked about a variety of subjects—local, provincial, national, international. His interest was the education of his people, the upliftment of the masses. In his endearing and relaxed voice he spun on and on and people never tired of listening to him. Some of the most obvious things sounded fresh when they came from his lips, and some of his strangest utterances carried instant conviction with his audience. During his whirlwind election tours, he converted millions of people by his eloquence and sincerity and the magic of his personality.

Spontaneity was the hallmark of Nehru's public speeches. There was no prefabricated pattern to make him sound complex. He fumbled, he searched for the exact word (sometimes even the audience provided it), he had his own pet phrases which he repeated often. He gave what appeared to be wrong pauses, his timing did not conform to any set design, and yet he held his audience spellbound.

Excepting, perhaps, for some of his broadcast talks which inevitably acquired a formal note, the important utterances made in Parliament and addresses delivered on formal occasions, Nehru never gave the impression that he had a premeditated argument to offer or planned statement to make. He stimulated thinking and put his audiences onto new paths...

...Nehru knew his audience as few people did. He communicated facts and ideas at an assimilable rate. He conveyed information painlessly and in small doses. He adjusted himself to the tempo of the audience. It was not the speaker but the audience that set the pace in Nehru's public speeches. Nehru needed the people no less than they needed him.

He moulded his words with an uncanny musical perception. Essentially an artist, he at times rose to truly poetic heights in his phrases. With his sensitive mind, he seemed to be restoring to literature values which it had lost since it was divorced from the spoken word.

Nehru symbolized the most significant five decades in Indian history—the period of struggle, the hour of triumph, and the days of reconstruction. When he spoke to the people, they saw in him the hero of a drama, in which the entire nation had participated, reappearing on the stage to carry the story forward. He remained their beau ideal till his last breath.

~

Some Early Memories[5]

Ali Sardar Jafri

Ali Sardar Jafri (1913–2000) was a noted Urdu writer, poet, critic and film lyricist. In the following essay he recalls his interactions with Nehru as a student at the Aligarh Muslim University in early 1930s, and how he was a shining beacon in the social and political life of the subcontinent.

~

Years before he became the Prime Minister of free India, Jawaharlal Nehru, speaking in Lucknow, declared: 'Hindustan ek shaandaar mulk hai. Aur mein bhi ek shaandaar admi hoon.' ('India is a magnificent country; I too am such a person.') He said this with the simple candour of a child identifying himself with his mother. There was a sense of pride but no false note in his voice. And the audience applauded.

---

[5] *From* Jawaharlal Nehru: Centenary Volume, *1989.*

Nehru was a dazzling personality. He was a very handsome man, who had been brought up in an aristocratic family and given the best of modern education. Three great cultural traditions found harmony in his life: the essence of the ancient Indian civilization, sometimes called Hindu culture; the refined Mughal way of life; and the modern European scientific temper. Proud and detached, Nehru was yet a man of the masses who loved to swim in the ocean of humanity. He looked at thousands of years of Indian history with vast erudition. He tried to shape the destiny of India in the modern age in the spirit of Ghalib: he was aware of the conflict between the burden of the past and the lure of the future. He wrote, in *The Discovery of India*: 'If the past has given us some part of the truth, the future also hides many aspects of the truth, and invites us to search for them. But often the past is jealous of the future and holds us in a terrible grip, and we have to struggle with it to get free to face and advance towards the future.' This reveals a modern mind fascinated by science, yet inside lived a man as old as the Vedas.

In Jawaharlal Nehru's concept of democracy, there could be no place for narrow nationalism, revivalism or communalism. He had formulated his ideas very clearly as early as 1930. In an article published in *The Bombay Chronicle* in October 1933, he wrote: 'Whither India? Surely to the great human goal of social and economic equality, to the ending of all exploitation of nation by nation and class by class, the national freedom within the framework of an international co-operative socialist world federation.' He was not discouraged by the delay in the realization of the goal as long as the movement was in the right direction. 'For in the pursuit of a mighty purpose there is joy and happiness and a measure of achievement.'

Nehru burnt like a flame, and illumined the hearts of millions of freedom fighters. They responded by giving their love to him. He was the ideal of the youth. His writings were read eagerly. His voice was heard with great attention. He was approachable. People gathered around him just to have a look at him. Sometimes he lost his temper. His admirers liked to see him in all his moods.

I remember a winter night which I, along with some other students of Delhi's Anglo-Arabic College, spent on the railway platform of Ghaziabad to catch Jawaharlal Nehru early in the morning on the Kalka Mail coming from Allahabad to Delhi. He was alone in a second class compartment, busy packing his bedding. We told him that he could not be invited to the college to address the students, but our English Principal, Mr Walker, had permitted us to have him with us for a tea party. It was a delightful evening. He was a fine conversationalist. He did not indulge in any political talk, and this was highly appreciated by Principal Walker, and we got the freedom to invite Nehru whenever we wished.

About two years earlier, perhaps in 1934, he had been brought to the Aligarh Muslim University by the students without the permission of the Vice Chancellor, Sir Ross Masood. His entry into the university was not actually banned. But it was known that the Viceroy of India would frown on his visit. Aligarh at that time was the storm centre of the anti-fascist movement. Dr K.M. Ashraf, teaching history, Dr Abdul Aleem, lecturer in Arabic, students like Akhtar Husain Raipuri, Sibte Hasan, Hayatullah Ansari, Ansar Harvani and poets and writers like K.A. Abbas, Majaz, Janisar Akhtar, and Sa'adat Hasan Manto were the leaders of the radical movement.

One day we came to know that Pandit Jawaharlal Nehru was in Delhi and would soon return to Allahabad. Three students, Hayatullah Ansari, K.A. Abbas, and Akhtar Husain Raipuri, rushed to Delhi and persuaded him to break his journey at Aligarh for a day to meet the students. Nehru liked the idea and agreed. But when the Kalka-Howrah Mail arrived at the Aligarh railway station, at ten in the morning, the Vice Chancellor, Sir Ross Masood, and Professor Mohammad Habib, were present to receive the great leader. The student hosts of Nehru jumped out of the compartment on the other side. Sir Ross Masood welcomed Nehru formally and accompanied him to the residence of Professor Mohammad Habib, where he stayed for a day and a night. The news of the visit had been conveyed to the Vice

Chancellor by Dr Ansari, Nehru's host in Delhi. This had not been anticipated by the students.

The whole university turned out for the formal reception given by the Vice Chancellor that evening. Sir Ross Masood in his opening speech said that he was welcoming the son of Pandit Motilal Nehru who was a personal friend of his father, Dr Mahmood. But it could not save the situation. Sir Ross Masood had to pay the price. His term was not extended by the Viceroy and Dr Sir Ziauddin was appointed the new Vice Chancellor. Within two years Dr K.M. Ashraf and Dr Abdul Aleem had to leave the university. After a student strike in 1936, I also left the university along with Qazi Jalil Abbasi, now a Congress Member of Parliament.

Three different versions of this happening have been written by Akhtar Husain Raipuri, K.A. Abbas and Hayatullah Ansari. Mine is the fourth version. This is how legends arise.

This was the most glorious period of Nehru's leadership. His impact was felt on the changing political climate of India. His name was associated with the magic word socialism. The resolution for complete independence had been passed at the Lahore session of the Congress under his leadership. It was he who had drafted the Remembrance Day pledge. Then his personal association with poets, writers, artists, scientists and intellectuals all over the world was so wide that his great contemporaries seemed to look like various aspects of his personality, or his personality an extension of their intellectual achievements.

At the time of the Lahore session, when the resolution demanding complete independence was passed, Dr Mohammad Iqbal was writing his great dramatic poem in Persian called the *Javid Namah* in the style of Dante's *Divine Comedy.* What was going on in the mind and the soul of the poet is not known, nor has he left any record except the poem itself.

When the poem was published in 1932, it contained Iqbal's vision of a free India with a rich tribute to Pandit Jawaharlal Nehru and his family. Here India's freedom is within the framework of a free Asia. The joyful tidings come to the poet from the Indian sage, Vishwamitra, on the Sphere of Moon.

It is the hour of the East's arising; the East has a new sun
shining in its breast.
Happy are the people whose soul has fluttered, that has created
itself anew out of its clay.

Further on, in a valley, the teachings of four prophets are revealed to him, Gautama Buddha, Zoroaster, Christ and Mohammad.

The poet goes higher and higher and in the Sphere of Mars visits the city of his Utopia, free from class struggle and the power of silver and gold, free from armies and squadrons, where none gains his livelihood by killing and murder.

On the Sphere of Saturn, the poet sees those vile spirits which have betrayed the nation and have been rejected by Hell and Death and are suffering eternal torture. They are the spirits of Jafar, who betrayed Sirajuddaula, and Sadiq, who betrayed Tipu Sultan. Here appears the Spirit of India in all her beauty and glory in chains. She laments and denounces everything which is responsible for her slavery. She says: 'Jafar is dead, but his spirit is living still; as soon as it escapes from the chains of one body at once it makes its nest in another flesh. God save me from the spirit of Jafar, save me from the Jafars of the present time.'

The poet moves beyond the Spheres and enters Paradise. There he meets the souls of Shah-i-Hamadan, saint of Kashmir, and Ghani Kashmiri, the poet of Kashmir. There he hears praise of Jawaharlal Nehru and the Nehru family from Ghani Kashmiri:

Who gave India this yearning for freedom?
Who gave the quarry this passion to be the hunter?
Those scions of Brahmans, with vibrant hearts,
Whose glowing cheeks put the red tulip to shame—
Keen of eye, mature and strenuous in action,
Whose very glance puts Europe into commotion.
Their origin is from this protesting soil of ours,
The rising place of these stars is our Kashmir.

Here Iqbal, himself of Kashmiri descent, in a very subtle

and poetic way identifies himself with the aspirations of these Brahman sons of Kashmir when Ghani Kashmiri tells him:

> If you suppose our earth is without spark,
> Cast a glance for a moment within your heart:
> Whence comes all this ardour you possess,
> Where comes this breath of the breeze of spring?
> It is from the self-same wind's influence
> That our mountains derive their colour and scent.

I do not know if Pandit Jawaharlal Nehru was aware of this poem, but he expresses identical sentiments when he writes, in *Discovery of India,* about his meeting with Iqbal in 1938: 'As I talked to him about many things, I felt, in spite of differences, how much we had in common and how easy it would be to get on with him.... I admired him and his poetry and it pleased me greatly that he liked me and had a good opinion of me.'

Today we need, more than anything else, Jawaharlal Nehru's vision to save our country and take us forward.

~

'Mahatma ji and Pundit Ji are Great Souls of Our Times...'[6]

Bhagwadacharya

The period referred to here is the fourth decade of the twentieth century. The national movement had not left the Sadhus untouched. The sampradayas and establishments were sharply divided on the question of untouchability. The conservatives hated Gandhi and Nehru, but even among sadhus there were many who actively supported not only the temple entry and other aspects of Harijanoddhar, but other activities of the Congress as well. Many of them even went to jail during the civil disobedience.

Bhagwadacharya was a leading inspiration for such sadhus and also

---

[6] From the first volume of his autobiography, *Swami Bhagwadacharya* (Alwar: Ramanand Sahitya Mandir, 1958), 232-235.

for the Vaishnava laity. He was a great scholar of traditional knowledge with a very progressive bent of mind, also he was a powerhouse of energy with remarkable focus on his goals in the politics of memory and symbols within the Vaishnava fold.

His activities literally changed the history of the Ramanandi sampradaya and transformed the figure of Ramanand himself forever.[7]

~

...I continued to deliver sermons every chatrumasya (i.e the four months of rainy season) for almost eight years at the Jagadish Mandir of Ahmedabad. For the initial two years I lectured on Valmiki Ramayana and after that for the remaining period I was speaking on Gita.

People have their own conceptions of vices and virtues. I have always maintained that all these are mere constructs. An act might seem virtuous to some people and wicked to some others. I generally used to refer to universally revered Mahatma Gandhi and Pundit Jawaharlal Nehru ji. Many people in the Jagadish Mandir felt uncomfortable with this. They found my act of mentioning Mahatmaji and Punditji during a religious discourse in a temple, highly inappropriate. They felt, the characters from the Mahabharata and the Puranas ought to be mentioned during a religious sermon, not the contemporary mortals like Gandhi and Nehru. They considered it a sin on my part that I insisted on referring to Mahatmaji and Punditji during my discourses.

What they thought to be "sin" was a great virtue to me. I never knew the Mahabharata close and first hand, could not as a period of 5000 years lay between me and them. The same goes for the characters from the Ramayana and the Puranas. I cannot be sure how true their available representations are. How can I talk of something with confidence, that I am not sure of? This is not the

---

[7] For an account see my essay, 'The impact of Sectarian Lobbying on Hindi Literary Historiography: The Fascinating Story Bhagwadacharya Ramanandi,' in *Literature and Nationalist Ideology,* ed. Hans Harder (New Delhi: Social Science Press, 2010).

case with Mahatmaji and Panditji. They are the great souls of our own times.

Mahatmaji in fact, is a case apart. I knew him personally. He commanded the faith of the whole country. He was truly the greatest leader of Bharatvarsha. To me, he was the only 'Mahatma'. Mohandas Karamchand Gandhi was the soul source of my goodness. His name purified me.

To my mind, religious discourse are not mere formality. They must lead to purification of hearts and minds. So, I continued to refer to the acts and ideas of Mahatmaji and Punditji. In spite of the sharp (sometimes even abusive and violent) opposition from some quarters, the Pujari of the temple Shri Sewadasji remained consistent in his support to me. My discourses continued to help the listeners to get rid of bad habits and pettiness and thus evolve into better human beings.

Translated by Purushottam Agrawal

~

Nehru and the Making of the Constitution[8]

Subhash C. Kashyap

Subhash C. Kashyap is an eminent politician and scholar, and Secretary-General of five Lok Sabha sessions from 1984 to 1990. He was a Member of the National Commission to Review the Working of Constitution and Chairman of its Drafting and Editorial Committee.

~

It is not entirely correct to say that the Constitution of India was framed by the Constituent Assembly during 1946–9. Actually our Constitution had an organic growth. It was being framed all through the period of the national struggle for independence

[8] For a fuller study of the theme see Subhash C. Kashyap, *Jawaharlal Nehru and the Constitution* (New Delhi: Metropolitan, 1982). This essay was published in the *Jawaharlal Nehru: Centenary Volume* (1989).

and the successive doses of constitutional reforms conceded by the British in response to national demands. Also, ever since its commencement on 26 January, 1950, the Constitution has been further evolving and growing through and during its actual operation. It is a continuous process. Of the many eminent men who contributed to this process, the most outstanding role, both before and after Independence, has been played by Pandit Jawaharlal Nehru, who once modestly described himself as 'one of those humble individuals who had something to do with the making of the Constitution.'

Pandit Nehru's contribution to the very conception, birth and work of the Constituent Assembly, as also to the framing and functioning of the Constitution of India was unique. He gave to it its spirit and soul, its philosophy and vision. It was he who laid down the basic principles and the broad structure of the Constitution through the Objectives Resolution, through crucial interventions in the Constituent Assembly and through his very active role in committees and in behind-the-scene informal discussions and party meetings. In this sense, the Constitution is, indeed, his handiwork. In the words of Indira Gandhi: 'The spirit of our Constitution bears the imprint of his [Nehru's] inspiration even though the forms might have been devised by professional lawyers.'

The task of framing the Constitution for independent India would always be remembered as a task of 'tremendous magnitude'; it was second in importance only to the achievement of the country's independence from foreign rule. The Prime Minister of the newly independent India, deeply involved in several pressing issues with national and international ramifications, could not be expected to find much time for the exercise of drafting the detailed provisions of the Constitution. Nevertheless, he was the Assembly's philosopher and its prime constitutional thinker. Himself an erudite scholar, he looked at the issues from intellectual and idealist angles. While he did not bother about what he considered to be petty details, he paid the most meticulous personal attention to the fundamentals.

Nehru was the most charismatic leader in the Constituent Assembly, with enormous popularity and mass appeal outside it. He had the power to sway opinion. But, committed democrat that he was, he saw to it that decision making in the Assembly was in accordance with the best democratic norms and traditions. He stood for full and free debate on all issues and, so far as possible, wanted decisions by unanimity or near unanimity. This is amply clear from his observations made in the Constituent Assembly:

> **Let us not trouble ourselves too much about the petty details of what we do; those details will not survive for long if they are achieved in conflict. What we achieve in unanimity, what we achieve by co-operation is likely to survive.**

Jawaharlal Nehru gave to the nation the concept of the Constituent Assembly. The Assembly, as envisaged by Nehru, was to be a fully sovereign body; it could not come as a gift from the imperialist power; it had to be elected by adult franchise and its function was to be 'only to frame a Constitution and nothing more'. Practically all the Congress resolutions on the subject of the Constituent Assembly were drafted by Nehru, though not always moved by him. By the end of 1939, Mahatma Gandhi had been fully converted by Nehru to the concept of a Constituent Assembly. In fact, Gandhiji categorically declared that it was Jawaharlal Nehru who 'compelled' him to study the implications of a Constituent Assembly, who introduced the idea in Congress resolutions, and finally made him (Gandhiji) a 'convert' to the idea.

Nehru believed that the Constituent Assembly was a new kind of organ 'which, once it meets, is self-governing and self-determining and will receive no directions from any one outside it,' even though it had to work within a certain framework. Nevertheless, Nehru was fully alive to the onerous responsibility of the Constituent Assembly in framing a Constitution, and conscious of the substantial and pivotal role expected of the Congress organization in the process. Nehru, the President of the

Congress Working Committee, on being appointed Chairman of the Committee of Experts to prepare material and draft proposals for the Constituent Assembly, himself did the original draft of the Objectives Resolution which he moved in the first session of the Constituent Assembly on 13 December, 1946, and made a memorable speech in the Assembly. As the leader and the hero of the Indian revolution, Nehru believed that it was important and necessary for him to tell the people of India and the world at large what the Constituent Assembly stood for and what it wanted the nation to be.

The Objectives Resolution which, according to Nehru, was 'in the nature of a pledge', guaranteed fundamental rights to citizens, and safeguards for the minorities. It was through this Resolution that the Constituent Assembly pledged itself to drawing up a Constitution for the country wherein, (it) 'shall be guaranteed and secured to all the citizens of India justice—social, economic and political; equality of status and of opportunity before the law; freedom of thought, expression, belief, faith, worship, vocation, association and action, subject to law and public morality' and wherein adequate safeguards would be provided for the minorities, backward and tribal areas and depressed and other classes. The preamble to the Constitution, which outlines in brief the basic philosophy as enshrined in its provisions, was carved out of this Objectives Resolution.

Thus, while Nehru's Objectives Resolution gave to the Constituent Assembly its guiding principles and the philosophy that was to permeate its task of constitution-making, his eloquent and inspiring address, full of the spirit of hope, determination and defiance, set the tenor and the tone for future Assembly deliberations. Commending the resolution for unanimous adoption by the Assembly, Nehru expressed the hope that it would lead to a Constitution on the suggested lines and the Constitution would lead the people to real freedom from hunger, want and poverty.

Of the most important committees of the Constituent Assembly, Nehru himself was the chairman of as many as three, namely the States Committee, the Union Powers Committee and the Union Constitution Committee. Without in any way meaning to detract from the unique role performed by Sardar Patel in the field of integration of the princely States with the rest of India, it may be pointed out that it is often forgotten that the first most crucial steps in the direction were actually taken by Nehru in his capacity as chairman of the States Committee appointed to negotiate with the States Negotiating Committee. Nehru showed remarkable statesmanship and through a display of the requisite firmness and a spirit of genuine accommodation and conciliation, he succeeded in bringing round a large number of States to agree to send their representatives to the Assembly under the formula of representation settled during negotiations. The Union Constitution Committee and the Union Powers Committee under his chairmanship similarly played crucial roles by settling the principles of the Constitution and the nature of the polity.

On the fundamental rights provisions of the Constitution, Nehru took very active part in the debates in the Constituent Assembly and later, while speaking on the First and the Fourth Constitution Amendment Bills. He supported the provision of adequate safeguards for minorities, tribals and backward classes. Intervening during the debate on the Interim Report of the Committee of Fundamental Rights, Nehru asked for the protection of the tribal areas and the tribal people in every possible way. However, he pointed out that the various safeguards were not to be confused with fundamental rights. the ultimate national objective was to build a united organic nation based on the rich variety and unity of Indian culture, and not to perpetuate separatist tendencies on privileges and class or caste discrimination.

Nehru dwelt at length on the changing concept of property in the history of mankind. In the Constituent Assembly, as a 'just compromise' between 'the right of the individual and the right of the community', he moved the most important and far-reaching amendment to the property clause providing for the compulsory acquisition of property. After a fairly long discussion, the amendment was adopted on 12 September, 1949.

Nehru spoke at length on the respective roles of and relationship between the legislature and the judiciary. Within the terms of the Constitution, he felt, the will of Parliament was supreme and the judiciary could not be allowed to function as a third member to thwart social reform measures. He supported Dr Ambedkar's amendment to Article 39A of the Draft Constitution regarding the separation of the judiciary from the executive in the public service of the state. The original article had prescribed a time limit of three years which the amendment sought to delete.

Nehru pleaded strongly for a parliamentary system as opposed to the presidential and other systems. In the words of K.M. Munshi, 'as a middle-of-the-way socialist, impatient to transform India's life, Nehru favoured parliamentary supremacy.' Sardar Patel was 'cynical' about parliamentary supremacy while C. Rajagopalachari would have favoured what may be termed 'a state of national democratic government on Gandhian lines'. The system of parliamentary democracy was finally adopted by deliberate choice, in Nehru's words, 'not only because, to some extent we had always thought on those lines previously, but because we thought it was in keeping with our old traditions also.'

Among the several important resolutions moved by Nehru were those concerning the preparation of electoral rolls for the elections to be held in 1950 on the basis of the provisions of the new Constitution agreed to by the Constituent Assembly, ratification of the decision of India's continued membership of the Commonwealth, the inclusion of Bhutan and Sikkim within the scope of the Negotiating Committee, and the adoption of the national flag of India. On the question of the adoption of the international form for numerals as against the Hindi or Devanagari numerals, Nehru was 'immediately convinced' that the right approach was to accept the form used internationally. Also, on the question of language, generally, Nehru spoke forcefully, and while agreeing with the need for India having one language, he deprecated any imposition and stressed the desirability of the all India language growing from the people. Worth recalling is the significant role played by him in the evolution and final acceptance in the Constituent Assembly of the Ayyangar formula on language.

Intervening in the debate on the citizenship provisions, in an important obiter dictum on secularism, Nehru said:

> It is brought in in all contexts, as if by saying that we are a secular state we have done something amazingly generous, given something out of our pocket to the rest of the world, something which we ought not to have done, so on and so forth. We have only done something which every country does, except a very few misguided and backward countries in the world.

Writing on 13 July, 1947, as chairman of the Union Constitution Committee, he recommended to the president of the Constituent Assembly the draft of a provision for the amendment of the Constitution. This formed the basis of all subsequent discussions regarding the amendment clause and finally took the shape of Article 368 of the Constitution.

During Nehru's premiership, as many as seventeen constitutional amendments were enacted. Of these, four affected fundamental rights and three sought to amend property provisions.

The Constitution (First Amendment) Act of 1951 made some vital changes in Articles 15, 19 and 31 dealing with the fundamental rights of equality, freedom of expression and of property. To clarify the position and to give effect to what was believed to be the real intention of the framers of the Constitution, new Articles 31A and 31B and the Ninth Schedule were inserted in the Constitution. The new provisions specially secured the constitutional validity of the Zamindari Abolition laws in general and certain specific state acts in particular by excepting laws providing for acquisition of any estate or any rights therein, from the operation of the Fundamental Rights provisions.

By 1955, when it became necessary to reiterate the principle that the 'responsibility for the economic and social welfare policies of the nation should be with Parliament, not with courts', the Constitution (Fourth Amendment) Act made substantial changes in Articles 31 and 31A. When the Fourth Amendment Bill was being discussed, it was argued by Pandit Nehru that the amendment of Article 31 became essential in order to create a 'socialist pattern of society' and to realize the ideal of a 'Welfare State' in India, and that it sought to remove an inherent contradiction in the Constitution between the Fundamental Rights and Directive Principles of State Policy. Amendments were later made to clauses 2, 3 and 4 of Article 19 by the Constitution (Sixteenth Amendment) Act, 1963, concerning the right of freedom of speech and expression, assembly and forming associations or unions in the interests of the sovereignty and integrity of India.

Pandit Nehru was a strong advocate of the need for flexibility in the Constitution. No constitution, howsoever good, could bind succeeding generations. In order to be lasting, it must be amenable to change in accordance with changing societal needs and aspirations. Nehru said, 'A Constitution to be living must be growing; must be adaptable; must be flexible; must be changeable.' He believed that 'however good a Constitution might be at any time, after working it for some little time, flaws appear. Nothing is perfect, and then it becomes necessary to make changes to remove those flaws.' In fact, a Constitution gets its real meaning and content only by the manner in which it is worked. So, the Constitution of India was really being made during the early years of its life when it was being actually put to work and test under the stewardship of Jawaharlal Nehru. Nehru's role in building the national edifice on firm foundations and giving to the Constitution its life and soul by working it for the first fourteen years was most remarkable. Many loopholes were detected in the process of working, and Nehru took it upon himself to plug them by bringing in the necessary constitutional amendments which clarified the real intent of the framers of the Constitution.

While piloting the Constitution amendment bills and

otherwise speaking on important issues, Nehru made a significant contribution to constitutional thinking on subjects like fundamental rights vs. directive principles, limits to freedom of speech, etc., rights of the individual vs. the interests of society, the supremacy of parliament and the jurisdiction of courts, right to property, protection of backward classes, resolution of the language problem, and relationship between President and the Prime Minister.

When a grateful nation celebrates the centenary of Pandit Nehru, it is pertinent to recall, among other things, his role in the evolution and operation of the Constitution of India not only as a matter of historical interest or to pay homage to the great builder of modern India, but because Nehru's vision and views, and his words and warnings on the crucial problems of the Indian polity are as relevant today as they were when he moved in flesh and blood and guided the destiny of the nation. What he told the Constituent Assembly, he could as well be saying today:

> At present the greatest and most important question in India is how to solve the problem of the poor and the starving. Wherever we turn, we are confronted with this problem. If we cannot solve this problem soon, all our paper Constitution will become useless and purposeless.

On 13 April, 1948, the Constituent Assembly adopted a resolution to the effect that 'for the proper functioning of democracy, and the growth of national unity and solidarity' it was essential that 'communalism should be eliminated from Indian life' and 'no communal organization ... should be permitted to engage in any of the activities other than those essential for the bona fide religious, cultural, social and educational needs of the community.' Pandit Nehru told the Constituent Assembly:

> We must have it clearly in our minds, and in the mind of the country, that the alliance of religion and politics in the shape of communalism is a most dangerous alliance, and it yields the most abnormal kind of illegitimate brood .... This combination is

harmful to the country as a whole; it is harmful to any minority that seeks to have some advantage from it.

~

Nehru and the Tribals[9]

B.K. Roy Burman

B.K. Roy Burman was a renowned anthropologist and social scientist. He joined the freedom movement in his college days in Calcutta, before receiving his doctorate in anthropology and subsequently serving as Director of the Tribal Research Institute in West Bengal, chairman of the Study Group on Land Holding System of Tribals, Planning Commission (1985–86), and chairman of the Committee on Forest and Tribals Backward Classes Unit, Ministry of Home Affairs (1980–82). In the following essay, Burman discusses how Nehru linked the tribals' freedom struggle with that of the rest of India and secured tribal rights to land and forests.

~

Jawaharlal Nehru was thrown 'almost without any will' of his own 'into contact with the peasantry'. Early in June 1920, about two hundred kisans marched fifty miles from the interior of Parbatgarh district to Allahabad city with the intention of drawing the attention of prominent politicians there to their woebegone condition. They persuaded Nehru to accompany them to their place. And then, as he records in his autobiography: 'A new picture of India seemed to rise before me, naked, starving, crushed and utterly miserable. And their faith in us, casual visitors from the distant city, embarrassed me and filled me with a new responsibility that frightened me.' This was an important milestone in the journey of a fighter for national freedom towards a deeper humanist commitment.

Another milestone was Nehru's participation for the first time in the All India Trade Union Congress, which was held in 1928

[9] From *Jawaharlal Nehru: Centenary Volume.*

at Jharia, the centre of a coal mining area which also had a large concentration of tribal population. He found a vast difference in the outlook between two sections of the trade unionists at the congress. There was the old trade union group, moderate in politics and indeed distrustful of politics in industrial matters. The other group was militant, believed in political action, and wanted to link up the struggle of the workers with the struggle against imperialism. Nehru's sympathy was with the latter group.

His ardent spirit, committed to human betterment, unreserved in its opposition to every kind of oppression, made him a natural friend of the tribals. In the 1930s when the legendary Naga freedom fighter, Gaidinliu, was incarcerated in a British gaol for the crime of leading a revolt against the British after her preceptor, Jadunang, had been taken to the gallows, she was hailed by Nehru as the Rani of the Nagas. Nehru promised to employ whatever means he had in his ability and influence to obtain her release.

Though this was perhaps Nehru's first important public pronouncement linking up the freedom struggle of a tribal community with the freedom struggle of India, the tribals themselves had been forging this link in many parts of the country for some time. Mention might be made of the Koya revolts led by Alluri Sitarama Raju in the Agency tract of what is today Andhra Pradesh in 1922–4. Raju is said to have been greatly influenced by the Indian National Movement and particularly by Gandhi. The Tana Bhagat movement of the Oraons of Chhota Nagpur, the Halapati movement of south Gujarat and many other such movements were more closely linked with the National Struggle at the ideological and organizational levels. Jawaharlal Nehru was aware of this. In 1952, he recalled how his general impression about the tribes had been derived from such people as the Bhils, the Santhals and the Gonds, whose habitats he had visited during his election tours in the 1930s. Although they lived in backward conditions, he had noted many strong points in them.

The crushing poverty in which they lived did not subdue the indomitable will of the tribals, and they participated in the Freedom Struggle. This must have reinforced Nehru's own view which regarded the quest for freedom as the music of the human spirit. When Nehru spoke of learning from the tribal people, he must have meant it in more than one sense.

The tribes of north-east India touched a different chord. As Nehru said:

> The North-East Border area deserves our special attention, not only of the government but of the people of India. Our contact with them [the people there] will do us good and will do them good also. They add to the strength, variety and cultural richness of India. As one travels there, a new and vaster picture of India comes before the eyes and the narrowness of outlook which sometimes obsesses us begins to fade away. One feels that India is not just one particular part which we might know intimately but something infinitely more, a meeting place of all manners of races, languages and cultures.

Nehru envisaged a freeing of the collective psyche of the rest of the country through building up a sense of community with the tribal people of north-east India. He said:

> Just as the hills breed different types of persons from those in the plains, so also the frontier breeds a different type of persons from those who live away from the frontier. My own predilection is rather for the mountains than for the plains, rather for the hill-folk than the plains people, so also I prefer the frontier, not the frontier physically, but the conception of living near the frontier, because living near the frontier, or round about it, prevents one from becoming complacent.

The implication of this unusual observation can perhaps be fully appreciated if one cares to cast even a passing glance at the diverse creative uses to which tribal people have put simple materials like bamboo and cane, pieces of wood, and animal horn.

Nehru had five cardinal principles in dealing with the tribal population: Firstly, they should be helped to develop along the lines of their own genius and we should avoid imposing anything on them. We should try to encourage in every way their own traditional arts and crafts. Secondly, tribal rights to land and forests should be respected. Third, we should try to train and build up a team of their own people to do the work of administration and development. Some technical personnel from outside might be needed, especially in the beginning. But we should avoid introducing too many outsiders into tribal territory. Fourth, we should not overadminister these areas or overwhelm them with a multiplicity of schemes. We should rather work through, and not in rivalry with, their own social and cultural institutions. Finally, we should judge results, not by statistics or the amount of money spent, but by the quality of human character evolved.

The second point, namely the recognition of tribal rights in land and forests is reminiscent of Gandhi's concept of trusteeship as refined in 1945 with the help of Dantwala. This might be elaborated as follows.

1. Trusteeship provides a means of transforming the present capitalist order of society into an egalitarian one. It gives no quarter to capitalism but affords the present owning class a chance to reform itself. It is based on the faith that human nature is never beyond redemption.
2. It does not recognize any right to private ownership of property except inasmuch as it may be permitted by society for its own welfare.
3. It does not exclude legislative regulation of the ownership and use of wealth.
4. Under state-regulated trusteeship, an individual will not be free to hold or use his wealth for selfish satisfaction or in disregard of the interest of society.
5. Just as it is proposed to fix a decent minimum living wage, even so a limit should be fixed for the maximum income that could be allowed to any person in society. The difference between such minimum and maximum income should be reasonable, equitable and variable from time to time, so

much so that the trend would be towards the obliteration of the difference.

6. Under the Gandhian economic order, the character of production will be determined by social necessity and not by personal whim or greed.

Thus, so far as the basic survival system of peasants or the tribals is concerned there is a common Gandhi-Nehru framework. This is not surprising for two reasons. The first is the accommodative dialogue, although in very different idioms, that the two leaders carried on throughout the Freedom Struggle. The second is the fact that while in the 'enchanting frontier' Nehru found rich material for strengthening the forces of creative humanism in the rest of the country, sizeable sections of the tribal population, especially in the central belt of India, had been drawn to the Gandhian movement much earlier and made their contribution to the composite anti-colonial struggle.

The implications of the Gandhi-Nehru framework in the approach to the basic survival system of the tribals have not, however, been worked out in detail.

When Nehru speaks of the tribal people developing along the lines of their own genius and opposes external intervention, one may ask what the long-range implication of this would be. In finding an answer to this question, two views prevailing among anthropologists about the future of tribal societies might be taken into account. The predominant view is to look upon tribal social formation as a stage in the evolution of human societies. The second is to look upon a tribe as a type of society incorporating a world view of attaining fulfilment through communication and reciprocity between man and man and between man and nature; rather than being held together through institutional arrangements based on coercive state power and market competition. Though Nehru has not spoken on this matter in theoretical terms, he has, by implication, shown his preference for the second point of view in his many utterances.

It would be useful to examine whether, in post-Independence

India, tribal policy has been formulated on this premise. When Nehru said that we should not overadminister the tribal areas, he was obviously speaking not in philosophical terms but in operational terms. Gandhi, however, spoke both in philosophical and operational terms. Gandhi regarded state organization as an evil, but he envisaged a 'minimal state' as a transitional arrangement. An examination of the evolution of administrative arrangements in tribal areas reveals trends leading away from what Nehru had envisaged at the operational level and what Gandhi had envisaged at both operational and philosophical levels. The deviation is greatest in the matter of the recognition of tribal rights in land and forests. The source of this deviation is not merely the manipulative pressure of vested interests, but also the continuation of a colonial legacy in the cognitive paradigm informing the legal system. Until recently, studies on the land question were predominantly informed by an empirico-positivistic orientation. But the recent trend seems to be moving towards a historico-comparative method. These two approaches are tied up with two approaches to law, namely legal positivism and legal pluralism (or, more appropriately, epistemological-anxiology inherent in social formation). According to legal positivism, all command laws of the state are legitimate. As against this, legal pluralism avers that social behaviour rather than the compulsive norm of the state is the source of the legitimization of law. When applied to land rights, two conflicting approaches result from these two orientations. One is res nuttius, according to which rights to property accrue to individuals from the property of nobody. Thus the state has superior right over all lands. The other is lex loci re sitae (law of the place where the thing is situated). During the colonial period, the first approach held the ground and even now judicial thinking, by and large, continues to be guided by it. But, as pointed out by Justice Hidayatullah, the Indian tradition is entirely different. Besides, among many tribal communities, the rights of individuals are subsumed within the rights of communities. If the community is removed in the name of abolition of the intermediary, the age-old rights of the individual also disappear.

Fresh rights are conferred by the state according to criteria laid down by the state apparatus during preparation of the record of rights. As a result, it has been found that in some states hardly one per cent of the land traditionally occupied by the tribals has been recorded in their favour. Again, it has been found that when a large number of persons are dislodged from their habitat for the purpose of implementation of massive development projects, no compensation is paid as a sequel to the non-recognition of traditional rights. Much of the unrest and upsurge in tribal areas appears to be due to a continuation of this colonial legacy which it has become possible to implement more vigorously now, because the requisite administrative, communication and other infrastructures have also come into existence.

The nation is paying the price for deviation from the Gandhi-Nehru framework. It is high time we looked back in order to move forward.

~

Nehru as Seen by an Economist[10]

Jan Tinbergen

Jan Tinbergen (1903–1994) was one of the most influential economists of the twentieth century, one of the founding fathers of econometrics and the first Nobel Prize winner in economics (with Ragnar Frisch) in 1969. In the following essay he highlights Nehru's prescient approach to economic and social planning, relying in equal parts on industrialization and justice for the less privileged.

~

When I was invited to contribute to [the] book to celebrate the centenary of Jawaharlal Nehru's birthday, I wondered what subject would best entitle me to participate. Since the main area I have given thought to in a serious way is that of economic policy in the wider sense, I decided to honour the great Indian leader by a sketch

---

[10] From *Jawaharlal Nehru: Centenary Volume.*

of his ideas on and activities in this field of a Prime Minister's responsibilities. Since the many facets of governing a country—even the largest democracy of the world—are interdependent, it is unavoidable that I shall, now and then, transgress the frontiers of my subject. There is much interdependence, both in the outside world and in Nehru's personality. It will be interesting, in particular, to compare Nehru's views with the views of other leading statesmen twenty-five years after his death.

Like all leading Indian personalities, Nehru was attracted by Mahatma Gandhi's philosophy of life. Jawaharlal Nehru lived fifty-seven years under colonial rule, with all its restrictions: he was in prison nine times, and Indians were not supposed to travel in first class railway compartments or to swim or sail in certain lakes.

The first problem he had to face together with all Indians was how to become the citizen of an independent nation. The solution of that problem required as much unity as possible and Indian leaders in this followed Gandhi, until some time before Independence the Muslim leader, Jinnah, changed his mind.

Once Independence had been attained, Nehru, as the nation's leader, had to pay attention to the continued changes in the rest of the world, to choose his own answers and to formulate his own policies. His answers were inspired by pragmatism, on the one hand, and a scientific approach, on the other hand. I still remember how, in his address to the members of the International Statistical Institute in 1951 in New Delhi, he reminded us that a scientist's task consisted in solving problems and added that in India these were abundant, since the survival of almost each of the hundreds of millions of inhabitants was a problem.

India had been free only four years when this Congress took me there for the first time. It was in this period that many former colonies had to learn that political independence did not automatically bring in economic independence. A development policy had to be identified. It was necessary to raise production in order to reduce the widespread poverty. The core of this process required investment in machines, in means of transportation, in factory buildings, and also investment in 'human beings', that is, to teach and to train them so as to become more productive.

The Congress Party, created in 1885, had been actively discussing these and many related problems and Jawaharlal Nehru, who for a considerable period had been its President, felt inspired by socialist ideas, which he integrated into the guidelines he set for himself and his country. He evidently did not want to give up democracy, which he had seen at work in Great Britain. But he was also impressed by planning as a means of coordinating the use of instruments of economic policy, and the desirability of a public sector as a framework of private production. In his admirable book on development planning,[11] Sukhamoy Chakravarty presents Nehru as the 'chief architect of Indian plans'. Thus, Nehru's choice was a mixed economy. In other words, he wanted to avoid extremism: neither the capitalist order nor the completely centrally-planned communist order of the Soviet Union appealed to him. In the light of recent changes in that country, and in the light of the Western European and Japanese systems as distinct from the American, Nehru's choice was clearly ahead of the world's actual development.

The planning concept, quite rightly, has also been introduced into population policy: it was only too clear that this form of self-restraint is basic to a balanced development policy. In many underdeveloped countries too, a large part of production increases is absorbed by a high increase in population. Smaller families are desirable not only because they imply a lower rate of growth of total population. They also imply—and that is even more important—that a better education can be given to the children and that the level of capability of the population can be thus enhanced.

Science points to coordination of the use of various instruments of economic policy, in particular it will assist development in the applied forms of technology. India had already participated in

---

[11] Sukhamoy Chakravarty, *Development Planning: The Indian Experience* (New Delhi: Oxford University Press, 1987).

scientific fields such as mathematics and statistics, as illustrated by names such as Mahalanobis, followed soon by physicists like Bhabha. The most important contributions to international development were the joint result of institutions and scholars of developed and developing countries, as illustrated by the 'green revolution': the emergence of high-yielding grains and other agricultural products. This was one of the causes of the increase of foodgrain production between 1951 and 1971 from 58 million to 108 million tonnes, and, as a consequence, Indian self-sufficiency in foodgrains. Another factor was the planned extension of irrigation.

As an illustration of industrial development, the rate of growth of steel and steel products may be quoted: between 1951 and 1961 steel production rose 2.2 times and production of machines 5 times; industrial production as a whole almost doubled.[12]

As observed, investment in human capital was also aimed at, and between 1951 and 1971, the number of children at school rose from 23.8 to 83 million. This was not only economically important, but it also meant a cultural development of considerable importance.

One dimension of democracy we have not yet mentioned is the geographical aspect. India is a federal nation, composed of about twenty states, under their own state governments, which implies a cultural pluralism, but also the possibility of a better economic policy. Problems of a local and regional character can be solved in a more efficient way if decision-making is an activity at more than one level. In contrast, some problems, such as international security and environmental considerations require a policy on the part of the Centre. The unity of India is as important as that of the superpowers (the United States and the Soviet Union) or, for Western Europe, its integration into the European Community, and for Eastern Europe, the Council of Mutual Economic Aid (COMECON).

Nehru saw the importance of these problems from the start. He referred to poverty as a 'world problem'. He emphasized the

---

[12] Ibid., 89.

necessity of development cooperation as he did when addressing the General Assembly of the United Nations in 1961. This was the year in which the 'Development Decade' was proclaimed, later called the First Development Decade. In 1970, the Second Development Decade was proclaimed, as proposed by the United Nations Development Planning Committee, over which I had the pleasure to preside.[13] Here again, Nehru was well ahead of his colleagues.

It was clear that the developed countries—with a few exceptions among the smaller ones—were hardly interested. Until today, with the possible exception of France, the large and the middle-sized industrial countries have not applied the criteria suggested by their own experts in the Pearson Commission,[14] to take part in financing the development of developing countries with an amount of 0.7 per cent of their gross national product. (One of the consequences is the debt problem we face today.)

The pressure had to come from the developing countries themselves. Here, already in 1955, Nehru was the leading personality in the convocation of the meeting at Bandung, Indonesia, of Asian and African politicians, and again in Belgrade, 1961, where the Group of Non-Aligned Nations was established. This group did not want to join either of the 'blocs', the 'capitalist' or the 'communist' bloc. In a sense this attitude is in conformity with an attitude of tolerance, one of the personal characteristics of Nehru. At the same time, it aims at strengthening the position of the low income countries, in order to approach a more equitable income distribution. Three years after Nehru's death, the Group of Seventy-Seven (G-77) was established, at a meeting at Algiers in 1967, in which the Latin American nations also participated. This

---

[13] United Nations, *Towards Accelerated Development: Proposal for the Second United Nations Development Decade*, New York, 1970; United Nations, *International Development Strategy: Action Programme of the General Assembly for the Second United Nations Development Decade*, New York, 1970.

[14] L.B. Pearson et al., *Partners in Development: Report of the Commission on International Development*, New York, 1969.

Group now includes over one hundred member nations and is able to exert more pressure in favour of the Third World. They too have learned to listen to the argument of the other side, however.

Asia is becoming more and more important. Japan competes with the United States of America in the field of technology. China experiments, like the Soviet Union, with a new social system. The centre of the world is shifting from the Atlantic to the Pacific. Nehru as an Asian contributed to the importance of Asia. He was not only the leading politician of India, he was one of the great statesmen of the world, and as a matter of fact, gave guidance to a large part of the Third World. Few, if any, other political leaders can be compared to him. For Latin America, Raul Prebisch was 'the grand old man' but he did not have responsibility for a national government simultaneously with supranational responsibility. For Africa, Julius Nyerere is the spiritual leader, who simultaneously had both national and international responsibility; but Tanzania is a much smaller country than India. Western Europe looks at Jean Monnet, the father of West European integration, as their great man, who had supranational responsibility, especially for the European Coal and Steel Community. Another European with an international, or even a world vision is, of course, Willy Brandt. It is to this class of statesmen that Jawaharlal Nehru belongs.

~

Poet, Thinker and Man of Action[15]

Sheikh Mohammad Abdullah

Sheikh Mohammad Abdullah (1905–1982), also known as Sher-e-Kashmir, was one of the most prominent Kashmiri politicians. He served as the second Chief Minister of the state post-Independence. He worked closely with Nehru throughout the freedom struggle and later, while bringing Kashmir into the Indian fold.

~

[15] From *Nehru Abhinandan Granth*, 6 April, 1949.

Pandit Nehru's achievement consists in the integration of the Indian struggle for independence into a united and successful upsurge against foreign domination. The Indian National Movement has evolved through definite stages of an increasing measure of concretization of its economic and political programme, as well as of increase in its volume. Pandit Nehru has contributed in a distinct and prominent way to the shaping of such programmes. Before and after he strode into the Indian political arena, people in many parts of the country were fighting local freedom battles which were operationally unrelated to the broad national movement in the country, for instance, in some of the states, or the North-West Frontier Province. It is his dynamic personality which is responsible for channelizing all these streams into a stormy torrent which swept away a mighty empire.

To start with, the National Movement was confined to the so-called British India. The great mass of humanity inhabiting Indian India had yet not been awakened to sufficient militancy to be able to play an effective role in the liberation of the country. The people in the States continued to groan under the weight of slavery. The princely order was the greatest ally of the British in India. No struggle against alien rule could succeed without the reduction of this stronghold of imperialism. With a profound insight into the future, Pandit Nehru was among the first to realize that to achieve national ideals it was essential to organize the states' people, to weld the rising, isolated movements in the states into one political framework, on one platform, with a united programme of action.

Such an organization had necessarily got to be separated from the Indian National Congress, because the problems facing the people in the states were different in many respects from the problems of the people in British India. The conditions prevalent in the states were different. Panditji had the opportunity of experiencing them when he was arbitrarily detained by the Nabha State authorities. The situation there was complicated by the fact that the fight against foreign rule involved the priority of liquidating the unhampered autocratic power wielded by the princes. Hence, the need for the States People's Conference which was to lead the attack against the princely order. Panditji was the guiding source of inspiration in forging the States People's Conference.

In our own state, the expression of grievances on the part of the people was confined to presenting appeals to the Prince before 1925. The year 1925, for the first time in history, saw the people involved in an organized political campaign: the State-owned silk factory workers struck work, demanding more education and better wages. However, the large mass of people remained unmoved. By 1931, the unrest had become universal. The causes operating were the same as those which culminated in the Civil Disobedience Movement in India. The peasant could no longer tolerate the gruelling conditions of poverty and starvation; there was mass unemployment in the country. The only solution was the abolition of the old order. The whole of the State was shaken by a colossal political earthquake. The tiller demanded his right to the fruit of his labour; the right to employment and the right to a popular share in the administration were insisted upon.

One of the weaknesses of the movement was that it was isolated. There were people who slandered it as being communal in import and purpose. It goes to the undying credit of Pandit Nehru that he stood up to defend the movement against slander. He characterized it as an expression of the progressive will of the Kashmiris to throw away the yoke of autocracy and foreign rule. It is he who was responsible for ushering in our movement into the fold of the States People's Conference.

Likewise the role of Pandit Nehru with regard to the freedom movement of the Pathans is significant. Living along strategically the most important and the most vulnerable of India's frontiers, the Pathans have ever refused to submit to any of India's conquerors, from Alexander to the British. The British tried to rule them through ruthless use of force, by bribery, and by fomenting internecine feuds. The Khan brothers united the Pathans as one people, and led them against the common enemy, suffering untold hardships and sacrifices. In their bitter struggle what they needed most was allies. People who were posing as the guardians of the claims of the Mussalmans of India refused to show them any quarter. Pandit Nehru embraced them with welcoming arms and was instrumental in getting the Khudai Khidmatgars (literally, Servants of God, the name given to followers of Khan Abdul Ghaffar Khan), linked up with the Indian National Congress.

Pandit Nehru has been a fighter not only for national freedom. His activities have had a vaster canvas. He has all along fought for the liberation of all the oppressed peoples of the world. Endowed with a historical perspective, he knew that national freedom and international progress are interlinked. There are two contending camps in the world—the camp of progress and the camp of reaction, the camp of democracy and the camp of tyranny. The victory of freedom and democracy depends on unity within the camp of progress. Any setback to progress in one country would result in a weakening of its forces in others. That explains why his heart wept when the Nazis tramped across the beautiful squares of Vienna; that is why he was so keenly interested in the issue of the Spanish Civil War. His support for the Arabs of Palestine was unstinted. His one recent concern is the Dutch aggression against Indonesian freedom. The loudest in protest against injustice and tyranny, he is the Shelley of our times, with the added capacity of being able to translate his ideals into action.

This comparison is not unfair to Shelley, for Panditji is a poet at heart. Possessed of a refined sensibility and a Catholic intellect, he has all the ingredients in his personality which constitute a poet. The urgent problems of poverty and ignorance of his people forced him to dedicate his entire faculties and energy to the stress and storm of politics. But whenever he could get opportunities to recollect emotion in tranquillity, i.e. in the cloistered solitude of a prison cell, he poured forth lyrics in prose, which his writings are.

I have known Panditji intimately for over a decade now. He has been to me not only a comrade-in-arms, but also a friend, philosopher and guide. He has always regarded me with deep affection, and his love has flown abundantly to the people of Jammu and Kashmir to whose rescue he always came in moments of crisis. During the 'Quit Kashmir' days, when we were engaged in a last-ditch battle against autocracy, he arrived post-haste in Kashmir and did all he could to steer us successfully through a sorely trying period.

Pandit Nehru rose to magnificent heights of personality during the communal disturbances in the Punjab and Delhi. In a frenzied world, when man had ceased to be human, when civilization was carried back to the primitive period, when crime had ceased to be a crime, when killing and rape were regarded as patriotic acts, Nehru, along with Gandhiji, stood firm as a rock in a turbulent ocean, emanating the light of love, peace and fellow feeling. And it is his stand that has finally been vindicated. He has been able to establish that the path of progress lies in the direction of communal concord, towards the setting up of a non-communal, secular state.

In the world today, torn as it is by bitter strife, Pandit Nehru emerges as a glorious symbol of peace and progress. There are forces which are driving the world in the direction of a devastating conflagration, although it has not yet recovered from the ravages of the last great war. The forces of aggression are polarising in two camps, a clash between which will mean the destruction of mankind. A race for armaments has already started, and we know from past experience where this race leads to. The need of the moment is the marshalling of all forces of peace, to abolish war as a method of international arbitration. The single biggest factor which can turn the balance in favour of peace is Pandit Nehru.

~

The Will to Peace

Martin Luther King, Jr[16]

Martin Luther King, Jr (1929–1968) was the most visible spokesperson and leader in the civil rights movement in America from 1955 until his

---

[16] *The Legacy of Nehru: A Memorial Tribute*, ed. Natwar-Singh, Kanwar (New York: John Day, 1965).

assassination in 1968. He famously embraced the Gandhian principles of nonviolence and civil disobedience. He was an admirer too of Nehru for providing inspiration to black Americans fighting segregation. The two corresponded briefly and actually met once in 1959 in New Delhi, and are thought to have discussed various political and social concerns.

~

Jawaharlal Nehru was a man of three extraordinary epochs. He was a leader in the long anti-colonial struggle to free his own land and to inspire a fighting will in other lands under bondage.

He lived to see victory and to move then to another epochal confrontation—the fight for peace after the Second World War. In this climactic struggle he did not have Gandhi at his side, but he did have the Indian people, now free in their own great Republic.

It would be hard to overstate Nehru's and India's contributions in this period. It was a time fraught with the constant threat of a devastating finality for mankind. There was no moment in this period free from the peril of atomic war. In these years Nehru was a towering world force skilfully inserting the peace will of India between the raging antagonisms of the Great Powers of East and West.

The world needed a mediator and an 'honest broker' lest, in its sudden acquisition of overwhelming destructive force, one side or the other might plunge the world into mankind's last war. Nehru had the prestige, the wisdom, and the daring to play the role.

The markedly relaxed tensions of today are Nehru's legacy to us, and at the same time they are our monument to him.

It should not be forgotten that the treaty to end nuclear testing accomplished in 1963 was first proposed by Nehru. Let us also remember that the world dissolution of colonialism now speedily unfolding, had its essential origins in India's massive victory. And let it also be remembered that Nehru guided into being the 'Asian-African Bloc' as a united voice for the billions who were groping toward a modern world.

He was the architect of the policy of non-alignment or neutralism which was calculated to give independent expression to the emerging nations while enabling them to play a constructive role in world affairs.

The third epoch of Nehru's work is unfolding after his death. Even though his physical presence is gone, his spiritual influence retains a living force. The Great Powers are not yet in harmonious relationship to each other, but with the help of the non-aligned world they have learned to exercise a wise restraint. In this is the basis for a lasting détente. Beyond this, Nehru's example in daring to believe and act for peaceful coexistence gives mankind its most glowing hope.

In this period my people, the Negroes of the United States, have made strides toward freedom beyond all precedent in our history. Our successes directly derive from our employment of the tactics of nonviolent direct action and non-cooperation with evil which Nehru effectively employed under Gandhi's inspiration.

The peculiar genius of imperialism was found in its capacity to delude so much of the world into the belief that it was civilizing primitive cultures even though it was grossly exploiting them.

Satyagraha made the myth transparent as it revealed the oppressed to be the truly civilized party. They rejected violence but maintained resistance, while the oppressor knew nothing but the use of violence.

My people found that satyagraha, applied in the United States to our oppressors, also clarified who was right and who was wrong. On this foundation of truth as irresistible, a majority could be organized for just solutions.

Our fight is not yet won, just as the struggle against colonialism is still unfinished, and above all, the achievement of a stable peace still lies ahead of and not behind us.

In all of these struggles of mankind to rise to a true state of civilization, the towering figure of Nehru sits unseen but felt at all council tables. He is missed by the world, and because he is so wanted, he is a living force in the tremulous world of today.

~

Ever Human[17]

Anu Bandyopadhyaya

Anu Bandyopadhyaya was a journalist and a Gandhian scholar. In the following recollections about Nehru, his generosity of spirit and tolerance, even in personal interactions, shines through. Nehru wrote the foreword to her book Bahuroopee Gandhi (1964).

~

I first came in direct contact with Jawaharlal Nehru when I was twenty-seven. He was thirty years older. Like many I was his admirer. I had not yet developed the critical acumen to judge his speeches and actions. I was then working in Bombay with the late D.G. Tendulkar on a birthday volume for Gandhiji.

One evening, after coming to my hostess's palatial residence, I found the place enveloped in a hush. Flowers were being arranged. The lights shone under artistic shades. My hostess, elegant in an austere but tasteful khadi sari, looked a bit flushed.

On enquiry I learnt that Jawaharlal Nehru was to come there soon. I seldom bothered about my dress. Yet I looked piteously at my crumpled salwar and khameez, but strode straight to the terrace where he was to sit and chat. The demeanour and artistic khadi saris of the ladies around suggested that Jawaharlal Nehru was a lady killer.

I never feel easy in front of outsiders. I am tonguetied in a group. I sought an exclusive interview with Jawaharlal Nehru the next day. In spite of being frugal, I went to Krishna Hutheesing's house in a taxi so as to be punctual. I walked up the stairs, rang the bell and, on entering the sitting room, found huge dogs. They really frightened me. In a minute Jawaharlal Nehru came in and, with a smile, asked, 'Are you scared?' 'Yes, a bit,' I said.

Politics is not my beat. After exchanging formal greetings, the feminist in me asked, 'Do you truly believe in the equality

---

[17] From *Jawaharlal Nehru: Centenary Volume.*

of man and woman, I mean, in spite of the physical handicaps women have?'

This is a favourite question of mine. I have addressed it at different times to my learned father, to Tagore, to Mahatma Gandhi, and to Badshah Khan.

Jawaharlal frowned, then beamed, and said, 'Of course I do. It looks as if you are aggressively conscious of women's rights and handicaps.' And then, after a pause, he added, 'Why did you not marry?'

I was taken aback at the suddenness of the question, but said, 'I am afraid I won't make a good wife. I am pretty choosy about a life partner.'

With a twinkle in his eyes he asked, 'What about me?'

'Oh, you are too old for me.'

'Otherwise?'

I smiled.

'What will you do after this work is over?'

'I am ashamed to admit I am not political-minded. I appreciate Gandhi's constructive social work, particularly the uplift of the weaker sections of society—the neglected, downtrodden women, not just Harijans.'

'Without winning freedom, which involves politics, can it be done effectively?'

'True, but it is equally true that in many so-called liberated countries women are not liberated, they are trampled upon or pampered, or even worshipped—all as nauseating as placing offerings to a god on a pedestal.'

'You don't like puja?'

'I don't believe in God or His bestowal of grace and all that. I don't want to encroach upon your precious time, just wanted to meet you. Moreover…'

'Moreover what?'

'I have made an ass of myself. I was nervous and forgot to pay the taxi driver. The fare must have shot up high. It will be a pretty costly interview with Betaj Jawaharlal!'

He smiled and patted me and we parted.

Our next encounter was years later when he was the Prime Minister of free India. I was then staying in the Bombay Government House, working on the *Collected Works of Mahatma Gandhi.* In a letter I had complained to him about the irregularities in our department. He had come to Bombay on some important work. On my return from the library, I found a note. 'The Prime Minister wants to meet you in the Golden Hall at 7 pm' I felt shaky. There was no means or time to consult my friend Tendulkar. I remembered my father. And I told myself that I should not seek any favour.

I went to the hall and waited for hardly three minutes when in came Jawaharlal with his brisk stride. We exchanged greetings. He said, 'Well, Anu, you are quarrelsome and fight with all.'

'Maybe. Can I open my mind, even if in a quarrelling tone?'

His benign smile encouraged me. 'What wrong has Gandhiji done that his devoted followers are putting nails into his coffin? Coffin perhaps is not a proper Hindu term.'

'What do you mean?'

'If your speech is not properly reported in the papers you flare up and say it is like murdering you. Why is Gandhiji's English, which even professors of English in Oxford dare not change, being tampered with? Why has a half-literate person been employed as my assistant just to please a Union Minister? [I mentioned his name]. Why this nepotism? He could have found a job in Khadi Bhandar if he needed a paid job. I am going to resign.'

'I shall look into it. But you honest, upright persons won't work with me. I have to run the Government with such Xs.'

'Luckily I don't have to. I don't have to lose my gadi (seat) if I flout hem.'

Jawaharlal Nehru, known for his impatience and short temper, looked offended but did not hit back at me. Instead he asked: 'What will you do after leaving this research work? Will you take up any work in Delhi? I know you hate flats. I shall have a bungalow given to you with a lawn and trees.'

I was stupefied. 'Very nice and kind of you to say this. I am a poor Brahman teacher's daughter. I shall go back to my Calcutta home, cook for my old, widowed mother and scrub floors.'

'You are not coming to Delhi?'

'I am afraid not.'

'Another complaint against you is at hand. Y is a very polite and good-natured person, not belligerent like you. Why have you quarrelled with him regarding your stay here?'

I was taken aback, and said, 'Good heavens, I never imagined that such a private affair and a trifle could be a matter of discussion between the Governor of a state and the Prime Minister.' I explained what the problem was and asked, 'What would you have done if you were in my position?'

He looked annoyed (not with me, though). Covering his disgust with a bewitching smile and patting me on my back, he said, 'I am sorry. I shall see that the awkward situation is smoothened.'

That look of pathos, which I often noticed in many of his photographs, grieved me. I wished I had not burdened him with my tale of woe. With tearful eyes I bowed and bade him goodbye.

The influence of Tendulkar, who was a very close friend of Jawaharlal Nehru from 1937, when they worked on the China Aid Committee, gave me the opportunity to correspond off and on with Jawaharlal. In spite of being so hard pressed with various activities and worries, he never failed to be human, courteous and considerate. I was delighted to get such notes as: 'Thank you for the pedas [actually sandesh made by me] and the date gur that you have sent me. I shall certainly try it.' (He referred to the specially made solid date gur of Bengal, the Indian chocolate.) 'I am enclosing an autograph for the little boy. I am sorry I cannot sign in the Bengali characters.'

I requested him to write a foreword for my small book on Gandhiji, provided he glanced through the manuscript. He agreed to do so 'if it does not take me too much time. If you will send me the manuscript or, better, the proofs, I shall be able to decide.' Just two months before his death he sent me the foreword in which he wrote: 'This is a book for children. But I am sure that many grown-ups will read it with pleasure and profit.... It will perhaps give us a greater insight into him [Gandhiji].'

I met Jawaharlal Nehru last when he visited Tendulkar's house with his grandson Sanjay. He had come to Bombay to open the Apsara. I jokingly told Tendulkar, 'Your friend comes to Bombay but never cares to see your cottage.' Immediately Tendulkar went to Government House, came back after half an hour, and told me, 'Jawaharlal is coming here this afternoon.'

I felt very nervous. Ours was such a spare life. I was all alone, with no helping hand. How to entertain him with barely three hours to prepare? We were told to observe strict confidence and not to call friends, not even next-door neighbours. The security men felt annoyed and exasperated when they found there was no hedge or gate to bar intruders. They fumed and fidgeted. One told me: 'Listen, please don't spread the news that the Prime Minister is coming. It will be very difficult for us to control the crowd.' 'I do not have to do it. You people are doing it much better.' 'How?' 'No pilot car with riders using special badges and caps ever came to this humble house. All are drawing the conclusion that some V.I.P. is coming and that too not the Governor.'

The balloon burst. After opening the Apsara, Jawaharlal came to Rocky Hills in the afternoon. He walked briskly and surveyed the cottage built on land graciously allotted by him to Tendulkar for his lifelong use. Gazing on the expanse of sea in front he said: 'It looks like an ashram. Where is your kitchen?' I felt embarrassed and worried. The verandah leading to it was narrow. Supposing he slipped and hurt himself.

'Won't you taste anything prepared by me in this kitchen? They are homemade.'

He quipped, 'So what? Gulab-jamuns, pedas and namkin made in shops are not necessarily bad.'

I too can be quick on the draw. I retorted: 'I never said these are better. There is some logic behind my statement. My preparations may not be very tasty but I am sure they won't upset you. Why are your attendants not eating anything?'

I was ignorant of protocol. Jawaharlal took a bite or two, sipped the orange juice and asked others to follow suit.

When he was about to enter the car, he looked around and asked, 'Who are these people?'

'They are the drivers, dhobis and servants of the high dignitaries who are our neighbours.'

He stepped down, went near them and did namaste. I still remember how grateful and happy they were. They told us, 'It is due to you that we saw the Betaj Samrat of India from such close quarters.'

Three years later, on my return from a trip to Kedar Badri, when I halted at Dehra Dun, the ailing Jawaharlal was there. I felt a great urge to meet him but thought it would not be proper to disturb him there. The day after, when I reached Calcutta, All India Radio's monotonous drone froze me.

~

Remembering Nehru[18]

Amritlal Nagar

Amritlal Nagar (1916–1990) was a prominent twentieth-century Hindi writer. In the following piece he recalls Nehru's early intellectual influence on him, observing him and his personal travails from close quarters in Lucknow, the colourful rumours about his family and his commitment to democracy and accountability.

~

I recall how during the days of the national Non-Cooperation Movement and Jallianwala Bagh, our innocent minds picked up effortlessly lines such as Maithili Sharan Gupta's

Jo bhara nahin hai bahvon se
Behti jisme ras dhar nahin
Woh hridaya nahin hai patthar hai
Jisme Swadesh ka pyar nahin

(He whose mind is not inundated by a flood of sweet patriotic emotions, has verily a stone in his chest in place of a heart.)

---

[18] From *Jawaharlal Nehru: Centenary Volume.*

We grew up listening to the marvellous cries of our local news vendors announcing the day's headlines from the two-page afternoon tabloid *Anand,* that told us how many of our leaders had been marched to gaol, and how many had been subjected to lathi charges by the police. The names of Mahatma Gandhi and the father-son duo of Motilal Nehru and Jawaharlal were then fast catching the nation's fancy.

Today it is hard for me to recollect exactly when the young Jawaharlal entered our hearts through his myriad photographs that were regularly appearing in all the national dailies, but I remember that it was some time around 1927 or 1928 that I first saw the Nehrus, father and son, at the Jhandewalan Park. One had heard how while defying the notorious Simon Commission, the brave Jawaharlal had been beaten mercilessly by the police. As a member of the vast crowd that he had led on the occasion, I felt the bonds of a nameless relationship develop within me. When Gandhiji selected the new Congress President with the words, 'Our Jawahar shall wear this crown of thorns this time,' my teenage heart did a somersault once again.

By the time Nehruji became Congress President, the youth of India had become firm supporters of his. He was often called the emperor of the young hearts of India. By now I had grown into an avid bookworm. When one of our teachers talked at length about this wonderful book by one Jawaharlal called *Inside Soviet Russia,* I immediately went out and bought it. This was the first book in the English language I read. I must confess that I only half understood it, but the ideals of socialism it presented began to churn in my mind. Even to date, Socialism, Nehru and Soviet Russia are inextricably intertwined in my mind.

Motilalji passed away in 1931 at the Kalakankar House in Lucknow. I remember Gandhiji was sitting in the car that carried Motilalji's body, and an immense crowd of Indians milled around, trying to bid a last farewell to a much-loved leader. I also recall how Nehru seemed to have aged suddenly when I saw him next a few months after his father's death, addressing a public meeting at the Jhandewalan Park in Lucknow. Those days, when we took out our morning processions called prabhat pheris, we sang a popular song which said how the brave Jawahar had carried the name of his country far and wide, and how he had taught his countrymen to fight for freedom. Bismil Allahabadi's couplet had a much quoted line:

> *Sham-e-mahfd dekh le, ye ghar ka ghar parvana hai*
> O candle of the *mahjil* (gathering), see, this entire clan is turned into a moth.

In 1933 Jawaharlalji's mother Swarup Rani fell ill, and was admitted to the King George Medical Hospital. It was by sheer chance that I had the opportunity to tend to her. Jawaharlalji was in gaol, by then, but he was released so he could take care of his mother. For about a month I met Panditji regularly in the evenings, and sometimes in the mornings as well. At that time Kitabistan, Allahabad, had published two small booklets by Panditji. I recall only one title, *Window in the Prison Land.* One day when I reached the place, this book had just been delivered by the publishers. Panditji had finished reading it and had put it down on his mother's bedside table. When Panditji caught me eyeing the book rather avidly, he smiled and said that I could take it home to read if I wanted to, adding that he had other copies.

Since that day Jawaharlalji has been enshrined in my heart like a deity. Later I may often have disagreed with his views, but the veneration he inspired within me that evening remained always. There are many leaders for whom I have an abiding respect, but I must confess that Gandhiji and Pandit Nehru were two men who left the deepest impression on my mind.

Our town was constantly churning out the most colourful rumours about the great Nehrus. One of them said that Jawaharlal was a classmate and a bosom friend of the Prince of Wales in England, and another said that Pandit Motilalji's dirty linen was sent to a French dhobikhana (laundromat) in France for washing. Many other tales also circulated freely, such as the one which said that the Governor of the United Provinces, one Mr Butler, smuggled in bottles of champagne for Pandit Motilal Nehru, when the latter was in gaol, while yet another maintained that when Jawaharlalji was a student, the Queen of England used to pack his lunch, along with her son's, with her own hands, in tiffin carriers that were despatched daily from Buckingham Palace to the school. One wonders whether the innocent minds that spun these yarns with great love for the Nehrus realized that they were not exactly adding to the prestige of their heroes by linking their names with such mannerisms and exaggerated claims of friendship with celebrities from the West.

The visible facts, however, contradicted all this. In Rae Bareli district, one could see the same supposed bosom pal of the Prince of Wales and the alleged eater of those royal packed lunches, go around in the blazing heat of the summer months with dusty chappals on his feet, and a wet towel over his head to protect it from the sun, as he carried the flame of independence from village to village, castigating the feudal talukdars and zamindars for sucking the blood of the poor of Awadh and making them poorer. So what, I finally said to myself, if he has high family connections? Friendship with the high and mighty might be a dishonest man's weakness, but had it not been an extra source of strength for the wise and the just? And, when the British police beat him up as the leader of the crowds protesting against the Simon Commission, all my misgivings dissolved and I was won over completely, along with most young Indians who had had similar doubts. We even took great delight in his weaknesses; his unbridled temper, his rushing in against all barriers to mingle with the crowds so effortlessly, the occasional fracas that resulted from all this. We just loved it all. Once, when one of my friends was praising the translucent beauty of the waters of the Ganga, I burst out, 'They are as clear as Jawaharlal's heart.' The conversation then turned from religion to politics.

Talking of Jawaharlalji and religion, most of us wondered aloud from time to time whether Jawaharlal was an atheist or a believer? He was known to be somewhat disdainful towards the

Hindu religion, but as I said, in his case it was often hard to sift facts from lore.

My own mind was deeply steeped in a combination of the new learning and traditional Hindu philosophy. I disliked the superstitions and the vulgar rituals of Hinduism, but a deep faith in my religion was the only touchstone I had to test my own honesty. I was keen to listen to logic and reason, but I was also aware that my religious faith was necessary for me to make up my mind about the veracity of the new ideas. Here I admired Gandhi deeply. I often felt that since Jawaharlal was very close to Gandhiji, he must have a deeply religious core to his psyche, notwithstanding his public statements about his atheist ideals. I found the actual answer to this after a long time, when I read *The Discovery of India*. At that time, however, I had only read *Inside Soviet Russia,* and felt charged with a new intellectual energy. The Brave New World that the book talked about, reminded me of the Brave New World of Soviet Russia, heralded by our Hindi journalists like Ganesh Shankar Vidyarthi in his weekly paper *Pratap.* Jawaharlalji's book offered a further glimpse into this phenomenon.

This was when I first heard of Karl Marx, although I still did not know anything about Marxism. Jawaharlalji's book had attracted our attention towards the principles of Marxism. He had toured Russia with his father some ten years after the Great October Revolution. His book was full of glowing references to Russia's decade of miracles. One felt charged with the same magic as one read through his descriptions. However, the book *Inside Russia* also went into graphic details about the cruelties inflicted on the dropouts from this great race towards new nation-building by the communists. The rumours about the communists' cruelty were many, and often they were as highly exaggerated as the rumours about Jawaharlal's family background. They served to prejudice the minds of some people against communism, just as stories about Motilal's Parisian dhobi and Jawaharlal's legendary culinary camaraderie with the Prince of Wales had done. The small lending libraries in our suburbs and smaller towns, were suddenly full of English spy novels that narrated hair raising tales of the tortures inflicted by the Bolsheviks. These and their Hindi translations were read avidly in our houses. Both those who were for Bolshevism, and those who were against, competed with each other in exaggerating stories about the Brave New World, and this had the result of confusing young boys like me totally. Jawaharlal's book about Russia served to clean many cobwebs and wipe off much dust from our minds.

By then most of my friends had opted for open ideological allegiance to either socialism or capitalism. The former firmly believed that they must, like the Russians, set their countrymen free from the stranglehold of the dirty capitalists and reform our society, so that India also became a brave new world.

Often we wondered how a fiery young man like Jawaharlal managed to pull on with a disciplined man like Gandhi, who was forever experimenting with strange ideas like the Salt Satyagraha. We felt this was a silly act, and as far as I recall, Nehru too had expressed feelings of surprise at this move initially in his *Autobiography*. Then suddenly we found the idea spreading like a virus in the Indian society. The Nehru women broke the law by making salt and went to gaol, so making salt became an unfailing method of following the patriots into gaol. A lot of intellectuals like me, who were initially opposed to the Salt Satyagraha, now joined the salt movement with great gusto.

I now realize that what joined Nehru and Gandhi and kept them together was Gandhi's capacity for struggle even while indulging in the most awkward and inexplicable acts; and Nehru's deep and abiding faith in the human capacity for struggle. He wanted the country to struggle hard till the British had no option but to leave, and the Indians could go back to living as a proud and free race in a free country. From members of Gandhi's Banar Sena to the youthful workers of Congress, this matching of Gandhi's controlled vision and Nehru's fiery idealism fired us Indians with great enthusiasm.

On the occasion of the Dandi march, one often heard the lines of the Hindi poet, Sohan Lal Dwivedi, being quoted: 'Wherever those two feet marched, crores of feet followed.' Truly at that time people followed the young Jawahar with closed eyes. Nehru's socialism that hovered on the brink of communism did not clash with Gandhi's passive theory of nonviolence, but acquired a new shine by this association.

Nehru shocked several of us, when after India won freedom, he declared India to be a secular nation. But I believe secularism to him meant something quite different from what it has come to mean today. Dr Radhakrishnan understood it perfectly when he explained how being secular is not synonymous with being irreligious, but acquiring a deep tolerance and respect for all religions.

Nehru did not wish to make India into a Hindu Rashtra, as a parallel to the Islamic Pakistan. This country, he felt, must give an equal place and consideration to all religions, and this, I feel, is the biggest contribution of this profoundly wise man to the new India.

Nehru's penchant for working methodically came from his admiration for the Russian five-year plans. He wished to set his country, ossified by centuries of redundant custom, on to a path of new learning as the Russians had managed to do in theirs. This was the reason why he brought forward the hotly-challenged Hindu Code Bill. But Nehru did not have the same resistance to facing criticism while advocating social change as Gandhi had. Gandhi managed to introduce some revolutionary social changes, like the removal of untouchability and purdah, which perhaps Jawahar could not have brought about due to a different mental attitude and temperament. But one must acknowledge a debt to him for having introduced the country to true secularism.

Nehru's fiscal policies are another important contribution. A decade prior to India's freedom he had formed the National Planning Committee within the Congress Party, while other leaders were only focusing on achieving freedom. In the first *Report* of the National Planning Committee, Nehru wrote how the ideal of his party was to found a true democracy in India, where each citizen gets a chance and develops the ability to express himself.

Nehru was not only a democrat, he was also very careful about maintaining healthy parliamentary traditions. This was why he accepted the resignation of trusted lieutenants like Shastriji (after a major railway accident) and T.T. Krishnamachari (after the Mundra scandal). In the Congress legislative party he was as democratic as he was in Parliament. He gave full freedom to all his party members for self-expression and he never ignored the people's verdict.

Years ago, when I had gone to meet Shri C.B. Gupta, then Chief Minister of Uttar Pradesh, he showed me a letter of Pandit Nehru's, which he was in the habit of sending to all his Chief Ministers each week. In this letter Panditji had asked them specifically to help artists, writers and other makers of artistic traditions. Like Tagore, he was ultimately a worshipper of art and beauty, and to my mind, a man who genuinely respects and admires beauty, can never be an irreligious atheist.

Translated from the original Hindi by Mrinal Pande

~

The Genius of Nehru[19]

John Grigg

John Grigg (1924–2001) was a British writer, historian and politician. The following essay is a frank assessment of Nehru's failures and his undeniably crucial role in shaping modern India.

~

Among the great personalities of history, Jawaharlal Nehru is one of the most appealing. We are drawn to him not only by his talents, virtues and achievements, but also, and no less powerfully, by faults and failures which enhance his interest as a human being while commanding our sympathy. The pathos of his life affects us at least as much as its glory. Moreover, since he was rare among

[19] From *Jawaharlal Nehru: Centenary Volume.*

those who have made history in being capable also of writing it, and in being prepared to reveal some of his innermost thoughts, we can feel all the closer to him.

He was, of course, a world figure in an age when mass communications were making the human race for the first time conscious of itself as a whole. His impact upon people throughout the world would have been considerable even if he had stayed at home; but since, as Prime Minister of independent India, he acted as his own Minister of External Affairs, paying very frequent visits to other countries, his impact abroad was all the greater. In the 1950s, when his career was at its zenith, he was beyond question one of the half dozen most familiar and prestigious statesmen on the international stage.

He belonged then to the whole world, and to the whole world he will never cease to belong.

Yet despite his global stature, there are two countries to which he belongs in a more profound and intimate sense. The first, obviously, is India, the land of his birth, to whose service he devoted his life and whose 'discovery' inspired his adult mind. But the other, surely, is my own country, England, whose language, literature and political tradition were vital influences throughout his life. Dom Moraes probably goes too far in describing him as 'a prototype manufactured in England (though with parts supplied in India)'. But even Mahatma Gandhi once said that he was 'more English than Indian in thoughts and make-up'.

The same was to some extent true of Gandhi himself, and this must have been one of the chief bonds between two men otherwise so dissimilar. Gandhi went to England by his own free choice, defying caste taboos and leaving his wife and children at home in Gujarat. It was the first extraordinarily bold act of his career, and the key to all the others. As a result he became a fascinating blend of Hindu mystic and Victorian liberal eccentric: mutatis mutandis, a sort of Indian Mr Gladstone. (One of many flaws in the all-too-popular Attenborough film about him is that it begins the story in South Africa, instead of showing him, aged nineteen, leaving his family and community and crossing the 'black waters' to England. The enormous biographical significance of this journey is ignored, and so is the intensely formative effect of Gandhi's two years as a student in London.)

Nehru was more anglicized than Gandhi, because he was brought up in a very anglophile home before being sent to an English boarding school and then to an English university. His response to England was in many ways different from Gandhi's, since he was a romantic but sceptical idealist, whereas Gandhi was above all religious. But both men absorbed a lot of Englishness of one kind or another, and shared an acceptance of certain English values which bound them together hardly less strongly than their love of India and commitment to the cause of national emancipation.

They were, indeed, finer exponents of those values than most of the native British products with whom they had to deal, at any rate at the political level. This was Britains's tragedy as well as theirs. Beatrice Webb noted in 1912 that 'the aristocracy of India' was subject to 'the mediocrity of Great Britain', and when we consider the small-mindedness of British policy towards India after the First World War, the remark seems just. Gandhi's vision of Indian Swaraj within a wider empire offered an opportunity for constructive statecraft that has seldom been matched; but British politicians, alas, squandered the opportunity. Similarly, Nehru's principled opposition to Hitler and Mussolini during the 1930s should have earned for him and his country equal status in the ensuing struggle. Instead, war was declared on behalf of India in 1939 without reference to India's elected leaders, and Nehru, who should have joined Churchill and Roosevelt in the higher direction of the war and in planning the peace, was forced back into the sterile role of an agitator.

But to return to his early life. One might have expected an Indian boy at that date to be miserably unhappy in the alien environment of Harrow, but in fact Nehru was not; on the contrary, he tells us that he wept when he left the school. British boarding schools have often been compared with prisons, and Nehru's equanimity at Harrow may be said to have anticipated that taste for prison life which was to become so marked a characteristic in his middle years. 'One feels almost lonely outside the jail,' he wrote in 1922, 'and selfishness prompts a quick return.' And soon afterwards his father, Motilal, had occasion to write to him: 'I was pained to find that ... my visit of yesterday only had the effect of disturbing the even tenor of your happy jail life ... . I am as happy outside the jail as you are in it.'

Clearly Nehru was a quite abnormally introverted character—in many ways a natural solitary. Yet his political convictions and aspirations led him into a life requiring the utmost gregariousness. When he was out of prison he had to deal all the time with his fellow human beings, both individually and in the mass. But he could not change his nature, and whether as a leader of the national movement before Independence, or as Prime Minister after it, his life was—in Sarvepalli Gopal's brilliant phrase—'a life of crowded loneliness'.

This contradiction or tension in him adds immensely to his value as an author, just as his welcome stretches in prison gave him the leisure to write. But other consequences were less fortunate. Gratifying his desire for solitude, with full cooperation from the British authorities, involved abandoning his wife and daughter for long periods. This was particularly regrettable since Kamala, who was not very well treated by other members of his family, was for much of the time ailing and eventually dying, and since Indira was an only child. Moreover, his habit of introspection made him a better judge of himself than of others; as Prime Minister his record as a picker of colleagues was less than masterly. Finally, his solitariness made him vulnerable to anybody who could win his confidence and seem to be protecting him against the outside world, as the affair of M.O. Mathai[20] was to demonstrate.

---

[20] Private Secretary to Nehru who was later embroiled in communist allegations of spying and misuse of power. Nehru, however, maintained contact with him even after these allegations and his subsequent resignation.

His sense of style, manifest in his books and letters, was no less so in his talk and bearing. He had a personal magic which—having admired him from afar—I was able to experience at first hand in 1957, when visiting Delhi with an international group of journalists. Meeting him with the group and subsequently on my own, I was altogether charmed. On the second occasion I was greeted by Indira Gandhi, who talked to me for a few minutes until her father came in, when she left us. (I later got to know her better.) Nehru then spoke with remarkable frankness, and with more humility than conceit, about his unique prestige as the leader under whom Independence had been won. Because of this, there could be no effective opposition during his lifetime. But his special authority would die with him, and then normal politics with an alternation of governments would evolve.

The conversation sticks in my mind, as does the figure of Nehru with his close-fitting white trousers, long brown coat, and rose in the third buttonhole; his quiet, melodious voice, turning sharp when he was ordering coffee; above all, his beautiful, rather enigmatic smile. But in retrospect, the figure of Mrs Indira Gandhi seems no less important, providing as it were an ironic comment on her father's expressed belief that the Nehru magic would be for his life only.

In fact it was, of course, transmitted to her, and after her to her surviving son. The Nehrus have become a political dynasty from which the leader of India is liable to be chosen, whatever his or her prior experience of government. Some have argued that it was by Nehru's wish and contrivance that his daughter succeeded him after a brief interlude, but this seems to me a quite unconvincing argument. If, as could more easily be argued, he set the stage for Lal Bahadur Shastri to succeed him, how could he have foreseen that the Shastri premiership would be as brief as it was? The most that can reasonably be suspected is that he wanted his daughter to play a part in national politics after his death, having earlier (in 1959) acquiesced in, if not promoted, her election as Congress President.

Rather than speculate about his ambitions for her, it seems, in any case, more worthwhile to discuss how and why she came to be so close to him towards the end of his life, and how that closeness determined, in a sense, the future course of events. This is a subject about which Dr Gopal is understandably reticent; he was writing Nehru's official biography while Mrs Gandhi was alive and, for most of the time, in power. (The first and third volumes were published while she was in office, the second during the period of the Janata government.) Yet it must surely be a subject of compelling interest to any student of Nehru.

His neglect of her during her childhood has already been noted. Some may regard this as a price that had to be paid if he was to fulfil his patriotic destiny; but we know that he did not, himself, take so simple or comforting a view of the matter. Sensitive as he was, and always prone to soul-searching, he was well aware that his long absences in prison might have been due as much to self-indulgence as to patriotism. He had a bad conscience about his wife, and this compounded his feelings of guilt about Indira, since he knew that for long periods in her youth she had had to look after her sick mother alone. It was natural that he should wish to compensate, later, for the mental suffering he had inflicted; and by making her, when he was Prime Minister, his closest companion and confidante, he must have hoped and intended to do so.

Once again, however, his good intentions were to some extent alloyed with selfishness, since he needed her also for his own comfort: not only as a hostess but as somebody he felt he could trust, more especially after the enforced resignation of Mathai in 1959. Moreover, just as his own marriage had been sacrificed to his political and temperamental needs, so with a tragic symmetry, her marriage in turn was sacrificed, when she decided to put her father's interests above those of her husband and children. In marrying Feroze Gandhi she had defied Nehru, who was opposed to the marriage not because it was intercommunal—that would have made nonsense of his secularism—but because of his reservations about Feroze Gandhi's impetuousness.

Relations between him and his son-in-law were, in due course, further complicated by politics. Feroze was a fiercely independent politician, who for that reason alone could never have consented to be a hanger-on in the Prime Minister's house. He wanted to be free to attack backsliding Congress grandees and to expose corruption in high places: a mission in which he achieved some success, but usually at the cost of adding to the difficulties with his father-in-law, who was apt to defend any appointee of his beyond the defensible limit. If only Feroze could have established a true rapport with Nehru, he would have been as good and honest an adviser, and as able a colleague as the Prime Minister could have found. But it was not to be, and Indira was placed in the cruel position of having to choose, in effect, between her husband and her father.

She chose the latter, though without of course formally ending her marriage. It was plausible to maintain that her father had the stronger claim on her, because in serving him she was also serving the nation. But was there not, perhaps, a little self-interest in her decision? Was she, even at that stage, a complete stranger to personal ambition? If, like her father before her, she was in some measure suiting herself while making an ostensible sacrifice, then it is probable that, like him, she knew it and had a raw nerve of conscience, particularly in regard to her sons whom she had deprived of a normal home background by living apart from their father. If so, moreover, it is surely possible that Sanjay may, consciously or unconsciously, have worked upon her sense of guilt, so that she may have felt she had to compensate him as her father had compensated her, and with a similar admixture of self-interest. The symmetrical pattern may, therefore, have been reproduced in the next generation, with even more tragic results.

What is certain is that a dynasty was created, and that its existence has prevented the sort of democratic evolution that Nehru confidently forecast thirty odd years ago. Though India is still in most essential respects a democracy, and the only experience of dictatorship in its independent history was happily short-lived, it has proved impossible, so far, for a strong opposition or viable alternative government to emerge, or for any political personalities to rival the automatic all-India status of the Nehrus. Other democracies have other weaknesses; none is perfect. But since Nehru's supreme achievement was establishing and nurturing Indian democracy, the extent to which its progress since his death has been hindered by the hereditary prestige attaching to his family cannot be overlooked in any frank review of his legacy.

What are the legacy's other major components? Of course he was the leader of the Indian National Movement—Gandhi having stood aside—at the time when Independence was attained 'not wholly or in full measure, but very substantially'. Can it be said that his legacy includes a divided subcontinent? Was the calamitous partition of India to any significant degree his fault? Much has been made by some critics of his failure to accept the 1946 Cabinet Mission plan in unqualified terms, when Jinnah had ostensibly accepted it; and it is surely hard to deny that that was a serious tactical error. But it is equally hard to doubt that Jinnah was inflexible in his determination to have Pakistan, and that Nehru's mistake merely gave him an immediate pretext for escaping from a commitment which, in any case, he would soon have found some other occasion to repudiate. The blame for Partition seems to me overwhelmingly attributable—though I hate to have to say it—to British government policy from the First World War onwards, in which communal differences were deliberately played up and exploited. There are very large pluses, as well as minuses, in the record of British rule, as Indian writers have been generous in acknowledging. But to my mind the most terrible minus is the paramount share of responsibility that British governments bear for the tragedy of Partition. Jinnah, too, has a very important share. Nehru's share seems to me negligible.

He has been vilified for intransigence over Kashmir, but in truth he is more open to criticism for weakness at the outset. He should never have given any countenance to the idea of a plebiscite there. All his subsequent troubles derived from that initial mistake.

In the wider international sphere, his distinctive contribution was the policy of non-alignment. This was fully justified on grounds of national self-interest, but perhaps unduly trumpeted as an ethically superior concept. There were, moreover, times when he seemed less than even-handed in his attitude towards the protagonists in the Cold War; somewhat reluctant to condemn Soviet iniquities, while all too ready to condemn the Western democracies with which, in reality, he had far more in common. Yet his motives were often crassly misunderstood by Western leaders. In the Suez crisis, for instance, his policy was by no means unhelpful to Britain and France, and might have served to resolve the dispute to the satisfaction of all concerned. But the British and French governments chose to spurn it and to embark instead on a course which was as disastrous as it was dishonourable.

His own misreading of the Chinese needs no elaboration. It led to the most traumatic and humiliating episode of his career, which probably hastened his death. But though his heart was, in a sense, broken by it, he did not lose his nerve, while the country's reaction to the Chinese challenge strikingly demonstrated its underlying strength and unity, which owed so much to his leadership.

In the balance sheet of his foreign statesmanship nothing stands more to his credit than the decision that independent and republican India should remain a member of the Commonwealth, recognizing the British sovereign as its titular head. He was under heavy pressure from some quarters to withdraw, and by withdrawing he could have rid himself of his excessively 'British' image. But he had the magnanimity to resist this temptation, and the prescience to see what the Commonwealth might become as the fact and the memory of British dominance faded. The modern Commonwealth, whose value is increasingly appreciated, is largely his monument.

At home his greatest bequest to posterity, apart from the state itself, was the industrial base that he established—for the first time in history—in conditions of political freedom. Though he was much attacked, by Jayaprakash Narayan and others, for the 'giganticism' of his projects, he knew what he was doing. It was lucky for India that its first Prime Minister was a science graduate. Thanks to him India is now one of the world's leading industrial nations.

Did he neglect agriculture? Perhaps he might have done more to develop it, but at least he avoided the folly of Marxist experiments to which, theoretically, he might have been drawn. It is safe to say that if Indian agriculture had been collectivized there would have been no green revolution.

In general he tended to be cautious in his approach to India's economic and social problems. If this was an error, it was surely the right way to err. Despite his mental energy and itch for action, he schooled himself to be patient when handling problems that he knew to be profound and complex. All the same, what he did for the country's material development was on a huge scale, and would have been marked by a dramatic improvement in the people's standard of life, had it not coincided with the medical revolution that kept so many more of them alive.

Their affection for him was not misplaced. He was a patriot who cared for his countrymen as human beings, as well as for the ideal of country. Remote though he may have been from most of them intellectually and culturally, he was in tune with them at the level of feeling. Such was the genius of Nehru. Such is the genius of India.

~

Dinkar on Nehru

Ramdhari Singh Dinkar

*Ramdhari Singh Dinkar (1908–1974), an eminent Hindi poet and writer, came in close contact with Nehru as a member of Rajya Sabha for twelve years. Nehru liked him and wrote a preface for his ambitious history of Indian culture—*Sanskriti ke Char Adhyay.

After Nehru's demise, Dinkar wrote a book containing his memoirs and evaluation of Nehru. It was titled Lok Devta Nehru *(Nehru: The People's Deity). An extract from the same follows. It is taken from the collected works of Dinkar.*[21]

~

[21] *Dinkar Rachnavali, vol xiii*, ed. *Nand Kishore Nawal and Tarun Kumar* (New Delhi: Lokbharati Prakashan, 2011).

A Symbol of Defeated Virtue

Panditji respected poets, but never got too excited by listening to poetry. I came very close to him after becoming a member of parliament. In his eyes, I could always see love and encouragement, probably he had started liking me. Dear friend Feroze Gandhi used to lightheartedly call me 'Mahakavi', maybe Panditji sometime overheard it. He also couple of times called me 'Mahakavi' but never with an invitation to recite any poem.

I was always eager to know his reaction to poetry, but it was rather difficult to catch. Once, in a holi gathering at his residence Josh Malihabadi read out his poem, *Utho ki naubahar hai*; Panditji heard it very attentively and at one point impulsively reacted as well. I also read out my poem, but could not see Panditji's face. As soon as I sat down, he got up and announced an end to the poetry session. I am not sure, if he was happy with my poem and wanted it to be the last one, or was apprehensive of two poets launching some sort of poetry reading match.

In my first meeting with him as an MP, I carried some books for him. He received these as if the most valuable gift he has ever got, and said affectionately, 'great, some books for me, will have a look.'

I said, 'you are hardly going to get time to go through these, I would be happy to see them in your library.'

'Will keep them in my bed-room', he said, 'I read a little before sleeping.'

In the very first meeting I made so bold as to ask him, 'Panditji, what all you have read?'

'Well, don't have any Persian. Besides English and French, I studied Hindi. A little bit of Sanskrit as well, and you know, I know by heart all that I read in Sanskrit.'

It has been reported after his death, that he used to read *Gita* occasionally, but Feroze once told me that he read the second chapter of Gita quite frequently and in fact knew it by heart.

Another thing comes to light in what Pyarelal ji has written about Motilal ji. He had passed away around six in the morning and Jawaharlal ji was with him throughout the night, In the morning, he told Gandhiji, 'Father told me in the night that as a child you were taught Gayatri mantra, but you hardly ever recite it. I had indeed forgotten this mantra, but strangely, it suddenly came back to me, last night.'

The late Pandit Ramnaresh Tripathi wanted to come to Parliament. He wanted me to take up this matter with Panditji. Once, in the course of this discussion, he informed me that requested by Motilal ji, he had helped Jawaharlal ji study *Ramcharitmanas* by Tulsidas.

History might record some things about him, leave out some things, but it has to perforce record the amazing effort Jawaharlal Nehru made to modernise the Indian mind. But in spite of being such a vocal flag bearer of modernity, he had a soft corner for ancient India. Once he took me along to a small gathering where he had to speak to a group of African students. He told them, 'You have come to a very old country. Its civilisation consists of many layers which you will come across when you go around. You will see some things here which you may see in USA and Europe as well, and some you will find troubling. Each one is important, because India whatever it is, consists of each and every one of them. Even the civilizational layers which seem hollow today had some significance at some point in history.'

Once, the Hindi committee of parliament was meeting at his residence. He joined us a bit late, and when he arrived I was speaking about the hurdles in the way of unity of Indian people. When, his turn came, Panditji mentioned his recent trip to Odisha where he had heard the discontent of adivasis against the Aryans, 'They say, Dronacharya the Aryan deprived Eklavya the Adivasi of his thumb.' Listening to this, some members of the committee started laughing, which made Panditji very upset, 'As a matter of fact, I feel very angry with Dronacharya for this act.'

Dwaper (the traditional era, during which Mahabharata and the Eklavya ancient epics took place) is so far from Kaliyuga—our own era. But true humanity transcends such distance. Nehru—the true human while living in Kaliyuga, felt deeply angry about an injustice committed in Dwaper.

As a minister, his remarks on files were never confined to 'as proposed'. Files coming from his table always had some sentences in fine English. He cared a lot of correspondence with members of parliament. There would hardly be a MP whose letter was not replied with Panditji's own signature. Often the case was that you sent the letter and the very next day the PM's peon will be at your door carrying his reply.

He felt sorry, whenever he failed to maintain the appointed hour. Once he gave me an appointment in the external affirms ministry for nine in the morning, but himself arrived late by forty minutes, apologising with some irritation, 'Mahakavi, like Red Fort and Qutab Minar, I have also become some kind of exhibit of Delhi. Everyday throngs of people arrive to "see" me, today, the number was much more than expected, hence this delay.'

He was quite pained with violent slogan-mongering in the wake of Chinese aggression. He articulated his pain in many ways, one being this, 'Even now, I can not like the brutalisation of my country.' When he declared this in the parliament, I responded with a poem, which is collected in *Parshuram ki Pratiksha* (waiting for Parshuram). I admired the height of Panditji's agony, but my conclusion however remained, 'brutes can be handled with brutal force only.'

From October 1962 to March 1963, he passed through multiple trials by fire. There was anger all around, he was the target of bitterest criticisms, frustrations were bursting like volcanos, but he remained calm and composed. There were rumours and hearsay that his leadership is over, but the fact is that during this period his leadership was put to most arduous test and by remaining calm and composed, he truly proved his leadership as never before.

Victory is always limited. Most of the times, history gets light from those who are defeated on the path of virtue. Krishna and

Ashoka, Kabir and Akbar, Gandhi and Jawaharlal are the symbols of the defeated virtue.

Translated by Purushottam Agrawal

~

Man and Symbol, A Fragmentary Appreciation[22]

Norman Cousins

Norman Cousins (1915–1990) was an American political journalist, author, professor, and peace activist. In the following piece he recollects the many facets of Nehru's personality: the selfless side, putting himself in harm's way to protect the vulnerable; his playful, private side as witnessed at an afternoon lunch at the Prime Minister's residence; and his sweeping intellect and charismatic, self-aware leadership.

~

He was not one man but a procession of men. In him you witnessed a national hero, statesman, philosopher, historian, author, educator.

He was also a triumphant assortment of paradoxes. He was a supreme rationalist who presided over a nation with the most pervasive and complex religious make-up in the world.

He was an intellectual product of Western civilization who was accepted as symbolic leader by many hundreds of millions of Asians and Africans who feared the West.

He was an accomplished logician who lived on intimate terms with the imponderables and intangibles.

He was an avowed optimist who found it difficult to keep from brooding.

He had sensitivities so finely attuned that he could be jarred by the slightest vibrations, but he was able to make history-jolting decisions.

He believed the highest function of the state was to help develop the individuality of the individual, but no nation in the

---

[22] From *Jawaharlal Nehru: Centenary Volume.*

world contained as many natural obstacles to the emergence of that individuality as the nation he governed for seventeen years.

With such a man, you cannot essay a full evaluation or appreciation. The best you can do is to pursue certain qualities and attributes.

First, the courage of the man

August 1947. With national Independence and Partition of the subcontinent between India and Pakistan, four hundred and fifty million people became caught up in a vast convulsion. Hindus and Muslims, with a long history of tension between them, became part of a chain reaction of violence and horror. No one knows how many died. But twelve million people became homeless. Rumours of atrocities and actual atrocities interacted to produce a spiralling madness.

For a while, the situation was relatively calm in New Delhi, with its large Muslim population. Then, suddenly, the storm broke. Late one night a Hindu mob, inflamed by stories of Muslim terror to the north-west, swept into Connaught Circus, the main shopping area in New Delhi. The rioters smashed their way into Muslim stores, destroying and looting and ready to kill.

Even before the police arrived in force, Jawaharlal Nehru was on the scene. He plunged into the crowd in the darkness, trying to bring people to their senses. He spied a Muslim who had just been seized by Hindus. He interposed himself between the man and his attackers.

Suddenly a cry went up, 'Jawaharlal is here! Jawaharlal is here! Don't hurt Jawaharlal!'

The cry spread through the crowd. It had a magical effect. People stood still and dropped their arms to their sides. Looted merchandise was dropped. The mob psychology disintegrated. By the time the police arrived people were dispersing. The riot was over.

The next day, friends rushed to Nehru, admonishing him for exposing himself to a mob at the height of its frenzy.

'You could have been killed,' one of them said. 'Then what?'

'That's for you to determine,' he replied quietly. 'Many others could have been killed last night. Then what?'

The fact that Nehru had risked his life to save a single Muslim had a profound effect far beyond New Delhi. Many thousands of Muslims who had intended to flee to Pakistan now stayed in India, staking their lives on Nehru's ability to protect them and assure them justice. In years to come, this confidence of India's Muslims in Nehru was to become a major factor in building a nation and holding it together.

Not many weeks after the communal rioting subsided, the Prime Minister and a foreign guest were driving in his private car about fifteen miles south of Delhi. The traffic piled up behind a caravan of camels in a village preponderantly populated by Muslims. Only recently, this village had figured in mass violence.

The combination of the heat, the heavy chalky dust from the dry dirt road, the temper of the camel drivers, and the screams of people in the stalled buses, trucks, wagons, and automobiles provided the combustible materials for a communal riot. Young Muslims from the village suddenly appeared with knives. They surrounded Nehru's car. One of them recognized the Prime Minister and shouted angry words at him.

Nehru stepped out of his car, walked up to the young man, spoke to him quietly. Suddenly, a cheer went up for the Prime Minister. The Muslims surrounded him, expressing their devotion and loyalty. Then some of them began to weep in shame for their actions. Nehru spoke with them, answering their questions, telling them of his hopes.

On the drive back to New Delhi, his guest expressed concern for the Prime Minister's safety. Mr Nehru agreed the risk might be real, but he said he could not let it get in the way of things that had to be done.

The human quality of the man

January 1951, Sunday. The desk clerk at the Imperial Hotel in New Delhi handed us a message. It was from Miss Sindhi at the Prime Minister's House. The Prime Minister was having some people over that afternoon and hoped we could come. Nothing special. Just relaxed talk.

Primed for a long bull session on philosophy and politics, we arrived at the Prime Minister's house at about three o'clock. Mr Nehru was at the door, greeting his guests. He seemed to be in excellent spirits. We were ushered to a large enclosed veranda. We looked around the room and recognized Dr Sarvepalli Radhakrishnan, the eminent philosopher and Vice-President of India; also, Shiva Rau, prominent author and long-time friend of the Prime Minister. Among the other guests to whom we were introduced were two cabinet ministers and a justice.

Mr Nehru came into the room, his young grandson riding his shoulders, kicking grandpa's ribs and demanding more speed.

'The gallop comes later,' Mr Nehru said, hoisting the boy over his head and placing him on the floor. He told the youngster he had a surprise for him. 'In fact, I've got a surprise for everyone. This afternoon we shall all have a good time. I've arranged for entertainment.'

The entertainer was a magician who went through a bewildering assortment of tricks. He caused long knives to turn into short knives, wine to turn into milk, and he made a chicken emerge from a paper cup. Then he demonstrated his accuracy with a bow and arrow, hitting a vertical thread at about twenty feet. Finally, he invited a member of the company to step forward. Mr Nehru, enjoying himself hugely, prodded the Finance Minister into joining the act.

As soon as the Finance Minister discovered he was to be a living prop in a latter- day version of a William Tell episode, he seemed to waver somewhat. Mr Nehru gently chided him into going on with the act. The Finance Minister was seated in a chair directly above which, six inches from his head, a circular wreath was suspended by several thin threads.

The magician announced that with one arrow he would sever all the threads, causing the wreath to fall around the Finance Minister's distinguished shoulders. Almost as an afterthought, he added that he would perform this feat while blindfolded.

Mr Nehru spoke up.

'They tell me that good Finance Ministers are hard to find these days,' he said. 'I don't know whether we ought to allow him to go through with this.'

The magician clapped for silence, put on his blindfold, picked up his bow, tested its tautness, and inserted the arrow. Then he paused and, still blindfolded, paced off the steps to his target, groping and stumbling on the way. Finally, he retraced his steps, assumed his battle station, and raised the bow and arrow.

'No, no,' Mr Nehru cried. 'You're aiming at the wrong man! You're aiming at the Justice. We can't afford to lose *him*. The man you want is about sixty degrees to the left.'

Suddenly the magician let fly. The arrow pierced the strings and the garland fell neatly over the shoulder of the Finance Minister, who, suddenly released from his encounter with non-fiscal suspense, joined in the general laughter.

After a while, the group exchanged stories. The Prime Minister presided over the ice-cream and punch bowl, the youngster at his side tugging at grandpa's pants and asking when he could have a fast horseback ride.

The closest anyone got to serious talk was when Mr Nehru told of a visit he had had the previous day from an old school chum who was now a wealthy industrialist.

According to the Prime Minister, the industrialist came up to him and complained that things had gone much too far. Taxes were crippling him and something had to be done about it. He said he had to pay a stiff tax on his private house in New Delhi. He also had to pay a tax on his hunting estate. As if this were not enough, he had to pay a tax on a house he kept in Bangalore. But worst of all was the tax he had to pay on his beach home in Juhu.

'Now I ask you, Jawaharlal, how do you expect me to keep up these houses with taxes like this?'

'Have you ever considered giving up a house or two?' Nehru asked.

'Now, what kind of advice is this to give a life-long friend?' the man asked.

The group laughed.

'What makes the story so ironic,' Mr Nehru said, 'is that here I am, fighting back legislation to confiscate luxurious property, and this chap wants me to give him a tax refund. I suppose each man has to have his own dream world.'

In this manner the afternoon passed. After the farewells, Dr Radhakrishnan said we had just seen a side of Nehru that few people knew.

'There is something eternally young, even boyish, about the Prime Minister,' he said. 'People tend to think of him as a man lost in brooding, not even knowing how to laugh. Not so; he loves to laugh, as we have seen. It is very good for the nation that he can laugh. It helps to freshen his spirits. The important thing about Nehru is that he continues to think young. A man like this can never grow old. He will never look old, no matter how old he is. But he must take better care of himself. He works too hard.'

The man as author, poet, historian, philosopher, thinker

He liked to write, felt incomplete when he was unable to assemble his thoughts and commit them to paper. He regarded writing as the most demanding, the most exhausting, but also the most satisfying of the creative arts. Writing enabled him to discipline his mind, to think sequentially and creatively. Being able to give life to a concept through words; using language as a vehicle of persuasion or as a voyage of intellectual exploration and discovery—these meant much to him.

At times he could write like the most detached and aseptic historian. At other times he would write with extreme sensitivity and grace. In describing a natural setting, he could be all poet. In his writing, as in his life, he was many men.

For many years, his writing, quite literally, kept him from losing his mind. This was during his various imprisonments as agitator for Indian freedom. No one knows how many hundreds of thousands or millions of words he wrote while in gaol. His autobiography came out of prison. He did a work on history, *The Discovery of India.* There were also, to be sure, the various pamphlets and tracts that made him the intellectual leader of the fight for freedom.

Of all his prison writings, however, perhaps none is more remarkable than the collection of letters to his daughter, Indira, later published under the title, *Glimpses of World History.* The letters, running to almost 1,000 pages in the book, constituted something of a liberal university education, ranging as it did over the whole of the human historical record—European, Asian, African, American, Australian. It took in not just the development of national and continental civilization but the creative thrust and splendour of mankind. Nehru's own insights and his appreciation of the human potential are in evidence throughout. What made the book unique in the history of literature was that his prison was totally bereft of historical materials. He wrote *Glimpses of World History,* with its thousands of facts and events and names, without reference books or notes of any kind. As a demonstration of human intellectual capacity, the book stands by itself.

It is doubtful whether any writer before or since has fused in one person more thoroughly the complex essences of East and West. He was a fascinating amalgam of two cultures; his formal education was English but his traditions were Indian. His intellect was rooted in the Enlightenment but his spirit in the Vedas. Few men of our time have been so avowedly rationalist, yet there were the strongest spiritual connotations in his feelings about India and her people.

He wrote in his will:

> I have been attached to the Ganga and Jamuna Rivers in Allahabad ever since my childhood and, as I have grown older, this attachment has also grown. I have watched their varying moods as the seasons changed, and have often thought of the history and myth and tradition and song and story that have become attached to them through the long ages and become part of their flowing waters....The Ganga reminds me of the snow-covered peaks and the deep valleys of the Himalayas, which I have loved so much, and of the rich and vast plains below, where my life and work have been cast.

> Smiling and dancing in the morning sunlight, and dark and gloomy and full of mystery as evening shadows fall; a narrow, slow, and graceful stream in winter, and a vast, roaring thing during monsoon, broad-bosomed almost as the sea, and with something of the sea's power to destroy, the Ganga has been to me a symbol and a memory of the past of India, running into the present, and flowing on to the great ocean of the future.

Intellectually, he could never quite comprehend, and sometimes he had difficulty in coping with, India's numberless castes. We disclaimed any affiliation with or affinity for the religious aspect of Hinduism, yet he presided over a nation that sensed and responded to a profoundly spiritual quality in him. Gandhi was a godhead; he easily fitted into a theology. Not so Nehru, a supreme logician. Yet when Gandhi's mantle passed on, it passed to Nehru. No one questioned its appropriateness. There might be all the difference in the world between the thought, style, and outlook of the two men, but there was a seamless connection between the two in their devotion to the Indian people and in the response of the Indian people to them.

Nehru wrote:

> I have received so much love and affection from the Indian people that nothing I can do can repay even a small fraction of it. Many have been admired, some have been revered, but the affection of all classes of the Indian people has come to me in such abundant measure that I have been overwhelmed by it.

The leadership capacities and charismatic quality of the man

April 1955. The Asian-African Conference in Bandung. An event of profound importance for most of the world's peoples, symbolizing not just their freedom from outside rule but their full membership in the human race. Much of the drama flowed out of the juxtaposed presence of the two men who represented the two largest nations in the world—Jawaharlal Nehru of India and Chou En-lai of the People's Republic of China.

Both men knew that what was happening in their countries

would have a great bearing on the way most of the newly-independent nations would be developed.

Chou En-lai, speaking in English through an interpreter, was the first of the two to address the meeting. He identified China with the aspirations of Asia and Africa. He said that history was riding with China. This was done more in the form of an announcement than a claim. He invited the Bandung delegates to visit China and see the marked progress made under socialism. His manner was not bombastic or aggressive but matter-of-fact, austere.

When Nehru spoke some time later, the contrast between the two men couldn't have been more startling. It wasn't only that he spoke without a manuscript or without an interpreter. He had warmth, personal rapport. He was creating strength, awakening the individual's capacity and his hopes rather than attempting to convert a man to any large impersonal system. He held up no glorious certainties of historical determinism, only the saturating uncertainties of the human situation. But this was in the nature of freedom, which guaranteed nothing except a chance to do better; and freedom was within their reach.

At Bandung, the delegates may have been impressed by Chou En-lai, but they believed Nehru. And even when they did not agree with Nehru, they believed in him. This was the way it was with his own people. They might not have comprehended him at times, but they believed in him and knew that good would come out of such a man. Even though they were unable to connect themselves to his intellectuality, they never had trouble in understanding[1] his integrity. And they knew that where he wanted to go was where India had to be.

At Bandung, Chou En-lai was surrounded by bodyguards, Nehru by men who wanted to talk to him—men from new nations who suddenly were obligated to make history and needed the kind of confidence that a Nehru could impart to them. He was Olympian but he was never aloof.

The morning before the last session of the conference at Bandung, Nehru invited us to breakfast with him at his villa in the hills several miles outside the city. We sat on a veranda overlooking a flowering countryside. Nehru had already been down among the flowers, sniffing with satisfaction. His mood was deeply reflective. He spoke of the future of Asia with special reference to China and India. He said he had given the matter much thought. It was obvious, he said, that what happened inside India would have important effects outside India—not just in Asia but Africa. Here were two giant display cases for millions of people. The Indian display case, with all its complexities and difficulties, showed it was possible to have a progressive society without taking individuality away from the individual. The state should never subordinate the individual; rather, the state itself had the obligation to be infinitely inventive in trying to serve him and ennoble him. India had four hundred million people; most of them were poor. They needed jobs and food and medicine and schools and homes. It was precisely the kind of total need that the Chinese Communists said could never be met outside of a totally controlled society. They said what had to be done couldn't come fast enough or deep enough without the machinery available to a total Marxist state.

These were the questions most of the world's peoples had to decide, Nehru said. And he believed that India, despite all the difficulties, was making progress and could do even better.

We asked what he considered to be the main strengths and weaknesses in the development of Communist China.

He said, characteristically, that it was not for him to dispense such judgements; this was a task more appropriately done by history. But he added, also quite characteristically, that he would suppose that any leader of a state might have a certain caution in applying rigidly and literally economic or ideological doctrines that were based on the world as it was a century ago.

Was this a reference to the ideas of Marx and Engels?

Yes, he replied. There was much that was valid and valuable in Marx. But the world had undergone profound changes since Marx published his theories and the attempt to pursue these doctrines as though they were natural law was itself retrogressive, in a sense.

Moreover, he added, Marxism provided too narrow a creed for

the problems it had to meet. It gave so much emphasis to economic factors that it underestimated the power of all other concerns of man. Life consisted of much more than economic growth. He was not at all certain, he added, that the Marxist ideas were completely understood by all those who attempted to apply them.

Then his eyes twinkled and he sat back in his chair and -told of an incident at the conference involving Chou En-lai to illustrate his point:

'We were assigned to a sub-committee whose job it was to prepare a draft for a short statement for the conference. It was a simple statement that was required, and we were able to agree readily on the general substance. I invited Chou En-lai to write the first draft. He declined, saying he preferred that I do it.

'I did—in English, of course, and then read it to him through his interpreter. He was appreciative but said there were several key words that tended to change the meaning from what he understood the statement was supposed to say.

'Again we discussed the purpose of the statement in general and the troublesome words in particular. We had no difficulty in agreeing on the intended sense of the draft. All that remained now was to translate a few English words into Chinese. The attempt to do this took several hours—and even then, I was not completely satisfied that the translation was precise.

'Do you know what came to my mind when I left that meeting? I said to myself: "Good Lord, just imagine what Karl Marx must be like in Chinese!"

'He laughed, then said: "I'm perfectly serious, you know."'

There came to my mind a conversation with the Prime Minister in New Delhi some years earlier. Then, too, we were discussing what Stuart Chase called 'the tyranny of words.' In particular, words like 'inevitability', 'free will', and 'determinism'.

Imprecise though these terms were bound to be, I had asked Nehru whether he accepted the idea of implacable historical forces beyond man's reach.

In matters such as these, he had replied, it was well to avoid absolute judgments. Even so, I had said, it was perhaps fair to ask how he reacted philosophically to the eternal debate over free will versus determinism.

'I would still try to avoid absolute judgments,' he had replied. 'Actually, I think it possible to reconcile the two. Do you play bridge?'

'Very little and very poorly,' I had said.

'No matter,' he resumed 'determinism is like the cards that are dealt you. Free will is how you play them. The interaction between the two determines what you are as a person—or even a nation.'

The man as prophet and politician

Jawaharlal Nehru may have been able to reconcile free will and determinism, but he was never able to reconcile the conflict inside himself between prophet and politician.

As prophet, he had profound kinship with Mahatma Gandhi. Whenever you asked him about his innermost beliefs he was certain to say that the most important conviction of his life—one taught him by Gandhi—was that good ends never justified bad means. Violence, even in a good cause, defeated the good.

'We must not appease evil,' he had said in our recorded conversation in 1951, 'but we must also remember that evil is not surmounted by wrong methods that themselves produce more evil. I have felt more and more that the basic lesson Gandhi taught was right, the means should not be subordinated to ends.

'I know these ideas cannot easily be translated into life. A political leader cannot function like a prophet. He has to limit himself to people's understanding of him; otherwise, he cannot function at all.'

'What happens when the moralist becomes the politician and is faced with the need to get things done?' we asked.

> **'I am not a moralist or even a very good politician. I have dabbled in various things because they interest me. The politician has to compromise. That is what makes him a politician. But it may make a difference if he at least begins with certain convictions or principles.**

Anyway, I think Gandhi was right about ends and means and about violence. I hope to come as close as I can to making this a working philosophy.'

Some years later, in a letter, he returned to this theme.

'A leader must not only feel what is right,' he wrote, 'but he has also to convince masses of people about it. Thus, he tends to compromise or else he would cease to be the leader. The only example I know in contemporary history of a leader who refused to compromise with what he thought was right is Gandhi—and Gandhi was assassinated in the end, as prophets often are.'

Yet even Gandhi, faced with the terrible gravitational pull of events, could acquiesce in compromise, even if he was not an architect of it. Shortly after Independence, armed raiders from the north-west moved into Kashmir. Nehru didn't hesitate. He ordered military action. He didn't wait to consult Gandhi.

Once having acted, Nehru told Gandhi he had decided to use force in Kashmir because this was the only course open to him. He was sorry if what he had done had brought pain to Gandhi.

Gandhi put his arm around Nehru's shoulders. He didn't have to say anything.

The battle between politician and prophet inside Nehru never left him. Before he had the responsibility for governing a nation, he could define goals in terms of necessity instead of workability or attainability; he could move toward an objective without having to develop a consensus in order to achieve it; he could advocate rather than legislate. Once in office, he found himself plagued by some of the very tactics that had been so effective in gaining independence for India. Separatist movements sprang up throughout the country; this or that state would want its own language or cultural or political autonomy. The methods used to advance these objectives, naturally enough, were the same ones that had been used to such good effect against the British. In order to deal with these methods, it was necessary for Nehru to be tougher than his personal make-up would warrant.

We were in India in 1961 when the Prime Minister was having

severe difficulties with Master Tara Singh, the Sikh separatist leader. In quest of his objectives, Singh went on a hunger strike. We asked Nehru how it felt being the target of this device, as contrasted to the time when he himself was an agitator identified with Gandhi, who made personal hunger and suffering into one of the most potent political weapons in history.

His face clouded over. I could tell it was painful for him to think about it.

'Frankly,' he said, 'I don't like it. I don't think this is the right way to go about persuading a government.'

For the first time in the years we had known him, he seemed to stammer somewhat. Then he realized the irony of the situation. He smiled.

'I think I told you that a politician has to act in a certain way,' he said. 'What else is there to be done? I can't give in to the man and allow India to become a mass of splinters.'

'Do you feel the hunger strike is—well, hitting below the belt?'

'In a sense, yes.'

'How did you feel about it when Gandhi used it?'

'To tell the truth, I didn't feel quite right about it even then. If I analyse my feelings, I suppose I felt rather awkward about it. But you don't have to try very hard if you want to catch me in an inconsistency. This is the occupational disease of any philosopher who finds himself in the position of an operating leader.'

It was at that 1961 meeting that I discerned for the first time the visible evidence in Nehru of physical deterioration. One side of his face seemed rigid, as though he had suffered a stroke. His posture was no longer as erect as it had once been. The fatigue came through in his voice. For more than a half century he had made India his life and work. Thinking he might be looking forward to a time when he might lay down his burden and return to his writing and thinking, we asked what he would do if it became possible for him to be freed of his government responsibilities.

'You mean, what would I do if I retired?'

'Yes.'

We had thought his face would light up at the prospect. Just the opposite. He looked as though nothing would be more unwelcome.

'Well, I suppose there are some things I might do,' he said without any particular enthusiasm in his voice. 'I like to walk quite a bit, in the mountains. I might want to read a bit. But I really haven't thought much about it.'

More than ever, we realized that Nehru loved his job and had no thought of leaving it; he loved everything about it, the contradictions, the inner struggle, the endless pressures and counterpressures, the physical strain and the anguish and the multiple problems and complexities and the insolubles. Most of all, he loved the direct connection he had with the people of India and the destiny of his nation.

Before leaving him, we had one more question to ask—even though we knew he was annoyed whenever it came up. But everyone was asking the question all through India, and indeed, throughout the world: After Nehru, who? In talking to newspaper editors and members of the government, we had encountered considerable feeling, some of it bitter, because Nehru had not selected a successor. One editor said he couldn't understand why Nehru couldn't anticipate the chaos and disintegration that would afflict India upon his death in the absence of a designated successor. A prominent member of the Congress Party told us that the battle for his successor might go on for months. He said Nehru was neglecting his responsibility.

We put the question to the Prime Minister. But we approached the subject somewhat gingerly.

'People say that the greatest part of Gandhi's legacy to India was you,' we said. 'Now who is your legacy to India?'

He didn't hesitate a moment.

'Four hundred million people who are capable of selecting a leader for themselves. I am not going to do it for them. It would be insolent of me to do it.'

'But suppose they don't have that capacity?'

'They do. Anyway, it is rather depressing to me to believe that everything we have tried to do about preparing people to rule themselves has failed. I don't believe we have failed, at least not in that respect.'

'They say—even some of your friends say—that if you fail to designate a successor, the attempt to choose one would tear the country to pieces. They say that all your good work could be undone if you don't train a man to take your place.'

'I think we will do all right. I think the country will do quite all right.'

The Indian people have vindicated Nehru's confidence. They have also justified his highest aspirations. Nehru's death, in a real sense, marked the coming of age of a free and mature India. His legacy is what he wished it to be.

~

Memories of the Making of *Gandhi*[23]

Richard Attenborough

Richard Attenborough (1923–2014) was an English actor and filmmaker. He is best known for directing the Oscar-winning film Gandhi (1982) based on the life of the Mahatma. The following is a fascinating account of a meeting he had with Nehru before starting work on the film, in which the latter warned him about not deifying his subject.

~

Our first encounter was strange because I carried him home in my arms. It was about half-past one in the morning and I was returning from a charity art auction where each supporter present had either donated a work of art or undertaken, as I had, to buy one.

When I'd received the catalogue it simply said 'A Bust by Epstein'—no mention of the subject. At the auction, the handsome head and shoulders, cast in bronze, proved to be those

[23] From *Jawaharlal Nehru: Centenary Volume.*

of Pandit Jawaharlal Nehru, one of the wisest, kindest, most statesmanlike and compelling men it has ever been my good fortune to encounter.

The year was 1962 and, as I carried my purchase home, I had no idea of the profound impact that name and everything surrounding him and his country was soon to have on the rest of my life.

A few hours later, without any warning or preparation, I received a telephone call from a gentleman called Motilal Kothari—later to become my partner—who hoped to persuade me to make a film devoted to the life of Mahatma Gandhi. At that time I was not a director of motion pictures. I was an actor who had only very recently become a producer. Within a matter of weeks, however, I too had fallen completely under the Mahatma's spell and, for the first time ever, desperately wanted to become a director simply in order to make this one particular film.

It was evident, right from the outset, that unless the backing of the Indian Government could be obtained, such a project would be unthinkable. The sole link that I had with India at that time was my friendship with Earl Mountbatten of Burma and I asked for his assistance. There could hardly be, I thought, a better advocate than the last Viceroy and first Governor-General of the Republic who also happened to be a close friend of both Mahatma Gandhi and Pandit Nehru.

Lord Louis, who was fortuitously about to spend a week in Delhi, kindly expressed himself willing to put forward my proposals. To my total delight, I received a letter from him early in May 1963 assuring me of Pandit Nehru's agreement in principle to a film. I wrote immediately to the Prime Minister's Private Secretary, Mr S.P. Khanna, requesting that he express my gratitude for the interest that had already been displayed in the project and asking whether, together with Motilal Kothari, I might seek an appointment to discuss it in person. Within a few days came a reply saying the Prime Minister would be happy to see us both on 26 May, a Sunday.

At the last moment Moti fell ill with recurrent heart trouble and was unable to travel, so it was with a feeling of sadness that, alone, I boarded the plane for my first visit to India.

On the Sunday, accompanied by Moti's brother Vala, I found myself in Mr Khanna's office a little after eight in morning. Despite the hour and the day, the place was already a hive of activity with people streaming in and out, bearing the various files and messages that testified to the multitude of activities surrounding the leader of one of the greatest nations in the world.

Prior to our going in to see Mr Nehru, Mr Khanna had a confidential word. Would I please be conscious of the passage of time while I was with the Prime Minister, since his day was very tightly scheduled and it had only been possible to allocate me thirty minutes with him. Naturally I agreed at once.

At precisely half-past eight, Vala and I were shown into the Prime Minister's office. Mr Nehru, who had been sitting behind a large desk, got to his feet and greeted us with a pranam, inviting us to sit.

Very often, when one is familiar with a famous figure by virtue of photographs or report, the actual person does not seem quite the same when you meet him for the first time. In this particular instance, my reaction was completely the opposite. Mr Nehru was exactly as I had expected; he was of medium height, dressed in his familiar sherwani, churidar and Gandhi topi. He had a most sweet face and gentle voice but my abiding memory is of his eyes—dark brown, compassionate, attentive, with the ability to convince you immediately that you had his absolute and entire attention.

He told us of his conversations with Lord Louis and repeated his feeling of pleasure at the possibility of a film on the life of Gandhiji. Managing immediately to dispel any feeling of formality, he encouraged me to talk freely about my enthusiasm and aspirations as far as the film was concerned. It was not the minutiae, the precise dates and times of events, which he felt were important. His concern was that the spirit and fundamental truth of Gandhiji's life should be apparent in all that we might attempt to convey.

He asked me to enumerate what I thought would be some of

the highlights of the film. I mentioned several major dramatic moments in Gandhi's life. Immediately Panditji—as I came to call him—launched into personal reminiscences, illustrating their particular impact upon his own life and that of his contemporaries and, ultimately, on the whole future of India.

He seemed convinced that the film, by simply telling Gandhi's story, could communicate the incredible worth of this man to millions of people and, indeed, reminded me that Gandhiji himself, when asked what message he wished to convey to the world, replied, 'My life is my message.'

I was bubbling over with excitement. We seemed to have been talking only for five or six minutes when I glanced at my watch and, to my horror, it was nine o'clock. I started to make a move—'What is it, where are you going?' asked the Prime Minister.

'Well, sir, it's nine o'clock.'

'Yes, yes, but we haven't finished,' he said. 'Do sit down.' Eventually he got up from his desk and took out an album full of photographs. Each one recalled some historic incident or some unique private moment. I longed to have a tape recorder in order to secure for the future these unique personal anecdotes which would bring such magical life and veracity to a screenplay.

The Prime Minister and I were by now on our hands and knees poring over more and more photographs. There was a knock at the door and a secretary came in. Somewhat startled not to find the Prime Minister in his usual place, he rather embarrassedly handed him a note. Mr Nehru glanced at it without getting up. 'Yes, yes,' he said, 'yes, yes,' and the secretary left. We went on with our talk. Every moment seemed to reveal some new element which should be considered and adjudged when putting together the script.

I am not certain exactly how long we remained. I only know that it went well beyond the allotted time. 'I want you to meet a number of people here,' the Prime Minister told me finally, 'including some of our officials and, of course, my daughter.'

He got up, went to the phone and rang what was obviously his home.

'I am sending the English actor and producer, Richard Attenborough, to see you. He's going to make a film about Bapu.'

At the end of the call he said, 'My daughter will be delighted to see you and you must come and visit me again.' He opened the door to the outer office. By now the anteroom seemed like Connaught Place with a positive multitude of people, all of whom had been kept waiting for their appointments. I immediately suffered a dreadful pang of conscience as I saw Mr Khanna's kind but plainly stricken face, looking towards us.

In November of the same year at Teen Murti House in Delhi, I met Panditji for the second and last time. Moti was with me on this occasion and I was really quite shocked to see how markedly the Prime Minister had aged during the six months that had elapsed since our previous encounter. He did not seem at all well; nevertheless, despite whatever effort was required, he summoned up his usual warmth in greeting us and enquiring as to the progress of our project. We were very much aware of the pressures on him, almost overwhelming at this particular time, and I was most anxious that the meeting should not take longer than was absolutely necessary.

He was conscious of our need for a contact in India, someone who, on a day-to-day basis, could answer the innumerable questions that were bound to arise, put us in touch with experts in every conceivable field and generally keep the project alive. The person he had selected for this task was his daughter, Indira.

It might have seemed a strange choice since, at that time, she held no official position. But she did, of course, know everyone and, as I had learned during my previous visit, she was also passionately interested in films. The Prime Minister said that whenever we had a query she would help us. This indeed she did through all the ups and downs of the next seventeen years and in the end, of course, it was entirely due to Indiraji's help, advocacy, interest and magnanimity that the Gandhi film came to be made.

Panditji told us that he had had the opportunity of looking at our script but, owing to pressure of work, had not read it very thoroughly. However, he thought we should give a great deal of thought to the selection of the principal figures we ultimately decided to portray in the film. He readily accepted that it would be impossible to include all the main statesmen involved in the Indian struggle for independence or all the British figures who had participated. He was totally opposed to dragging in a series of names by somewhat cursory reference, just to have them mentioned. He felt that we should settle on a relatively small number of people and allow them, in a way, to represent all the major figures concerned.

He accepted the necessity in a film to adopt the concertina approach—to truncate events—to construct circumstances in which certain debates and ultimate resolutions could be staged dramatically and succinctly.

After some further discussions about casting, we took our leave and he came to the door to say goodbye. I was just about to get into the taxi when he made one further observation. It was to remain my touchstone throughout all the years that would follow.

'Whatever you do,' he said, 'do not deify Gandhiji—that is what we have done in India—and he was too great a man to be deified.'

Those were the last words that Pandit Nehru ever spoke to me. I am eternally grateful to him, both for them and for his unique contribution in making possible a film that not only changed my life but also allowed millions of others around the world to learn something of Mahatma Gandhi and to understand that change can come about without violence.

Panditji's own impact on modern political thinking has, of course, been profound. Although passionate and capable of intense anger, he was, essentially, a man of peace. He was also, as I learned from personal experience, capable of consuming and infectious enthusiasm. The pain and deprivation suffered by many of his compatriots affected him deeply. To them and to those around him who had earned his trust he displayed a loyalty that was burning in its intensity. Most importantly of all, he accepted absolutely the responsibilities that had been thrust upon him although they were of a weight and magnitude most of us would find unbearable. In this he was sustained by a phenomenal sense of compassion and a steadfast determination to protect and enhance the rights and dignities of his fellow human beings.

~

First of the Afro-Asians[24]

Lee Kuan Yew

Lee Kuan Yew (1923–2015) was the first prime minister of Singapore who oversaw its transformation from a British crown colony to a flourishing sovereign nation. In the following tribute he recalls Nehru's influence for anti-colonial movements throughout the world.

~

Nehru was already a legend in the 1930s. As a schoolboy in Singapore, then a colony of the British Empire, I had read of him. I could recognize his handsome features in the newspapers. I had read his letters to his daughter, Indira, in *Glimpses of World History,* and admired his elegant and lucid prose style.

I was a student in England at the time of India's Independence. I heard his speech on BBC I can never forget his stirring words: 'Long years ago we made a tryst with destiny, and now the time comes when we shall redeem our pledge.... A moment comes, which comes but rarely in history... when the soul of a nation, long suppressed, finds utterance.' Powerful words that could come only from one who felt passionately for his country and his people.

The first time I saw him in person was in January 1959 when I attended a conference in New Delhi of the International Commission of Jurists at the Vigyan Bhawan. He arrived in a modest Morris Oxford. It was made in India and called the Hindustan. He had no script. He spoke for about thirty minutes. I was disappointed. He was not as crisp as his books, and rambled in parts. Perhaps it was his off day. Had he scripted it, it could have

[24] From *Jawaharlal Nehru: Centenary Volume.*

been polished and tightened into twenty minutes. But he was probably busy, and it was the age before ghostwriters. Or, more likely, Nehru never read ghosted speeches. I cannot remember what he said about the rule of law and the independence of the judiciary, but his philosophy came through as that of a liberal-minded humanist.

I spoke to him for the first time in April 1962 when I visited New Delhi as Prime Minister of a then self-governing, and not yet independent, Singapore. I sought his support for Singapore's proposed merger with the Federation of Malaya, together with the Borneo territories, to form the Federation of Malaysia. He approved of my views, especially my hope of building a multiracial nation. I remember vividly the lunch he gave at Flagstaff House, now Teen Murti House, which is the Nehru Memorial Museum. We sat at a long rectangular table. We each had a large silver platter with a raised rim. From this we picked rice and delicious north Indian curries with our fingers. This was something my wife and I had not done for many years—not since our childhood days. I was awkward. But he put me at ease, discussing the virtues of the different kinds of mangoes in India and comparing them with those he had tasted in other parts of the world, including Singapore, which he had visited shortly after the war.

I left New Delhi deeply grateful for the time he had given me, the graciousness with which he had listened to me and the friendship which he extended.

Six months later, in October, came the clashes with the Chinese across the Himalaya. The Singapore Government issued a statement which fell short of a condemnation for aggression.

When I next met him again in February 1964, in New Delhi, on my way back from a tour of Africa, he touched on this. I thought there was a trace of disappointment and reproach in his voice. I explained the problems of governing Singapore with one man one vote. Three quarters of the population were Chinese, more than half of them born in China. Their sentiments were with China, right or wrong. I would not say he was placated. But it might have lessened his disappointment at the ambivalence of the Singapore Government statement.

It was only one and a half years since I had last met him in April 1962. Then he was full of vigour. Now he looked tired and weary. I did not know what were the medical reasons for this appearance of fatigue. I thought then that it was because of the disappointment with what happened in the Himalaya.

He died about two months later. On 30 May, 1964, a vast crowd gathered at the Jalan Besar football stadium to pay homage to a great man. I said to them:

'Nehru was the first of the Afro-Asians. He started on the anti-colonial struggle fifty years ago when joining an anti-colonial movement meant not the glory of quick independence and high office, but a grim prospect of interminable hardship and repression ... .It was different for those who joined in anti-colonial movements after the Second World War ... .He gave his unceasing support to all the anti-colonial revolutions elsewhere in Asia and Africa ... .We ... also received his support and were inspired by India's struggle for freedom.'

~

A.B. Vajpayee's Tribute to Nehru[25]

Atal Bihari Vajpayee

After Prime Minister Jawaharlal Nehru's death in May 1964, Atal Bihari Vajpayee, then a Rajya Sabha member, paid homage in Parliament to India's first Prime Minister.

~

Sir, a dream has been shattered, a song silenced, a flame has vanished in the infinite. It was the dream of a world without fear and without hunger, it was the song of an epic that had the echo of the Gita and the fragrance of the rose. It was the flame of a lamp

---

25 https://theprint.in/opinion/vajpayee-on-nehrus-death-bharat-mata-has-lost-her-favourite-prince/99455/

that burnt all night, fought with every darkness, showed us the way, and one morning attained Nirvana.

Death is certain, the body is ephemeral. The golden body that yesterday we consigned to the funeral pyre of sandalwood was bound to end. But did death have to come so stealthily? When friends were asleep and guards were slack, we were robbed of a priceless gift of life.

Bharat Mata is stricken with grief today—she has lost her favourite prince. Humanity is sad today—it has lost its devotee. Peace is restless today—its protector is no more. The downtrodden have lost their refuge. The common man has lost the light in his eyes. The curtain has come down. The leading actor on the stage of the world displayed his final role and taken the bow.

In the Ramayana, Maharashi Valmiki has said of Lord Rama that he brought the impossible together. In Panditji's life, we see a glimpse of what the great poet said. He was a devotee of peace and yet the harbinger of revolution, he was a devotee of nonviolence but advocated every weapon to defend freedom and honour.

He was an advocate of individual freedom and yet was committed to bringing about economic equality. He was never afraid of a compromise with anybody, but he never compromised with anyone out of fear. His policy towards Pakistan and China was a symbol of this unique blend. It had generosity as well as firmness. It is unfortunate that this generosity was mistaken for weakness, while some people looked upon his firmness as obstinacy.

I remember I once saw him very angry during the days of the Chinese aggression when our Western friends were trying to prevail upon us to arrive at some compromise with Pakistan on Kashmir. When he was told we would have to fight on two fronts if there was no compromise on the Kashmir problem, he flared up and said we would fight on both fronts if necessary. He was against negotiating under pressure.

Sir, the freedom of which he was the general protector is today in danger. We have to protect it with all our might. The national unity and integrity of which he was the apostle is also in danger today. We have to preserve it at any cost. The Indian democracy he established, and of which he made a success is also faced with a doubtful future. With our unity, discipline and self-confidence we have to make this democracy a success.

The leader is gone, the followers remain. The sun has set, now we have to find our way by the light of the stars. This is a highly testing time. If we all could dedicate ourselves to the great ideal of a mighty and prosperous India that could make an honourable contribution to world peace for ever, it would indeed be a true tribute to him.

The loss to Parliament is irreparable. Such a resident may never grace Teen Murti again. That vibrant personality, that attitude of taking even the opposition along, that refined gentlemanliness, that greatness we may not again see in the near future. In spite of a difference of opinion we have nothing but respect for his great ideals, his integrity, his love for the country and his indomitable courage. With these words, I pay my humble homage to that great soul.

Select Bibliography

Ambedkar, B.R. "Pakistan or the Partition of India." In *Writings and Speeches Vol. 8*. Bombay: Education Department, Government of Maharashtra, 1990.

Akbar, M.J. *Nehru: The Making of India*. New Delhi: Roli Books, 2002.

Dikshit, Sheila, K. Natwar Singh, G. Parthasarathi, H.Y. Sharada Prasad, S. Gopal and Ravinder Kumar, eds. *Jawaharlal Nehru: Centenary Volume*. New Delhi: Oxford University Press, 1989.

Dixit, Rajiv. "Nehru Was Died OF STD (sexually Tranmitted Disease).Jinna,Nehru,Edwina Exposed By Rajiv Dixit." YouTube video, 27:04. Posted by Rajiv Dixit, October 5, 2012. https://www.youtube.com/watch?time_continue=33&v=5XtcFiZwENY.

Karanjia, R.K. *The Mind of Mr. Nehru*. London: George Allen and Unwin, 1960.

Kashyap, Subhash C. *Jawaharlal Nehru and the Constitution*. New Delhi: Metropolitan, 1982.

King, Martin Luther Jr. "The Will to Peace." In *The Legacy of Nehru: A Memorial Tribute*. Edited by Natwar Singh. New York: John Day, 1965.

Nehru Abhinandan Granth: A Birthday Book. New Delhi: Nehru Abhinandan Granth Committee, 1949.

Nehru, Jawaharlal. *An Autobiography*. New Delhi: Penguin, 2004.

———*A Bunch of Old Letters*. Bombay: Asia Publishing House, 1960.

——— *The Discovery of India*. New Delhi: Penguin, 2010.

———*Glimpses of World History*. New Delhi: Penguin, 2004.

——— *Jawaharlal Nehru: Selected Speeches 1949–1953* Vol. 2. New Delhi: Publication Division, 1954.

———*Jawaharlal Nehru's Speeches 1953–57*. New Delhi: Publications Division, 1958.

———*Selected Speeches Vol. 3*. New Delhi: Publications Division, 1958.

——— *Selected Works of Jawaharlal Nehru Vol. 1*. Edited by S. Gopal. New Delhi: Orient Longman, 1972.

——— *Selected Works of Jawaharlal Nehru Vol. 6*. Edited by S. Gopal. New Delhi: Orient Longman, 1974.

——— *Selected Works of Jawaharlal Nehru Volume VI*. New Delhi: Jawaharlal Nehru Memorial Fund, 1987.

——— *The Unity of India: Collected Writings 1937–1940*. New York: John Day Company, 1942.

Mitra, Anirban. "The Netaji Files Reveal a Tale of Nehru's Warmth – Not Sinister Conspiracy." The Wire. May 27, 2017. https://thewire.in/137206/netaji-files-family-nehru/.

Raghavan, Shrinath. *War and Peace in Modern India: A Strategic History of the Nehru Years*. Ranikhet: Permanent Black, 2017.

Sidharth, Arjun. "Did Jawaharlal Nehru ever say "I am English by education, Muslim by culture and Hindu by accident"?." Altnews. November 5, 2018. https://www.altnews.in/did-jawaharlal-nehru-ever-say-i-am-english-by-education-muslim-by-culture-and-hindu-by-accident/.

Vajpayee, A.B. "Vajpayee on Nehru's death: Bharat Mata has lost her favourite prince." The Print. August 16, 2018. https://theprint.in/opinion/vajpayee-on-nehrus-death-bharat-mata-has-lost-her-favourite-prince/99455/.

Editor's Note and Acknowledgements

I have been fascinated by the personality and thoughts of Jawaharlal Nehru for nearly five decades. This fascination did not wane even when all around me Nehru's memories seemed to be fading. With the regime change in 2014, Nehru was targeted with renewed fury, particularly with the charge—which I can only call slanderous—that he was not rooted in Indian tradition, and that he was contemptuous of culture and religion, particularly Hinduism. It was in this context that during an informal conversation in 2017 with Ravi Singh of Speaking Tiger, the idea of this volume took shape.

I am very grateful to Smt. Sonia Gandhi who graciously permitted the use of copyright material.

My dear friend, historian Ramachandra Guha, gave the wonderful suggestion that a phrase from Nehru himself, that underlines the democratic content of the slogan '*Bharat Mata ki Jai*', could work best as the title of this collection. Thank you, Ram, here it is: '*Who is Bharat Mata?*'

~

Before I thank the several other people who have helped me with this project, I must put on record my appreciation for and gratitude to the young women and men who attended my lectures and talks over the last couple of years at JNU, Ashoka University (Sonipat), Lady Shri Ram college and Hindu college (Delhi University), Azim Premji Foundation (Raipur), Aghaz Sanskritik Manch, Delhi, ITM university (Gwalior), Kavita Singh Memorial lecture (Patna) and the Rajiv Gandhi Study Circles at Jaipur, Chandigarh and Varanasi. Interactions at these events helped me with my ideas and gave me hope by underlining the fact that young Indians are genuinely concerned about India's future and interested in learning from rather than blindly valorizing or dismissing our past.

A number of conversations with so many wonderful people have helped immensely in the shaping of my ideas on the Indian national movement and the roles played in it by Gandhi, Nehru and others.

Shri Prakash Dikshit, a magnetic figure in the Gwalior of my childhood and early youth, first introduced Nehru to me by making me read *Hindustan ki Kahani*. I wish him a very, very long life.

I remember fondly the animated discussions with the Late Shri Rajendra Mathur, then editor of *Navbharat Times* and a diehard Nehruvian. The late Dr. B.D. Sharma, the legendary civil servant, social activist and a family elder, gave me rare insights into Indian, particularly tribal, life. Prof. Namwar Singh, Prof. Bipan Chandra and Shri Mohit Sen were constant sources of inspiration and intellectual provocation, as were Faruque Sheikh, Anupam Mishra and Khurshid Anwar. I remember them all with gratitude.

I'm grateful to Shyam Benegal, the creator of the unforgettable TV serial *Bharat: Ek Khoj*, and to Ashok Vajpayee, Javed Akhtar, Shabana Azmi, Ahmad Patel, Dilip Simeon, Devi Prasad Tripathi, Krishna Kumar, Harbans Mukhia, Bhagwan Josh, Mahesh Rangarajan, Gurdeep Singh Sappal, Om Thanvi, Rajeev Bhargava, Tani Bhargava, Ali Javed, Jamal Kidwai, Deokishan Sarada, Ashok Singh, Rambabu Agrawal and Ramashankar Singh (an old Lohiaite fast turning into a Nehru admirer!) for insights gained in conversations over many years.

Anu Prasad of ILSS (Indian Leaders for Social Sector), Aniha Brar of the Young India Fellowship programme at Ashoka University, V.K. Gupta, Kundan Yadav, Prakash Bindu and Neelakshi Tiwari have been helpful in many ways. Awadhesh Pande and Nabnita Baruah enthusiastically made it possible for me to have most of the material required for this volume. Thank you all.

I also wish to put on record my appreciation for the Nehru Memorial Museum and Library, the JNU library and the Sahitya Akademi library for their support.

Nothing would move without the constant emotional support and intellectual engagement provided by my wife Suman, son Ritwik and daughter Ritambhara, and by Saraswati.

Last, but not least, I thank eight more family members—our lovely, free-minded cats.